Mastering Node.js

Second Edition

Build robust and scalable real-time server-side web applications efficiently

Sandro Pasquali
Kevin Faaborg

BIRMINGHAM - MUMBAI

Mastering Node.js

Second Edition

First published: November 2013

Second edition: December 2017

Production reference: 1271217

Published by Packt Publishing Ltd.
Livery Place
35 Livery Street
Birmingham
B3 2PB, UK.
ISBN 978-1-78588-896-0

www.packtpub.com

Credits

Authors
Sandro Pasquali
Kevin Faaborg

Reviewer
Glenn Geenen

Commissioning Editor
Ashwin Nair

Acquisition Editor
Reshma Raman

Content Development Editor
Onkar Wani

Technical Editor
Sachin Sunilkumar

Copy Editor
Shaila Kusanale

Project Coordinator
Devanshi Doshi

Proofreader
Safis Editing

Indexer
Rekha Nair

Graphics
Jason Monteiro

Production Coordinator
Shantanu Zagade

About the Authors

Sandro Pasquali formed Simple.com in 1997, a technology company that sold the world's first JavaScript-based application development framework and was awarded several patents for deployment and advertising technologies that anticipated the future of internet-based software. Node represents, for him, the natural next step in the inexorable march toward the day when JavaScript powers nearly every level of software development.

Sandro has led the design of enterprise-grade applications for some of the largest companies in the world, including Nintendo, Major League Baseball, Bang and Olufsen, LimeWire, AppNexus, Conde Nast, and others. He has displayed interactive media exhibits during the Venice Biennial, won design awards, built knowledge management tools for research institutes and schools, and started and run several start-ups. Always seeking new ways to blend design excellence and technical innovation, he has made significant contributions across all levels of software architecture, from data management and storage tools to innovative user interfaces and frameworks.

He is the author of *Deploying Node.js*, also by Packt Publishing, which aims to help developers get their work in front of others.

Sandro runs a software development company in New York and trains corporate development teams interested in using Node and JavaScript to improve their products. He spends the rest of his time entertaining his beautiful daughter and his wife.

You can follow him on Twitter at `@spasquali`, at `github.com/sandro-pasquali`, and read more of his writing on Node, JavaScript, and software engineering at `exploringnode.com`.

> *I would, first of all, like to thank my coauthor, Kevin Faaborg, for his perspective on this book, and my family for their support. The team at Packt deserves a lot of credit for gracefully encouraging me to keep writing about a topic I love. I'd also like to thank all those who bought the first edition and wrote to thank me for the book, especially those who took up Node more seriously because of it. If it wasn't for them, I wouldn't have written another. To the ones who wrote negative reviews, I thank you even more.*

Kevin Faaborg is a professional software developer and an avid software hobbyist. At Harvard, he learned C programming from visiting professor Brian Kernighan. He witnessed and contributed to how digital technology has shaped music distribution, working first at MTV Networks, then at Lime Wire LLC, and now at Spotify AB, where he designed and started the patent program.

Kevin travels frequently, spending time each year in San Francisco, Colorado, NYC, and Stockholm. You can follow him on Twitter at `@zootella`, at `github.com/zootella`, and read more of his writing on Node, JavaScript, and software engineering at `exploringnode.com`.

To my parents, for keeping a place and being people I can always go home to.
And to all the tinkers who have ever been told, "you're doing it wrong."
You're not.

About the Reviewer

Glenn Geenen is a Node.js developer who lives in Belgium. He studied digital arts and entertainment at HOWEST (Hogeschool West Vlaanderen). He worked for several years as a mobile (iOS) developer. After discovering Node.js, he embraced web development and became a Node.js consultant for his own company, GeenenTijd.

www.PacktPub.com

For support files and downloads related to your book, please visit www.PacktPub.com. Did you know that Packt offers eBook versions of every book published, with PDF and ePub files available? You can upgrade to the eBook version at www.PacktPub.com and as a print book customer, you are entitled to a discount on the eBook copy. Get in touch with us at service@packtpub.com for more details.

At www.PacktPub.com, you can also read a collection of free technical articles, sign up for a range of free newsletters and receive exclusive discounts and offers on Packt books and eBooks.

https://www.packtpub.com/mapt

Get the most in-demand software skills with Mapt. Mapt gives you full access to all Packt books and video courses, as well as industry-leading tools to help you plan your personal development and advance your career.

Why subscribe?

- Fully searchable across every book published by Packt
- Copy and paste, print, and bookmark content
- On demand and accessible via a web browser

Customer Feedback

Thanks for purchasing this Packt book. At Packt, quality is at the heart of our editorial process. To help us improve, please leave us an honest review on this book's Amazon page at `www.amazon.in/dp/178588896X`.

If you'd like to join our team of regular reviewers, you can email us at `customerreviews@packtpub.com`. We award our regular reviewers with free eBooks and videos in exchange for their valuable feedback. Help us be relentless in improving our products!

Table of Contents

Preface

The internet is no longer a collection of static websites to be passively consumed. The browser (and mobile) user has come to expect a much richer and interactive experience. Over the last decade or so, network applications have come to resemble desktop applications. Also, recognition of the social characteristics of information has inspired the development of new kinds of interfaces and visualizations modeling dynamic network states, where the user is viewing change over real time rather than fading snapshots trapped in the past.

Even though our expectations for software have changed, the tools available to us as software developers have not changed much. Computers are faster, and multicore chip architectures are common. Data storage is cheaper, as is bandwidth. Yet we continue to develop with tools designed before billion-user websites and push-button management of cloud-based clusters of virtual machines.

The development of network applications remains an overly expensive and slow process because of this. Developers use different languages, programming styles, complicating code maintenance, debugging, and more. Very regularly, scaling issues arrive too early, overwhelming the ability of what is often a small and inexperienced team. Popular modern software features, such as real-time data, multiplayer games, and collaborative editing spaces, demand systems capable of carrying thousands of simultaneous connections without bending. Yet we remain restricted to frameworks designed to assist us in building CRUD applications, binding a single relational database on a single server to a single user running a multipage website in a browser on a desktop computer.

Node helps developers build more resilient network applications at scale. Built on C++ and bundled with Google's V8 engine, Node is fast, and it understands JavaScript. Node has brought together the most popular programming language in the world and the fastest JavaScript compiler around, and has given easy access to an operating system through C++ bindings. Node represents a change in how network software is designed and built.

What this book covers

Chapter 1, *Understanding the Node Environment*, gives a brief description of the particular problems Node attempts to solve, their history and roots in the Unix design philosophy, and Node's power as a systems language. We will also learn how to write optimized, modern JavaScript on V8 (the engine powering Node), including a brief tour of the newest features of the language that will help you upgrade your code.

Chapter 2, *Understanding Asynchronous Event-Driven Programming*, digs deep into the fundamental characteristics of Node's design: event-driven, asynchronous programming. By the end of this chapter, you will understand how events, callbacks, and timers are used in Node as well as how the event loop works to enable high-speed I/O across filesystems, networks, and processes. We'll also learn about modern concurrency modeling constructs, from the default Node callback pattern to Promises, Generators, async/await, and other flow control techniques.

Chapter 3, *Streaming Data Across Nodes and Clients*, describes how streams of I/O data are knitted through most network software, emitted by file servers or broadcast in response to an HTTP GET request. Here, you will learn how Node facilitates the design, implementation, and composition of network software, using examples of HTTP servers, readable and writable file streams, and other I/O focused Node modules and patterns. You will take a deep dive into the Streams implementation, mastering this fundamental part of the Node stack.

Chapter 4, *Using Node to Access the Filesystem*, lays out what you need to know when accessing the filesystem with Node, how to create file streams for reading and writing, along with techniques for handling file uploads and other networked file operations. You will also implement a simple file browsing application using Electron.

Chapter 5, *Managing Many Simultaneous Client Connections*, shows you how Node helps in solving problems accompanying the high-volume and high-concurrency environments that contemporary, collaborative web applications demand. Through examples, learn how to efficiently track user state, route HTTP requests, handle sessions, and authenticate requests using the Redis database and Express web application framework.

Chapter 6, *Creating Real-Time Applications*, explores AJAX, Server-Sent-Events, and the WebSocket protocol, discussing their pros and cons when building real-time systems, and how to implement each using Node. We finish the chapter by building a collaborative document editing application.

Chapter 7, *Using Multiple Processes,* teaches how to distribute clusters of Node processes across multicore processors, and other techniques for scaling Node applications. An investigation of the differences between programming in single and multithreaded environments leads to a discussion on how to spawn, fork, and communicate with child processes in Node, including a section on using the PM2 process manager. We also build an analytics tool that records, and displays, the mouse actions of multiple, simultaneous clients connected through a cluster of web sockets.

Chapter 8, *Scaling Your Application,* outlines some techniques for detecting when to scale, deciding how to scale, and scaling Node applications across multiple servers and cloud services, with examples, including how to use RabbitMQ as a message queue, using NGINX to proxy Node servers, and using Amazon Web Services in your application. The chapter closes with us building a robust customer service application deployed on Heroku, where you will learn how to use the Twilio SMS gateway with Node.

Chapter 9, *Microservices,* introduces the concept of microservices—small, independent services—and how we got from monolithic and 3-Tier stacks to large fleets of independent services whose collaboration patterns are dynamic. We'll learn how to use Seneca and Node to create an autodiscovering services mesh, AWS Lambda to create serverless applications infinitely scalable in the cloud, and finally, how to create Docker containers and orchestrate their deployment with Kubernetes.

Chapter 10, *Testing Your Application,* explains how to implement unit, functional, and integration tests with Node. We will go deep, exploring how to use native debugging and testing modules, heap dumps and CPU profiling, eventually building test suites with Mocha and Chai. We'll cover mocks, stubs, and spies with Sinon, live debugging of running Node processes with Chrome DevTools, and how to use tools like Puppeteer to implement headless testing of your UI code.

Appendix A, *Organizing Your Work into Modules,* gives tips on using the npm package management system. Here, you will learn how to create, publish, and manage packages.

Appendix B, *Creating your own C++ Add-ons,* provides a brief introduction on how to build your own C++ add-ons and how to use them from within Node. We also cover the new **NAN (Native Abstractions for Node)** tool and how that can help you with writing cross-platform, future-proofed add-ons.

What you need for this book

You will need to have some familiarity with JavaScript, and have a copy of Node installed on your development machine or server, Version 9.0 or higher. You should know how to install programs on this machine, as you will need to install Redis, along with other libraries like Docker. Having Git installed, and learning how to clone GitHub repositories, will greatly improve your experience.

You should install RabbitMQ so that you can follow with the examples using message queues. The sections on using NGINX to proxy Node servers will, of course, require that you can install and use that web server. To build C++ add-ons, you will need to install the appropriate compiler on your system.

The examples in this book are built and tested within UNIX-based environments (including Mac OS X), but you should be able to run all Node examples on Windows-based operating systems as well. You can obtain installers for your system, and binaries, from `http://www.nodejs.org`.

Who this book is for

This book is for developers who want to build high-capacity network applications, such as social networks, collaborative document editing environments, real-time data-driven web interfaces, networked games, and other I/O-heavy software. If you're a client-side JavaScript developer, reading this book will teach you how to become a server-side programmer using a language you already know. If you're a C++ hacker, Node is an open source project built using that language, offering you an excellent opportunity to make a real impact within a large and growing community, even gaining fame, by helping to develop this exciting new technology.

This book is also for technical managers and others seeking an explanation of the capabilities and design philosophy of Node. The book is filled with examples of how Node solves the problems modern software companies are facing in terms of high-concurrency, real-time applications pushing enormous volumes of data through growing networks. Node has already been embraced by the enterprise, and you should consider it for your next project.

We are using the bleeding-edge version of Node (9.x at the time of writing). This is the only book you need to be ready for in the next few years as Node continues its march through the enterprise.

Conventions

In this book, you will find a number of text styles that distinguish between different kinds of information. Here are some examples of these styles and an explanation of their meaning.

Code words in text, database table names, folder names, filenames, file extensions, pathnames, dummy URLs, user input, and Twitter handles are shown as follows: "If we take a look at our `find-byte.c` file, we will see that our `render` method returns content wrapped in the `View` component".

A block of code is set as follows:

```
const s1 = "first string";
const s2 = "second string";
let s3 = s1 + s2;
```

Any command-line input or output is written as follows:

```
$ node --version
```

When we wish to draw your attention to a particular part of a code block, the relevant lines or items are set in bold:

```
const char *s1 = "first string";
const char *s2 = "second string";
int size = strlen(s1) + strlen(s2);
char *buffer = (char *)malloc(size + 1);
strcpy(buffer, s1);
strcat(buffer, s2);
free(buffer);
```

New terms and **important words** are shown in bold. Words that you see on the screen, for example, in menus or dialog boxes, appear in the text like this: "Clicking the **Next** button moves you to the next screen."

Warnings or important notes appear in a box like this.

 Tips and tricks appear like this.

Reader feedback

Feedback from our readers is always welcome. Let us know what you think about this book-what you liked or disliked. Reader feedback is important for us as it helps us develop titles that you will really get the most out of.

To send us general feedback, simply e-mail feedback@packtpub.com, and mention the book's title in the subject of your message.

If there is a topic that you have expertise in and you are interested in either writing or contributing to a book, see our author guide at www.packtpub.com/authors .

Customer support

Now that you are the proud owner of a Packt book, we have a number of things to help you to get the most from your purchase.

Downloading the example code

You can download the example code files for this book from your account at http://www.packtpub.com. If you purchased this book elsewhere, you can visit http://www.packtpub.com/support and register to have the files e-mailed directly to you.

You can download the code files by following these steps:

1. Log in or register to our website using your e-mail address and password.
2. Hover the mouse pointer on the **SUPPORT** tab at the top.
3. Click on **Code Downloads & Errata**.
4. Enter the name of the book in the **Search** box.
5. Select the book for which you're looking to download the code files.
6. Choose from the drop-down menu where you purchased this book from.
7. Click on **Code Download**.

You can also download the code files by clicking on the **Code Files** button on the book's webpage at the Packt Publishing website. This page can be accessed by entering the book's name in the **Search** box. Please note that you need to be logged in to your Packt account.

Once the file is downloaded, please make sure that you unzip or extract the folder using the latest version of:

- WinRAR / 7-Zip for Windows
- Zipeg / iZip / UnRarX for Mac
- 7-Zip / PeaZip for Linux

The code bundle for the book is also hosted on GitHub at `https://github.com/PacktPublishing/Mastering-Node.js-Second-Edition`. We also have other code bundles from our rich catalog of books and videos available at `https://github.com/PacktPublishing/`. Check them out!

Errata

Although we have taken every care to ensure the accuracy of our content, mistakes do happen. If you find a mistake in one of our books-maybe a mistake in the text or the code-we would be grateful if you could report this to us. By doing so, you can save other readers from frustration and help us improve subsequent versions of this book. If you find any errata, please report them by visiting `http://www.packtpub.com/submit-errata`, selecting your book, clicking on the **Errata Submission Form** link, and entering the details of your errata. Once your errata are verified, your submission will be accepted and the errata will be uploaded to our website or added to any list of existing errata under the Errata section of that title.

To view the previously submitted errata, go to `https://www.packtpub.com/books/content/support` and enter the name of the book in the search field. The required information will appear under the **Errata** section.

Piracy

Piracy of copyrighted material on the Internet is an ongoing problem across all media. At Packt, we take the protection of our copyright and licenses very seriously. If you come across any illegal copies of our works in any form on the Internet, please provide us with the location address or website name immediately so that we can pursue a remedy.

Please contact us at `copyright@packtpub.com` with a link to the suspected pirated material.

We appreciate your help in protecting our authors and our ability to bring you valuable content.

Questions

If you have a problem with any aspect of this book, you can contact us at `questions@packtpub.com`, and we will do our best to address the problem.

1
Understanding the Node Environment

Introduction – JavaScript as a systems language

When *John Bardeen*, *Walter Brattain*, and *William Shockley* invented the transistor in 1947, they changed the world in ways we are still discovering today. From their revolutionary building block, engineers could design and manufacture digital circuits far more complex than those possible earlier. Each decade that followed has seen a new generation of these devices: smaller, faster, and cheaper, often by orders of magnitude.

By the 1970s, corporations and universities could afford mainframe computers small enough to fit in a single room, and powerful enough that they could serve multiple users simultaneously. The minicomputer, a new and different kind of device, needed new and different kinds of technologies to help users get the most out of the machine. *Ken Thompson* and *Dennis Ritchie* at Bell Labs developed the operating system Unix, and the programming language **C** to write it. They built constructs into their system, like processes, threads, streams, and the hierarchical filesystem. Today, these constructs are so familiar, that it's hard to imagine a computer working any other way. However, they're just constructs, made up by these pioneers, with the goal of helping people like us understand the otherwise inscrutable patterns of data in memory and storage inside the machine.

C is a systems language, and it is a safe and powerful shorthand alternative for developers familiar with keying in assembly instructions. Given its familiar setting of a microprocessor, C makes low-level system tasks easy. For instance, you can search a block of memory for a byte of a specific value:

```
// find-byte.c
int find_byte(const char *buffer, int size, const char b) {
    for (int i = 0; i < size; i++) {
        if (buffer[i] == b) {
            return i;
        }
    }
    return -1;
}
```

By the 1990s, what we could build with transistors had evolved again. A *personal computer (PC)* was light and cheap enough to be found on workplace and dormitory desktops. Increased speed and capacity allowed users to boot from a character-only teletype to graphical environments, with pretty fonts and color images. And with an Ethernet card and cable, your computer got a static IP address on the internet, where network programs could connect to send and receive data with any other computer on the planet.

It was within this landscape of technology that *Sir Tim Berners-Lee* invented the *World Wide Web,* and *Brendan Eich* created **JavaScript**. Designed for coders familiar with HTML tags, JavaScript was a way to move beyond static pages of text with animation and interactivity. Given its familiar setting of a webpage, JavaScript makes high-level tasks easy. Web pages are filled with text and tags, so combining two strings is easy:

```
// combine-text.js
const s1 = "first string";
const s2 = "second string";
let s3 = s1 + s2;
```

Now, let's port each program to the other language and platform. First, from the preceding `combine-text.js`, let's write `combine-text.c`:

```
// combine-text.c
const char *s1 = "first string";
const char *s2 = "second string";
int size = strlen(s1) + strlen(s2);
char *buffer = (char *)malloc(size + 1); // One more for the 0x00 byte that
terminates strings
strcpy(buffer, s1);
strcat(buffer, s2);
free(buffer); // Never forget to free memory!
```

The two string literals are easy to define, but after that, it gets a lot harder. Without automatic memory management, it's your responsibility as a developer to determine how much memory you need, allocate it from the system, write to it without overwriting the buffer, and then free it afterwards.

Secondly, let's attempt the reverse: from the find-byte.c code prior, let's write find-byte.js. Before Node, it was not possible to use JavaScript to search a block of memory for a specific byte. In the browser, JavaScript can't allocate a buffer, and doesn't even have a type for byte. But with Node, it's both possible and easy:

```
// find-byte.js
function find_byte(buffer, b) {
  let i;
  for (i = 0; i < buffer.length; i++) {
    if (buffer[i] == b) {
      return i;
    }
  }
  return -1; // Not found
}
let buffer = Buffer.from("ascii A is byte value sixty-five", "utf8");
let r = find_byte(buffer, 65); // Find the first byte with value 65
console.log(r); // 6 bytes into the buffer
```

Emerging from generations of computing decades apart, when both computers and what people were doing with them were wildly different, there's no real reason the design, purpose, or use that drives these two languages, C and JavaScript, should necessarily come together. But they did, because in 2008 Google released Chrome, and in 2009, *Ryan Dahl* wrote **Node.js.**

Applying design principles previously only considered for operating systems. Chrome uses multiple processes to render different tabs, ensuring their isolation. Chrome was released open source and built on WebKit, but one part inside was completely new. Coding from scratch in his farmhouse in Denmark, *Lars Bak*'s V8 used hidden class transitions, incremental garbage collection, and dynamic code generation to execute (not interpret) JavaScript faster than ever before.

With V8 under the hood, how fast can Node run JavaScript? Let's write a little program to show execution speed:

```
// speed-loop.js
function main() {
  const cycles = 1000000000;
  let start = Date.now();
  for (let i = 0; i < cycles; i++) {
```

```
    /* Empty loop */
  }
  let end = Date.now();
  let duration = (end - start) / 1000;
  console.log("JavaScript looped %d times in %d seconds", cycles,
duration);
}
main();
```

The following is the output for `speed-loop.js`:

```
$ node --version
v9.3.0
$ node speed-loop.js
JavaScript looped 1000000000 times in 0.635 seconds
```

There's no code in the body of the `for` loop, but your processor is busy incrementing `i`, comparing it to `cycles`, and repeating the process. It's late 2017 as I write this, typing on a MacBook Pro with a 2.8 GHz Intel Core i7 processor. Node v9.3.0 is current, and takes *less than a second* to loop a *billion* times.

How fast is pure C? Let's see:

```
/* speed-loop.c */
#include <stdio.h>
#include <time.h>
int main() {
  int cycles = 1000000000;
  clock_t start, end;
  double duration;
  start = clock();
  for (int i = 0; i < cycles; i++) {
    /* Empty loop */
  }
  end = clock();
  duration = ((double)(end - start)) / CLOCKS_PER_SEC;
  printf("C looped %d times in %lf seconds\n", cycles,duration);
  return 0;
}
```

The following is the output for `speed-loop.c`:

```
$ gcc --version
Apple LLVM version 8.1.0 (clang-802.0.42)
$ gcc speed-loop.c -o speed-loop
$ ./speed-loop
C looped 1000000000 times in 2.398294 seconds
```

For additional comparison, let's try an interpreted language, like Python:

```python
# speed-loop.py

import time

def main():

  cycles = 1000000000
  start = time.perf_counter()

  for i in range(0, cycles):
    pass # Empty loop

  end = time.perf_counter()
  duration = end - start
  print("Python looped %d times in %.3f seconds" % (cycles, duration))

main()
```

The following is the output for `speed-loop.py`:

```
$ python3 --version
Python 3.6.1
$ python3 speed-loop.py
Python looped 1000000000 times in 31.096 seconds
```

Node runs code fast enough so that you don't have to worry that your application might be slowed down by the execution speed. You'll still have to think about performance, of course, but constrained by factors beyond language and platform choice, such as algorithms, I/O, and external processes, services, and APIs. As V8 compiles JavaScript rather than interpreting it, Node lets you enjoy high-level language features like automatic memory management and dynamic types, without having to give up the performance of a natively-compiled binary. Earlier, you had to choose one or the other; but now, you can have both. It's great.

Computing in the 1970s was about the microprocessor, and computing in the 1990s was about the web page. Today, in 2017, another new generation of physical computing technology has once again changed our machines. The smartphone in your pocket communicates wirelessly with scalable, pay-as-you-go software services in the cloud. Those services run on virtualized instances of Unix, which in turn run on physical hardware in data centers, some of which are so large they were strategically placed to draw current from a neighboring hydroelectric dam. With such new and different machines as these, we shouldn't be surprised that what's possible for users and what's necessary for developers is also new and different, once again.

Node.js imagines JavaScript as a systems language, like C. On the page, JavaScript can manipulate headers and styles. As a systems language, JavaScript can manipulate memory buffers, processes and streams, and files and sockets. This anachronism, made possible by the performance V8 gives the language, sends it back two decades, transplanting it from the web page to the microprocessor die.

"Node's goal is to provide an easy way to build scalable network programs."

– Ryan Dahl, creator of Node.js

In this book, we will study the techniques professional Node developers use to tackle the software challenges of today. By mastering Node, you are learning how to build the next generation of software. In this chapter, we will explore how a Node application is designed, the shape and texture of its footprint on a server, and the powerful base set of tools and features Node provides for developers. Throughout, we will examine progressively more intricate examples demonstrating how Node's simple, comprehensive, and consistent architecture solves many difficult problems well.

The Unix design philosophy

As a network application scales, the volume of information it must recognize, organize, and maintain increases. This volume, in terms of I/O streams, memory usage, and processor load, expands as more clients connect. This expansion of information volume also burdens the software developer. Scaling issues appear, usually demonstrating a failure to accurately predict the behavior of a large system from the behavior of its smaller predecessors:

- Can a data layer designed for storing a few thousand records accommodate a few million?
- Are the algorithms used to search a handful of records efficient enough to search many more?
- Can this server handle 10,000 simultaneous client connections?

The edge of innovation is sharp and cuts quickly, presenting less time for deliberation precisely when the cost of error is magnified. The shape of objects comprising the whole of an application becomes amorphous and difficult to understand, particularly as ad hoc modifications are made, reactively, in response to dynamic tension in the system. What is described in a specification as a small subsystem may have been patched into so many other systems, that its actual boundaries are misunderstood. When this happens, it becomes impossible to accurately trace the outline of the composite parts of the whole.

Eventually, an application becomes unpredictable. It is dangerous when one cannot predict all future states of an application, or the side effects of change. Any number of servers, programming languages, hardware architectures, management styles, and so on, have attempted to subdue the intractable problem of risk following growth, of failure menacing success. Oftentimes, systems of even greater complexity are sold as the cure. The hold that any one person has on information is tenuous. Complexity follows scale; confusion follows complexity. As resolution blurs, errors happen.

Node chose clarity and simplicity instead, echoing a philosophy from decades earlier:

> *"Write programs that do one thing and do it well.*
> *Write programs to work together.*
> *Write programs to handle text streams, because that is a universal interface."*

> *-Peter H. Salus, A Quarter-Century of Unix, 1994*

From their experiences creating and maintaining Unix, *Ken Thompson* and *Dennis Ritchie* came up with a philosophy for how people should best build software. Using this philosophy as his guide, *Ryan Dahl* made a number of decisions in the design of Node:

- Node's design favors simplicity over complexity
- Node uses familiar POSIX APIs, rather than attempting an improvement
- Node does everything with events, and doesn't need threads
- Node leverages the existing C libraries, rather than trying to reimplement their functionality
- Node favors text over binary formats

Text streams are the language of Unix programs. JavaScript got good at manipulating text from its beginning as a web scripting language. It's a natural fit.

POSIX

POSIX, the **Portable Operating System Interface**, defines the standard APIs for Unix. It's adopted in Unix-based operating systems and beyond. The IEEE created and maintains the POSIX standard to enable systems from different manufacturers to be compatible. Write your C program using POSIX APIs on your laptop running macOS, and you'll have an easier time later building it on a Raspberry Pi.

As a common denominator, POSIX is old, simple, and most importantly, well-known to developers of all stripes. To make a new directory in a C program, use this API:

```
int mkdir(const char *path, mode_t mode);
```

And here it is in Node:

```
fs.mkdir(path[, mode], callback)
```

The Node documentation for the filesystem module starts out by telling the developer, there's nothing new here:

> *File I/O is provided by simple wrappers around standard POSIX functions.*
> `https://nodejs.org/api/fs.html`

For Node, *Ryan Dahl* implemented proven POSIX APIs, rather than trying to come up with something on his own. While such an attempt might be better in some ways, or some situations, it would lose the instant familiarity that POSIX gives to new Node developers trained in other systems.

In choosing POSIX for the API, Node is in no way limited to the standards from the 1970s. It's easy for anyone to write their own module that calls down to Node's API, while presenting a different one upwards. These fancier alternatives can then compete in a Darwinian quest to prove themselves better than POSIX.

Events for everything

If a program asks the operating system to open a file on the disk, that task might complete right away. Or, it might take a moment for the disk to spin up, or for other file system activity the operating system is working on to finish before it can perform this new request. Tasks that go beyond manipulating the memory of our application's process space to more distant hardware in the computer, network, and internet are not fast or reliable enough to program in the same way. Software designers needed a way to code these tasks, which can be slow and unreliable, without making their applications slow and unreliable as a whole. For systems programmers using languages like C and Java, the standard and accepted tool to use to solve this problem is the **thread.**

```
pthread_t my_thread;
int x = 0;
/* Make a thread and have it run my_function(&x) */
pthread_create(&my_thread, NULL, my_function, &x);
```

If a program asks the user a question, the user might respond right away. Or, the user may take a moment to think before clicking **Yes** or **No**. For web developers using HTML and JavaScript, the way to do this is the event as follows:

```
<button onclick="myFunction()">Click me</button>
```

At first glance, these two scenarios may seem completely distinct:

- In the first, a low-level system is shuttling blocks of memory from program to program, with delays milliseconds can be too big to measure
- In the second, the very top surface of a huge stack of software is asking the user a question

Conceptually, however, they're the same. Node's design realizes this, and uses events for both. In Node, there is one thread, bound to an event loop. Deferred tasks are encapsulated, entering and exiting the execution context via callbacks. I/O operations generate evented data streams, and these are piped through a single stack. Concurrency is managed by the system, abstracting thread pools, and simplifying shared access to memory.

Node showed us that JavaScript doesn't need threads to be useful as a systems language. Additionally, by not having threads, JavaScript and Node avoid concurrency issues that create performance and reliability challenges that developers expert in a code base can still have difficulty reasoning about. In Chapter 2, *Understanding Asynchronous Event-Driven Programming*, we'll go deeper into events, and the event loop.

Standard libraries

Node is built on standard open source C libraries. For example, the *TLS* and *SSL* protocols are implemented by *OpenSSL*. More than just adopting an API, the C source code of OpenSSL is included and complied into Node. When your JavaScript program hashes a cryptographic key, it's not JavaScript that's actually doing the work. Your JavaScript, run by Node, has called down to the C code of OpenSSL. Essentially, you are scripting the native library.

This design choice of using the existing and proven open source libraries helped Node in a number of ways:

- It meant that Node could arrive on the scene very rapidly, with the core set of functionality systems programmers needed and expected already there
- It ensures performance, reliability, and security continues to match the libraries

- It also didn't break cross-platform use, as all of these C libraries have been written and maintained to compile for different architectures for years

Previous platforms and languages have made a different choice in trying to achieve software portability. The *100% Pure Java™ Standard*, for instance, was a *Sun Microsystems* initiative to promote the development of portable applications. Rather than leveraging the existing code in a hybrid stack, it encouraged developers to rewrite everything in Java. Developers had to keep features, performance, and security up to the standard by writing and testing new code. Node, on the other hand, picked a design that gets this all for free.

Extending JavaScript

When he designed Node, JavaScript was not *Ryan Dahl*'s original language choice. Yet, upon exploration, he found a good modern language without opinions on streams, the filesystem, handling binary objects, processes, networking, and other capabilities one would expect to exist in a systems language. JavaScript, strictly limited to the browser, had no use for, and had not implemented, these features.

Guided by the Unix philosophy, Dahl was guided by a few rigid principles:

- A Node program/process runs on a single thread, ordering execution through an event loop
- Web applications are I/O intensive, so the focus should be on making I/O fast
- Program flow is always directed through asynchronous callbacks
- Expensive CPU operations should be split off into separate parallel processes, emitting events as results arrive
- Complex programs should be assembled from simpler programs

The general principle is, operations must never block. Node's desire for speed (high concurrency) and efficiency (minimal resource usage) demands the reduction of waste. A waiting process is a wasteful process, especially when waiting for I/O.

JavaScript's asynchronous, event-driven design fits neatly into this model. Applications express interest in some future event, and are notified when that event occurs. This common JavaScript pattern should be familiar to you:

```
Window.onload = function() {
  // When all requested document resources are loaded,
  // do something with the resulting environment
}
```

```
element.onclick = function() {
  // Do something when the user clicks on this element
}
```

The time it will take for an I/O action to complete is unknown, so the pattern is to ask for notification when an I/O event is emitted, whenever that may be, allowing other operations to be completed in the meantime.

Node adds an enormous amount of new functionality to JavaScript. Primarily, the additions provide evented I/O libraries offering the developer system access not available to browser-based JavaScript, such as writing to the filesystem or opening another system process. Additionally, the environment is designed to be modular, allowing complex programs to be assembled out of smaller and simpler components.

Let's look at how Node imported JavaScript's event model, extended it, and used it in the creation of interfaces to powerful system commands.

Events

Many functions in the Node API emit events. These events are instances of `events.EventEmitter`. Any object can extend `EventEmitter`, providing Node developers with a simple and uniform way to build tight, asynchronous interfaces to object methods.

The following code sets Node's `EventEmitter` object as the prototype of a function constructor we define. Each constructed instance has the `EventEmitter` object exposed to its prototype chain, providing a natural reference to the event API. The counter instance methods emit events, and code after that listens for them. After making a `Counter`, we listen for the incremented event, specifying a callback Node will call when the event happens. Then, we call the increment twice. Each time, our `Counter` increments the internal count it holds, and then emits the incremented event. This calls our callback, giving it the current count, which our callback logs:

```
// File counter.js
// Load Node's 'events' module, and point directly to EventEmitter there
const EventEmitter = require('events').EventEmitter;
// Define our Counter function
const Counter = function(i) { // Takes a starting number
  this.increment = function() { // The counter's increment method
    i++; // Increment the count we hold
    this.emit('incremented', i); // Emit an event named incremented
  }
}
```

```
// Base our Counter on Node's EventEmitter
Counter.prototype = new EventEmitter(); // We did this afterwards, not
before!
// Now that we've defined our objects, let's see them in action
// Make a new Counter starting at 10
const counter = new Counter(10);
// Define a callback function which logs the number n you give it
const callback = function(n) {
  console.log(n);
}
// Counter is an EventEmitter, so it comes with addListener
counter.addListener('incremented', callback);
counter.increment(); // 11
counter.increment(); // 12
```

The following is the output for counter.js:

```
$ node counter.js
11
12
```

To remove the event listeners bound to counter, use this:

```
counter.removeListener('incremented', callback).
```

For consistency with browser-based JavaScript, counter.on and counter.addListener
are interchangeable.

Node brought EventEmitter to JavaScript and made it an object your objects can extend.
This greatly increases the possibilities available to developers. With EventEmitter, Node
can handle I/O data streams in an event-oriented manner, performing long-running tasks
while keeping true to Node's principles of asynchronous, non-blocking programming:

```
// File stream.js
// Use Node's stream module, and get Readable inside
let Readable = require('stream').Readable;
// Make our own readable stream, named r
let r = new Readable;
// Start the count at 0
let count = 0;
// Downstream code will call r's _read function when it wants some data
from r
r._read = function() {
  count++;
  if (count > 10) { // After our count has grown beyond 10
    return r.push(null); // Push null downstream to signal we've got no
more data
```

```
    }
    setTimeout(() => r.push(count + '\n'), 500); // A half second from now,
  push our count on a line
  };
  // Have our readable send the data it produces to standard out
  r.pipe(process.stdout);
```

The following is the output for `stream.js`:

```
$ node stream.js
1
2
3
4
5
6
7
8
9
10
```

This example creates a readable stream `r`, and pipes its output to the standard out. Every 500 milliseconds, code increments a counter and pushes a line of text with the current count downstream. Try running the program yourself, and you'll see the series of numbers appear on your terminal.

On what would be the 11th count, `r` pushes null downstream, indicating that it has no more data to send. This closes the stream, and with nothing more to do, Node exits the process.

Subsequent chapters will explain streams in more detail. Here, just note how pushing data onto a stream causes an event to fire, how you can assign a custom callback to handle this event, and how the data flows downstream.

Node consistently implements I/O operations as asynchronous, evented data streams. This design choice enables Node's excellent performance. Instead of creating a thread (or spinning up an entire process) for a long-running task like a file upload that a stream may represent, Node only needs to commit the resources to handle callbacks. Additionally, in the long stretches of time in between the short moments when the stream is pushing data, Node's event loop is free to process other instructions.

As an exercise, re-implement `stream.js` to send the data `r` produces to a file instead of the terminal. You'll need to make a new writable stream `w`, using Node's `fs.createWriteStream`:

```
  // File stream2file.js
```

```
// Bring in Node's file system module
const fs = require('fs');
// Make the file counter.txt we can fill by writing data to writeable
stream w
const w = fs.createWriteStream('./counter.txt', { flags: 'w', mode: 0666
});
...
// Put w beneath r instead
r.pipe(w);
```

Modularity

In his book, *The Art of Unix Programming, Eric Raymond* proposed the **Rule of Modularity**:

> *"Developers should build a program out of simple parts connected by well-defined interfaces, so problems are local, and parts of the program can be replaced in the future versions to support new features. This rule aims to save time on debugging complex code that is complex, long, and unreadable."*

Large systems are hard to reason about, especially when the boundaries of internal components are fuzzy, and the interactions between them are complex. This principle of building large systems out of small, simple, and loosely-coupled pieces is a good idea for software and beyond. Physical manufacturing, management theory, education, and government, all have benefited from this design philosophy.

When developers began employing JavaScript for larger and more complex software challenges, they encountered this challenge. There was not yet a good way (and later, no common standard way) to assemble a JavaScript program from smaller ones. For example, you've probably seen HTML pages with tags like these at the top:

```
<head>
<script src="fileA.js"></script>
<script src="fileB.js"></script>
<script src="fileC.js"></script>
<script src="fileD.js"></script>
...
</head>
```

This works, but leads to a number of problems:

- The page must declare all potential dependencies before any are needed or used. If, while running, your program encounters a situation where it needs an additional dependency, dynamically loading another module is possible, but a separate hack.

- The scripts are not encapsulated. Code in every file writes to the same global object. Adding a new dependency may break an earlier one because of a name collision.
- `fileA` cannot address `fileB` as a collection. An addressable context like `fileB.function1` isn't available.

The `<script>` tag would be a nice place for useful module services such as dependency awareness and version control, but it doesn't have these features.

These difficulties and dangers made creating and using JavaScript modules feel more treacherous than effortless. A good module system with features like encapsulation and versioning can reverse this, encouraging code organization and sharing, and leading to a robust ecosystem of high-quality open source software components.

JavaScript needed a standard way to load and share discreet program modules, and found one in 2009 with the CommonJS Modules specification. Node follows this specification, making it easy to define and share bits of reusable code called **modules** or **packages.**

Choosing a delightfully simple design, a package is just a directory of JavaScript files. Metadata about the package, such as its name, version, and software license, lives in an additional file named `package.json`. The JSON contents of this file are easily both human and machine-readable. Let's take a look:

```
{
    "name": "mypackage1",
    "version": "0.1.2",
    "dependencies": {
        "jquery": "^3.1.0",
        "bluebird": "^3.4.1",
    },
    "license": "MIT"
}
```

This `package.json` defines a package named `mypackage1`, which depends on two other packages: **jQuery** and **Bluebird.** Alongside the package names is a version number. Version numbers follow the **Semantic Versioning (SemVer)** rules, with a pattern like Major.Minor.Patch. Looking at the incremented version numbers of a package your code has been using, here's what that means:

- **Major:** There's a change in the purpose or outcome of the API. If your code calls an updated function, it may break or produce an unintended result. Figure out what's changed, and determine if it affects your code.

- **Minor:** The package has added functionality, but remains compatible. Run all your tests, and you're good to go. Check out the documentation if you're curious, as there might be new, more advanced parts of the API alongside the functions and objects you're familiar with.
- **Patch:** The package fixed a bug, improved performance, or refactored a little. Run all your tests, and you're good to go.

Packages enable the construction of large systems from many small, interdependent systems. Perhaps even more importantly, packages encourage sharing. More detailed information about SemVer is available in Appendix A, *Organizing Your Work Into Modules*, where npm and packages are discussed in more depth.

> *"What I'm describing here is not a technical problem. It's a matter of people getting together and making a decision to step forward and start building up something bigger and cooler together."*

> *– Kevin Dangoor, creator of CommonJS*

 Not just about modules, CommonJS is actually a whole collection of standards founded with the goal of removing everything that was holding JavaScript back from world domination, open source developer *Kris Kowal* explained in a 2009 post evangelizing the initiative. He names the first of these impediments as the absence of a good module system. The second? The absence of a standard library, including such systems-level fundamentals as access to the filesystem, manipulation of I/O streams, and types for bytes and blocks of binary data. Today, CommonJS is known for giving JavaScript a module system, while Node is what gave JavaScript systems-level access:

```
https://arstechnica.com/information-technology/2009/12/commonjs-
effort-sets-javascript-on-path-for-world-domination/
```

CommonJS gave JavaScript packages. With packages, the next thing JavaScript needed was a package manager. Node provided one with npm.

A registry of packages, npm is accessible in two ways. First, at the website www.npmjs.com, you can link to and search for packages, essentially shopping for the right one. Stats that count how many times a package has been downloaded in the last day, week, and month show popularity and usage. Most packages link to a developer profile page and open source code on GitHub, so you can see the code, visualize recent development activity, and judge the reputations of the authors and contributors.

The second way to access npm is through the command-line tool npm, which is installed with Node. Using npm as a traditional package manager for your workstation, you can install packages globally, creating new command-line tools on your shell's path. npm also knows how to create, read, and edit `package.json` files, and can start you out with a new, empty Node package, add the dependencies it needs, download all the code, and keep everything up to date.

Along with Git and GitHub, npm is now achieving a dream of software development identified in the 1970s: that code could be reused more often, and software projects would be written entirely from scratch less frequently.
Earlier attempts at reaching this goal through version control systems like CVS and Subversion, and open source code sharing websites like `SourceForge.net`, focused on bigger units of both code and people, and didn't achieve as much.

GitHub and npm took a different approach in two important ways:

- Favoring individual developers working alone over communities meeting and discussing, developers could focus more on code and less on conversation
- Favoring small, atomic software components over complete applications, encapsulated composition started happening not just at a micro-level of subroutines and objects, but at the more important macroscale of application design

Even documentation is better with the new approach: in a monolithic software application, documentation was too often the afterthought that may or may not have happened after the product shipped.
With components, great documentation is necessary to sell your package to the world, getting it a larger public daily download count, and the social media accounts you keep as a developer of more followers.

In no small part, Node's success is due to the number and quality of packages available to you as a Node developer.

More extensive information on creating and managing Node packages can be found in `Appendix A`, *Organizing Your Work into Modules*.

The key design philosophy to follow is this: build programs out of packages where possible, and share those packages when possible. The shape of your applications will be clearer and easier to maintain. Importantly, the efforts of thousands of other developers can be linked into applications via npm, directly by inclusion, and indirectly as shared packages are tested, improved, refactored, and repurposed by members of the Node community.

 Contrary to popular belief, npm is not an abbreviation for Node Package Manager, and *should never be used or explained as an acronym*:
`https://docs.npmjs.com/policies/trademark`

The network

I/O in the browser is mercilessly hobbled, for very good reasons - if the JavaScript on any given website could access your filesystem, for instance, users could only click links to new sites they trusted, rather than ones they simply wanted to try out. Keeping pages in a limited sandbox, the design of the web made navigating from thing1.com to thing2.com not have the consequences of double-clicking thing1.exe and thing2.exe.

Node, of course, recasts JavaScript in the role of a systems language, giving it direct and unfettered access to operating system kernel objects such as files, sockets, and processes. This lets Node create scalable systems with high I/O requirements. It's likely the first thing you coded in Node was a HTTP server.

Node supports standard network protocols in addition to HTTP, such as TLS/SSL, and UDP. With these tools we can easily build scalable network programs, moving far beyond the comparatively limited AJAX solutions JavaScript developers know from the browser.

Let's write a simple program that sends a UDP packet to another node:

```
const dgram = require('dgram');
let client = dgram.createSocket("udp4");
let server = dgram.createSocket("udp4");
let message = process.argv[2] || "message";
message = Buffer.from(message);
server
.on('message', msg => {
  process.stdout.write(`Got message: ${msg}\n`);
  process.exit();
})
.bind(41234);
client.send(message, 0, message.length, 41234, "localhost");
```

Go ahead and open two terminal windows and navigate each to your code bundle for `Chapter 8`, *Scaling Your Application*, under the `/udp` folder. We're now going to run a UDP server in one window, and a UDP client in another.

In the right window, run `receive.js` with a command like the following:

```
$ node receive.js
```

On the left, run `send.js` with a command, as follows:

```
$ node send.js
```

Executing that command will cause the message to appear on the right:

```
$ node receive.js
Message received!
```

A UDP server is an instance of `EventEmitter`, emitting a message event when messages are received on the bound port. With Node, you can use JavaScript to write your application at the I/O level, moving packets and streams of binary data with ease.

Let's continue to explore I/O, the process object, and events. First, let's dig into the machine powering Node's core, V8.

V8, JavaScript, and optimizations

V8 is Google's JavaScript engine, written in C++. It compiles and executes JavaScript code inside of a VM (Virtual Machine). When a webpage loaded into Google Chrome demonstrates some sort of dynamic effect, like automatically updating a list or news feed, you are seeing JavaScript, compiled by V8, at work.

V8 manages Node's main process thread. When executing JavaScript, V8 does so in its own process, and its internal behavior is not controlled by Node. In this section, we will investigate the performance benefits that can be had by playing with these options, learning how to write *optimizable* JavaScript, and the cutting-edge JavaScript features available to users of the latest Node versions (such as 9.x, the version we use in this book).

Flags

There are a number of settings available to you for manipulating the Node runtime. Try this command:

```
$ node -h
```

In addition to standards such as --version, you can also flag Node to --abort-on-uncaught-exception.

You can also list the options available for v8:

```
$ node --v8-options
```

Some of these settings can save the day. For example, if you are running Node in a restrained environment like a Raspberry Pi, you might want to limit the amount of memory a Node process can consume, to avoid memory spikes. In that case, you might want to set the --max_old_space_size (by default ~1.5GB) to a few hundred MB.

You can use the -e argument to execute a Node program as a string; in this case, logging out of the version of V8 your copy of Node contains:

```
$ node -e "console.log(process.versions.v8)"
```

It's worth your time to experiment with Node/V8 settings, both for their utility and the path, to give you a slightly stronger understanding of what is happening (or might happen) *under the hood*.

Optimizing your code

The simple optimizations of smart code design can really help you. Traditionally, JavaScript developers working in browsers did not need to concern themselves with memory usage optimizations, having quite a lot to use for what were typically uncomplicated programs. On a server, this is no longer the case. Programs are generally more complicated, and running out of memory takes down your server.

The convenience of a dynamic language is in avoiding the strictness that compiled languages impose. For example, you need not explicitly define object property types, and can actually change those property types at will. This dynamism makes traditional compilation impossible, but opens up some interesting new opportunities for exploratory languages such as JavaScript. Nevertheless, dynamism introduces a significant penalty in terms of execution speeds when compared to statically compiled languages. The limited speed of JavaScript has regularly been identified as one of its major weaknesses.

V8 attempts to achieve the sorts of speeds one observes for compiled languages for JavaScript. V8 compiles JavaScript into native machine code, rather than interpreting bytecode, or using other just-in-time techniques. Because the precise runtime topology of a JavaScript program cannot be known ahead of time (the language is dynamic), compilation consists of a two-stage, speculative approach:

1. Initially, a first-pass compiler (the *full* compiler) converts your code into a runnable state as quickly as possible. During this step, type analysis and other detailed analysis of the code is deferred, prioritizing fast compilation – your JavaScript can begin executing as close to instantly as possible. Further optimizations are accomplished during the second step.

2. Once the program is up and running, an optimizing compiler then begins its job of watching how your program runs, and attempting to determine its current and future runtime characteristics, optimizing and re-optimizing as necessary. For example, if a certain function is being called many thousands of times with similar arguments of a consistent type, V8 will re-compile that function with code optimized on the optimistic assumption that future types will be like the past types. While the first compile step was conservative with as-yet unknown and un-typed functional signature, this `hot` function's predictable texture impels V8 to assume a certain optimal profile and re-compile based on that assumption.

Assumptions help us make decisions more quickly, but can lead to mistakes. What if the `hot` function V8's compiler just optimized against a certain type signature is now called with arguments violating that optimized profile? V8 has no choice, in that case: it must de-optimize the function. V8 must admit its mistake and roll back the work it has done. It will re-optimize in the future if a new pattern is seen. However, if V8 must again de-optimize at a later time, and if this optimize/de-optimize binary switching continues, V8 will simply *give up*, and leave your code in a de-optimized state.

Let's look at some ways to approach the design and declaration of arrays, objects, and functions, so that you are helping, rather than hindering the compiler.

Numbers and tracing optimization/de-optimization

The ECMA-262 specification defines the Number value as a "primitive value corresponding to a double-precision 64-bit binary format IEEE 754 value". The point is that there is no Integer type in JavaScript; there is a Number type defined as a double-precision floating-point number.

V8 uses 32-bit numbers for all values internally, for performance reasons that are too technical to discuss here. It can be said that one bit is used to point to another 32-bit number, should greater width be needed. Regardless, it is clear that there are two types of values tagged as numbers by V8, and switching between these types will cost you something. Try to restrict your needs to 31-bit signed Integers where possible.
Because of the type ambiguity of JavaScript, switching the types of numbers assigned to a slot is allowed. For example, the following code does not throw an error:

```
let a = 7;
a = 7.77;
```

However, a speculative compiler like V8 will be unable to optimize this variable assignment, given that its *guess* that a will always be an Integer turned out to be wrong, forcing de-optimization.

We can demonstrate the optimization/de-optimization process by setting some powerful V8 options, executing V8 native commands in your Node program, and tracing how v8 optimizes/de-optimizes your code.

Consider the following Node program:

```
// program.js
let someFunc = function foo(){}
console.log(%FunctionGetName(someFunc));
```

If you try to run this normally, you will receive an **Unexpected Token** error – the modulo (%) symbol cannot be used within an identifier name in JavaScript. What is this strange method with a % prefix? It is a V8 native command, and we can turn on execution of these types of functions by using the --allow-natives-syntax flag:

```
node --allow-natives-syntax program.js
// 'someFunc', the function name, is printed to the console.
```

Now, consider the following code, which uses native functions to assert information about the optimization status of the square function, using the %OptimizeFunctionOnNextCall native method:

```
let operand = 3;
function square() {
    return operand * operand;
}
// Make first pass to gather type information
square();
// Ask that the next call of #square trigger an optimization attempt;
// Call
```

```
%OptimizeFunctionOnNextCall(square);
square();
```

Create a file using the previous code, and execute it using the following command: `node --allow-natives-syntax --trace_opt --trace_deopt myfile.js`. You will see something like the following returned:

```
[deoptimize context: c39daf14679]
[optimizing: square / c39dafca921 - took 1.900, 0.851, 0.000 ms]
```

We can see that V8 has no problem optimizing the square function, as operand is declared once and never changed. Now, append the following lines to your file and run it again:

```
%OptimizeFunctionOnNextCall(square);
operand = 3.01;
square();
```

On this execution, following the optimization report given earlier, you should now receive something like the following:

```
**** DEOPT: square at bailout #2, address 0x0, frame size 8
  [deoptimizing: begin 0x2493d0fca8d9 square @2]
  ...
  [deoptimizing: end 0x2493d0fca8d9 square => node=3, pc=0x29edb8164b46,
  state=NO_REGISTERS, alignment=no padding, took 0.033 ms]
  [removing optimized code for: square]
```

This very expressive optimization report tells the story very clearly: the once-optimized square function was de-optimized following the change we made in one number's type. You are encouraged to spend some time writing code and testing it using these methods.

Objects and arrays

As we learned when investigating numbers, V8 works best when your code is predictable. The same holds true with arrays and objects. Nearly all of the following *bad practices* are bad for the simple reason that they create unpredictability.

Remember that in JavaScript, an object and an array are very similar *under the hood* (resulting in strange rules that provide no end of material for those poking fun at the language!). We won't be discussing those differences, only the important similarities, specifically in terms of how both these data constructs benefit from similar optimization techniques.

Avoid mixing types in arrays. It is always better to have a consistent data type, such as *all integers* or *all strings*. As well, avoid changing types in arrays, or in property assignments after initialization if possible. V8 creates *blueprints* of objects by creating hidden classes to track types, and when those types change the optimization, blueprints will be destroyed and rebuilt—if you're lucky. Visit https://github.com/v8/v8/wiki/Design%20Elements for more information.

Don't create arrays with gaps, such as the following:

```
let a = [];
a[2] = 'foo';
a[23] = 'bar';
```

Sparse arrays are bad for this reason: V8 can either use a very efficient linear storage strategy to store (and access) your array data, or it can use a hash table (which is much slower). If your array is sparse, V8 must choose the least efficient of the two. For the same reason, always start your arrays at the zero index. As well, do not ever use *delete* to remove elements from an array. You are simply inserting an *undefined* value at that position, which is just another way of creating a sparse array. Similarly, be careful about populating an array with empty values—ensure that the external data you are pushing into an array is not incomplete.

Try not to preallocate large arrays—grow as you go. Similarly, do not preallocate an array and then exceed that size. You always want to avoid spooking V8 into turning your array into a hash table. V8 creates a new hidden class whenever a new property is added to an object constructor. Try to avoid adding properties after an object is instantiated. Initialize all members in constructor functions in the same order. Same properties + same order = same object.

Remember that JavaScript is a dynamic language that allows object (and object prototype) modifications after instantiation. Since the shape and volume of an object can, therefore, be altered *after the fact*, how does V8 allocate memory for objects? It makes some reasonable assumptions. After a set number of objects are instantiated from a given constructor (I believe 8 is the trigger amount), the largest of these is assumed to be of the maximum size, and all further instances are allocated that amount of memory (and the initial objects are similarly resized). A total of 32 fast property slots, inclusive, are then allocated to each instance based on this assumed maximum size. Any extra properties are slotted into a (slower) overflow property array, which can be resized to accommodate any further new properties.

With objects, as with arrays, try to define as much as possible the shape of your data structures in a *futureproof* manner, with a set number of properties, of types, and so on.

Functions

Functions are typically called often, and should be one of your prime optimization focuses. Functions containing try-catch constructs are not optimizable, nor are functions containing other unpredictable constructs, like `with` or `eval`. If, for some reason, your function is not optimizable, keep its use to a minimum.

A very common optimization error involves the use of polymorphic functions. Functions that accept variable function arguments will be de-optimized. Avoid polymorphic functions.

An excellent explanation of how V8 performs speculative optimization can be found here: `https://ponyfoo.com/articles/an-introduction-to-speculative-optimization-in-v8`

Optimized JavaScript

The JavaScript language is in constant flux, and some major changes and improvements have begun to find their way into native compilers. The V8 engine used in the latest Node builds supports nearly all of the latest features. Surveying all of these is beyond the scope of this chapter. In this section, we'll mention a few of the most useful updates and how they might be used to simplify your code, helping to make it easier to understand and reason about, to maintain, and perhaps even become more performant.

We will be using the latest JavaScript features throughout this book. You can use **Promises**, **Generators**, and **async/await** constructs as of Node 8.x, and we will be using those throughout the book. These concurrency operators will be discussed at depth in `Chapter 2`, *Understanding Asynchronous Event-Driven Programming,* but a good takeaway for now is that the callback pattern is losing its dominance, and the Promise pattern in particular is coming to dominate module interfaces.

In fact, a new method `util.promisify` was recently added to Node's core, which converts a callback-based function to a Promise-based one:

```
const {promisify} = require('util');
const fs = require('fs');

// Promisification happens here
let readFileAsync = promisify(fs.readFile);
```

```
let [executable, absPath, target, ...message] = process.argv;

console.log(message.length ? message.join(' ') : `Running file ${absPath}
using binary ${executable}`);

readFileAsync(target, {encoding: 'utf8'})
.then(console.log)
.catch(err => {
  let message = err.message;
  console.log(`
    An error occurred!
    Read error: ${message}
  `);
});
```

Being able to easily *promisify* `fs.readFile` is very useful.

Did you notice any other new JavaScript constructs possibly unfamiliar to you?

Help with variables

You'll be seeing `let` and `const` throughout this book. These are new variable declaration types. Unlike `var`, `let` is *block scoped*; it does not apply outside of its containing block:

```
let foo = 'bar';

if(foo == 'bar') {
    let foo = 'baz';
    console.log(foo); // 1st
}
console.log(foo); // 2nd

// baz
// bar
// If we had used var instead of let:
// baz
// baz
```

For variables that will never change, use `const`, for *constant*. This is helpful for the compiler as well, as it can optimize more easily if a variable is guaranteed never to change. Note that `const` only works on assignment, where the following is illegal:

```
const foo = 1;
foo = 2; // Error: assignment to a constant variable
```

However, if the value is an object, `const` doesn't protect members:

```
const foo = { bar: 1 }
console.log(foo.bar) // 1
foo.bar = 2;
console.log(foo.bar) // 2
```

Another powerful new feature is **destructuring**, which allows us to easily assign the values of arrays to new variables:

```
let [executable, absPath, target, ...message] = process.argv;
```

Destructuring allows you to rapidly map arrays to variable names. Since `process.argv` is an array, which always contains the path to the Node executable and the path to the executing file as the first two arguments, we can pass a file target to the previous script by executing `node script.js /some/file/path`, where the third argument is assigned to the `target` variable.

Maybe we also want to pass a message with something like this:

```
node script.js /some/file/path This is a really great file!
```

The problem here is that `This is a really great file!` is space-separated, so it will be split into the array on each word, which is not what we want:

```
[... , /some/file/path, This, is, a, really, great, file!]
```

The **rest pattern** comes to the rescue here: the final argument `...message` collapses all remaining destructured arguments into a single array, which we can simply `join(' ')` into a single string. This also works for objects:

```
let obj = {
    foo: 'foo!',
    bar: 'bar!',
    baz: 'baz!'
};

// assign keys to local variables with same names
let {foo, baz} = obj;

// Note that we "skipped" #bar
console.log(foo, baz); // foo! baz!
```

This pattern is especially useful for processing function arguments. Prior to rest parameters, you might have been grabbing function arguments in this way:

```
function (a, b) {
    // Grab any arguments after a & b and convert to proper Array
    let args = Array.prototype.slice.call(arguments, f.length);
}
```

This was necessary previously, as the `arguments` object was not a true **Array**. In addition to being rather clumsy, this method also triggers de-optimization in compilers like V8.

Now, you can do this instead:

```
function (a, b, ...args) {
    // #args is already an Array!
}
```

The **spread pattern** is the rest pattern in reverse—you expand a single variable into many:

```
const week = ['mon','tue','wed','thur','fri'];
const weekend = ['sat','sun'];

console.log([...week, ...weekend]); //
['mon','tue','wed','thur','fri','sat','sun']

week.push(...weekend);
console.log(week); // ['mon','tue','wed','thur','fri','sat','sun']
```

Arrow functions

Arrow functions allow you to shorten function declarations, from `function() {}` to simply `() => {}`. Indeed, you can replace a line like this:

```
SomeEmitter.on('message', function(message) { console.log(message) });
```

To:

```
SomeEmitter.on('message', message => console.log(message));
```

Here, we lose both the brackets and curly braces, and the tighter code works as expected.

Another important feature of arrow functions is they are not assigned their own `this`—arrow functions inherit `this` from the call site. For example, the following code does not work:

```
function Counter() {
```

```
    this.count = 0;

    setInterval(function() {
        console.log(this.count++);
    }, 1000);
}

new Counter();
```

The function within `setInterval` is being called in the context of `setInterval`, rather than the `Counter` object, so this does not have any reference to count. That is, at the function call site, `this` is a `Timeout` object, which you can check yourself by adding `console.log(this)` to the prior code.

With arrow functions, this is assigned at the point of definition. Fixing the code is easy:

```
setInterval(() => { // arrow function to the rescue!
  console.log(this);
  console.log(this.count++);
}, 1000);
// Counter { count: 0 }
// 0
// Counter { count: 1 }
// 1
// ...
```

String manipulation

Finally, you will see a lot of backticks in the code. This is the new **template literal** syntax, and along with other things, it (finally!) makes working with strings in JavaScript much less error-prone and tedious. You saw in the example how it is now easy to express multiline strings (avoiding 'First line\n' + 'Next line\n' types of constructs). String interpolation is similarly improved:

```
let name = 'Sandro';
console.log('My name is ' + name);
console.log(`My name is ${name}`);
// My name is Sandro
// My name is Sandro
```

This sort of substitution is especially effective when concatenating many variables, and since the contents of each `${expression}` can be any JavaScript code:

```
console.log(`2 + 2 = ${2+2}`)   // 2 + 2 = 4
```

You can also use `repeat` to generate strings: `'ha'.repeat(3) // hahaha`.

Strings are now iterable. Using the new `for...of` construct, you can pluck apart a string character by character:

```
for(let c of 'Mastering Node.js') {
    console.log(c);
    // M
    // a
    // s
    // ...
}
```

Alternatively, use the spread operator:

```
console.log([...'Mastering Node.js']);
// ['M', 'a', 's',...]
```

Searching is also easier. New methods allow common substring seeks without much ceremony:

```
let targ = 'The rain in Spain lies mostly on the plain';
console.log(targ.startsWith('The', 0)); // true
console.log(targ.startsWith('The', 1)); // false
console.log(targ.endsWith('plain')); // true
console.log(targ.includes('rain', 5)); // false
```

The second argument to these methods indicates a search offset, defaulting to **0**. The is found at position **0**, so beginning the search at position **1** fails in the second case.

Great, writing JavaScript programs just got a little easier. The next question is what's going on when that program is executed within a V8 process?

The process object

Node's **process object** provides information on and control over the current running process. It is an instance of `EventEmitter` is accessible from any scope, and exposes very useful low-level pointers. Consider the following program:

```
const size = process.argv[2];
const n = process.argv[3] || 100;
const buffers = [];
let i;
for (i = 0; i < n; i++) {
  buffers.push(Buffer.alloc(size));
```

```
        process.stdout.write(process.memoryUsage().heapTotal + "\n");
    }
```

Have Node run `process.js` with a command like this:

```
$ node process.js 1000000 100
```

The program gets the command-line arguments from `process.argv`, loops to allocate memory, and reports memory usage back to standard out. Instead of logging back to the terminal, you could stream output to another process, or a file:

```
$ node process.js 1000000 100 > output.txt
```

A Node process begins by constructing a single execution stack, with the global context forming the base of the stack. Functions on this stack execute within their own local context (sometimes referred to as **scope**), which remains enclosed within the global context. This way of keeping the execution of a function together with the environment the function runs in is called **closure**. Because Node is evented, any given execution context can commit the running thread to handling an eventual execution context. This is the purpose of callback functions.

Consider the following schematic of a simple interface for accessing the filesystem:

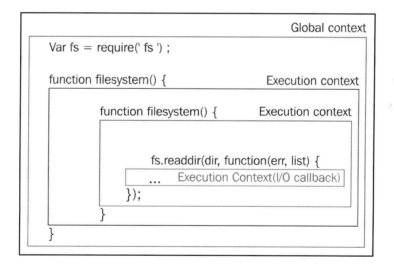

If we were to instantiate `Filesystem` and call `readDir`, a nested execution context structure would be created:

```
(global (fileSystem (readDir (anonymous function) ) ) )
```

Inside Node, a C library named `libuv` creates and manages the event loop. It connects to low-level operating system kernel mode objects that can produce events, such as timers that go off, sockets that receive data, files that open for reading, and child processes that complete. It loops while there are still events to process, and calls callbacks associated with events. It does this at a very low level, and with a very performant architecture. Written for Node, `libuv` is now a building block of a number of software platforms and languages.

The concomitant execution stack is introduced to Node's single-process thread. This stack remains in memory until `libuv` reports that `fs.readdir` has completed, at which point the registered anonymous callback fires, resolving the sole pending execution context. As no further events are pending, and the maintenance of closures no longer necessary, the entire structure can be safely torn down (in reverse, beginning with anonymous), and the process can exit, freeing any allocated memory. This method of building up and tearing down a single stack is what Node's event loop is ultimately doing.

The REPL

Node's **REPL (Read-Eval-Print-Loop)** represents the Node shell. To enter the shell prompt, enter Node via your terminal without passing a filename:

```
$ node
```

You now have access to a running Node process, and may pass JavaScript commands to this process. Additionally, if you enter an expression, the REPL will echo back the value of the expression. As a simple example of this, you can use the REPL as a pocket calculator:

```
$ node
> 2+2
4
```

Enter the 2+2 expression, and Node will echo back the value of the expression, 4. Going beyond simple number literals, you can use this behavior to query, set, and again, query the values of variables:

```
> a
ReferenceError: a is not defined
  at repl:1:1
  at sigintHandlersWrap (vm.js:22:35)
```

```
   at sigintHandlersWrap (vm.js:96:12)
   at ContextifyScript.Script.runInThisContext (vm.js:21:12)
   at REPLServer.defaultEval (repl.js:346:29)
   at bound (domain.js:280:14)
   at REPLServer.runBound [as eval] (domain.js:293:12)
   at REPLServer.<anonymous> (repl.js:545:10)
   at emitOne (events.js:101:20)
   at REPLServer.emit (events.js:188:7)
> a = 7
7
> a
7
```

Node's REPL is an excellent place to try out, debug, test, or otherwise play with JavaScript code.

As the REPL is a native object, programs can also use instances as a context in which to run JavaScript interactively. For example, here we create our own custom function `sayHello`, add it to the context of a REPL instance, and start the REPL, emulating a Node shell prompt:

```
require('repl').start("> ").context.sayHello = function() {
  return "Hello";
};
```

Enter `sayHello()` at the prompt, and the function will send `Hello` to standard out.

Let's take everything we've learned in this chapter and create an interactive REPL that allows us to execute JavaScript on a remote server:

1. Create two files, `client.js` and `server.js`, and type in the following code.
2. Run each in its own terminal window, keeping both windows side by side on your screen:

```
// File client.js
let net = require("net");
let sock = net.connect(8080);
process.stdin.pipe(sock);
sock.pipe(process.stdout);

// File server.js
let repl = require("repl")
let net = require("net")
net.createServer((socket) => {
  repl
  .start({
    prompt: "> ",
```

```
        input: socket,
        output: socket,
        terminal: true
    }).on('exit', () => {
        socket.end();
    })
}).listen(8080);
```

The `client.js` program creates a new socket connection to port `8080` through `net.connect`, and pipes any data coming from standard in (your terminal) through to that socket. Similarly, any data arriving from the socket is piped to standard out (back to your terminal). With this code, we've created a way to take terminal input and send it via a socket to port `8080`, listening for any data that the socket may send back to us.

The other program, `server.js`, closes the loop. This program uses `net.createServer` and `.listen` to create and start a new TCP server. The callback the code passes to `net.createServer` receives a reference to the bound socket. Within the enclosure of that callback, we instantiate a new REPL instance, giving it a nice prompt (> here, but could be any string), indicating that it should both listen for input from, and broadcast output to, the passed socket reference, indicating that the socket data should be treated as terminal data (which has special encoding).

We can now type something like `console.log("hello")` into the client terminal, and see `hello` displayed.

To confirm that the execution of our JavaScript commands is occurring in the server instance, type `console.log(process.argv)` into the client, and the server will display an object containing the current process path, which will be `server.js`.

With just a few lines of code, we've created a way to remotely control Node processes. It's the first step towards multi-node analytics tools, remote memory management, automatic server administration, and more.

Summary

Experienced developers have all struggled with the problems that Node aims to solve:

- How to serve many thousands of simultaneous clients efficiently
- Scaling networked applications beyond a single server

- Preventing I/O operations from becoming bottlenecks
- Eliminating single points of failure, thereby ensuring reliability
- Achieving parallelism safely and predictably

As each year passes, we see collaborative applications and software responsible for managing levels of concurrency that would have been considered rare just a few years ago. Managing concurrency, both in terms of connection handling and application design, is the key to building scalable architectures.

In this chapter, we've outlined the key problems Node's designers sought to solve, and how their solution has made the creation of easily scalable, high-concurrency networked systems easier for an open community of developers. We've seen how JavaScript has been given very useful new powers, how its evented model has been extended, and how V8 can be configured to further customize the JavaScript runtime. Through examples, we've learned how I/O is handled by Node, how to program the REPL, as well as how to manage inputs and outputs to the process object.

Node turns JavaScript into a systems language, creating a useful anachronism of scripting sockets as well as buttons, and cutting across decades of learning from the evolution of computing.

Node's design restores the virtues of simplicity the original Unix developers discovered in the 1970s. Interestingly, computer science rebelled against that philosophy in the intervening time period. C++ and Java favored object-oriented design patterns, serialized binary data formats, subclassing rather than rewriting, and other policies that caused codebases to often grow to one million lines or more before finally collapsing under the weight of their own complexity.

But then came the web. The browser's **View**, **Source** feature is a gentle on-ramp that brought millions of web users into the ranks of a new generation of software developers. Brendan Eich designed JavaScript with this novice prospective developer in mind. It's easy to start by editing tags and changing styles, and soon be writing code. Talk to the young employees of newly growing start-ups, now professional developers, engineers, and computer scientists, and many will recount **View**, **Source** as how they got their start.

Riding Node's time warp back, JavaScript found a similar design and philosophy in the founding principles of Unix. Perhaps connecting computers to the internet gave smart people new, more interesting computing problems to solve. Perhaps another new generation of students and junior employees arrived and rebelled against their mentors once again. For whatever reason, small, modular, and simple make up the prevailing philosophy today, as they did much earlier before.

In the decades ahead, how many more times will computing technology change enough to prompt the designers of the day to write new software and languages quite different from the practices taught and accepted as correct, finished, and permanent just a few years earlier? As *Arthur C. Clarke* noted, trying to predict the future is a discouraging and hazardous occupation. Perhaps we'll see several more revolutions in computers and code. Alternatively, it's possible that computing technology will soon plateau for a stretch of years, and within that stability, computer scientists will find and settle on the best paradigms to teach and use. Nobody knows the best way to code right now, but perhaps soon, we will. If that's the case, then this time now, when creating and exploring to find these answers is anyone's game, is a wonderfully compelling time to be working and playing with computers.

Our goal of demonstrating how Node allows applications to be intelligently constructed out of well-formed pieces in a principled way has begun. In the next chapter, we will delve deeper into asynchronous programming, learn how to manage more complex event chains, and develop more powerful programs using Node's model.

2
Understanding Asynchronous Event-Driven Programming

"The best way to predict the future is to invent it."

– Alan Kay

Eliminating blocking processes through the use of event-driven, asynchronous I/O is Node's primary organizational principle. We've learned how this design helps developers in shaping information and adding capacity. Node lets you build and organize lightweight, independent, and share-nothing processes that communicate through callbacks and synchronize with a predictable event loop.

Accompanying the growth in the popularity of Node is a growth in the number of well-designed event-driven systems and applications. For a new technology to be successful, it must eliminate the existing problems, and/or offer to consumers a better solution at a lower cost in terms of time, effort, or price. In its young and fertile lifespan, the Node community has collaboratively proven that this new development model is a viable alternative to the existing technologies. The number and quality of Node-based solutions powering enterprise-level applications provides further proof that these new ideas are not only novel, but preferred.

In this chapter, we will delve deeper into how Node implements event-driven programming. We will begin by unpacking the ideas and theories that event-driven languages and environments derive from and grapple with, in an effort to clear away misconceptions and encourage mastery. Following this introduction to events, we'll look at the key Node.js technology—the event loop. We'll then go into more detail on how Node implements timers, callbacks, and I/O events, and how you as a Node developer can use them. We'll further discuss management of concurrency using modern tools such as **Promises**, **Generators**, and **async/await**. We'll practice the theory as we build up some simple but exemplary file and data-driven applications. These examples highlight Node's strengths, and show how Node is succeeding in its ambition to simplify network application designs.

Node's unique design

First, let's take an accurate look at the total time cost when your program asks the system to perform different kinds of services. I/O is expensive. In the following chart (taken from *Ryan Dahl*'s original presentation on Node), we can see how many clock cycles typical system tasks consume. The relative cost of I/O operations is striking:

L1 cache	3 cycles
L2 cache	14 cycles
RAM	250 cycles
Disk	41,000,000 cycles
Network	240,000,000 cycles

The reasons are clear enough: a disk is a physical device, a spinning metal platter — storing and retrieving that data is much slower than moving data between solid-state devices (such as microprocessors and memory chips), or indeed optimized on-chip L1/L2 caches. Similarly, data does not move from point to point on a network instantaneously. Light itself needs 0.1344 seconds to circle the globe! In a network used by many billions of people regularly interacting across great distances at speeds much slower than the speed of light, with many detours and few straight lines, this sort of latency builds up.

When our software ran on personal computers on our desks, little or no communication was happening over the network. Delays or hiccups in our interactions with a word processor or spreadsheet had to do with disk access time. Much work was done to improve disk access speeds. Data storage and retrieval became faster, software became more responsive, and users now expect this responsiveness in their tools.

With the advent of cloud computing and browser-based software, your data has left the local disk and exists on a remote disk, and you access this data via a network—the internet. Data access times have slowed down again, dramatically. Network I/O is slow. Nevertheless, more companies are migrating sections of their applications into the cloud, with some software being entirely network-based.

Node is designed to make I/O fast. It is designed for this new world of networked software, where data is in many places and must be assembled quickly. Many of the traditional frameworks to build web applications were designed at a time when a single user working on a desktop computer used a browser to periodically make HTTP requests to a single server running a relational database. Modern software must anticipate tens of thousands of simultaneously connected clients concurrently altering enormous, shared data pools via a variety of network protocols, on any number of unique devices. Node is designed specifically to help those building that kind of network software.

The breakthrough in thinking reflected by Node's design is simple to understand once one recognizes that most worker threads spend their time waiting—for more instructions, a sub-task to complete, and so on. For example, a process assigned to service the command *format my hard drive* will dedicate all of its allotted resources to managing a workflow, something like the following:

- Communicate to a device driver that a format request has been made
- Idle, waiting for an *unknowable* length of time
- Receive the signal format as complete
- Notify the client
- Clean up; shut down:

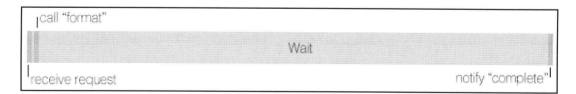

In the preceding figure, we see that an expensive worker is charging the client a fixed fee per unit of time, regardless of whether any useful work is being done (the client is paying equally for activity and idleness). To put it another way, it is not necessarily true, and most often not true, that the sub-tasks comprising a total task each require similar effort or expertise. It's therefore wasteful to pay a premium price for such cheap labor.

Sympathetically, we must also recognize that this worker can do no better even if ready and able to handle more work — even the best-intentioned worker cannot do anything about I/O bottlenecks. The worker here is **I/O bound**.

Instead, imagine an alternative design. What if multiple clients could share the same worker, such that the moment a worker announces availability due to an I/O bottleneck, another job from another client can start?

Node has commoditized I/O through the introduction of an environment where system resources are (ideally) **never** idle. Event-driven programming as implemented by Node reflects the simple goal of lowering overall system costs by encouraging the sharing of expensive labor, mainly by reducing the number of I/O bottlenecks to **zero**. We no longer have a powerless chunk of rigidly-priced unsophisticated labor; we can reduce all effort into discrete units with precisely delineated shapes, and therefore admit much more accurate pricing.

What would an environment within which many client jobs are cooperatively scheduled look like? And how is this message passing between events handled? Additionally, what do concurrency, parallelism, asynchronous execution, callbacks, and events mean to the Node developer?

Collaboration

What would be preferable to the blocking system described previously is a collaborative work environment, where workers are regularly assigned new tasks to do, instead of idling. In order to achieve such a goal, what we need is a virtual switchboard, where requests for services are dispatched to available workers, and where workers notify the switchboard of their availability.

One way to achieve this goal is to have a pool of available labors, improving efficiency by delegating tasks to different workers as the tasks come in:

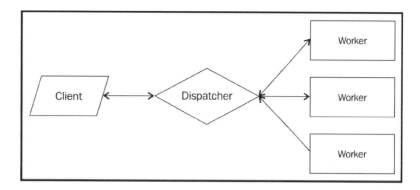

One drawback to this method is the amount of scheduling and worker surveillance that needs to be done. The dispatcher must field a steady stream of requests, while managing messages coming from workers about their availability, neatly breaking up requests into manageable tasks and efficiently sorting them, so that the fewest number of workers are idling.

Perhaps most importantly, what happens when all workers are fully booked? Does the dispatcher begin to drop requests from clients? Dispatching is resource-intensive as well, and there are limits even to the dispatcher's resources. If requests continue to arrive and no worker is available to service them, what does the dispatcher do? Manage a queue? We now have a situation where the dispatcher is no longer doing the right job (dispatching), and has become responsible for bookkeeping and keeping lists, further extending the time each task takes to complete. Each task takes some amount of time, and must be processed in arrival order. This task execution model stacks fixed time intervals — *ticks* of time. This is *synchronous* execution.

Queueing

In order to avoid overwhelming anyone, we might add a buffer between the clients and the dispatcher. This new worker is responsible for managing customer relations. Instead of speaking directly with the dispatcher, the client speaks to the services manager, passing the manager requests, and at some point in the future, getting a call that their task has been completed. Requests for work are added to a prioritized work queue (a stack of orders with the most important one on top), and this manager waits for another client to walk through the door.

The following figure describes the situations:

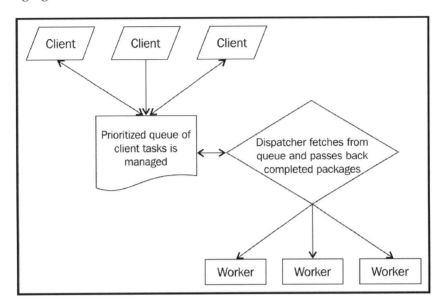

The dispatcher tries to keep all workers busy by pulling tasks from this queue, passing back any packages workers have completed, and generally maintaining a sane work environment where nothing gets dropped or lost. Rather than proceeding task-by-task along a single timeline, multiple simultaneous jobs, on their own timelines, run in parallel. If it comes to a point where all the workers are idle and the task queue is empty, the office can sleep for a while, until the next client arrives.

This is a rough schematic of how Node gains speed by working *asynchronously,* rather than *synchronously*. Now, let's dive deeper into how Node's event loop works.

Understanding the event loop

The following three points are important to remember, as we break down the event loop:

- The event loop runs in the same (single) thread your JavaScript code runs in. Blocking the event loop means blocking the entire thread.
- You don't start and/or stop the event loop. The event loop starts as soon as a process starts, and ends when no further callbacks remain to be performed. The event loop may, therefore, run forever.

- The event loop delegates many I/O operations to `libuv`, which manages these operations (using the power of the OS itself, such as thread pools), notifying the event loop when results are available. An easy-to-reason-about single-threaded programming model is reinforced with the efficiency of multithreading.

For example, the following `while` loop will never terminate:

```
let stop = false;
setTimeout(() => {
  stop = true;
}, 1000);

while (stop === false) {};
```

Even though one might expect, in approximately one second, the assignment of a Boolean `true` to the variable `stop`, tripping the `while` conditional and interrupting its loop; this will never happen. Why? This `while` loop starves the event loop by running infinitely, greedily checking and rechecking a value that is never given a chance to change, as the event loop is never given a chance to schedule our timer callback for execution. This proves the event loop (which manages timers), and runs on the same thread.

According to the Node documentation, "The event loop is what allows Node.js to perform non-blocking I/O operations — despite the fact that JavaScript is single-threaded — by offloading operations to the system kernel whenever possible." The key design choice made by Node's designers was the implementation of an event loop as a concurrency manager. For example, notifying your Node-based HTTP server of network connections to your local hardware is handled by the OS passing along, via `libuv`, network interface events.

The following description of event-driven programming (taken from: `http://www.princeton.edu/~achaney/tmve/wiki100k/docs/Event-driven_programming.html`) clearly not only describes the event-driven paradigm, but also introduces us to how events are handled in Node, and how JavaScript is an ideal language for such a paradigm.

In computer programming, event-driven programming or event-based programming is a programming paradigm in which the flow of the program is determined by events—that is, sensor outputs or user actions (mouse clicks, key presses) or messages from other programs or threads. Event-driven programming can also be defined as an application architecture technique in which the application has a main loop that is clearly divided down to two sections: the first is event selection (or event detection), and the second is event handling [...]. Event-driven programs can be written in any language, although the task is easier in languages that provide high-level abstractions, such as closures. Visit `https://www.youtube.com/watch?v=QQnz4QHNZKc` for more information.

Node makes a single thread more efficient by delegating many blocking operations to OS subsystems to process, bothering the main V8 thread only when there is data available for use. The main thread (your executing Node program) expresses interest in some data (such as via fs.readFile) by passing a callback, and is notified when that data is available. Until that data arrives, no further burden is placed on V8's main JavaScript thread. How? Node delegates I/O work to libuv, as quoted at: http://nikhilm.github.io/uvbook/basics. html#event-loops.

In event-driven programming, an application expresses interest in certain events, and responds to them when they occur. The responsibility of gathering events from the operating system or monitoring other sources of events is handled by libuv, and the user can register callbacks to be invoked when an event occurs.

Matteo Collina has created an interesting module for benchmarking the event loop, which is available at: https://github.com/mcollina/ loopbench.

Consider the following code:

```
const fs = require('fs');
fs.readFile('foo.js', {encoding:'utf8'}, (err, fileContents) => {
  console.log('Then the contents are available', fileContents);
});
console.log('This happens first');
```

The output of this program is:

```
> This happens first
> Then the contents are available, [file contents shown]
```

Here's what Node does when executing this program:

1. A process object is created in C++ using the V8 API. The Node.js runtime is then imported into this V8 process.
2. The fs module is attached to the Node runtime. V8 exposes C++ to JavaScript. This provides access to native filesystem bindings for your JavaScript code.

3. The `fs.readFile` method has passed instructions and a JavaScript callback. Through `fs.binding`, `libuv` is notified of the file read request, and is passed a specially prepared version of the callback sent by the original program.

4. `libuv` invokes the OS-level functions necessary to read a file.

5. The JavaScript program continues, printing `This happens first`. Because there is a callback outstanding, the event loop continues to spin, waiting for that callback to resolve.

6. When the file descriptor has been fully read by the OS, `libuv` (via internal mechanisms) is informed, and the callback passed to `libuv` is invoked, which essentially prepares the original JavaScript callback for re-entrance into the main (V8) thread.

7. The original JavaScript callback is pushed onto the event loop, and is invoked on a near-future tick of the loop.

8. The file contents are printed to the console.

9. As there are no further callbacks in flight, the process exits.

Here, we see the key ideas that Node implements to achieve fast, manageable, and scalable I/O. If, for example, there were 10 read calls made for `foo.js` in the preceding program, the execution time would, nevertheless, remain roughly the same. Each call will be managed by `libuv` as efficiently as possible (by, for example, parallelizing the calls using threads). Even though we wrote our code in JavaScript, we are actually deploying a very efficient multithreaded execution engine while avoiding the difficulties of OS asynchronous process management.

Now that we know how a filesystem operation might work, let's dig into how every type of asynchronous operation Node capable of spawning is treated on the event loop.

Event loop ordering, phases, and priorities

The event loop proceeds through phases, and each phase has a queue of events to process. From the Node documentation:

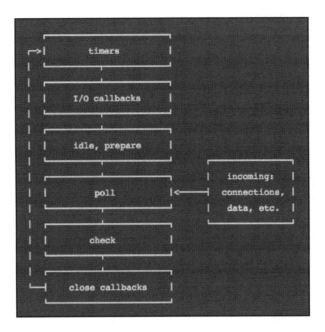

The phases relevant to developers are the following:

- **Timers**: Callbacks deferred to some time in the future specified in milliseconds, such as `setTimeout` and `setInterval`
- **I/O callbacks**: Prepared callbacks returned to the main thread after being delegated to Node's managed thread pool, such as filesystem calls and network listeners
- **Poll/check**: Mainly the functions slotted on the stack according to the rules of `setImmediate` and `nextTick`

When data becomes available on a socket or other stream interface, we cannot simply execute our callback immediately. JavaScript is single-threaded, so results must be synchronized. We can't suddenly change the state in the middle of an event loop tick — this would create some of the classic multithreaded application problems of race conditions, memory access conflicts, and so on.

To learn more about how Node is bound to `libuv` and other core libraries, parse through the `fs` module code at: `https://github.com/nodejs/node/blob/master/lib/fs.js`. Compare the `fs.read` and the `fs.readSync` methods to observe the difference between how synchronous and asynchronous actions are implemented; note the wrapper callback that is passed to the native `binding.read` method in `fs.read`. To take an even deeper dive into the very heart of Node's design, including the queue implementation, read through the Node source at: `https://github.com/joyent/node/tree/master/src`. Follow `FSEventWrap` within `fs_event_wrap.cc`. Investigate the `req_wrap` class, a wrapper for the V8 engine, deployed in `node_file.cc` and elsewhere and defined in `req_wrap.h`.

Upon entering an event loop, Node, in effect, makes a copy of the current instruction queue (also known as **stack**), empties the original queue, and executes its copy. The processing of this instruction queue is referred to as a **tick**. If `libuv`, asynchronously, receives results while the chain of instructions copied at the start of this tick are being processed on the single main thread (V8), these results (wrapped as callbacks) are queued. Once the current queue is emptied and its last instruction has completed, the queue is again checked for instructions to execute on the next tick. This pattern of checking and executing the queue will repeat (loop) until the queue is emptied, and no further data events are expected, at which point the Node process exits.

Next, let's look at the event interfaces of Node.

Listening for events

Modern network software, for various reasons, is growing in complexity and, in many ways, changing how we think about application development. Most new platforms and languages are attempting to address these changes. Node is no exception — and JavaScript is no exception.

Learning about Node means learning about event-driven programming, composing software out of modules, creating and linking data streams, and producing and consuming events and their related data. Node-based architectures are often composed of many small processes and/or services communicating with events — internally, by extending the `EventEmitter` interface and using callbacks, and externally, over one of several common transport layers (for example, HTTP, TCP), or through a thin messaging layer covering one of these transport layers (for example, 0MQ, Redis PUBSUB, and Kafka).

It is likely that these processes are composed of several free, open source, and high-quality npm modules, each distributed with unit tests and/or examples and/or documentation.

The previous chapter introduced you to the `EventEmitter` interface. This is the primary event interface we will be encountering as we move chapter to chapter, as it provides the prototype class for the many Node objects exposing evented interfaces, such as file and network streams. Various `close`, `exit`, `data`, and other events exposed by different module APIs signal the presence of an `EventEmitter` interface, and we will be learning about these modules and use cases as we progress.

In this section, our goal is to discuss some lesser-known event sources: signals, child process communication, filesystem change events, and deferred execution.

Signals

Evented programming is like hardware interrupt programming. Interrupts do exactly what their name suggests. They use their ability to interrupt whatever a controller, or the CPU, or any other device is doing, demanding that their particular need be serviced immediately.

In fact, the Node process object exposes standard **Portable Operating System Interface (POSIX)** signal names, such that a Node process can subscribe to these system events.

> *As* `http://en.wikipedia.org/wiki/POSIX_signal` *defines, "A signal is a limited form of inter-process communication used in Unix, Unix-like, and other POSIX-compliant operating systems. It is an asynchronous notification sent to a process, or to a specific thread, within the same process in order to notify it of an event that occurred."*

This is a very elegant and natural way to expose a Node process to operating system signal events. One might configure listeners to catch signals instructing a Node process to restart or update some configuration files, or simply clean up and shut down.

For example, the **SIGINT** signal is sent to a process when its controlling terminal detects a *Ctrl* + *C* (or equivalent) keystroke. This signal tells a process that an interrupt has been requested. If a Node process has bound a callback to this event, that function might log the request prior to terminating, do some other cleanup work, or even ignore the request:

```
// sigint.js
console.log("Running...");

// After 16 minutes, do nothing
setInterval(() => {}, 1e6); // Keeps Node running the process
```

```
// Subscribe to SIGINT, so some of our code runs when Node gets that signal
process.on("SIGINT", () => {
    console.log("We received the SIGINT signal!");
    process.exit(1);
});
```

The following is the output for `sigint.js`:

```
$ node sigint.js
Running...
(then press Ctrl+C)
We received the SIGINT signal!
```

This example starts a long interval, so Node doesn't exit with nothing else to do. When you send a *Ctrl + C* from your keyboard through the terminal controlling the process, Node gets the signal from the operating system. Your code has subscribed to that event, and Node runs your function.

Now, consider a situation in which a Node process is doing some ongoing work, such as parsing logs. It might be useful to be able to send that process a signal, such as update your configuration files, or restart the scan. You may want to send such signals from the command line. You might prefer to have another process do so — a practice known as **Inter-Process Communication** (IPC).

Create a file named `ipc.js`, and type in the following code:

```
// ipc.js
setInterval(() => {}, 1e6);
process.on("SIGUSR1", () => {
    console.log("Got a signal!");
});
```

Run the following command:

```
$ node ipc.js
```

As before, Node will wait for around 16 minutes before running the empty function, keeping the process open, so you'll have to *Ctrl + C* to get your prompt back. Note that this works just fine even though here, we haven't subscribed to the SIGINT signal.

`SIGUSR1` (and `SIGUSR2`) are user-defined signals, triggered by no specific action known to the operating system. They're meant for custom functionality.

To send a command to a process, you must determine its **process ID.** With a PID in hand, you can address a process and communicate with it. If the PID assigned to `ipc.js` after being run through Node is `123`, then we can send that process a `SIGUSR1` signal using the `kill` command:

```
$ kill -s SIGUSR1 123
```

> A simple way to find the PID for a given Node process in UNIX is to search the system process list for the name of the program that says the process is running. If `ipc.js` is currently executing, its PID is found by entering the following command line in the console/terminal: `ps aux | grep ipc.js`. Try it.

Child processes

A fundamental part of Node's design is to create or fork processes when parallelizing execution or scaling a system, as opposed to creating a thread pool, for instance. We will be using these child processes in various ways throughout this book. Right now, the focus will be on understanding how to handle communication events between child processes.

To create a child process, require Node's `child_process` module, and call the `fork` method. Pass the name of the program file the new process should execute:

```
let cp = require("child_process");
let child = cp.fork(__dirname + "/lovechild.js");
```

You can keep any number of subprocesses running with this method. On multicore machines, the operating system will distribute forked processes across the available hardware cores. Spreading Node processes across cores, even onto other machines, and managing IPC is one way to scale a Node application in a stable, understandable, and predictable way.

Extending the preceding example, we can now have the forking process (`parent`) send, and listen for, messages from the forked process (`child`). Here's the code for `parent.js`:

```
// parent.js
const cp = require("child_process");
let child = cp.fork(__dirname + "/lovechild.js");

child.on("message", (m) => {
  console.log("Child said: ", m); // Parent got a message up from our child
});
child.send("I love you"); // Send a message down to our child
```

The following is the output for `parent.js`:

```
$ node parent.js
Parent said:  I love you
Child said:  I love you too
(then Ctrl+C to terminate both processes)
```

Alongside that file, make another one and name it `lovechild.js`. The code of the child in here can listen for messages and send them back up:

```
// lovechild.js
process.on("message", (m) => {
  console.log("Parent said: ", m); // Child got a message down from the
parent
  process.send("I love you too"); // Send a message up to our parent
});
```

Don't run `lovechild.js` yourself; `--parent.js` will do that for you with fork!

Running `parent.js` should fork a child process and send that child a message. The child should respond in kind:

```
Parent said:  I love you
Child said:  I love you too
```

With `parent.js` running, check your operating system's task manager. There will be two Node processes, not one, as there were with preceeding examples.

Another very powerful idea is to pass a network server an object to a child. This technique allows multiple processes, including the parent, to share the responsibility for servicing connection requests, spreading load across cores.

For example, the following program will start a network server, fork a child process, and pass the server reference from the parent down to the child:

```
// net-parent.js
const path = require('path');
let child = require("child_process").fork(path.join(__dirname, "net-
child.js"));
let server = require("net").createServer();

server.on("connection", (socket) => {
  socket.end("Parent handled connection");
});

server.listen(8080, () => {
```

```
    child.send("Parent passing down server", server);
});
```

In addition to passing a message to a child process as the first argument to send, the preceding code also sends the server handle to itself as a second argument. Our child server can now help out with the family's service business:

```
// net-child.js
process.on("message", function(message, server) {
  console.log(message);
  server.on("connection", function(socket) {
    socket.end("Child handled connection");
  });
});
```

This child process should print out the sent message to your console, and begin listening for connections, sharing the sent server handle.

Repeatedly connecting to this server at `localhost:8080` will result in either child-handled connection or parent-handled connection being displayed; two separate processes are balancing the server load. This technique, when combined with the simple inter-process messaging protocol discussed previously, demonstrates how *Ryan Dahl's* creation succeeds in providing an easy way to build scalable network programs.

We've connected two nodes with just a few lines of code.

 We will discuss Node's new cluster module, which expands and simplifies the previously discussed technique in `Chapter 7`, *Using Multiple Processes*. If you are interested in how server handles are shared, visit the cluster documentation: `https://nodejs.org/dist/latest-v9.x/docs/api/cluster.html`

File events

Most applications make some use of the filesystem, in particular, those that function as web services. As well, a professional application will likely log information about usage, cache pre-rendered data views, or make other changes to files and directory structures. Node allows developers to register for notifications on file events through the `fs.watch` method. The `watch` method broadcasts changed events on both files and directories.

The `watch` method accepts three arguments, in order:

- The file or directory path being watched. If the file does not exist, an **ENOENT (no entity)** error will be thrown, so using `fs.exists` at some prior useful point is encouraged.
- An optional options object, including:
    - Persistent (Boolean default true): Node keeps processes alive, as long as there is *something to do*. Set this option to *false* to let Node close the process even if your code still has a file watcher watching.
    - Recursive (Boolean default false): Whether to automatically descend into subdirectories. Note: This is not consistently implemented across platforms. For this reason, and for performance reasons, you should explicitly control the file list you are watching, rather than randomly watching directories.
    - Encoding (String default `utf8`): Character encoding of passed filenames. You probably don't need to change this.
- The `listener` function, which receives two arguments:
    - The name of the change event (one of rename or change)
    - The filename that was changed (important when watching directories)

This example will set up a watcher on itself, change its own filename, and exit:

```
const fs = require('fs');
fs.watch(__filename, { persistent: false }, (event, filename) => {
  console.log(event);
  console.log(filename);
})

setImmediate(function() {
  fs.rename(__filename, __filename + '.new', () => {});
});
```

Two lines, `rename` and the name of the original file, should have been printed to the console.

Close your watcher channel whenever you want to use code like this:

```
let w = fs.watch('file', () => {});
w.close();
```

It should be noted that `fs.watch` depends a great deal on how the host OS handles file events, and the Node documentation says this:

> *"The fs.watch API is not 100% consistent across platforms, and is unavailable in some situations."*

The author has had very good experiences with the module across many different systems, noting only that the filename argument is null in callbacks on OS X implementations. Different systems may also enforce case sensitivity, one way or the other. Nevertheless, be sure to run tests on your specific architecture — trust, but verify.

 Alternatively, use a third-party package! If you encounter difficulties with a Node module, check npm for alternatives. Here, as a problem-fixing wrapper on top of `fs.watch`, consider *Paul Miller's chokidar*. It is used as the file-watching tool for build systems like gulp, and in many other projects. Refer to: `https://www.npmjs.com/package/chokidar`.

Deferred execution

One occasionally needs to defer the execution of a function. Traditional JavaScript uses timers for this purpose, with the well-known `setTimeout` and `setInterval` functions. Node introduces another perspective on defers, primarily as means of controlling the order in which a callback executes in relation to I/O events, as well as timer events properly.

As we saw earlier, managing timers is one of the main jobs of Node's event loop. Two types of deferred event sources that give a developer the ability to schedule callback executions to occur either before, or after, the processing of queued I/O events are `process.nextTick` and `setImmediate`. Let's look at those now.

process.nextTick

A method of the native Node process module, `process.nextTick` is similar to the familiar `setTimeout` method in which it delays execution of its callback function until some point in the future. However, the comparison is not exact; a list of all requested `nextTick` callbacks are placed at the head of the event queue, and is processed, in its entirety and in order, before I/O or timer events and after execution of the current script (the JavaScript code executing synchronously on the V8 thread).

The primary use of nextTick in a function is to postpone the broadcast of result events to listeners on the current execution stack until the caller has had an opportunity to register event listeners, giving the currently executing program a chance to bind callbacks to EventEmitter.emit events.

Think of this as a pattern to use wherever you want to create your own asynchronous behavior. For instance, imagine a lookup system that may either fetch from a cache, or pull fresh data from a data store. The cache is fast and doesn't need callbacks, while the data I/O call would need them.

The need for callbacks in the second case argues for emulation of the callback behavior, with nextTick in the first case. This allows a consistent API, improving clarity of implementation without burdening the developer with the responsibility of determining whether or not to use a callback.

The following code seems to set up a simple transaction; when an instance of EventEmitter emits a start event, log Started to the console:

```
const events = require('events');
function getEmitter() {
  let emitter = new events.EventEmitter();
  emitter.emit('start');
  return emitter;
}

let myEmitter = getEmitter();

myEmitter.on("start", () => {
  console.log("Started");
});
```

However, the result you might expect will not occur! The event emitter instantiated within getEmitter emits start previous to being returned, wrong-footing the subsequent assignment of a listener, which arrives a step late, missing the event notification.

To solve this race condition, we can use process.nextTick:

```
const events = require('events');
function getEmitter() {
  let emitter = new events.EventEmitter();
  process.nextTick(() => {
    emitter.emit('start');
  });
  return emitter;
}
```

```
let myEmitter = getEmitter();
myEmitter.on('start', () => {
  console.log('Started');
});
```

This code attaches the on("start") handler before Node gives us the start event, and works properly.

Erroneous code can recursively call nextTick, causing an unending loop of code to run. Note that unlike a recursive call to a function within a single turn of the event loop, doing this won't cause a stack overflow. Rather, it will starve the event loop, churn your process on the microprocessor, and could prevent your program from discovering the I/O that Node has finished.

setImmediate

setImmediate is technically a member of the class of timers, along with setInterval and setTimeout . However, there is no sense of time associated with it — there is no *number of milliseconds* to wait for an argument to be sent.

This method is really more of a sibling to process.nextTick, differing in one very important way: while callbacks queued by nextTick will execute before I/O and timer events, callbacks queued by setImmediate will be called after I/O events.

 The naming of these two methods is confusing: Node will actually run the function you give to nextTick before the one you pass to setImmediate.

This method does reflect the standard behavior of timers in that its invocation will return an object that can be passed to clearImmediate, cancelling your request to run your function later on in the same way clearTimeout cancels timers set with setTimeout.

Timers

Timers are used to schedule events in the future. They are used when one seeks to delay the execution of some block of code until a specified number of milliseconds have passed, to schedule periodic execution of a particular function, and so on.

JavaScript provides two asynchronous timers: `setInterval()` and `setTimeout()`. It is assumed that the reader is fully aware of how to set (and cancel) these timers, so very little time will be spent discussing the syntax. We'll instead focus more on gotchas and less well-known details about timeouts and intervals.

The key takeaway will be this: when using timers, one should make no assumptions about the amount of actual time that will expire before the callback registered for this timer fires, or about the ordering of callbacks. Node timers are not interrupts. Timers simply promise to execute as close as possible to the specified time (though never before), beholden, as with every other event source, to event loop scheduling.

 At least one thing you may not know about timers-we are all familiar with the standard arguments to `setTimeout`: a callback function and timeout interval. Did you know that many additional arguments are passed to the `callback` function? `setTimeout(callback, time, [passArg1, passArg2...])`

setTimeout

Timeouts can be used to defer the execution of a function until some number of milliseconds into the future.

Consider the following code:

```
setTimeout(a, 1000);
setTimeout(b, 1001);
```

One would expect that function b would execute after function a. However, this cannot be guaranteed — a may follow b, or the other way around.

Now, consider the subtle difference present in the following code snippet:

```
setTimeout(a, 1000);
setTimeout(b, 1000);
```

The execution order of a and b are predictable in this case. Node essentially maintains an object map grouping callbacks with identical timeout lengths. *Isaac Schlueter*, a former leader of the Node project and now CEO of npm Inc., puts it in this way:

> *As we can find on* https://groups.google.com/forum/#!msg/nodejs-dev/ kiowz4iht4Q/TORuSwAeJVOJ, *"[N]ode uses a single low level timer object for each timeout value. If you attach multiple callbacks for a single timeout value, they'll occur in order, because they're sitting in a queue. However, if they're on different timeout values, then they'll be using timers in different threads, and are thus subject to the vagaries of the [CPU] scheduler."*

The ordering of timer callbacks registered within an identical execution scope does not predictably determine the eventual execution order in all cases. Additionally, there exists a minimum wait time of one millisecond for a timeout. Passing a value of zero, -1, or a non-number will be translated into this minimum value.

To cancel a timeout, use clearTimeout(timerReference).

setInterval

One can think of many cases where being able to periodically execute a function would be useful. Polling a data source every few seconds and pushing updates is a common pattern. Running the next step in an animation every few milliseconds is another use case, as is collecting garbage. For these cases, setInterval is a good tool:

```
let intervalId = setInterval(() => { ... }, 100);
```

Every 100 milliseconds the sent callback function will execute, a process that can be cancelled with clearInterval(intervalReference).

Unfortunately, as with setTimeout, this behavior is not always reliable. Importantly, if a system delay (such as some badly written blocking while loop) occupies the event loop for some period of time, intervals set prior and completing within that interim will have their results queued on the stack. When the event loop becomes unblocked and unwinds, all the interval callbacks will be fired in sequence, essentially immediately, losing any sort of timing delays they intended.

Luckily, unlike browser-based JavaScript, intervals are rather more reliable in Node, generally able to maintain expected periodicity in normal use scenarios.

unref and ref

A Node program does not stay alive without a reason to do so. A process will keep running for as long as there are callbacks still waiting to be processed. Once those are cleared, the Node process has nothing left to do, and it will exit.

For example, the following silly code fragment will keep a Node process running forever:

```
let intervalId = setInterval(() => {}, 1000);
```

Even though the set callback function does nothing useful or interesting, it continues to be called. This is the correct behavior, as an interval should keep running until `clearInterval` is used to stop it.

There are cases of using a timer to do something interesting with external I/O, or some data structure, or a network interface, where once those external event sources stop occurring or disappear, the timer itself becomes unnecessary. Normally, one would trap that irrelevant state of a timer somewhere else in the program, and cancel the timer from there. This can become difficult or even clumsy, as an unnecessary tangling of concerns is now necessary, an added level of complexity.

The `unref` method allows the developer to assert the following instructions: when this timer is the only event source remaining for the event loop to process, go ahead and terminate the process.

Let's test this functionality to our previous silly example, which will result in the process terminating rather than running forever:

```
let intervalId = setInterval(() => {}, 1000);
intervalId.unref();
```

Note that `unref` is a method of the opaque value returned when starting a timer, which is an object.

Now, let's add an external event source, a timer. Once that external source gets cleaned up (in about 100 milliseconds), the process will terminate. We send information to the console to log what is happening:

```
setTimeout(() => {
  console.log("now stop");
}, 100);

let intervalId = setInterval(() => {
  console.log("running")
```

```
}, 1);

intervalId.unref();
```

You may return a timer to its normal behavior with `ref`, which will undo an `unref` method:

```
let intervalId = setInterval(() => {}, 1000);
intervalId.unref();
intervalId.ref();
```

The listed process will continue indefinitely, as in our original silly example.

Snap quiz! After running the following code, what is the expected order of logged messages?

```
const fs = require('fs');
const EventEmitter = require('events').EventEmitter;
let pos = 0;
let messenger = new EventEmitter();

// Listener for EventEmitter
messenger.on("message", (msg) => {
  console.log(++pos + " MESSAGE: " + msg);
});

// (A) FIRST
console.log(++pos + " FIRST");

// (B) NEXT
process.nextTick(() => {
  console.log(++pos + " NEXT")
})

// (C) QUICK TIMER
setTimeout(() => {
  console.log(++pos + " QUICK TIMER")
}, 0)

// (D) LONG TIMER
setTimeout(() => {
  console.log(++pos + " LONG TIMER")
}, 10)

// (E) IMMEDIATE
setImmediate(() => {
  console.log(++pos + " IMMEDIATE")
```

```
})

// (F) MESSAGE HELLO!
messenger.emit("message", "Hello!");

// (G) FIRST STAT
fs.stat(__filename, () => {
  console.log(++pos + " FIRST STAT");
});

// (H) LAST STAT
fs.stat(__filename, () => {
  console.log(++pos + " LAST STAT");
});

// (I) LAST
console.log(++pos + " LAST");
```

The output of this program is:

```
FIRST (A).
MESSAGE: Hello! (F).
LAST (I).
NEXT (B).
QUICK TIMER (C).
FIRST STAT (G).
LAST STAT (H).
IMMEDIATE (E).
LONG TIMER (D).
```

Let's break the preceding code down:

A, F, and I execute in the main program flow, and as such, they will have the first priority in the main thread. This is obvious; your JavaScript executes its instructions in the order they are written, including the synchronous execution of the emit callback.

With the main call stack exhausted, the event loop is now almost reading to process I/O operations. This is the moment when `nextTick` requests are honored, slotting in at the head of the event queue. This is when B is displayed.

The rest of the order should be clear. Timers and I/O operations will be processed next, (C, G, H) followed by the results of the `setImmediate` callback (E), always arriving after any I/O and timer responses are executed.

Finally, the long timeout (D) arrives, being a relatively far-future event.

Note that reordering the expressions in this program will not change the output order outside of possible reordering of the STAT results, which only implies that they have been returned from the thread pool in a different order, remaining as a group in the correct order as related to the event queue.

Concurrency and errors

Members of the Node community develop new packages and projects every day. Because of Node's evented nature, callbacks permeate these codebases. We've considered several of the key ways in which events might be queued, dispatched, and handled through the use of callbacks. Let's spend a little time outlining the best practices, in particular, about conventions for designing callbacks and handling errors, and discuss some useful patterns when designing complex chains of events and callbacks. In particular, let's look at the new **Promise**, **Generator**, and **async/await** patterns that you will see in this book, and other examples of modern Node code.

Managing concurrency

Simplifying control flows has been a concern of the Node community since the very beginning of the project. Indeed, this potential criticism was one of the very first anticipated by *Ryan Dahl*, who discussed it at length during the talk in which he introduced Node to the JavaScript developer community.

Because deferred code execution often requires the nesting of callbacks within callbacks, a Node program can sometimes begin to resemble a sideways pyramid, also known as *The Pyramid of Doom*. You've seen it: deeply nested code, 4 or 5 or even more levels deep, curly braces everywhere. Apart from syntactical annoyances, you can also imagine that tracking errors across such a call stack might be difficult—if a callback at the third level throws, who is responsible for handling that error? The second level? Even if level 2 is reading a file and level 3 is querying a database? Does that make sense? It can be hard to make sense of asynchronous program flows.

Callbacks

Luckily, Node creators agreed upon sane conventions on how to structure callbacks early on. It is important to follow this tradition. Deviation leads to surprises, sometimes very bad surprises, and in general, to do so automatically makes an API awkward, a characteristic other developers will rapidly tire of.

One is either returning a function result by executing a `callback`, handling the arguments received by a `callback`, or designing the signature for a `callback` within your API. Whichever situation is being considered, one should follow the convention relevant to that case.

The first argument returned to a `callback` function is any error message, preferably in the form of an error object. If no error is to be reported, this slot should contain a null value.

When passing a `callback` to a function, it should be assigned the last slot of the function signature. APIs should be consistently designed this way.

Any number of arguments may exist between the error and the `callback` slots.

To create an error object: `new Error("Argument must be a String!")`

Promises

Like some politicians, the Node core was against Promises before it was for them. *Mikeal Rogers*, in discussing why Promises were removed from the original Node core, makes a strong argument for why leaving feature development to the community leads to a stronger core product. You can view this discussion at: `https://web.archive.org/posts/broken-promises.html`

Promises have gained a very large following since then, and Node core has changed in response. Promises are essentially a replacement for the standard callback pattern seen everywhere in Node. Once, you might have written this:

```
API.getUser(loginInfo, function(err, user) {
    API.getProfile(user, function(err, profile) {
        // ...and so on
    }
});
```

If API was instead "Promisified" (recall `util.promisify` from the previous chapter?), your description of the preceding asynchronous control flow would be described using a Promise chain:

```
let promiseProfile = API.getUser(loginInfo)
.then(user => API.getProfile(user))
.then(profile => {
    // do something with #profile
})
.catch(err => console.log(err))
```

This is at least a tighter syntax that reads a little more easily, with long chains of operations; however, there is much more going on here that is of value.

`promiseProfile` references a Promise object. Promises only execute once, reaching either an error state (unfulfilled) or fulfilled state, where you can extract the last, immutable value via `then`, as we did with **profile**, previously. Of course, Promises can be assigned to a variable, and that variable can be passed around to as many consumers as you'd like, even prior to resolving. Since `then` is only called when there is a value available, whenever that may be, Promises are aptly named as promises of a future state.

Perhaps most importantly, Promises, unlike callbacks, are able to manage errors across many asynchronous actions. If you go back and look at the example callback code at the head of this section, you'll see **err** parameters in each callback, reflecting the core error-first callback style of Node. Each of those error objects must be handled individually, so the preceding code would actually start to look more like this:

```
API.getUser(loginInfo, function(err, user) {
  if(err) {
    throw err;
  }
  API.getProfile(user, function(err, profile) {
    if(err) {
      throw err;
    }
    // ...and so on
  }
});
```

Observe how each error condition must be handled individually. In practice, developers would like to be responsible for "hand-rolling" a wrapper around this code, such as a `try...catch` block, which would, in some way, catch all errors in this logical unit and manage them in a centralized way.

With Promises, you get that for free. Any `catch` statement will catch any errors thrown by any `then` prior to it in the chain. This makes creating a common error handler a snap. Even more, Promises allows the execution chain to continue past an error. You can add the following to the previous Promise chain:

```
.catch(err => console.log(err))
.then(() => // this happens no matter what happened previously)
```

In this way, Promises allows you to compose rather complex, asynchronous, logical flows in much less space, with limited indentation, where error handling is much easier to work with and values are immutable and exchangeable.

Another extremely useful feature of the Promise object is that these future-resolving states can be managed as a block. For instance, imagine that to fulfill a query for a user profile, you needed to make three database calls. Rather than chaining these calls which always run serially, one at a time in order, you might use `Promise.all`:

```
const db = {
  getFullName: Promise.resolve('Jack Spratt'),
  getAddress: Promise.resolve('10 Clean Street'),
  getFavorites: Promise.resolve('Lean'),
};

Promise.all([
  db.getFullName()
  db.getAddress()
  db.getFavorites()
])
.then(results => {
  // results = ['Jack Spratt', '10 Clean Stree', 'Lean']
})
.catch(err => {...})
```

Here, all three of the Promises will be triggered *simultaneously,* and will *run in parallel.* Running calls in parallel is, of course, much more efficient than running them serially. Also, `Promise.all` guarantees that the final thennable receives an array of results ordered to synchronize result position with caller position.

It would be good for you to familiarize yourself with the full Promise API, which you can read about at MDN: `https://developer.mozilla.org/en-US/docs/Web/JavaScript/Reference/Global_Objects/Promise`

Even though Promises are now native, there remains a "userland" module, **bluebird**, which continues to offer a compelling alternative Promises implementation, with added features and oftentimes faster execution speed. You can read more about **bluebird** here: `http://bluebirdjs.com/docs/api-reference.html`.

async/await

Rather than wrap fulfillment in a specialized data structure like a Promise with so many function blocks and parentheses and special contexts, why not simply make it so that asynchronous expressions can have their cake and eat it, too? These expressions do not block the process (asynchronous execution), but they nevertheless halt further execution of a program (synchronous) until resolved.

The `await` operator is used to wait for a Promise. It only executes within an `async` function. The `async/await` concurrency modeling syntax has been available since Node 8.x. Here's a demonstration of `async/await` being used to replicate the preceding `Promise.all` example:

```
const db = {
  getFullName: Promise.resolve('Jack Spratt'),
  getAddress: Promise.resolve('10 Clean Street'),
  getFavorites: Promise.resolve('Lean'),
}

async function profile() {
  let fullName = await db.getFullName() // Jack Spratt
  let address = await db.getAddress() // 10 Clean Street
  let favorites = await db.getFavorites() // Lean

  return {fullName, address, favorites};
}

profile().then(res => console.log(res) // results = ['Jack Spratt', '10
Clean Street', 'Lean'
```

Nice, right? You'll note that `profile()` returned a Promise. An `async` function *always* returns a Promise, though as we see here, the function itself can return anything it would like.

Promises and `async/await` work together like old pals. Here is a recursive directory walker that demonstrates this teamwork:

```
const {join} = require('path');
const {promisify} = require('util');
```

```
const fs = require('fs');
const readdir = promisify(fs.readdir);
const stat = promisify(fs.stat);

async function $readDir (dir, acc = []) {
  await Promise.all((await readdir(dir)).map(async file => {
    file = join(dir, file);
    return (await stat(file)).isDirectory() && acc.push(file) &&
$readDir(file, acc);
  }));
  return acc;
}

$readDir(`./dummy_filesystem`).then(dirInfo => console.log(dirInfo));

// [ 'dummy_filesystem/folderA',
// 'dummy_filesystem/folderB',
// 'dummy_filesystem/folderA/folderA-C' ]
```

It's a testament to how terse the code is for this recursive directory walker, that it is only slightly longer than the setup code above it. Since `await` expects a Promise, which `Promise.all` will return, run through every file that the `readDir` Promise returns, and map each file to another awaited Promise that will handle any recursive descent into subdirectories, updating the accumulator where appropriate. Read like this, the `Promise.all((await readdir(dir)).map` construct reads not unlike a basic looping construct, where deep asynchronous recursion is being modelled in a simple and easy-to-follow procedural, synchronous way.

A pure Promise drop-in replacement version might look like this, assuming the same dependencies as the `async/await` version:

```
function $readDir(dir, acc=[]) {
  return readdir(dir).then(files => Promise.all(files.map(file => {
    file = join(dir, file);
    return stat(file).then(fobj => {
      if (fobj.isDirectory()) {
        acc.push(file);
        return $readDir(file, acc);
      }
    });
  }))).then(() => acc);
};
```

Both versions are cleaner than what you would have with callbacks.
The `async/await` version does take the best of both worlds, and creates a succinct representation resembling synchronous code, making it perhaps easier to follow and reason about.

Error handling with `async/await` is also quite easy, as it requires no special new syntax. With Promises and `catch`, there is a slight problem with synchronous code errors. Promises catch errors that occur in `then` blocks. If, for example, a third-party library your code is calling throws, that code is not wrapped by the Promise and that error *will not be caught by* `catch`.

With `async/await`, you can use the familiar `try...catch` statement:

```
async function makeError() {
    try {
        console.log(await thisDoesntExist());
    } catch (error) {
        console.error(error);
    }
}

makeError();
```

This avoids all problems with special error-catching constructs. This native, rock-solid method will catch anything that throws anywhere in the `try` block, regardless of whether execution is synchronous or not.

Generators and Iterators

Generators are function execution contexts that can be paused and resumed. When you call a normal function, it will likely `return` a value; the function fully executes, then terminates. A Generator function will yield a value then stop but the function context of a Generator is not disposed of (as it is with normal functions). You can re-enter the Generator at a later point in time and pick up further results.

An example might help:

```
function* threeThings() {
    yield 'one';
    yield 'two';
    yield 'three';
}

let tt = threeThings();
```

```
console.log(tt); // {}
console.log(tt.next()); // { value: 'one', done: false }
console.log(tt.next()); // { value: 'two', done: false }
console.log(tt.next()); // { value: 'three', done: false }
console.log(tt.next()); // { value: undefined, done: true }
```

A Generator is declared by marking it with an asterisk (*). On the first call to `threeThings`, we get don't get a result, but an Generator object.

Generators conform to the new JavaScript iteration protocols (`https://developer. mozilla.org/en-US/docs/Web/JavaScript/Reference/Iteration_protocols#iterator`), which for our purposes mean that a Generator object exposes a `next` method, which is used to pull out as many values from a Generator as it is willing to yield. This power comes from the fact that Generators implement the JavaScript Iteration protocol. So, what's an iterator?

> *As* `https://developer.mozilla.org/en-US/docs/Web/JavaScript/Guide/ Iterators_and_Generators` *says,*
> *"An object is an iterator when it knows how to access items from a collection one at a time, while keeping track of its current position within that sequence. In JavaScript an iterator is an object that provides a next() method which returns the next item in the sequence. This method returns an object with two properties: done and value."*

We can replicate the Generator example using just an Iterator:

```
function demoIterator(array) {
  let idx = 0;
  return {
    next: () => {
      return idx < array.length ? {
        value: array[idx++],
        done: false
      } : { done: true };
    }
  };
}
let it = demoIterator(['one', 'two', 'three']);
console.log(it); // { next: [Function: next] }
console.log(it.next()); // { value: 'one', done: false }
console.log(it.next()); // { value: 'two', done: false }
console.log(it.next()); // { value: 'three', done: false }
console.log(it.next()); // { done: true }
```

You'll note that the results are nearly identical with the Generator example, with one important difference we can see in the first result: an Iterator is simply an object with a next method. It must do all the work of maintaining its own internal state (tracking `idx` in the previous example). Generators are factories for Iterators; furthermore, they do all the work of maintaining and yielding their own state.

Descended from Iterators, Generators yield objects with two properties:

- **done** : A Boolean. If true, the Generator is indicating that it has nothing left to `yield`. If you were to think of Generators as streams (not a bad parallel), then you might compare this pattern to the pattern of `Readable.read()` returning **null** when a stream has ended (or if you prefer, the way a `Readable` will push **null** when finished).
- **value**: The value of the last `yield`. Should be ignored if `done` is true.

Generators are designed for iterative contexts, not unlike a loop, providing the powerful advantage of a function execution context. You may have written something like this:

```
function getArraySomehow() {
  // slice into a copy; don't send original
  return ['one','two','buckle','my','shoe'].slice(0);
}

let state = getArraySomehow();
for(let x=0; x < state.length; x++) {
    console.log(state[x].toUpperCase());
}
```

This is fine, but there are downsides, such as needing to create a local reference to an external data provider and maintaining that reference when this block or function terminates. Do we make `state` a global? Should it be immutable? If the underlying data changes, for example, a new element is added to the array, how do we make sure `state` is updated, disconnected as it is from the true state of our application? What if something accidentally overwrites `state`? Data observation and binding libraries exist, design theories exist, frameworks exist to properly encapsulate your data sources and inject immutable versions into execution contexts; but what if there was a better way?

Generators can contain and manage their own data and `yield` the right answer even through change. We can implement the previous code with Generators:

```
function* liveData(state) {
    let state = ['one','two','buckle','my','shoe'];
    let current;
```

```
        while(current = state.shift()) {
            yield current;
        }
    }

    let list = liveData([]);
    let item;
    while (item = list.next()) {
        if(!item.value) {
            break;
        }
        console.log('generated:', item.value);
    }
```

The Generator method handles all the "boilerplate" for sending back a value, and naturally encapsulates the state. But there doesn't seem to be a significant advantage here. This is because we are using a Generator to execute iterations that run sequentially and immediately. Generators are really for situations when a series of values are promised, with individual values being generated only when requested, over time. Rather than processing an array all at once and in order, what we really want to create is a sequential chain of communicating processes, each process "tick" calculating a result with visibility into previous process results.

Consider the following:

```
    function* range(start=1, end=2) {
        do {
            yield start;
        } while(++start <= end)
    }

    for (let num of range(1, 3)) {
        console.log(num);
    }
    // 1
    // 2
    // 3
```

You can pass arguments to Generators. We create a range state machine by passing range bounds, where further calls to the machine will cause an internal state change, and yield the current state representation to the caller. While for demonstration purposes we use the for...of method of traversing Iterators (and therefore Generators), this sequential processing (which blocks the main thread until it is finished) can be made *asynchronous*.

The run/halt (not run/stop) design of Generators means that we can think of iteration not as running through a list, but of capturing a set of transition events over time. This idea is central to the idea of **Reactive Programming** (https://en.wikipedia.org/wiki/Reactive_programming), for example. Let's think through another example where this particular advantage of Generators can be displayed.

There are many other things you can do with these sorts of data structures. It might be helpful to think this way: Generators are to a sequence of future values as Promises are to a single future value. Both Promises and Generators can be passed around the instant they are generated (even if some eventual values are still resolving, or haven't yet been queued for resolution), with one getting values via the `next()` interface, and the other via the `then()` interface.

Errors and exceptions

Generally in programming, the terms *error* and *exception* are often used interchangeably. Within the Node environment, these two concepts are not identical. Errors and exceptions are different. Additionally, the definition of error and exception within Node does not necessarily align with similar definitions in other languages and development environments.

Conventionally, an **error** condition in a Node program is a non-fatal condition that should be caught and handled, seen most explicitly in the *Error as first argument* convention displayed by the typical Node callback pattern. An **exception** is a serious error (a system error) that a sane environment should not ignore or try to handle.

One comes across four common error contexts in Node, and should respond predictably:

- **A synchronous context**: This will normally happen in the context of a function, where a bad call signature or another non-fatal error is detected. The function should simply return an error object; `new Error(...)`, or some other consistent indicator that the function call has failed.
- **An asynchronous context**: When expected to respond by firing a `callback` function, the execution context should pass an `Error` object, with appropriate message, as the first argument to that `callback`.
- **An event context**: Quoting the Node documentation: *"When an `EventEmitter` instance experiences an error, the typical action is to emit an error event. Error events are treated as a special case in node. If there is no listener for it, then the default action is to print a stack trace and exit the program."* Use events where events are expected.

- **A Promise context**: A Promise throws or is otherwise rejected, and this error is caught within a `.catch` block. Important note: you should *always* reject Promises with true `Error` objects. *Petka Antonov*, author of the popular *Bluebird* Promises implementation, discusses why: `https://github.com/petkaantonov/bluebird/blob/master/docs/docs/warning-explanations.md`

Clearly, these are situations where an error is caught in a controlled manner, prior to it destabilizing the entire application. Without falling too far into defensive coding, an effort should be made to check inputs and other sources for errors, and properly dismiss them.

An additional benefit of always returning a proper `Error` object is access to the stack property of that object. The error stack shows the provenance of an error, each link in the chain of function, and calls the function that led to the error. A typical `Error.stack` trace would look like this:

```
> console.log(new Error("My Error Message").stack);
Error: My Error Message
    at Object.<anonymous> (/js/errorstack.js:1:75)
    at Module._compile (module.js:449:26)
    at Object.Module._extensions..js (module.js:467:10)
    ...
```

Similarly, the stack is always available via the `console.trace` method:

```
> console.trace("The Stack Head")
Trace: The Stack Head
    at Object.<anonymous> (/js/stackhead.js:1:71)
    at Module._compile (module.js:449:26)
    at Object.Module._extensions..js (module.js:467:10)
    ...
```

It should be clear how this information aids in debugging, helping to ensure that the logical flow of our application is sound.

A normal stack trace truncates after a dozen or so levels. If longer stack traces are useful to you, try *Matt Insler's* **longjohn**: `https://github.com/mattinsler/longjohn`

As well, run and examine the `js/stacktrace.js` file in your bundle for some ideas on how stack information might be used when reporting errors, or even test results.

Exception handling is different. Exceptions are unexpected or fatal errors that have destabilized the application. These should be handled with care; a system in an exception state is unstable, with indeterminate future states, and should be gracefully shut down and restarted. This is the smart thing to do.

Typically, exceptions are caught in try/catch blocks:

```
try {
    something.that = wontWork;
} catch (thrownError) {
    // do something with the exception we just caught
}
```

Peppering a codebase with try/catch blocks and trying to anticipate all errors can become unmanageable and unwieldy. Additionally, what if an exception you didn't anticipate, an uncaught exception, occurs? How do you pick up from where you left off?

Node does not have a standard built-in way to handle uncaught critical exceptions. This is a weakness of the platform. An exception that is uncaught will continue to bubble up through the execution stack until it hits the event loop where, like a wrench in the gears of a machine, it will take down the entire process. The best we have is to attach an uncaughtException handler to the process itself:

```
process.on('uncaughtException', (err) => {
    console.log('Caught exception: ' + err);
});

setTimeout(() => {
    console.log("The exception was caught and this can run.");
}, 1000);

throwAnUncaughtException();

// > Caught exception: ReferenceError: throwAnUncaughtException is not
defined
// > The exception was caught and this can run.
```

While nothing that follows our exception code will execute, the timeout will still fire, as the process managed to catch the exception, saving itself. However, this is a very clumsy way of handling exceptions. The domain module aimed to fix this hole in Node's design, but it has since been deprecated. Properly handling and reporting errors remains a real weakness in the Node platform. Work continues by the core team to address this problem: https://nodejs.org/en/docs/guides/domain-postmortem/

Recently, a similar mechanism was introduced to catch runaway Promises, which occur when you do not attach a catch handler to your Promise chain:

```
process.on('unhandledRejection', (reason, Prom) => {
  console.log(`Unhandled Rejection: ${p} reason: ${reason}`);
});
```

The `unhandledRejection` handler is fired whenever a Promise is rejected and no error handler is attached to the Promise within one turn of the event loop.

Considerations

Any developer is regularly making decisions with a far-reaching impact. It is very hard to predict all the possible consequences resulting from a new bit of code, or a new design theory. For this reason, it may be useful to keep the shape of your code simple, and to force yourself to consistently follow the common practices of other Node developers. These are some guidelines you may find useful, as follows:

- Generally, try to aim for shallow code. This type of refactoring is uncommon in non-evented environments. Remind yourself of it by regularly re-evaluating entry and exit points, and shared functions.
- Consider building your systems using distinct, composable microservices, which we'll discuss in Chapter 9, *Microservices*.
- Where possible, provide a common context for `callback` re-entry. Closures are very powerful tools in JavaScript, and by extension, Node, as long as the context frame length of the enclosed callbacks is not excessive.
- Name your functions. In addition to being useful in deeply recursive constructs, debugging code is much easier when a stack trace contains distinct function names, as opposed to anonymous.
- Think hard about priorities. Does the order, in which a given result arrives or a `callback` is executed, actually matter? More importantly, does it matter in relation to I/O operations? If so, consider `nextTick` and `setImmediate`.
- Consider using finite state machines for managing your events. State machines are surprisingly under-represented in JavaScript codebases. When a `callback` re-enters program flow, it has likely changed the state of your application, and the issuing of the asynchronous call itself is a likely indicator that state is about to change.

Building a Twitter feed using file events

Let's apply what we've learned. The goal is to create a server that a client can connect to and receive updates from Twitter. We will first create a process to query Twitter for any messages with the hashtag #nodejs, and write any found messages to a tweets.txt file in 140-byte chunks. We will then create a network server that broadcasts these messages to a single client. Those broadcasts will be triggered by write events on the tweets.txt file. Whenever a write occurs, 140-byte chunks are asynchronously read from the last-known client read pointer. This will happen until we reach the end of the file, broadcasting as we go. Finally, we will create a simple client.html page, which asks for, receives, and displays these messages.

While this example is certainly contrived, it demonstrates:

- Listening to the filesystem for changes, and responding to those events
- Using data stream events for reading and writing files
- Responding to network events
- Using timeouts for polling state
- Using a Node server itself as a network event broadcaster

To handle server broadcasting, we are going to use the **Server Sent Events** (**SSE**) protocol, a new protocol being standardized as part of HTML5.

We're first going to create a Node server that listens for changes on a file and broadcasts any new content to the client. Open your editor and create a file server.js:

```
let fs = require("fs");
let http = require('http');

let theUser = null;
let userPos = 0;
let tweetFile = "tweets.txt";
```

We will be accepting a single user connection, whose pointer will be theUser. The userPos will store the last position this client read from in tweetFile:

```
http.createServer((request, response) => {
  response.writeHead(200, {
    'Content-Type': 'text/event-stream',
    'Cache-Control': 'no-cache',
    'Access-Control-Allow-Origin': '*'
  });
```

```
    theUser = response;

    response.write(':' + Array(2049).join(' ') + '\n');
    response.write('retry: 2000\n');

    response.socket.on('close', () => {
      theUser = null;
    });
  }).listen(8080);
```

Create an HTTP server listening on port 8080, which will listen for and handle a single connection, storing the `response` argument, representing the pipe connecting the server to the client. The `response` argument implements the writable stream interface, allowing us to write messages to the client:

```
let sendNext = function(fd) {
  let buffer = Buffer.alloc(140);
  fs.read(fd, buffer, 0, 140, userPos * 140, (err, num) => {
    if (!err && num > 0 && theUser) {
      ++userPos;
      theUser.write(`data: ${buffer.toString('utf-8', 0, num)}\n\n`);
      return process.nextTick(() => {
        sendNext(fd);
      });
    }
  });
};
```

We create a function to send the client messages. We will be pulling buffers of 140 bytes out of the readable stream bound to our `tweets.txt` file, incrementing our file position counter by one on each read. We write this buffer to the writable stream binding our server to the client. When done, we queue up a repeat call of the same function using `nextTick`, repeating until we get an error, receive no data, or the client disconnects:

```
function start() {
  fs.open(tweetFile, 'r', (err, fd) => {
    if (err) {
      return setTimeout(start, 1000);
    }
    fs.watch(tweetFile, (event, filename) => {
      if (event === "change") {
        sendNext(fd);
      }
    });
```

```
    });
  };

  start();
```

Finally, we start the process by opening the `tweets.txt` file and watching for any changes, calling `sendNext` whenever new tweets are written. When we start the server, there may not yet exist a file to read from, so we poll using `setTimeout` until one exists.

Now that we have a server looking for file changes to broadcast, we need to generate data. We first install the **TWiT** Twitter package for Node, via **npm.**

We then create a process whose sole job is to write new data to a file:

```
const fs = require("fs");
const Twit = require('twit');

let twit = new Twit({
  consumer_key: 'your key',
  consumer_secret: 'your secret',
  access_token: 'your token',
  access_token_secret: 'your secret token'
});
```

 To use this example, you will need a Twitter Developer account. Alternatively, there is also the option of changing the relevant code to simply write random 140-byte strings to `tweets.txt`: `require("crypto").randomBytes(70).toString('hex')`:

```
let tweetFile = "tweets.txt";
let writeStream = fs.createWriteStream(tweetFile, {
  flags: "a" // indicate that we want to (a)ppend to the file
});
```

This establishes a stream pointer to the same file that our server will be watching. We will be writing to this file:

```
let cleanBuffer = function(len) {
  let buf = Buffer.alloc(len);
  buf.fill('\0');
  return buf;
};
```

Because Twitter messages are never longer than 140 bytes, we can simplify the read/write operation by always writing 140-byte chunks, even if some of that space is empty. Once we receive updates, we will create a buffer that is *number of messages* x 140 bytes wide, and write those 140-byte chunks to this buffer:

```
let check = function() {
  twit.get('search/tweets', {
    q: '#nodejs since:2013-01-01'
  }, (err, reply) => {
    let buffer = cleanBuffer(reply.statuses.length * 140);
    reply.statuses.forEach((obj, idx) => {
      buffer.write(obj.text, idx*140, 140);
    });
    writeStream.write(buffer);
  })
  setTimeout(check, 10000);
};

check();
```

We now create a function that will be asked every 10 seconds to check for messages containing the hashtag #nodejs. Twitter returns an array of message objects. The one object property we are interested in is the #text of the message. Calculate the number of bytes necessary to represent these new messages (140 x message count), fetch a clean buffer, and fill it with 140-byte chunks until all messages are written. Finally, this data is written to our tweets.txt file, causing a change event to occur that our server is notified of.

The final piece is the client page itself. This is a rather simple page, and how it operates should be familiar to the reader. The only thing to note is the use of SSE that listens to port 8080 on localhost. It should be clear how, on receipt of a new tweet from the server, a list element is added to the unordered list container #list:

```
<!DOCTYPE html>
<html>
<head>
    <title></title>
</head>

<script>

window.onload = () => {
  let list = document.getElementById("list");
  let evtSource = new EventSource("http://localhost:8080/events");

  evtSource.onmessage = (e) => {
```

```
    let newElement = document.createElement("li");
    newElement.innerHTML = e.data;
    list.appendChild(newElement);
  }
}

</script>
<body>

<ul id="list"></ul>

</body>
</html>
```

 To read more about SSE, refer to `Chapter 6`, *Creating Real-time Applications*, or you can visit: `https://developer.mozilla.org/en-US/docs/Web/API/Server-sent_events`.

Summary

Programming with events is not always easy. The control and context switches, defining the paradigm, often confound those new to evented systems. This seemingly reckless loss of control and the resulting complexity drives many developers away from these ideas. Students in introductory programming courses normally develop a mindset in which program flow can be dictated, where a program whose execution flow does not proceed sequentially from A to B can bend understanding.

By examining the evolution of the architectural problems, Node is now attempting to solve for network applications—in terms of scaling and code organization, in general terms of data and complexity volume, in terms of state awareness, and in terms of well-defined data and process boundaries. We learned how managing these event queues can be done intelligently. We saw how different event sources are predictably stacked for an event loop to process, and how far-future events can enter and reenter contexts using closures and smart callback ordering. We also learned about the newer Promise, Generator, and async/await structures designed to help with managing concurrency.

We now have a basic domain understanding of the design and characteristics of Node, in particular, how evented programming is done using it. Let's now move on to larger, more advanced applications of this knowledge.

3

Streaming Data Across Nodes and Clients

"A jug fills drop by drop."

– Buddha

We now have a clearer picture of how the evented, I/O-focused design ethic of Node is reflected across its various module APIs, delivering a consistent and predictable environment for development.

In this chapter, we will discover how data, pulled from files or other sources, can be read, written, and manipulated just as easily using Node. Ultimately, we will learn how to use Node to develop networked servers with rapid I/O interfaces that support highly concurrent applications, sharing real-time data across thousands of clients, simultaneously.

Why use streams?

Presented with a fancy new language feature, design pattern, or software module, a novice developer may begin using it because it is new and fancy. An experienced developer, on the other hand, might ask, *why is this required?*

Streams are required because files are big. A few simple examples can demonstrate their necessity. To begin, let's say we want to copy a file. In Node, a naive implementation looks like this:

```
// First attempt
console.log('Copying...');
let block = fs.readFileSync("source.bin");
console.log('Size: ' + block.length);
fs.writeFileSync("destination.bin", block);
console.log('Done.');
```

It's very straightforward.

The call to `readFileSync()` blocks while Node copies the contents of `source.bin`, a file in the same folder as the script, into memory, returning a `ByteBuffer` here named `block`. Once we have `block`, we can check and print out its size. Then, the code hands `block` to `writeFileSync`, which copies the memory block to the contents of a newly made or overwritten file, `destination.bin`.

This code assumes the following things:

- It's OK to block the event loop (it's not!)
- We can read the whole file into memory (we can't!)

As you will recall from the previous chapter, Node processes one event after another, a single event at a time. Good asynchronous design allows a Node program to appear to be doing all sorts of things simultaneously, both to connected software systems and human users alike, while simultaneously offering developers in the code a straightforward presentation of logic that's easy to reason about and resistant to bugs. This is true, especially when compared to multithreaded code that might be written to solve the same task. Your team may have even turned to Node to make an improved replacement to such a classically multithreaded system. Also, good asynchronous design never blocks the event loop.

Blocking the event loop is bad because Node can't do anything else, while your one blocking line of code is blocking. The example prior, written as a rudimentary script that copies a file from one place to another, might work just fine. It would block the terminal of the user while Node copies the file. The file might be small enough that there's little time to wait. If not, you could open another shell prompt while you're waiting. In this way, it's really no different from familiar commands like `cp` or `curl`.

From the computer's perspective, this is quite inefficient, however. Each file copy shouldn't require its own operating system process.

Additionally, incorporating the previous code into a larger Node project could destabilize the system as a whole.

Your server-side Node app might be simultaneously letting three users log in, while sending large files to another two. If that app executes the previous code as well, two downloads will stick, and three browser throbbers will spin.

So, let's try to fix this, one step at a time:

```
// Attempt the second
console.log('Copying...');
fs.readFile('source.bin', null, (error1, block) => {
  if (error1) {
    throw error1;
  }
  console.log('Size: ' + block.length);
  fs.writeFile('destination.bin', block, (error2) => {
    if (error2) {
      throw error2;
    }
    console.log('Done.');
  });
});
```

At least now we're not using Node methods that have *Sync* in their titles. The event loop can breathe freely again.

But still:

- How about big files? (Big explosions)
- That's quite a pyramid you've got there (of doom)

Try the code prior with a 2 GB (2.0 x 2^30, or 2,147,483,648 byte) source file:

```
RangeError: "size" argument must not be larger than 2147483647
 at Function.Buffer.allocUnsafe (buffer.js:209:3)
 at tryCreateBuffer (fs.js:530:21)
 at Object.fs.readFile (fs.js:569:14)
 ...
```

If you're watching a video on YouTube at 1080p, 2 GB will last you about an hour. The previous `RangeError` happens because $2,147,483,647$ is 1111111111111111111111111111111 in binary, the largest 32-bit signed binary integer. Node uses that type internally to size and address the contents of a `ByteBuffer`.

What happens if you hand our poor example? Smaller, but still very large, files are less deterministic. When it works, it does because Node successfully gets the required amount of memory from the operating system. The memory footprint of the Node process grows by the file size during the copy operation. Mice may turn to hourglasses, and fans may noisily spin up. Would promises help?:

```
// Attempt, part III
console.log('Copying...');
fs.readFileAsync('source.bin').then((block) => {
  console.log('Size: ' + block.length);
  return fs.writeFileAsync('destination.bin', block);
}).then(() => {
 console.log('Done.');
}).catch((e) => {
  // handle errors
});
```

No, essentially. We've flattened the pyramid, but the size limitation and memory issues remain in force.

What we really need is some code that is both asynchronous, and also *piece by piece*, grabbing a little part of the source file, shuttling it over to the destination file for writing, and repeating that cycle until we're done, like a bucket brigade from antique fire fighting.

Here is a picture of an old Bucket Brigade. Firemen are passing pails of water up to the fire.

Such a design would let the event loop breathe freely the entire time. This is exactly what streams are:

```
// Streams to the rescue
console.log('Copying...');
fs.createReadStream('source.bin')
.pipe(fs.createWriteStream('destination.bin'))
.on('close', () => { console.log('Done.'); });
```

In practice, scaled network applications are typically spread across many instances, requiring that the processing of data streams be distributed across many processes and servers. Here, a streaming file is simply a stream of data partitioned into slices, where each slice can be viewed independently irrespective of the availability of others. You can write to a data stream, or listen on a data stream, free to dynamically allocate bytes, to ignore bytes, to reroute bytes. Streams of data can be chunked, many processes can share chunk handling, chunks can be transformed and reinserted, and data flows can be precisely emitted and creatively managed.

Recalling our discussion on modern software and the Rule of Modularity, we can see how streams facilitate the creation of independent share-nothing processes that do one task well, and in combination, can compose a predictable architecture whose complexity does not preclude an accurate appraisal of its behavior. If the interfaces to data are uncontroversial, the data map can be accurately modeled, independent of considerations about data volume or routing.

Managing I/O in Node involves managing data events bound to data streams. A Node Stream object is an instance of `EventEmitter`. This abstract interface is implemented in numerous Node modules and objects, as we saw in the previous chapter. Let's begin by understanding Node's Stream module, then move on to a discussion of how network I/O in Node is handled via various Stream implementations; in particular, the HTTP module.

Exploring streams

According to Bjarne Stoustrup in his book, *The C++ Programming Language*, (third edition):

"Designing and implementing a general input/output facility for a programming language is notoriously difficult... An I/O facility should be easy, convenient, and safe to use; efficient and flexible; and, above all, complete."

It shouldn't surprise anyone that a design team, focused on providing efficient and easy I/O, has delivered such a facility through Node. Through a symmetrical and simple interface, which handles data buffers and stream events so that the implementer does not have to, Node's Stream module is the preferred way to manage asynchronous data streams for both internal modules, and the module's developers will create.

A stream in Node is simply a sequence of bytes. At any time, a stream contains a buffer of bytes, and this buffer has a zero or greater length:

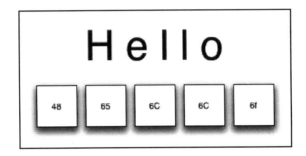

As each character in a stream is well-defined, and because every type of digital data can be expressed in bytes, any part of a stream can be redirected, or *piped*, to any other stream, different chunks of the stream can be sent to different handlers, and so on. In this way, stream input and output interfaces are both flexible and predictable, and can be easily coupled.

 Node also offers a second type of streams: object streams. Instead of chunks of memory flowing through the stream, an object stream shuttles JavaScript objects. Byte streams pass around serialized data like streaming media, while object streams are the right choice for parsed, structured data like JSON records.

Digital streams are well described using the analogy of fluids, where individual bytes (drops of water) are being pushed through a pipe. In Node, streams are objects representing data flows that can be written to and read from asynchronously.

The Node philosophy is a non-blocking flow, I/O is handled via streams, and so the design of the Stream API naturally duplicates this general philosophy. In fact, there is no other way of interacting with streams except in an asynchronous, evented manner—Node prevents developers, by design, from blocking I/O.

Five distinct base classes are exposed via the abstract Stream interface: **Readable**, **Writable**, **Duplex**, **Transform**, and **PassThrough**. Each base class inherits from `EventEmitter`, which we know of as an interface to which event listeners and emitters can be bound.

As we will learn, and here will emphasize, the Stream interface is an abstract interface. An abstract interface functions as a kind of blueprint or definition, describing the features that must be built into each constructed instance of a Stream object. For example, a Readable stream implementation is required to implement a `public read` method which delegates to the interface's `internal _read` method.

In general, all stream implementations should follow these guidelines:

- As long as data exists to send, write to a stream until that operation returns `false`, at which point the implementation should wait for a drain event, indicating that the buffered stream data has emptied.
- Continue to call read until a `null` value is received, at which point wait for a readable event prior to resuming reads.
- Several Node I/O modules are implemented as streams. Network sockets, file readers and writers, `stdin` and `stdout`, zlib, and so on are all streams. Similarly, when implementing a readable data source, or data reader, one should implement that interface as a Stream interface.

It is important to note that over the history of Node, the Stream interface changed in some fundamental ways. The Node team has done its best to implement compatible interfaces, so that (most) older programs will continue to function without modification. In this chapter, we will not spend any time discussing the specific features of this older API, focusing on the current design. The reader is encouraged to consult Node's online documentation for information on migrating older programs. As often happens, there are modules that *wrap* streams with convenient, reliable interfaces. A good one is: `https://github.com/rvagg/through2`.

Implementing readable streams

Streams producing data that another process may have an interest in are normally implemented using a `Readable` stream. A `Readable` stream saves the implementer all the work of managing the read queue, handling the emitting of data events, and so on.

To create a `Readable` stream, use this:

```
const stream = require('stream');
let readable = new stream.Readable({
  encoding: "utf8",
  highWaterMark: 16000,
  objectMode: true
});
```

As previously mentioned, `Readable` is exposed as a base class, which can be initialized through three options:

- `encoding`: Decode buffers into the specified encoding, defaulting to UTF-8.
- `highWaterMark`: Number of bytes to keep in the internal buffer before ceasing to read from the data source. The default is 16 KB.
- `objectMode`: Tell the stream to behave as a stream of objects instead of a stream of bytes, such as a stream of JSON objects instead of the bytes in a file. Default `false`.

In the following example, we create a mock `Feed` object whose instances will inherit the `Readable` stream interface. Our implementation need only implement the abstract `_read` method of `Readable`, which will push data to a consumer until there is nothing more to push, at which point it triggers the `Readable` stream to emit an `end` event by pushing a `null` value:

```
const stream = require('stream');

let Feed = function(channel) {
  let readable = new stream.Readable({});
  let news = [
    "Big Win!",
    "Stocks Down!",
    "Actor Sad!"
  ];
  readable._read = () => {
    if(news.length) {
      return readable.push(news.shift() + "\n");
    }
    readable.push(null);
  };
  return readable;
};
```

Now that we have an implementation, a consumer might want to instantiate the stream and listen for stream events. Two key events are `readable` and `end`.

The `readable` event is emitted as long as data is being pushed to the stream. It alerts the consumer to check for new data via the `read` method of `Readable`.

 Note again how the `Readable` implementation must provide a `private` `_read` method that services the `public read` method exposed to the consumer API.

The `end` event will be emitted whenever a `null` value is passed to the `push` method of our `Readable` implementation.

Here, we see a consumer using these methods to display new stream data, providing a notification when the stream has stopped sending data:

```
let feed = new Feed();

feed.on("readable", () => {
   let data = feed.read();
   data && process.stdout.write(data);
});
feed.on("end", () => console.log("No more news"));
// Big Win!
// Stocks Down!
// Actor Sad!
// No more news
```

Similarly, we can implement a stream of objects through the use of the `objectMode` option:

```
const stream = require('stream');

let Feed = function(channel) {
   let readable = new stream.Readable({
      objectMode : true
   });
   let prices = [{price : 1}, {price : 2}];
   readable._read = () => {
      if(prices.length) {
         return readable.push(prices.shift());
      }
      readable.push(null);
   };
   return readable;
};
```

Having been placed in objectMode, each chunk pushed is expected to be an object. The reader for this stream can then work on the assumption that each `read()` event will produce a single object:

```
let feed = new Feed();
feed.on("readable", () => {
   let data = feed.read();
   data && console.log(data);
});
feed.on("end", () => console.log("No more news"));
// { price: 1 }
// { price: 2 }
// No more news
```

Here, we see that each read event is receiving an object, rather than a buffer or string.

Finally, the `read` method of a `Readable` stream can be passed a single argument, indicating the number of bytes to be read from the stream's internal buffer. For example, if it was desired that a file should be read one byte at a time, one might implement a consumer using a routine similar to this:

```
let Feed = function(channel) {
    let readable = new stream.Readable({});
    let news = 'A long headline might go here';
    readable._read = () => {
        readable.push(news);
        readable.push(null);
    };
    return readable;
};
```

Note that we're pushing the entirety of news into the stream, and terminating with null. The stream is primed with the entire string of bytes. Now the consumer:

```
feed.on('readable', () => {
   let character;
   while(character = feed.read(1)) {
       console.log(character.toString());
   }
});
// A
//
// l
// o
// n
// ...
// No more bytes to read
```

Here, it should be clear that the `Readable` stream's buffer was filled with a number of bytes all at once, but was read from discretely.

Pushing and pulling

We have seen how a `Readable` implementation will use `push` to populate the stream buffer for reading. When designing these implementations, it is important to consider how volume is managed, at either end of the stream. Pushing more data into a stream than can be read can lead to complications around exceeding available space (memory). At the consumer end, it is important to maintain awareness of termination events, and how to deal with pauses in the data stream.

We might compare the behavior of data streams running through a network with that of water running through a hose.

As with water through a hose, if a greater volume of data is being pushed into the read stream than can be efficiently drained out of the stream at the consumer end through `read`, a great deal of back pressure builds, causing a data backlog to begin accumulating in the stream object's buffer. Because we are dealing with strict mathematical limitations, `read` simply cannot be compelled to release this pressure by reading more quickly—there may be a hard limit on available memory space, or other limitations. As such, memory usage can grow dangerously high, buffers can overflow, and so forth.

A stream implementation should therefore be aware of, and respond to, the response from a `push` operation. If the operation returns `false` , this indicates that the implementation should cease reading from its source (and cease pushing) until the next `_read` request is made.

In conjunction with the above, if there is no more data to push but more is expected in the future, the implementation should `push` an empty string `("")`, which adds no data to the queue but does ensure a future `readable` event.

While the most common treatment of a stream buffer is to `push` to it (queuing data in a line), there are occasions where you might want to place data on the front of the buffer (jumping the line). Node provides an `unshift` operation for these cases, whose behavior is identical to push, outside of the aforementioned difference in buffer placement.

Writable streams

A `Writable` stream is responsible for accepting some value (a stream of bytes, a string) and writing that data to a destination. Streaming data into a file container is a common use case.

To create a `Writable` stream:

```
const stream = require('stream');
let readable = new stream.Writable({
  highWaterMark: 16000,
  decodeStrings: true
});
```

The `Writable` streams constructor can be instantiated with two options:

- `highWaterMark`: The maximum number of bytes the stream's buffer will accept prior to returning `false` on writes. Default is 16 KB.
- `decodeStrings`: Whether to convert strings into buffers before writing. Default is `true`.

As with `Readable` streams, custom `Writable` stream implementations must implement a `_write` handler, which will be passed the arguments sent to the `write` method of instances.

One should think of a `Writable` stream as a data target, such as for a file you are uploading. Conceptually, this is not unlike the implementation of push in a `Readable` stream, where one pushes data until the data source is exhausted, passing `null` to terminate reading. For example, here, we write 32 "A" characters to a stream, which will log them:

```
const stream = require('stream');

let writable = new stream.Writable({
  decodeStrings: false
});

writable._write = (chunk, encoding, callback) => {
  console.log(chunk.toString());
  callback();
};

let written = writable.write(Buffer.alloc(32, 'A'));
writable.end();

console.log(written);
```

```
// AAAAAAAAAAAAAAAAAAAAAAAAAAAAAAAA
// true
```

There are two key things to note here.

First, our `_write` implementation fires the `callback` function immediately after writing a callback that is always present, regardless of whether the instance `write` method is passed a `callback` directly. This call is important for indicating the status of the write attempt, whether a failure (error) or a success.

Second, the call to write returned `true`. This indicates that the internal buffer of the `Writable` implementation has been emptied after executing the requested write. What if we sent a very large amount of data, enough to exceed the default size of the internal buffer?

Modifying the previous example, the following would return `false`:

```
let written = writable.write(Buffer.alloc(16384, 'A'));
console.log(written); // Will be 'false'
```

The reason this `write` returns `false` is that it has reached the `highWaterMark` option—default value of 16 KB (16 * 1,024). If we changed this value to `16383`, `write` would again return `true` (or one could simply increase its value).

What should you do when `write` returns `false`? You should certainly not continue to send data! Returning to our metaphor of water in a hose: when the stream is full, one should wait for it to drain prior to sending more data. Node's Stream implementation will emit a `drain` event whenever it is safe to write again. When `write` returns `false`, listen for the `drain` event before sending more data.

Putting together what we have learned, let's create a `Writable` stream with a `highWaterMark` value of 10 bytes. We'll then set up a simulation where we push the a string of data to `stdout` larger than the `highWaterMark` some number of times. We catch buffer overflows and wait for the drain event to fire prior to sending more data:

```
const stream = require('stream');

let writable = new stream.Writable({
   highWaterMark: 10
});

writable._write = (chunk, encoding, callback) => {
   process.stdout.write(chunk);
   callback();
```

```
};

function writeData(iterations, writer, data, encoding, cb) {
    (function write() {

        if(!iterations--) {
            return cb()
        }

        if (!writer.write(data, encoding)) {
            console.log(` <wait> highWaterMark of
${writable.writableHighWaterMark} reached`);
            writer.once('drain', write);
        }
    })()
}

writeData(4, writable, 'String longer than highWaterMark', 'utf8', () =>
console.log('finished'));
```

Each time we right we check if the stream write action returned **false**, and if so we wait for the next **drain** event before running our `write` method again.

You should be careful to implement proper stream management, respecting the "warnings" emitted by write events, and properly waiting for the drain event to occur prior to sending more data.

The fluid data in a `Readable` stream can be easily redirected to a `Writable` stream. For example, the following code will take any data sent by a terminal (`stdin` is a `Readable` stream) and echo it back to the destination `Writable` stream (`stdout`): `process.stdin.pipe(process.stdout)`. Whenever a `Writable` stream is passed to a `Readable` stream's pipe method, a **pipe** event will fire. Similarly, when a `Writable` stream is removed as a destination for a `Readable` stream, the **unpipe** event fires. To remove a pipe, use the following: `unpipe(destination stream)`

Duplex streams

A **duplex stream** is both readable and writeable. For instance, a TCP server created in Node exposes a socket that can be both read from, and written to:

```
const stream = require("stream");
```

```
const net = require("net");

net.createServer(socket => {
  socket.write("Go ahead and type something!");
  socket.setEncoding("utf8");
  socket.on("readable", function() {
    process.stdout.write(this.read())
  });
})
.listen(8080);
```

When executed, this code will create a TCP server that can be connected to via Telnet:

```
telnet 127.0.0.1 8080
```

Start the server in one terminal window, open a separate terminal, and connect to the server via telnet. Upon connection, the connecting terminal will print out `Go ahead and type something!`—writing to the socket. Any text entered in the connecting terminal (after hitting **ENTER**) will be echoed to the `stdout` of the terminal running the TCP server (reading from the socket), creating a sort of chat application.

This implementation of a bidirectional (duplex) communication protocol demonstrates clearly how independent processes can form the nodes of a complex and responsive application, whether communicating across a network or within the scope of a single process.

The options sent when constructing a `Duplex` instance merge those sent to `Readable` and `Writable` streams, with no additional parameters. Indeed, this stream type simply assumes both roles, and the rules for interacting with it follow the rules for the interactive mode being used.

As a `Duplex` stream assumes both read and write roles, any implementation is required to implement both _write and _read methods, again following the standard implementation details given for the relevant stream type.

Transforming streams

On occasion, stream data needs to be processed, often in cases where one is writing some sort of binary protocol or other *on the fly* data transformation. A `Transform` stream is designed for this purpose, functioning as a `Duplex` stream that sits between a `Readable` stream and a `Writable` stream.

A `Transform` stream is initialized using the same options used to initialize a typical `Duplex` stream, where `Transform` differs from a normal `Duplex` stream is in its requirement that the custom implementation merely provides a `_transform` method, excluding the `_write` and `_read` method requirement.

The `_transform` method will receive three arguments, first the sent buffer, an optional encoding argument, and finally a callback which `_transform` is expected to call when the transformation is complete:

```
_transform = function(buffer, encoding, cb) {
  let transformation = "...";
  this.push(transformation);
  cb();
};
```

Let's imagine a program that helps to convert **ASCII (American Standard Code for Information Interchange)** codes into ASCII characters, receiving input from `stdin`. You type in an ASCII code, and the program responds with the alphanumeric character corresponding to that code. Here we can simply pipe our input to a `Transform` stream, then pipe its output back to `stdout`:

```
const stream = require('stream');
let converter = new stream.Transform();

converter._transform = function(num, encoding, cb) {
    this.push(String.fromCharCode(new Number(num)) + "\n");
    cb();
};

process.stdin.pipe(converter).pipe(process.stdout);
```

Interacting with this program might produce an output resembling the following:

```
65 A
66 B
256 Ā
257 ā
```

A more involved example of a transform stream will be demonstrated in the example that ends this chapter.

Using PassThrough streams

This sort of stream is a trivial implementation of a `Transform` stream, which simply passes received input bytes through to an output stream. This is useful if one doesn't require any transformation of the input data, and simply wants to easily pipe a `Readable` stream to a `Writable` stream.

`PassThrough` streams have benefits similar to JavaScript's anonymous functions, making it easy to assert minimal functionality without too much fuss. For example, it is not necessary to implement an abstract base class, as one does with for the _read method of a `Readable` stream. Consider the following use of a `PassThrough` stream as an event spy:

```
const fs = require('fs');
const stream = require('stream');
const spy = new stream.PassThrough();

spy
.on('error', (err) => console.error(err))
.on('data', function(chunk) {
    console.log(`spied data -> ${chunk}`);
})
.on('end', () => console.log('\nfinished'));

fs.createReadStream('./passthrough.txt').pipe(spy).pipe(process.stdout);
```

Normally a Transform or Duplex stream is what you want (where you can set up a proper implementation of _read and _write), but in certain scenarios, such as tests, it can be useful to place "watchers" on a stream.

Creating an HTTP server

HTTP is a stateless data transfer protocol built upon a request/response model: clients make requests to servers, which then return a response. As facilitating this sort of rapid-pattern network communication is the sort of I/O Node was designed to excel at, Node gained early widespread attention as a toolkit for creating servers—though it can certainly be used to do much, much more. Throughout this book, we will be creating many implementations of HTTP servers, as well as other protocol servers, and will be discussing best practices in more depth, contextualized within specific business cases. It is expected that you have already had some experience doing the same. For both of these reasons, we will quickly move through a general overview into some more specialized uses.

At its simplest, an HTTP server responds to connection attempts, and manages data as it arrives and as it is sent along. A Node server is typically created using the `createServer` method of the `http` module:

```
const http = require('http');
let server = http.createServer((request, response) => {
    response.writeHead(200, {
        'Content-Type': 'text/plain'
    });
    response.write("PONG");
    response.end();
}).listen(8080);

server.on("request", (request, response) => {
    request.setEncoding("utf8");
    request.on("readable", () => console.log(request.read()));
    request.on("end", () => console.log("DONE"));
});
```

The object returned by `http.createServer` is an instance of `http.Server`, which extends `EventEmitter`, broadcasting network events as they occur, such as a client connection or request. The code prior is a common way to write Node servers. However, it is worth pointing out that directly instantiating the `http.Server` class is sometimes a useful way to distinguish distinct server/client interactions. We will use that format for the following examples.

Here, we create a basic server that simply reports when a connection is made, and when it is terminated:

```
const http = require('http');
const server = new http.Server();
server.on('connection', socket => {
    let now = new Date();
    console.log(`Client arrived: ${now}`);
    socket.on('end', () => console.log(`client left: ${new Date()}`));
});
// Connections get 2 seconds before being terminated
server.setTimeout(2000, socket => socket.end());
server.listen(8080);
```

When building multiuser systems, especially authenticated multiuser systems, this point in the server-client transaction is an excellent place for client validation and tracking code, including setting or reading of cookies and other session variables, or the broadcasting of a client arrival event to other clients working together in a concurrent real-time application.

By adding a listener for requests, we arrive at the more common request/response pattern, handled as a `Readable` stream. When a client POSTs some data, we can catch that data like the following:

```
server.on('request', (request, response) => {
    request.setEncoding('utf8');
    request.on('readable', () => {
        let data = request.read();
        data && response.end(data);
    });
});
```

Try sending some data to this server using **curl**:

```
curl http://localhost:8080 -d "Here is some data"
// Here is some data
```

By using connection events, we can nicely separate our connection handling code, grouping it into clearly defined functional domains correctly described as executing in response to particular events. In the example above we saw how to set a timer that kicks server connections after two seconds.

 If one simply wants to set the number of milliseconds of inactivity before a socket is presumed to have timed out, simply use `server.timeout = (Integer)num_milliseconds`. To disable socket timeouts, pass a value of 0 (zero).

Let's now take a look at how Node's HTTP module can be used to enter into more interesting network interactions.

Making HTTP requests

It is often necessary for a network application to make external HTTP calls. HTTP servers are also often called upon to perform HTTP services for clients making requests. Node provides an easy interface for making external HTTP calls.

For example, the following code will fetch the HTML front page of `www.example.org`:

```
const http = require('http');
http.request({
    host: 'www.example.org',
    method: 'GET',
    path: "/"
}, function(response) {
```

```
    response.setEncoding("utf8");
    response.on("readable", () => console.log(response.read()));
}).end();
```

As we can see, we are working with a `Readable` stream, which can be written to a file.

> A popular Node module for managing HTTP requests is Mikeal Roger's request: `https://github.com/request/request`

Because it is common to use `HTTP.request` in order to `GET` external pages, Node offers a shortcut:

```
http.get("http://www.example.org/", response => {
    console.log(`Status: ${response.statusCode}`);
}).on('error', err => {
    console.log("Error: " + err.message);
});
```

Let's now look at some more advanced implementations of HTTP servers, where we perform general network services for clients.

Proxying and tunneling

Sometimes, it is useful to provide a means for one server to function as a proxy, or broker, for other servers. This would allow one server to distribute a load to other servers, for example. Another use would be to provide access to a secured server to users who are unable to connect to that server directly. It is also common to have one server answering for more than one URL—using a proxy, that one server can forward requests to the right recipient.

Because Node has a consistent streams interface throughout its network interfaces, we can build a simple HTTP proxy in just a few lines of code. For example, the following program will set up an HTTP server on port `8080` which will respond to any request by fetching the front page of a website and piping that page back to the client:

```
const http = require('http');
const server = new http.Server();

server.on("request", (request, socket) => {
    console.log(request.url);
    http.request({
        host: 'www.example.org',
```

```
          method: 'GET',
          path: "/",
          port: 80
      }, response => response.pipe(socket))
      .end();
});

server.listen(8080, () => console.log('Proxy server listening on
localhost:8080'));
```

Go ahead and start this server, and connect to it. Once this server receives the client socket, it is free to push content from any readable stream back to the client, and here, the result of GET of www.example.org is streamed. One can easily see how an external content server managing a caching layer for your application might become a proxy endpoint, for example.

Using similar ideas, we can create a tunneling service, using Node's native CONNECT support. Tunneling involves using a proxy server as an intermediary to communicate with a remote server on behalf of a client. Once our proxy server connects to a remote server, it is able to pass messages back and forth between that server and a client. This is advantageous when a direct connection between a client and a remote server is not possible, or not desired.

First, we'll set up a proxy server responding to HTTP CONNECT requests, then make a CONNECT request to that server. The proxy receives our client's Request object, the client's socket itself, and the head (the first packet) of the tunneling stream:

```
const http = require('http');
const net = require('net');
const url = require('url');
const proxy = new http.Server();

proxy.on('connect', (request, clientSocket, head) => {
  let reqData = url.parse(`http://${request.url}`);
  let remoteSocket = net.connect(reqData.port, reqData.hostname, () => {
    clientSocket.write('HTTP/1.1 200 \r\n\r\n');
    remoteSocket.write(head);
    remoteSocket.pipe(clientSocket);
    clientSocket.pipe(remoteSocket);
  });
}).listen(8080);

let request = http.request({
  port: 8080,
  hostname: 'localhost',
  method: 'CONNECT',
```

```
    path: 'www.example.org:80'
});
request.end();

request.on('connect', (res, socket, head) => {
  socket.setEncoding("utf8");
  socket.write('GET / HTTP/1.1\r\nHost: www.example.org:80\r\nConnection:
close\r\n\r\n');
  socket.on('readable', () => {
      console.log(socket.read());
    });
  socket.on('end', () => {
    proxy.close();
  });
});
```

Once we make a request to our local tunneling server running on port 8080 it will set up a remote socket connection to our destination and maintain this "bridge" between the remote socket and the (local) client socket. The remote connection of course only sees our tunneling server, and in this way clients can connect in a sense anonymously to remote services (which isn't always a shady practice!).

HTTPS, TLS (SSL), and securing your server

The security of web applications has become a significant discussion topic in recent years. Traditional applications normally benefited from the well-tested and mature security models designed into the major servers and application stacks underpinning major deployments. For one reason or another, web applications were allowed to venture into the experimental world of client-side business logic and open web services shielded by a diaphanous curtain.

As Node is regularly deployed as a web server, it is imperative that the community begins to accept responsibility for securing these servers. HTTPS is a secure transmission protocol—essentially encrypted HTTP formed by layering the HTTP protocol on top of the SSL/TLS protocol.

Creating a self-signed certificate for development

In order to support SSL connections, a server will need a properly signed certificate. While developing, it is much easier to simply create a self-signed certificate, which will allow you to use Node's HTTPS module.

These are the steps needed to create a certificate for development. The certificate we create won't demonstrate identity, as a certificate from a third party does, but it is all we need to use the encryption of HTTPS. From a terminal:

```
openssl genrsa -out server-key.pem 2048
  openssl req -new -key server-key.pem -out server-csr.pem
  openssl x509 -req -in server-csr.pem -signkey server-key.pem -out server-cert.pem
```

These keys may now be used to develop HTTPS servers. The contents of these files need simply be passed along as options to a Node server:

```
const https = require('https');
const fs = require('fs');
https.createServer({
  key: fs.readFileSync('server-key.pem'),
  cert: fs.readFileSync('server-cert.pem')
}, (req, res) => {
  ...
}).listen(443);
```

Free low-assurance SSL certificates are available from `http://www.startssl.com/` for cases where self-signed certificates are not ideal during development. Additionally, `https://www.letsencrypt.org` has started an exciting initiative toward providing free certificates for all (and a safer web).

Installing a real SSL certificate

In order to move a secure application out of a development environment and into an internet-exposed environment, a real certificate will need to be purchased. The prices of these certificates has been dropping year by year, and it should be easy to find reasonably priced providers of certificates with a high-enough level of security. Some providers even offer free person-use certificates.

Setting up a professional cert simply requires changing the HTTPS options we introduced previously. Different providers will have different processes and filenames. Typically, you will need to download or otherwise receive from your provider a `private .key` file, your signed domain certificate `.crt` file, and a bundle describing certificate chains:

```
let options = {
  key: fs.readFileSync("mysite.key"),
  cert: fs.readFileSync("mysite.com.crt"),
  ca: [ fs.readFileSync("gd_bundle.crt") ]
};
```

It is important to note that the `ca` parameter must be sent as an *array*, even if the bundle of certificates has been concatenated into one file.

The request object

HTTP request and response messages are similar, consisting of the following:

- A status line, which for a request would resemble GET/`index.html` HTTP/1.1, and for a response would resemble HTTP/1.1 200 OK
- Zero or more headers, which in a request might include `Accept-Charset:` `UTF-8` or `From: user@server.com`, and in responses might resemble `Content-Type: text/html` and `Content-Length: 1024`
- A message body, which for a response might be an HTML page, and for a `POST` request might be some form data

We've seen how HTTP server interfaces in Node are expected to expose a request handler, and how this handler will be passed some form of a request and response object, each of which implement a readable or writable stream.

We will cover the handling of `POST` data and `Header` data in more depth later in this chapter. Before we do, let's go over how to parse out some of the more straightforward information contained in a request.

The URL module

Whenever a request is made to an HTTP server, the request object will contain URL property, identifying the targeted resource. This is accessible via `request.url`. Node's URL module is used to decompose a typical URL string into its constituent parts. Consider the following figure:

```
> console.log(url.parse("http://username:password@www.example.org:8080/events/today/?filter=sports&maxresults=20#football"));
{ protocol: 'http:',
  slashes: true,
  auth: 'username:password',
  host: 'www.example.org:8080',
  port: '8080',
  hostname: 'www.example.org',
  hash: '#football',
  search: '?filter=sports&maxresults=20',
  query: 'filter=sports&maxresults=20',
  pathname: '/events/today/',
  path: '/events/today/?filter=sports&maxresults=20',
  href: 'http://username:password@www.example.org:8080/events/today/?filter=sports&maxresults=20#football' }
```

We see how the `url.parse` method decomposes strings, and the meaning of each segment should be clear. It might also be clear that the `query` field would be more useful if it was itself parsed into key/value pairs. This is accomplished by passing `true` as the second argument of to the `parse` method, which would change the query field value given above into a more useful key/value map:

```
query: { filter: 'sports', maxresults: '20' }
```

This is especially useful when parsing GET requests. There is one final argument for `url.parse` that relates to the difference between these two URLs:

- `http://www.example.org`
- `//www.example.org`

The second URL here is an example of a (relatively unknown) design feature of the HTTP protocol: the protocol-relative URL (technically, a **network-path reference**), as opposed to the more common absolute URL.

 To learn more about how network-path references are used to smooth resource protocol resolution, visit: `http://tools.ietf.org/html/ rfc3986#section-4.2`.

The issue under discussion is this: `url.parse` will treat a string beginning with slashes as indicating a path, not a host. For example, `url.parse("//www.example.org")` will set the following values in the host and path fields:

```
host: null,
 path: '//www.example.org'
```

What we actually want is the reverse:

```
host: 'www.example.org',
 path: null
```

To resolve this issue, pass `true` as the third argument to `url.parse`, which indicates to the method that slashes denote a host, not a path:

```
url.parse("//www.example.org", null, true);
```

It is also the case that a developer will want to create an URL, such as when making requests via `http.request`. The segments of said URL may be spread across various data structures and variables, and will need to be assembled. You accomplish this by passing an object like the one returned from `url.parse` to the method `url.format`.

The following code will create the URL string `http://www.example.org`:

```
url.format({
  protocol: 'http:',
  host: 'www.example.org'
});
```

Similarly, you may also use the `url.resolve` method to generate URL strings in the common scenario of requiring the concatenating of a base URL and a path:

```
url.resolve("http://example.org/a/b", "c/d"); //'http://example.org/a/c/d'
url.resolve("http://example.org/a/b", "/c/d");
//'http://example.org/c/d'
url.resolve("http://example.org", "http://google.com");
//'http://google.com/'
```

The Querystring module

As we saw with the URL module, query strings often need to be parsed into a map of key/value pairs. The `Querystring` module will either decompose an existing query string into its parts, or assemble a query string from a map of key/value pairs.

For example, `querystring.parse("foo=bar&bingo=bango")` will return:

```
{
  foo: 'bar',
  bingo: 'bango'
}
```

If our query strings are not formatted using the normal "`&`" separator and "`=`" assignment character, the `Querystring` module offers customizable parsing.

The second argument to `Querystring` can be a custom separator string, and the third, a custom assignment string. For example, the following will return the same mapping as given previously on a query string with custom formatting:

```
let qs = require("querystring");
console.log(qs.parse("foo:bar^bingo:bango", "^", ":"));
// { foo: 'bar', bingo: 'bango' }
```

You can compose a query string using the `Querystring.stringify` method:

```
console.log(qs.stringify({ foo: 'bar', bingo: 'bango' }));
// foo=bar&bingo=bango
```

As with parse, `stringify` also accepts custom separator and assignment arguments:

```
console.log(qs.stringify({ foo: 'bar', bingo: 'bango' }, "^", ":"));
// foo:bar^bingo:bango
```

Query strings are commonly associated with GET requests, seen following the ? character. As we saw previously, in these cases, automatic parsing of these strings using the `url` module is the most straightforward solution. However, strings formatted in such a manner also show up when we're handling POST data, and in these cases, the `Querystring` module is of real use. We'll discuss this usage shortly, but first, something about HTTP headers.

Working with headers

Each HTTP request made to a Node server will likely contain useful header information, and clients normally expect to receive similar package information from a server. Node provides straightforward interfaces for reading and writing headers. We'll briefly go over those simple interfaces, clarifying some details. Finally, we'll discuss how more advanced header usage might be implemented in Node, studying some common network responsibilities a Node server will likely need to accommodate.

A typical request header will look something like the following:

```
{ host: '127.0.0.1:8080',
  'user-agent': 'Mozilla/5.0 (Macintosh; Intel Mac OS X 10.8; rv:19.0)
Gecko/20100101 Firefox/19.0',
  accept:
  'text/html,application/xhtml+xml,application/xml;q=0.9,*/*;q=0.8',
  'accept-language': 'en-US,en;q=0.5',
  'accept-encoding': 'gzip, deflate',
  connection: 'keep-alive',
  'if-modified-since': 'Sun Apr 07 2013 08:09:12 GMT-0400 (EDT)',
  'if-none-match': '1441a7909c087dbbe7ce59881b9df8b9',
  'cache-control': 'max-age=0' }
```

Headers are simple key/value pairs. Request keys are always lowercased. You may use any case format when setting response keys.

Reading headers is straightforward. Read header information by examining the `request.header` object, which is a 1:1 mapping of the header's key/value pairs. To fetch the *accept* header from the previous example, simply read `request.headers.accept`.

The number of incoming headers can be limited by setting the `maxHeadersCount` property of your HTTP server.

If it is preferred that headers are read programmatically, Node provides the `response.getHeader` method, accepting the header key as its first argument.

While request headers are simple key/value pairs, when writing headers, we need a more expressive interface. As a response typically must send a status code, Node provides a straightforward way to prepare a response status line and header group in one command:

```
response.writeHead(200, {
  'Content-Length': 4096,
  'Content-Type': 'text/plain'
});
```

To set headers individually, you can use `response.setHeader`, passing two arguments: the header key, followed by the header value.

To set multiple headers with the same name, you may pass an array to `response.setHeader`:

```
response.setHeader("Set-Cookie", ["session:12345", "language=en"]);
```

Occasionally, it may be necessary to remove a response header after that header has been *queued*. This is accomplished using `response.removeHeader`, passing the header name to be removed as an argument.

Headers must be written prior to writing a response. It is an error to write a header after a response has been sent.

Using cookies

The HTTP protocol is stateless. Any given request has no information on previous requests. For a server, this meant that determining if two requests originated from the same browser was not possible. Cookies were invented to solve this problem. Cookies are primarily used to share state between clients (usually a browser) and a server, existing as small text files stored in browsers.

Cookies are insecure. Cookie information flows between a server and a client in plain text. There is any number of tamper points in between. Browsers allow easy access to them, for example. This is a good idea, as nobody wants information on their browser or local machine to be hidden from them, beyond their control.

Nevertheless, cookies are also used rather extensively to maintain state information, or pointers to state information, particularly in the case of user sessions or other authentication scenarios.

It is assumed that you are familiar with how cookies function in general. Here, we will discuss how cookies are fetched, parsed, and set by a Node HTTP server. We will use the example of a server that echoes back the value of a sent cookie. If no cookie exists, the server will create that cookie and instruct the client to ask for it again.

Consider the following code:

```
const http = require('http');
const url = require('url');
http.createServer((request, response) => {
  let cookies = request.headers.cookie;
  if(!cookies) {
    let cookieName = "session";
    let cookieValue = "123456";
    let numberOfDays = 4;
    let expiryDate = new Date();
    expiryDate.setDate(expiryDate.getDate() + numberOfDays);

    let cookieText =
```

```
`${cookieName}=${cookieValue};expires=${expiryDate.toUTCString()};`;
    response.setHeader('Set-Cookie', cookieText);
    response.writeHead(302, {'Location': '/'});
    return response.end();
  }
  cookies.split(';').forEach(cookie => {
    let m = cookie.match(/(.*?)=(.*)$/);
    cookies[m[1].trim()] = (m[2] || '').trim();
  });

  response.end(`Cookie set: ${cookies.toString()}`);
}).listen(8080);
```

First, we create a server that checks request headers for cookies:

```
let server = http.createServer((request, response) => {
  let cookies = request.headers.cookie;
  ...
```

Note that cookies are stored as the `cookie` attribute of `request.headers`. If no cookies exist for this domain, we will need to create one, giving it the name `session` and a value of `123456`:

```
if (!cookies) {
  ...
  let cookieText =
`${cookieName}=${cookieValue};expires=${expiryDate.toUTCString()};`;
  response.setHeader('Set-Cookie', cookieText);
  response.writeHead(302, {
    'Location': '/'
  });
  return response.end();
}
```

If we have set this cookie for the first time, the client is instructed to make another request to this same server, using a **302 Found** redirect, instructing the client to call our server location again. As there is now a cookie set for this domain, the subsequent request will contain our cookie, which we handle next:

```
cookies.split(';').forEach(cookie => {
 let m = cookie.match(/(.*?)=(.*)$/);
 cookies[m[1].trim()] = (m[2] || '').trim();
});
response.end(`Cookie set: ${cookies.toString()}`);
```

Now if you visit `localhost:8080` you should see something like this displayed:

```
Cookie set: AuthSession=c3Bhc3F1YWxpOjU5QzkzRjQ3OosrEJ30gDa0KcTBhRk-
YGGXSZnT; io=QuzEHrr5tIZdH3LjAAAC
```

Understanding content types

A client will often pass along a request header indicating the expected response **MIME** (**Multi-purpose Internet Mail Extension**) type. Clients will also indicate the MIME type of a request body. Servers will similarly provide header information about the MIME type of a response body. The MIME type for HTML is text/html, for example.

As we have seen, it is the responsibility of an HTTP response to set headers describing the entity it contains. Similarly, a GET request will normally indicate the resource type, the MIME type, it expects as a response. Such a request header might look like this:

```
Accept: text/html
```

It is the responsibility of a server receiving such instructions to prepare a body entity conforming to the sent MIME type, and if it is able to do so, it should return a similar response header:

```
Content-Type: text/html; charset=utf-8
```

Because requests also identify the specific resource desired (such as /files/index.html), the server must ensure that the requested resource it is streaming back to the client is in fact of the correct MIME type. While it may seem obvious that a resource identified by the extension html is in fact of the MIME type text/html, this is not at all certain—a filesystem does nothing to prevent an image file from being given an html extension. Parsing extensions is an imperfect method of determining file type. We need to do more.

The UNIX file program is able to determine the MIME type of a system file. For example, one might determine the MIME type of a file without an extension (for example, resource) by running this command:

```
file --brief --mime resource
```

We pass arguments instructing file to output the MIME type of resource, and that the output should be brief (only the MIME type, and no other information). This command might return something like text/plain; charset=us-ascii. Here, we have a tool to solve our problem.

For more information about the file utility consult, go to: `http://man7.org/linux/man-pages/man1/file.1.html`

Recalling that Node is able to spawn child processes, we have a solution to our problem of accurately determining the MIME type of system files. We can use the Node command `exec` method of Node's `child_process` module in order to determine the MIME type of a file, like so:

```
let exec = require('child_process').exec;
exec("file --brief --mime resource", (err, mime) => {
  console.log(mime);
});
```

This technique is also useful when validating a file streamed in from an external location. Following the axiom "never trust the client", it is always a good idea to check whether the `Content-type` header of a file posted to a Node server matches the actual MIME type of the received file as it exists on the local filesystem.

Handling favicon requests

When visiting a URL via a browser, you will often notice a little icon in the browser tab or in the browser's address bar. This icon is an image named `favicon.ico`, and it is fetched on each request. As such, an HTTP GET request normally combines two requests—one for the favicon, and another for the requested resource.

Node developers are often surprised by this doubled request. Any implementation of an HTTP server must deal with favicon requests. To do so, the server must check the request type and handle it accordingly. The following example demonstrates one method of doing so:

```
const http = require('http');
http.createServer((request, response) => {
  if(request.url === '/favicon.ico') {
    response.writeHead(200, {
      'Content-Type': 'image/x-icon'
    });
    return response.end();
  }
  response.writeHead(200, {
    'Content-Type': 'text/plain'
  });
```

```
    response.write('Some requested resource');
    response.end();
}).listen(8080);
```

This code will simply send an empty image stream for the favicon. If there is a favicon to send, you would simply push that data through the response stream, as we've discussed previously.

Handling POST data

One of the most common REST methods used in network applications is POST. According to the REST specification, a POST is not idempotent, as opposed to most of the other well-known methods (GET, PUT, DELETE, and so on) that are. This is mentioned in order to point out that the handling of POST data will very often have a consequential effect on an application's state, and should therefore be handled with care.

We will now discuss the handling of the most common type of POST data, that which is submitted via forms. The more complex type of POST—multipart uploads—will be discussed in Chapter 4, *Using Node to Access the Filesystem*.

Let's create a server which will return a form to clients, and echo back any data that client submits with that form. We will need to first check the request URL, determining if this is a form request or a form submission, returning HTML for a form in the first case, and parsing submitted data in the second:

```
const http = require('http');
const qs = require('querystring');

http.createServer((request, response) => {
    let body = "";
    if(request.url === "/") {
        response.writeHead(200, {
            "Content-Type": "text/html"
        });
        return response.end(
            '<form action="/submit" method="post">\
            <input type="text" name="sometext">\
            <input type="submit" value="Send some text">\
            </form>'
        );
    }
}).listen(8080);
```

Note that the form we respond with has a single field named `sometext`. This form should POST data in the form `sometext=entered_text` to the path `/submit`. To catch this data, add the following conditional:

```
if(request.url === "/submit") {
    request.on('readable', () => {
        let data = request.read();
        data && (body += data);
    });
    request.on('end', () => {
        let fields = qs.parse(body);
        response.end(`Thanks for sending: ${fields.sometext}`);
    });
}
```

Once our POST stream ends we parse the body using `Querystring.parse`, giving us a key/value map from which we can pluck the value of the form element with name `sometext`, and respond to the client that we have received their data.

Creating and streaming images with Node

Having gone over the main strategies for initiating and diverting streams of data, let's practice the theory by creating a service to stream (aptly named) **PNG (Portable Network Graphics)** images to a client. This will not be a simple file server, however. The goal is to create PNG data streams by piping the output stream of an **ImageMagick** convert operation executing in a separate process into the response stream of an HTTP connection, where the converter is translating another stream of **SVG (Scalable Vector Graphics)** data generated within a virtualized **DOM (Document Object Model)**, existing in the Node runtime. Let's get started.

 The full code for this example can be found in your code bundle.

Our goal is to use Node to generate pie charts dynamically on a server based on client requests. A client will specify some data values, and a PNG representing that data in a pie will be generated. We are going to use the **D3.js** library, which provides a Javascript API for creating data visualizations, and the **jsdom** NPM package, which allows us to create a virtual DOM within a Node process. Additionally we'll use **ImageMagick** to transform a **SVG (Scalable Vector Graphics)** representation into a **PNG (Portable Network Graphics)** representation.

Visit `https://github.com/tmpvar/jsdom` to learn about how **jsdom** works, and `https://d3js.org/` to learn about using D3 to generate SVG.

Additionally, the PNG we create will be written to a file. If future requests pass the same query arguments to our service, we will then be able to rapidly pipe the existing rendering immediately, without the overhead of regenerating it.

A pie graph represents a range of percentages whose sum fills the total area of a circle, visualized as slices. Our service will draw such a graph based on the values a client sends. In our system, the client is required to send values adding up to 1, such as .5, .3, .2. Our server, when it receives a request, will therefore need to fetch query parameters as well as create a unique key that maps to future requests with the same query parameters:

```
let values = url.parse(request.url, true).query['values'].split(",");
let cacheKey = values.sort().join('');
```

Here, we see the URL module in action, pulling out our data values. As well, we create a key on these values by first sorting the values, then joining them into a string we will use as the filename for our cached pie graph. We sort values for this reason: the same graph is achieved by sending .5 .3 .2 and .3 .5 .2. By sorting and joining, these both become the filename .2 .3 .5.

In a production application, more work would need to be done to ensure that the query is well formed, is mathematically correct, and so on. In our example, we assume proper values are being sent.

Creating, caching, and sending a PNG representation

To start, install ImageMagick: `http://www.imagemagick.org/script/download.php`. We will spawn a Node process to interface with the installed binary, below.

Before we build the graph dynamically, assume that there already exists an SVG definition stored on variable `svg`, which will contain a string similar to this:

```
<svg width="200" height="200">
<g transform="translate(100,100)">
<defs>
  <radialgradient id="grad-0" gradientUnits="userSpaceOnUse" cx="0" cy="0"
```

```
r="100">
  <stop offset="0" stop-color="#7db9e8"></stop>
...
```

To convert that SVG to a PNG we would spawn a child process running the ImageMagick convert program, and stream our SVG data to the `stdin` of that process, which will output a PNG. In the example that follows we continue this idea to stream the generated PNG to the client.

We'll skip the server boilerplate -- suffice it to say that the server will be running on 8080 and will a client calling with some data to graph. What's important is how we generate and stream the pie chart back.

The client will send some querystring arguments indicating the `values` for this graph (such as **4,5,8**, the relative size of the slices). What the server will do is generate a "virtual DOM" using the jsdom module, into which the D3 graphics library is inserted, as well as some javascript (`pie.js` in your code bundle) to take the values we have received and draw an SVG pie chart using D3, all within this server-side virtual DOM. We then grab that generated SVG code and convert it to a PNG using ImageMagick. In order to allow caching we store this PNG using a string filename formed from the cache values as a cacheKey, and while writing we pipe the streaming PNG back to the client:

```
jsdom.env({
    ...
    html : `<!DOCTYPE html><div id="pie"
style="width:${width}px;height:${height}px;"></div>`,
    scripts : ['d3.min.js','d3.layout.min.js','pie.js'],
    done : (err, window) => {
        let svg = window.insertPie("#pie", width, height, values).innerHTML;
        let svgToPng = spawn("convert", ["svg:", "png:-"]);
        let filewriter = fs.createWriteStream(cacheKey);
        filewriter.on("open", err => {
            let streamer = new stream.Transform();
            streamer._transform = function(data, enc, cb) {
                filewriter.write(data);
                this.push(data);
                cb();
            };
            svgToPng.stdout.pipe(streamer).pipe(response);
            svgToPng.stdout.on('finish', () => response.end());
            // jsdom's domToHTML will lowercase element names
            svg = svg.replace(/radialgradient/g,'radialGradient');
            svgToPng.stdin.write(svg);
            svgToPng.stdin.end();
            window.close();
        });
```

```
    }
});
```

Recalling our discussion on streams, what is happening here should be clear. We generate a DOM (`window`) with jsdom, run the `insertPie` function to generate the SVG, and then spawn two streams: one to write the cache file, and one to the ImageMagick process. Using a `TransformStream` (both readable and writable) we implement its abstract `_transform` method to expect input from `stdout` of our ImageMagick stream, write that data to the local filesystem, and then re-push the data back into the stream, which is piped forward onto the response stream. We can now achieve the desired stream chaining:

```
svgToPng.stdout.pipe(streamer).pipe(response);
```

The client receives a pie graph, and a copy is written on the local file cache. In cases where the requested pie chart has already been rendered it can be directly streamed from a filesystem:

```
fs.exists(cacheKey, exists => {
  response.writeHead(200, {
    'Content-Type': 'image/png'
  });
  if (exists) {
    fs.createReadStream(cacheKey).pipe(response);
    return;
  }
...
```

If you start the server and paste the following into your browser:

```
http://localhost:8080/?values=3,3,3,3,3
```

You should see a pie chart displayed:

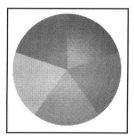

While somewhat artificial, hopefully this shows how chains of different processes can be connected via streams, avoiding any intermediate storage in memory, which can be especially useful when passing data through and out of a highly trafficked network server.

Summary

As we have learned, Node's designers have succeeded in creating a simple, predictable, and convenient solution to the challenging design problem of enabling efficient I/O between disparate sources and targets, while keeping code easy to manage. Its abstract Stream interface facilitates the instantiation of consistent readable and writable interfaces, and the extension of this interface into HTTP requests and responses, the filesystem, child processes, and other data channels makes stream programming with Node a pleasant experience.

Now that we've learned how to set up HTTP servers to handle streams of data arriving from many simultaneously connected clients, and how to feed those clients buffets of buffered streams, we can begin to engage more deeply with the task of building enterprise-grade concurrent real-time systems with Node.

4
Using Node to Access the Filesystem

"We have persistent objects - they're called files."

– *Ken Thompson*

A file is simply a chunk of data that is persisted, usually, on some hard medium such as a hard drive. Files are normally composed of a sequence of bytes whose encoding maps onto some other pattern, like a sequence of numbers or electrical pulses. A nearly infinite number of encodings are possible, with some common ones being text files, image files, and music files. Files have a fixed length, and to be read, their character encoding must be deciphered by some sort of reader, such as an MP3 player or a word processor.

When a file is in transit, moving through a cable after it's been siphoned off of some storage device, it is no different than any other data stream running through the wire. Its previous solid state is just a stable blueprint that can be easily and infinitely copied.

We've already seen how event streams reflect the core design principles informing Node's design, where byte streams are to be read from and written to, and piped into other streams, emitting relevant stream events, such as `end`. Files are easily understood as being containers of data, filled with bytes that can be extracted or inserted partially or as a whole.

In addition to their natural similarity to streams, files also display the characteristics of objects. Files have properties that describe the interface available for accessing file contents—data structures with properties and associated access methods.

A **filesystem** reflects some concept of how files should be organized—how they are identified, where they are stored, how they are to be accessed, and so forth. A common filesystem for UNIX users is the **UFS** (**Unix File System**), while Windows users may be familiar with **NTFS** (**New Technology File System**).

It is interesting that the designers of the Plan 9 operating system (a team including *Ken Thompson*) decided to have *all* control interfaces represented as filesystems, such that all system interfaces (across devices, across applications) are modeled as file operations. Treating files as first-class citizens is a philosophy the UNIX OS also uses; using files as references to named pipes and sockets, among other things, gives developers enormous power when shaping data flow.

File objects are also powerful, and the system they reside within exposes fundamental I/O interfaces that must be easy to use, consistent, and very fast. Not surprisingly, Node's `file` module exposes just such an interface.

We will be considering handling files in Node from these two perspectives: how file data content is streamed in and out (read from and written), and how the attributes of file objects are modified, such as changing file permissions.

Additionally, we will cover the responsibilities of the Node server, in terms of accepting file uploads and servicing file requests. By working through examples of directory iterators and file servers, the full range and behavior of Node's filesystem API should become clear.

Lastly, we'll take JavaScript back to the desktop, using GitHub's Electron framework to make our own desktop app, a simple file browser.

Directories, and iterating over files and folders

Typically, a filesystem groups files into collections, normally referred to as directories. One navigates through directories to find individual files. Once a target file is found, the file object must be wrapped by an interface exposing the file contents for reading and writing.

As Node development often involves the creation of servers that both accept and emit file data, it should be clear how important transfer speed at this active and important I/O layer is. As mentioned earlier, files can also be understood as objects, and objects have certain attributes.

Types of files

There are six types of files commonly encountered on a UNIX system:

- **Ordinary files**: These contain a one-dimensional array of bytes, and cannot contain other files.
- **Directories**: These are also files implemented in a special way such that they can describe collections of other files.
- **Sockets**: Used for IPC, allowing processes to exchange data.
- **Named pipe**: A command such as `ps aux | grep node` creates a pipe, which is destroyed once the operation terminates. Named pipes are persistent and addressable, and they can be used variously by multiple processes for IPC indefinitely.
- **Device files**: These are representations of I/O devices, processes that accept streams of data; `/dev/null` is commonly an example of a character device file (accepts serial streams of I/O), and `/dev/sda` is an example of a block device file (allowing random access I/O for blocks of data) representing a data drive.
- **Links**: These are pointers to other files of two types: hard links and symbolic links. Hard links directly point to another file and are indistinguishable from the target file. Symbolic links are indirect pointers and are distinguishable from normal files.

Most Node filesystem interactions encounter only the first two types, with the third only indirectly via the Node API. A deeper explanation of the remaining types is beyond the scope of this discussion. However, Node provides a full suite of file operations via the `file` module, and the reader should have at least some familiarity with the full range and power of file types.

Studying named pipes will reward the reader interested in understanding how Node was designed to work with streams and pipes. Try this from a terminal:

```
$ mkfifo namedpipe
```

If you get an expanded listing of the current directory `-ls -l`, a listing similar to this will be shown:

```
prw-r--r-- 1 system staff 0 May 01 07:52 namedpipe
```

Note the `p` flag in the file mode (the first segment, with the dashes). You've created a named `(p)`ipe. Now, enter this into the same terminal, pushing some bytes into the named pipe:

```
echo "hello" > namedpipe
```

It will seem like the process has hung. It hasn't—pipes, like water pipes, must be open on both ends to complete their job of flushing contents. We've pumped some bytes in... now what?

Open another terminal, navigate to the same directory, and enter this:

```
$ cat namedpipe.
```

hello will appear in the second terminal as the contents of namedpipe are flushed. Note that the first terminal is no longer hung—it has flushed. If you recall the discussion on Node streams in Chapter 3, *Streaming Data Across Nodes and Clients*, you will note something of a resemblance with Unix pipes, which is intentional.

File paths

Most of the filesystem methods provided by Node will require the manipulation of file paths, and for this purpose, we make use of the path module. We can compose, decompose, and relate paths with this module. Instead of hand rolling your own path string splitting and regexing and concatenating routines, try to normalize your code by delegating path manipulation to this module:

- Use path.normalize whenever working with a file path string whose source is untrusted or unreliable to ensure a predictable format:

```
const path = require('path');
path.normalize("../one////two/./three.html");
// -> ../one/two/three.html
```

- Use path.join whenever building a single path out of path segments:

```
path.join("../", "one", "two", "three.html");
// -> ../one/two/three.html
```

- Use path.dirname to snip the directory name out of a path:

```
path.dirname("../one/two/three.html");
// ../one/two
```

- Use `path.basename` to manipulate the final path segment:

```
path.basename("../one/two/three.html");
// -> three.html

// Remove file extension from the basename
path.basename("../one/two/three.html", ".html");
// -> three
```

- Use `path.extname` to slice from the last period (.) to the end of the path string:

```
var pstring = "../one/two/three.html";
path.extname(pstring);
// -> .html
```

- Use `path.relative` to find the relative path from one absolute path to another:

```
path.relative(
  '/one/two/three/four',
  '/one/two/thumb/war'
);
// -> ../../thumb/war
```

- Use `path.resolve` to resolve a list of path instructions into an absolute path:

```
path.resolve('/one/two', '/three/four');
// -> /three/four
path.resolve('/one/two/three', '../', 'four', '../../five')
// -> /one/five
```

Think of the arguments passed to `path.resolve` as being a sequence of cd calls:

```
cd /one/two/three
cd ../
cd four
cd ../../five
pwd
// -> /one/five
```

If the list of arguments passed to `path.resolve` fails to deliver an absolute path, the current directory name is used as well. For instance, consider that we are in `/users/home/john/`:

```
path.resolve('one', 'two/three', 'four');
// -> /users/home/john/one/two/three/four
```

These arguments resolve to a relative path `one/two/three/four` that is, therefore, prefixed with the current directory name.

File attributes

A file object exposes some of its attributes, comprising a useful set of metadata about the file data. If one is using Node to run an HTTP server, it will be necessary to determine the file length of any file requested via a GET, for example. Determining the time a file was last modified finds uses across many types of applications.

To read the attributes of a file, use `fs.stat`:

```
fs.stat("file.txt", (err, stats) => {
  console.log(stats);
});
```

In the preceding example, `stats` will be an `fs.Stats` object describing the file through a map of attributes:

```
dev: 2051, // id of device containing this file
mode: 33188, // bitmask, status of the file
nlink: 1, // number of hard links
uid: 0, // user id of file owner
gid: 0, // group id of file owner
rdev: 0, // device id (if device file)
blksize: 4096, // I/O block size
ino: 27396003, // a unique file inode number
size: 2000736, // size in bytes
blocks: 3920, // number of blocks allocated
atime: Fri May 3 2017 15:39:57 GMT-0500 (CDT), // last access
mtime: Fri May 3 2017 17:22:46 GMT-0500 (CDT), // last modified
ctime: Fri May 3 2017 17:22:46 GMT-0500 (CDT)  // last status change
```

An `fs.Stats` object exposes several useful methods for accessing file attribute data:

- Use `stats.isFile` to check for standard files
- Use `stats.isDirectory` to check for directories
- Use `stats.isBlockDevice` to check for block type device files
- Use `stats.isCharacterDevice` to check for character type device files
- Use `stats.isSymbolicLink` after an `fs.lstat` to find symbolic links

- Use `stats.isFIFO` to identify named pipes
- Use `stats.isSocket` to check for sockets

There are two further `stat` methods available:

- `fs.fstat(fd, callback)`: Similar to `fs.stat`, except that a file descriptor `fd` is passed rather than a file path
- `fs.lstat(path, callback)`: An `fs.stat` on a symbolic link will return an `fs.Stats` object for the target file, while `fs.lstat` will return an `fs.Stats` object for the link file itself

The following two methods simplify the file timestamp manipulation:

- `fs.utimes(path, atime, mtime, callback)`: Change the access and modify timestamps on a file at `path`. The access and modify times of a file are stored as instances of the JavaScript `Date` object. `Date.getTime` will, for example, return the number of milliseconds elapsed since midnight (UTC) on January 1, 1970.
- `fs.futimes(fd, atime, mtime, callback)`: Change the access and modify timestamps on a file descriptor `fd`; it's similar to `fs.utimes`.

 More information about manipulating dates and times with JavaScript can be found at:
`https://developer.mozilla.org/en-US/docs/Web/JavaScript/`
`Reference/Global_Objects/Date`.

Opening and closing files

One of the unofficial rules governing the Node project is to not unnecessarily abstract away from the existing OS implementation details. As we will see, references to file descriptors appear throughout Node's file API. For **POSIX (Portable Operating System Interface)**, a file descriptor is simply an (non-negative) integer uniquely referencing a specific file. Since Node modeled its filesystem methods on POSIX, not surprisingly, a file descriptor is represented in Node as an integer.

Recalling our discussion of how devices and other elements of the OS are represented as files, it would stand to reason that the standard I/O streams (stdin, stdout, stderr) would also have file descriptors. In fact, that is the case:

```
console.log(process.stdin.fd); // 0
console.log(process.stdout.fd); // 1
console.log(process.stderr.fd); // 2

fs.fstat(1, (err, stat) => {
  console.log(stat); // an fs.Stats object
});
```

File descriptors are easy to obtain and are convenient ways to pass around file references. Let's look at how file descriptors are created and used by examining how to perform low-level file open and close operations using Node. As the chapter progresses, we'll investigate more refined interfaces to file streams.

fs.open(path, flags, [mode], callback)

Trying to open a file at path. callback will receive any exceptions with the operation as its first argument, and a file descriptor as its second argument. Here, we open a file for reading:

```
fs.open("path.js", "r", (err, fileDescriptor) => {
  console.log(fileDescriptor); // An integer, like `7` or `23`
});
```

flags receives a string indicating the types of operations the caller expects to perform on the returned file descriptor. Their meanings should be clear:

- r: Opening a file for reading, throwing an exception if the file doesn't exist.
- r+: Opening a file for both reading and writing, throwing an exception if the file doesn't exist.
- w: Opening a file for writing, creating the file if it doesn't exist, and truncating the file to zero bytes if it does exist.
- wx: Like w, but it opens the file in exclusive mode, which means if the file already exists, it will **not be opened**, and the open operation will fail. This is useful if multiple processes may be simultaneously trying to create the same file.
- w+: Opening a file for reading and writing, creating the file if it doesn't exist, and truncating the file to zero bytes if it does exist.
- wx+: Like wx (and w), additionally opening the file for reading.

- a: Opening a file for appending, creating the file if it does not exist.
- ax: Like **a**, but opens the file in exclusive mode, which means if the file already exists, it will **not be opened**, and the open operation will fail. This is useful if multiple processes may be simultaneously trying to create the same file.
- a+: Open a file for reading and appending, creating the file if it does not exist.
- ax+: Like ax (and a), additionally opening the file for reading.

When an operation may create a new file, use the optional mode to set permissions for this file in octal digits, defaulting to 0666 (refer to fs.chmod for more information about octal permissions):

```
fs.open("index.html", "w", 755, (err, fd) => {
    fs.read(fd, ...);
});
```

fs.close(fd, callback)

The fs.close(fd, callback) method closes a file descriptor. The callback receives one argument, any exception thrown in the call. It's a good habit to close all the file descriptors that have been opened.

File operations

Node implements the standard POSIX functions for working with files, which a UNIX user will be familiar with. We will not be covering each member of this extensive collection in depth, instead focusing on some commonly used examples. In particular, we will go into depth discussing the methods for opening file descriptors and manipulating file data, reading and manipulating file attributes, and moving through filesystem directories. Nevertheless, the reader is encouraged to experiment with the entire set, which the following list briefly describes. Note that all of these methods are asynchronous, non-blocking file operations.

fs.rename(oldName, newName, callback)

The fs.rename(oldName, newName, callback) method renames file at oldName to newName. The callback receives one argument, any exception thrown in the call.

fs.truncate(path, len, callback)

The `fs.truncate(path, len, callback)` method changes the length of the file at `path` by `len` bytes. If `len` represents a length shorter than the file's current length, the file is truncated to that length. If `len` is greater, the file length is padded by appending null bytes (x00) until `len` is reached. The callback receives one argument, any exception thrown in the call.

fs.ftruncate(fd, len, callback)

The `fs.ftruncate(fd, len, callback)` method is like `fs.truncate`, except that instead of specifying a file, a file descriptor is passed as `fd`.

fs.chown(path, uid, gid, callback)

The `fs.chown(path, uid, gid, callback)` method changes the ownership of the file at `path`. Use this to set whether user `uid` or group `gid` has access to a file. The callback receives one argument, any exception thrown in the call.

fs.fchown(fd, uid, gid, callback)

The `fs.fchown(fd, uid, gid, callback)` method is like `fs.chown`, except that instead of specifying a file path, a file descriptor is passed as `fd`.

fs.lchown(path, uid, gid, callback)

The `fs.lchown(path, uid, gid, callback)` method is like `fs.chown`, except that in the case of symbolic links, ownership of the link file itself is changed, but not the referenced link.

fs.chmod(path, mode, callback)

The fs.chmod(path, mode, callback) method changes the mode(permissions) on a file at path. You are setting the read(4), write(2), and execute(1) bits for this file, which can be sent in octal digits:

	[r]ead	[w]rite	E[x]ecute	Total
Owner	4	2	1	7
Group	4	0	1	5
Other	4	0	1	5
				chmod(755)

You may also use symbolic representations, such as g+rw for group read and write, similar to the arguments we saw for file.open earlier. For more information on setting file modes, consult: http://en.wikipedia.org/wiki/Chmod.

The callback receives one argument, any exception thrown in the call.

fs.fchmod(fd, mode, callback) ----

The fs.fchmod(fd, mode, callback) method is like fs.chmod, except that instead of specifying a file path, a file descriptor is passed as fd.

fs.lchmod(path, mode, callback)

The fs.lchmod(path, mode, callback) method is like fs.chmod, except that in the case of symbolic links, permissions on the link file itself is changed, but not those of the referenced link.

fs.link(srcPath, dstPath, callback)

The fs.link(srcPath, dstPath, callback) creates a hard link between srcPath and dstPath. This is a way of creating many different paths to exactly the same file. For example, the following directory contains a target.txt file and two hard links—a.txt and b.txt—which each point to this file:

```
-rw-r--r-- 3 root root 0 May 11 15:45 a.txt
-rw-r--r-- 3 root root 0 May 11 15:45 b.txt
-rw-r--r-- 3 root root 0 May 11 15:45 target.txt
```

Note that target.txt is empty. If the content of the target file is changed, the length of the link files will also be changed. Consider changing the content of the target file:

```
echo "hello" >> target.txt
```

This results in this new directory structure, clearly demonstrating the hard references:

```
-rw-r--r-- 3 root root 6 May 11 15:50 a.txt
-rw-r--r-- 3 root root 6 May 11 15:50 b.txt
-rw-r--r-- 3 root root 6 May 11 15:50 target.txt
```

The callback receives one argument, any exception thrown in the call.

fs.symlink(srcPath, dstPath, [type], callback)

The fs.symlink(srcPath, dstPath, [type], callback) method creates a symbolic link between srcPath and dstPath. Unlike hard links created with fs.link, symbolic links are simply pointers to other files, and do not themselves respond to changes in the target file. The default link typeis file. Other options are directory and junction, the last being a Windows-specific type that is ignored on other systems. The callback receives one argument, any exception thrown in the call.

Compare and contrast the directory changes described in our fs.link discussion to the following:

```
lrwxrwxrwx 1 root root 10 May 11 16:11 a.txt -> target.txt
lrwxrwxrwx 1 root root 10 May 11 16:11 b.txt -> target.txt
-rw-r--r-- 1 root root  0 May 11 16:12 target.txt
```

Unlike hard links, symbolic links do not change in length when their target file (in this case `target.txt`) changes length. Here, we see how changing the target's length from zero bytes to six bytes has no effect on the length of any bound symbolic links:

```
lrwxrwxrwx  1 root  root    10 May 11 16:11 a.txt -> target.txt
lrwxrwxrwx  1 root  root    10 May 11 16:11 b.txt -> target.txt
-rw-r--r--  1 root  root     6 May 11 16:12 target.txt
```

fs.readlink(path, callback)

The given symbolic link at `path` returns the filename of the targeted file:

```
fs.readlink('a.txt', (err, targetFName) => {
  console.log(targetFName); // target.txt
});
```

fs.realpath(path, [cache], callback)

The `fs.realpath(path, [cache], callback)` method attempts to find the real path to file at `path`. This is a useful way to find the absolute path to a file, resolve symbolic links, and even clean up extraneous slashes and other malformed paths. Consider this example:

```
fs.realpath('file.txt', (err, resolvedPath) => {
  console.log(resolvedPath); // `/real/path/to/file.txt`
});
```

Alternatively, consider this:

```
fs.realpath('.////./file.txt', (err, resolvedPath) => {
  // still `/real/path/to/file.txt`
});
```

If some of the path segments to be resolved are already known, one can pass a `cache` of mapped paths:

```
let cache = {'/etc':'/private/etc'};
fs.realpath('/etc/passwd', cache, (err, resolvedPath) => {
  console.log(resolvedPath); // `/private/etc/passwd`
});
```

fs.unlink(path, callback)

The `fs.unlink(path, callback)` method removes the file at `path`—equivalent to deleting a file. The callback receives one argument, any exception thrown in the call.

fs.rmdir(path, callback)

The `fs.rmdir(path, callback)` method removes the directory at `path`, equivalent to deleting a directory.

Note that if the directory is not empty, this will throw an exception. The callback receives one argument, any exception thrown in the call.

fs.mkdir(path, [mode], callback)

The `fs.mkdir(path, [mode], callback)` method creates a directory at `path`. To set the mode of the new directory, use the permission bit map described in `fs.chmod`.

Note that if this directory already exists, an exception will be thrown. The callback receives one argument, any exception thrown in the call.

fs.exists(path, callback)

The `fs.exists(path, callback)` method checks whether a file exists at `path`. The callback will receive a Boolean true or false.

fs.fsync(fd, callback)

Between the instant a request for some data to be written to a file is made and that data fully exists on a storage device, the candidate data exists within core system buffers. This latency isn't normally relevant but, in some extreme cases, such as system crashes, it is necessary to insist that the file reflects a known state on a stable storage device.

`fs.fsync` copies all in-core data of a file referenced by file descriptor `fd` to disk (or other storage device). The callback receives one argument, any exception thrown in the call.

Synchronicity

Conveniently, Node's `file` module provides synchronous counterparts for each of the asynchronous methods we've covered, indicated by the `Sync` suffix. For example, the synchronous version of `fs.mkdir` is `fs.mkdirSync`.

A synchronous call is also able to directly return its result, obviating the need for callbacks. While demonstrating the creation of HTTPS servers in `Chapter 3`, *Streaming Data Across Nodes and Clients*, we saw both a good use case for synchronous code and an example of direct assignment of results without a callback:

```
key: fs.readFileSync('server-key.pem'),
cert: fs.readFileSync('server-cert.pem')
```

Hey! Doesn't Node strictly enforce asynchronous programming? Isn't blocking code always wrong? All developers are encouraged to adhere to non-blocking designs, and you are encouraged to avoid synchronous coding—if facing a problem where a synchronous operation seems the only solution, it is likely that the problem has been misunderstood. Nevertheless, edge cases requiring a file object existing fully in memory prior to executing further instructions (a blocking operation) do exist. Node give a developer the power to break with asynchronous tradition if it is the only possible solution (which it probably isn't!).

One synchronous operation developers regularly use (perhaps without realizing it) is the `require` directive:

```
require('fs')
```

Until the dependency targeted by require is fully initialized, subsequent JavaScript instructions will not execute (file loading blocks the event loop). *Ryan Dahl* struggled with this decision to introduce synchronous operations (file operations in particular) into Node, as he mentioned at a Google Tech Talk on July 2013:

> *According to* `http://www.youtube.com/watch?v=F6k8lTrAE2g`,
> *"I think this is an OK compromise. It pained me for months, to drop the purity of having an asynchronous module system. But, I think it's ok.*
>
> *...*

It simplifies the code a lot to be able to just stick in "require, require, require" and not have to do an onload callback...I think that's been a relatively OK compromise. [...] There's really two parts to your program: there's the loading and starting up phase...and you don't really care how fast that runs...you're going to load modules and stuff...the setup phase of your daemon, generally, is synchronous. It's when you get into your event loop for serving requests that you want to be very careful about this. [...] I will give people synchronous file I/O. If they do it in servers...it won't be terrible, right? The important thing is to never let them do synchronous network I/O."

Synchronous code does have the advantage of being eminently predictable, as nothing else happens until this instruction is completed. When starting up a server, which will happen only rarely, Dahl is suggesting that a little certainty and simplicity goes a long way. The loading of configuration files, for example, might make sense on server initialization.

Sometimes a desire to use synchronous commands in Node development is simply a cry for help; a developer being overwhelmed by deeply nested callback structures. If ever faced with this pain, try some of the callback-taming libraries mentioned in Chapter 2, *Understanding Asynchronous Event-Driven Programming*.

Moving through directories

Let's apply what we have learned and create a directory iterator. The goal for this project is to create a function that will accept a directory path and return a JSON object reflecting the directory hierarchy of files, its nodes composed of file objects. We will also make our directory walker a more powerful event-based parser, consistent with the Node philosophy.

To move through nested directories, one must first be able to read a single directory. Node's filesystem library provides the fs.readdir command for this purpose:

```
fs.readdir('.', (err, files) => {
  console.log(files); // list of all files in current directory
});
```

Remembering that everything is a file, we will need to do more than simply getting a directory listing; we must determine the type of each member of our file list. By adding fs.stat, we have already completed a large majority of the logic:

```
(dir => {
  fs.readdir(dir, (err, list) => {
    list.forEach(file => {
      fs.stat(path.join(dir, file), (err, stat) => {
        if (stat.isDirectory()) {
          return console.log(`Found directory: ${file}`);
```

```
        }
        console.log(`Found file: ${file}`);
      });
    });
  });
})(".");
```

This self-executing function receives a directory path argument (`"."`), folds that directory listing into an array of file names, fetches an `fs.Stats` object for each of these, and makes a decision based on the indicated file type (directory or not a directory) on what to do next. At this point, we also have the name of the current file and its attributes available to us. Clearly, we have already mapped a single directory.

We must now map directories within directories, storing results in a JSON object reflecting the nested filesystem tree, with each leaf on the tree a file object. Recursively passing our directory reader function paths to subdirectories and appending returned results as branches of the final object is the next step:

```
let walk = (dir, done) => {
  let results = {};
  fs.readdir(dir, (err, list) => {
    let pending = list.length;
    if (err || !pending) {
      return done(err, results);
    }
    list.forEach(file => {
      let dfile = require('path').join(dir, file);
      fs.stat(dfile, (err, stat) => {
        if(stat.isDirectory()) {
          return walk(dfile, (err, res) => {
            results[file] = res;
            !--pending && done(null, results);
          });
        }
        results[file] = stat;
        !--pending && done(null, results);
      });
    });
  });
};
walk(".", (err, res) => {
  console.log(require('util').inspect(res, {depth: null}));
});
```

We create a `walk` method that receives a directory path and a callback that receives the directory graph or an error when `walk` is complete, following Node's style. Not much code is needed to create a very fast, non-blocking file tree walker, complete with file stats.

Now, let's publish events whenever a directory or file is encountered, giving any future implementation flexibility to construct its own representation of the filesystem. To do this, we will use the friendly `EventEmitter` object:

```
let walk = (dir, done, emitter) => {
  ...
  emitter = emitter || new (require('events').EventEmitter);
  ...
  if (stat.isDirectory()) {
    emitter.emit('directory', dfile, stat);
    return walk(dfile, (err, res) => {
      results[file] = res;
      !--pending && done(null, results);
    }, emitter);
  }
  emitter.emit('file', dfile, stat);
  results[file] = stat;
  ...
  return emitter;
}
walk("/usr/local", (err, res) => {
  ...
}).on("directory", (path, stat) => {
  console.log(`Directory: ${path} - ${stat.size}`);
}).on("file", (path, stat) => {
  console.log(`File: ${path} - ${stat.size}`);
});
// File: index.html - 1024
// File: readme.txt - 2048
// Directory: images - 106
// File images/logo.png - 4096
// ...
```

Now that we know how to discover and address files, we can start reading from and writing to them.

Reading from a file

In our discussion of file descriptors, we touched on one method of opening a file, fetching a file descriptor, and ultimately pushing or pulling data through that reference. Reading files is a common operation. Sometimes, managing a read buffer precisely may be necessary, and Node allows byte-by-byte control. In other cases, one simply wants a no-frills stream that is simple to use.

Reading byte by byte

The `fs.read` method is the most low-level way Node offers for reading files.

fs.read(fd, buffer, offset, length, position, callback)

Files are composed of ordered bytes, and these bytes are addressable by their `position`, relative to the beginning of in the file (position zero [0]). Once we have a file descriptor `fd`, we can begin to read `length` number of bytes and insert those into a `Buffer` object `buffer`, insertion beginning at a given buffer `offset`. For example, to copy the 8,366 bytes beginning at `position` 309 of the readable file `fd` into a `buffer` beginning at an `offset` of 100, we will use `fs.read(fd, buffer, 100, 8366, 309, callback)`.

The following code demonstrates how to open and read a file in 512 byte chunks:

```
fs.open('path.js', 'r', (err, fd) => {
  fs.fstat(fd, (err, stats) => {
    let totalBytes = stats.size;
    let buffer = Buffer.alloc(totalBytes);
    let bytesRead = 0;
    // Each call to read should ensure that chunk size is
    // within proper size ranges (not too small; not too large).
    let read = chunkSize => {
      fs.read(fd, buffer, bytesRead, chunkSize, bytesRead, (err, numBytes,
bufRef) => {
        if((bytesRead += numBytes) < totalBytes) {
          return read(Math.min(512, totalBytes - bytesRead));
        }
        fs.close(fd);
        console.log(`File read complete. Total bytes read: ${totalBytes}`);
        // Note that the callback receives a reference to the
        // accumulating buffer
        console.log(bufRef.toString());
```

```
      });
    }
    read(Math.min(512, totalBytes));
  });
});
```

The resulting buffer can be piped elsewhere (including a server response object). It can also be manipulated using the methods of Node's `Buffer` object, such as conversion into a UTF8 string with `buffer.toString("utf8")`.

Fetching an entire file at once

Often, one simply needs to fetch an entire file, without any ceremony or fine control. Node provides a shortcut method for exactly this.

fs.readFile(path, [options], callback)

Fetching the data contained by the `path` file can be accomplished in one step:

```
fs.readFile('/etc/passwd', (err, fileData) => {
  if(err) {
    throw err;
  }
  console.log(fileData);
  // <Buffer 48 65 6C 6C 6F ... >
});
```

We see how `callback` receives a buffer. It may be more desirable to receive the file data in a common encoding, such as UTF8. We are able to specify the encoding of the returned data as well as the read mode using the `options` object, which has two possible attributes:

- **encoding**: A string, such as `utf8`, it defaults to null (no encoding)
- **flag**: The file mode as a string, it defaults to `r`

Modifying the previous example:

```
fs.readFile('/etc/passwd', (err, { encoding : "utf8" }, fileData) => {
  ...
  console.log(fileData);
  // "Hello ..."
});
```

Creating a readable stream

While `fs.readFile` is an excellent, simple way to accomplish a common task, it does have the significant drawback of requiring that an entire file be read into memory prior to any part of the file being sent to a callback. For large files or files of unknown size, this isn't a good solution.

In the last chapter, we learned about data streams and the `Stream` object. While files are easily and naturally handled using readable streams, Node provides a dedicated file streaming interface that offers a compact file streaming facility without the extra construction work, with more flexibility than that offered by `fs.readFile`.

fs.createReadStream(path, [options])

The `fs.createReadStream(path, [options])` method returns a readable stream object for file at `path`. You may then perform stream operations on the returned object, such as `pipe()`.

The following options are available:

- `flags`: File mode argument as a string. Defaults to `r`.
- `encoding`: One of `utf8`, `ascii`, or `base64`. Defaults to no encoding.
- `fd`: One may set `path` to null, instead passing the call a file descriptor.
- `mode`: Octal representation of file mode, defaulting to 0666.
- `bufferSize`: The chunk size, in bytes, of the internal read stream. Defaults to 64 * 1024 bytes. You can set this to any number, but memory allocation is strictly controlled by the host OS, which may ignore a request. Refer to: https://groups.google.com/forum/?fromgroups#!topic/nodejs/p5FuU1oxbeY.
- `autoClose`: Whether to automatically close the file descriptor (a la `fs.close`). Defaults to true. You may want to set this to false and close manually if you are sharing a file descriptor across many streams, as closing a descriptor will disrupt any other readers.
- `start`: Begin reading from this position. Default is 0.
- `end`: Stop reading at this position. Default is the file byte length.

Reading a file line by line

While reading a file stream byte-by-byte is sufficient for any file-parsing job, text files in particular are often more usefully read line by line, such as when reading logfiles. More precisely, any stream can be understood in terms of the chunks of data separated by newline characters, typically rn on UNIX systems. Node provides a native module whose methods simplify access to newline-separated chunks in data streams.

The Readline module

The Readline module has a simple but powerful goal, that is, to make reading a stream of data line-by-line easier. The bulk of its interface is designed to make command-line prompting easier, such that interfaces taking user input are easier to design.

Remembering that Node is designed for I/O, that I/O operations normally involve moving data between readable and writable streams, and that stdout and stdin are stream interfaces identical to the file streams returned by fs.createReadStream and fs.createWriteStream, we will look at how this module can be similarly used to prompt file streams for a line of text.

To start working with the Readline module, one must create an interface defining the input stream and the output stream. The default interface options prioritize usage as a terminal interface. The options we are interested in are as follows:

- input: Required. The readable stream being listened to.
- output: Required. The writable stream being written to.
- terminal: Set this to true if both the input and output streams should be treated like a Unix terminal, or **Teletypewriter** (**TTY**). For files, you will set this to false.

Reading the lines of a file is made easy through this system. For example, assuming that one has a dictionary file listing common words in the English language, one might want to read the list into an array for processing:

```
const fs = require('fs');
const readline = require('readline');

let rl = readline.createInterface({
  input: fs.createReadStream("dictionary.txt"),
  terminal: false
});
let arr = [];
rl.on("line", ln => {
```

```
    arr.push(ln.trim())
});
// aardvark
// abacus
// abaisance
// ...
```

Note how we disable TTY behavior, handling the lines ourselves without redirecting to an output stream.

As expected with a Node I/O module, we are working with stream events. The events listeners that may be of interest are as listed:

- `line`: Receives the most recently read line, as a string
- `pause`: Called whenever the stream is paused
- `resume`: Called whenever a stream is resumed
- `close`: Called whenever a stream is closed

Except for `line`, these event names reflect the `Readline` methods, pause a stream with `Readline.pause`, resume with `Readline.resume`, and `close` with `Readline.close`.

Writing to a file

As with reading files, Node provides a rich collection of tools for writing to files. We'll see how Node makes it as easy to target a file's contents byte-by-byte, as it is to pipe continuous streams of data into a single writable file.

Writing byte by byte

The `fs.write` method is the most low-level way Node offers for writing files. This method gives us precise control over where bytes will be written to in a file.

fs.write(fd, buffer, offset, length, position, callback)

To write the collection of bytes between positions 309 and 8,675 (length 8,366) of `buffer` to the file referenced by file descriptor `fd`, insertion beginning at position 100:

```
let buffer = Buffer.alloc(8675);
fs.open("index.html", "w", (err, fd) => {
  fs.write(fd, buffer, 309, 8366, 100, (err, writtenBytes, buffer) => {
    console.log(`Wrote ${writtenBytes} bytes to file`);
    // Wrote 8366 bytes to file
  });
});
```

 Note that for files opened in the append (a) mode, some operating systems may ignore `position` values, always adding data to the end of the file. Additionally, it is unsafe to call `fs.write` multiple times on the same file without waiting for the callback. Use `fs.createWriteStream` in those cases.

With such precise control, we can intelligently structure files. In the following (somewhat contrived) example, we create a file-based database containing indexed information for 6 months of baseball scores for a single team. We want to be able to quickly look up whether this team won or lost (or did not play) on a given day.

Since a month can have at most 31 days, we can (randomly) create a 6 x 31 grid of data in this file, placing one of three values in each grid cell: L (loss), W (win), N (no game). For fun, we also create a simple **CLI (Command-Line Interface)** to our database with a basic query language. This example should make it clear how `fs.read`, `fs.write`, and `Buffer` objects are used to precisely manipulate bytes in files:

```
const fs = require('fs');
const readline = require('readline');
let cells = 186; // 6 x 31
let buffer = Buffer.alloc(cells);
let rand;
while(cells--) {
  //  0, 1 or greater
  rand = Math.floor(Math.random() * 3);
  //  78 = "N", 87 = "W", 76 = "L"
  buffer[cells] = rand === 0 ? 78 : rand === 1 ? 87 : 76;
}
fs.open("scores.txt", "r+", (err, fd) => {
  fs.write(fd, buffer, 0, buffer.length, 0, (err, writtenBytes, buffer) =>
  {
    let rl = readline.createInterface({
```

```
    input: process.stdin,
    output: process.stdout
  });
  let quest = () => {
    rl.question("month/day:", index => {
      if(!index) {
        return rl.close();
      }
      let md = index.split('/');
      let pos = parseInt(md[0] -1) * 31 + parseInt(md[1] -1);
      fs.read(fd, Buffer.alloc(1), 0, 1, pos, (err, br, buff) => {
        let v = buff.toString();
        console.log(v === "W" ? "Win!" : v === "L" ? "Loss..." : "No
game");
        quest();
      });
    });
  };
  quest();
  });
});
```

Once running, we can simply type in a month/day pair and rapidly access that data cell. Adding in bounds checking for the input values would be a simple improvement. Pushing the file stream through a visualizing UI might be a nice exercise.

Writing large chunks of data

For straightforward write operations `fs.write` may be overkill. Sometimes, all that is needed is a way to create a new file with some content. Just as common is the need to append data to the end of a file, as one might do in a logging system. The `fs.writeFile` and `fs.appendFile` methods can help us with those scenarios.

fs.writeFile(path, data, [options], callback)

The `fs.writeFile(path, data, [options], callback)` method writes the contents of `data` to the file at `path`. The data argument can be either a buffer or a string. The following options are available:

- `encoding`: Defaults to `utf8`. If data is a buffer, this option is ignored.

- `mode`: Octal representation of file mode, defaulting to 0666.
- `flag`: Write flags, defaulting to `w`.

Usage is straightforward:

```
fs.writeFile('test.txt', 'A string or Buffer of data', err => {
  if (err) {
    return console.log(err);
  }
  // File has been written
});
```

fs.appendFile(path, data, [options], callback)

Similar to `fs.writeFile`, except that `data` is appended to the end of the file at `path`. Also, the `flag` option defaults to `a`.

Creating a writable stream

If the data being written to a file arrives in chunks (such as occurs with a file upload), streaming that data through a `WritableStream` object interface provides more flexibility and efficiency.

fs.createWriteStream(path, [options])

The `fs.createWriteStream(path, [options])` method returns a writable stream object for file at `path`.

The following options are available:

- `flags`: File mode argument as a string. Defaults to `w`.
- `encoding`: One of `utf8`, `ascii`, or `base64`. Defaults to no encoding.
- `mode`: Octal representation of file mode, defaulting to 0666.
- `start`: An offset indicating the position in the file where writing should begin.

For example, this little program functions as the world's simplest word processor, writing all terminal input to a file, until the terminal is closed:

```
let writer = fs.createWriteStream("novel.txt", 'w');
process.stdin.pipe(writer);
```

Caveats

The side effects of opening a file descriptor and reading from it are minimal, such that in normal development, very little thought is given to what is actually happening within the system. Normally, reading a file doesn't change it.

When writing to a file, a number of concerns must be addressed, such as these:

- Is there sufficient writable storage space available?
- Is another process simultaneously accessing this file, or even erasing it?
- What must be done if a write operation fails or is unnaturally terminated mid-stream?

We've seen the exclusive write mode flag (wx) that can help in the case of multiple write processes simultaneously trying to create a file. Full solutions to all the concerns one might face when writing to files are difficult to derive in general, or state briefly. Node encourages asynchronous programming. Nevertheless, with regard to the filesystem in particular, sometimes synchronous, deterministic programming is necessary. You are encouraged to keep these and other issues in mind, and to keep I/O non-blocking whenever possible.

Serving static files

Anyone using Node to create a web server will need to respond intelligently to HTTP requests. An HTTP request to a web server for a resource expects some sort of response. A basic file static file server might look like this:

```
http.createServer((request, response) => {
  if(request.method !== "GET") {
    return response.end("Simple File Server only does GET");
  }
  fs
  .createReadStream(__dirname + request.url)
  .pipe(response);
}).listen(8000);
```

This server services GET requests on port 8000, expecting to find a local file at a relative path equivalent to the URL path segment. We see how easy Node makes it for us to stream local file data, simply piping a ReadableStream into a WritableStream representing a client socket connection. This is an enormous amount of functionality to be safely implemented in a handful of lines.

Eventually, a great deal more will be added, such as handling routines for standard HTTP methods, handling errors and malformed requests, setting proper headers, managing favicon requests, and so forth.

Let's build a reasonably useful file server with Node, one that will respond to HTTP requests by streaming back a resource and which will respect caching requests. In the process, we will touch on how to manage content redirection. Later on in this chapter, we will also look at implementing file uploads. Note that a web server fully compliant with all features of HTTP is a complicated beast, so what we are creating should be considered a good start, not an end.

Redirecting requests

Sometimes, a client will try to GET a URL that is incorrect or incomplete in some way, the resource may have been moved, or there are better ways to make the same request. Other times, a POST may create a new resource at a new location the client cannot know, necessitating some response header information pointing to the newly created URI. Let's look at two common redirection scenarios someone implementing a static file server with Node might face.

Two response headers are fundamental to redirection:

- Location: This indicates a redirection to a location where said content body can be found
- Content-Location: This is meant to indicate the URL where the requester will find the original location of the entity enclosed in the response body

Also, there are two specific use cases for these headers:

- To provide information about the location of a newly created resource in response to a POST
- To inform the client of an alternate location for the requested resource in response to a GET

 There are many possible pairings of Location and Content-Location headers with HTTP status codes, the **3xx** (redirection) set in particular. In fact, these headers may even appear together in the same response. The user is encouraged to read the relevant sections of the HTTP/1.1 specification, as only a small set of common cases is discussed here.

Location

Responding to a `POST` with a `201` status code indicates that a new resource has been created its URI assigned to the `Location` header and that the client may go ahead and use that URI in the future. Note that it is up to the client to decide whether, and when, to fetch this resource. As such, this is not, strictly speaking, a redirect.

For example, a system might create new accounts by posting new user information to a server, expecting to receive the location of a new user page:

```
POST /path/addUser HTTP/1.1
Content-Type: application/x-www-form-urlencoded
name=John&group=friends
...
Status: 201
Location: http://website.com/users/john.html
```

Similarly, in cases where a resource creation request has been accepted but not yet fulfilled, a server will indicate a status of `202`. This will be the case in the preceding example if creation of the new user record had been delegated to a worker queue, which might at some point in the future create a record at the given `Location`.

We will see a realistic implementation demonstrating this usage later on in the chapter, when we discuss file uploads.

Content-Location

When a `GET` is made to a resource that has multiple representations and those can be found at distinct resource locations, a `content-location` header for the particular entity should be returned. For example, content format negotiation is a good candidate for `Content-Location` handling. One might be interested in retrieving all blog posts for a given month, perhaps available at a URL such as: `http://example.com/september/`. GET requests with an `Accept` header of `application/json` will receive a response in JSON format. A request for XML will receive that representation.

If a caching mechanism is being used those resources may have alternate permanent locations, such as `http://example.com/cache/september.json` or `http://example.com/cache/september.xml`. One will send this additional location information via `Content-Location`, in a response object resembling this:

```
Status: 200
Content-Type: application/json
Content-Location: http://blogs.com/cache/allArticles.json
... JSON entity body
```

In cases where the requested URL has been moved, permanently or temporarily, the **3xx** group of status codes can be used with `Content-Location` to indicate this state. For example, to redirect a request to a URL that has been permanently moved, one should send a 301 code:

```
function requestHandler(request,response) {
  let newPath = "/thedroids.html";
  response.writeHead(301, {
    'Content-Location': newPath
  });
  response.end();
}
```

Implementing resource caching

As a general rule, never expend resources delivering irrelevant information to clients. For an HTTP server, resending files that the client already possesses is an unnecessary I/O cost, exactly the wrong way to implement a Node server, increasing latency as well as the financial hit of paying for misappropriated bandwidth.

Browsers maintain a cache of the files they have already fetched, and an **Entity Tag (ETag)** identifies these files. An ETag is a response header sent by servers to uniquely identify entities they are returning, such as a file. When a file changes on a server, that server will send a different ETag for said file, allowing file changes to be tracked by clients.

When a client makes a request to a server for a resource contained within that client's cache, that request will contain an `If-None-Match` header set to the value of the ETag associated with the said cached resource. The `If-None-Match` header can contain one or multiple ETags:

```
If-None-Match : "686897696a7c876b7e"
If-None-Match : "686897696a7c876b7e", "923892329b4c796e2e"
```

A server understands this header and will return the full entity body of the requested resource only if none of the sent ETags match the current resource entity tag. If one of the sent ETags matches the current entity tag, the server will respond with a 304 (not modified) status, which should result in a browser, fetching the resource from its internal cache.

Assuming that we have an `fs.Stats` object available, managing cache controls on a resource can be done easily with Node:

```
let etag = crypto.createHash('md5').update(stat.size +
stat.mtime).digest('hex');
if(request.headers['if-none-match'] === etag) {
  response.statusCode = 304;
  return response.end();
} else {
  // stream the requested resource
}
```

We create an `etag` for the current file by creating an MD5 of the current file size and its last modified time, and match against the sent `If-None-Match` header. If the two do not match, the resource representation has changed, and the new version must be sent back to the requesting client. Note that the specific algorithm one should use to create an `etag` is not formally specified. The example technique should work well for most purposes.

Hey! What about `Last-Modified` and `If-Unmodified-Since`? These are fine headers and are also useful in the case of caching files. Indeed, one should set the `Last-Modified` header where possible when responding to entity requests. The techniques we're describing here using ETag will work similarly with these tags, and in fact, using both Etags and these other tags is encouraged. For more information, consult: http://www.w3.org/Protocols/rfc2616/rfc2616-sec13.html#sec13.3.4.

Handling file uploads

It is likely that anyone reading this sentence has had at least one experience with uploading a file from a client to a server. Some may have even implemented a file upload service, a server that will receive and do something useful with a multipart data stream. Within popular development environments, this task has been made very easy. In the PHP environment, for example, uploaded data is automatically processed and made globally available, neatly parsed and packaged into an array of files or form field values, without the developer having written a single line of code.

Unfortunately, Node leaves implementation of file upload handling to the developer, a challenging bit of work many developers may be unable to successfully or safely complete.

Fortunately, Felix Geisendorfer created the **Formidable** module, one of the most important early contributions to the Node project. A widely implemented, enterprise-grade module with extensive test coverage, it not only makes handling file uploads a snap, but can be used as a complete tool for handling form submissions. We will use this library to add file upload capability to our file server.

For more information about how HTTP file uploads are designed, and the tricky implementation problems developers must overcome, consult the multipart/form-data specification at `http://www.w3.org/TR/html401/` `interact/forms.html#h-17.13.4.2` and Geisendorfer's breakdown of how **Formidable** was conceived of and evolved at `http://debuggable.com/posts/parsing-file-uploads-at-500-mb-s-wit` `h-node-js:4c03862e-351c-4faa-bb67-4365cbdd56cb`.

First, install `formidable` via npm:

```
npm install formidable
```

You can now `require` it:

```
let formidable = require('formidable');
```

We will assume that file uploads will be posted to our server along a path of `/uploads/`, and that the upload arrives via a HTML form that looks like this:

```
<form action="/uploads" enctype="multipart/form-data" method="post">
Title: <input type="text" name="title"><br />
<input type="file" name="upload" multiple="multiple"><br />
<input type="submit" value="Upload">
</form>
```

This form will allow a client to write some sort of title for the upload, and to select one (or multiple) files for uploading. At this point, our only responsibility on our server is to properly detect when a POST request has been made and pass the relevant request object to Formidable.

We won't be covering every part of the comprehensive formidable API design, but we'll focus on the key POST events the library exposes. As formidable extends EventEmitter, we use the on(eventName, callback) format to catch file data, field data, and termination events, sending a response to the client describing what the server has successfully processed:

```
http.createServer((request, response) => {
  let rm = request.method.toLowerCase();
  if(request.url === '/uploads' && rm === 'post') {
    let form = new formidable.IncomingForm();
    form.uploadDir = process.cwd();
    let resp = "";
    form
    .on("file", (field, File) => {
      resp += `File: ${File.name}<br />`;
    })
    .on("field", (field, value) => {
      resp += `${field}: ${value}<br />`;
    })
    .on("end", () => {
      response.writeHead(200, {'content-type': 'text/html'});
      response.end(resp);
    })
    .parse(request);
    return;
  }
}).listen(8000);
```

We see here how a formidable instance receives an http.Incoming object through its parse method, and how the write path for incoming files is set using the uploadDir attribute of that instance. The example sets this directory to the local directory. A real implementation would likely target a dedicated upload folder, or even direct the received file to a storage service, receiving in return the final storage location (perhaps receiving it via HTTP and a Location header...).

Also note how the file event callback receives a formidable File object as a second argument, which contains important file information including the following:

- **size**: The size of the uploaded file, in bytes
- * **path**: The current location of the uploaded file on the local filesystem, such as /tmp/bdf746a445577332e38be7cde3a98fb3
- **name**: The original name of the file as it existed on the client filesystem, such as lolcats.jpg
- **type**: The file mime type, such as image/png

In a few lines of code, we've implemented a significant amount of POST data management. Formidable also provides tools for handling progress indicators, dealing with network errors, and more, which the reader can learn about by visiting: https://github.com/felixge/node-formidable.

Putting it all together

Recalling our discussion of favicon handling from the last chapter and adding what we've learned about file caching and file uploading, we can now construct a simple file server handling the GET and POST requests:

```javascript
http.createServer((request, response) => {
  let rm = request.method.toLowerCase();
  if(rm === "post") {
    let form = new formidable.IncomingForm();
    form.uploadDir = process.cwd();
    form
    .on("file", (field, file) => {
      // process files
    })
    .on("field", (field, value) => {
      // process POSTED field data
    })
    .on("end", () => {
      response.end("Received");
    })
    .parse(request);
    return;
  }
  // Only GET is handled if not POST
  if(rm !== "get") {
    return response.end("Unsupported Method");
  }
  let filename = path.join(__dirname, request.url);
  fs.stat(filename, (err, stat) => {
      if(err) {
        response.statusCode = err.errno === 34 ? 404 : 500;
      return response.end()
      }
    var etag = crypto.createHash('md5').update(stat.size +
stat.mtime).digest('hex');
    response.setHeader('Last-Modified', stat.mtime);
    if(request.headers['if-none-match'] === etag) {
      response.statusCode = 304;
      return response.end();
```

```
    }
    response.setHeader('Content-Length', stat.size);
    response.setHeader('ETag', etag);
    response.statusCode = 200;
    fs.createReadStream(filename).pipe(response);
  });
}).listen(8000);
```

Note the 404 (not found) and 500 (internal server error) status codes.

 `Content-Length` is measured in bytes, not characters. Normally, your data will be in single byte characters (hello is five bytes long), but this is not always the case. If you are determining the length of a stream buffer, use `Buffer.byteLength`.

A simple file browser

Now, let's take what we've learned about files and Node to do something that truly (and hopefully) no web page can; let's directly browse the entire hard disk of your personal computer! To make this possible, we'll use two powerful recent additions to the JavaScript and Node family: *Electron* and *Vue.js*.

Start out at your terminal with commands like these:

```
$ mkdir hello_files
$ cd hello_files
$ npm init
$ npm install -S electron
```

The default answers are fine, except for the entry point—instead of `index.js`, type `main.js`. When you're done, you should have a `package.json` file like this:

```
{
  "name": "hello_files",
  "version": "0.0.1",
  "description": "A simple file browser using Node, Electron, and Vue.js",
  "main": "main.js",
  "dependencies": {
    "electron": "^1.7.9"
  }
}
```

Now, let's take a look at these three commands:

```
$ ./node_modules/.bin/electron --version
$ ./node_modules/.bin/electron
$ ./node_modules/.bin/electron .
```

Try the first to ensure that npm got a working copy of Electron onto your computer. As of this writing, the current version is **v1.7.9**. The second command will execute electron "empty", that is, without giving it an app to run. The third command tells electron to run the app in this folder: Electron will read `package.json` to find and run `main.js`.

Alternatively, you can use `-g` to install Electron globally, and then reach the executable more easily with commands like these:

```
$ npm install -g electron

$ electron --version
$ electron
$ electron .
```

Electron

Let's run the second command. The result may be surprising: a graphical window appears on your screen!:

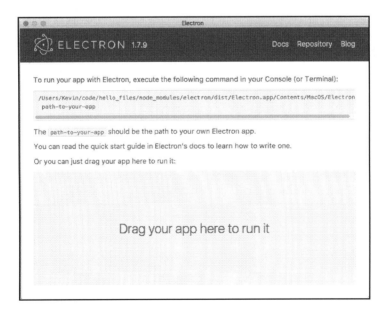

What is this? What is Electron? Let's answer that question several ways: to the end user, to the developer or product owner, under the hood, and at the end of the chapter, from the perspective of JavaScript's history and development.

To the end user, an Electron app is just a regular desktop app. Users can't even tell it's made with Electron. The unboxing flow is exactly the same: the user gets the app from their favorite app store, or downloads `setup.exe` from your website. The daily experience is also the same: the app has an icon on the Start menu or dock, menus where they should be, a `File|Open...` dialog—all the features users expect from a desktop application. You might use Slack on Windows or macOS, for instance, and may be surprised to learn that Slack is made with Electron.

To the developer or product owner, Electron is a great way to make desktop apps. Developers can use the modern and powerful technologies they learned for the web on the desktop now. All your favorite npm modules can come along, too. Product owners like being able to ship version 1.0 simultaneously on Windows, Mac, and Linux with very little additional development or testing required. Business stakeholders like being able to task a single group of web developers across web and desktop projects, instead of having to hire new individual dedicated teams (a separate one per target operating system) experienced in each individual native desktop stack.

Under the hood, Electron is pretty amazing. It's built from parts of both Chromium and Node, getting abilities like page rendering from Chromium, and abilities like buffers, files, and sockets from Node. Both Chromium and Node contain V8, and inside V8 a JavaScript event loop, of course. In an impressive engineering feat, Electron merges these two event loops together, allowing a single JavaScript event to run code that affects both the screen and the system.

Electron is made by GitHub, which also develops the Atom text editor. To make Atom as hackable as the web, GitHub built it using web technologies. Realizing that other software teams might want to construct desktop apps this way, GitHub released their tools first as Atom Shell, and simplified the name to Electron.

Now that we've got Electron running, let's make Electron an app of our own. The `electron` `.` command causes Electron to look in `package.json` to see what it should do. There, we're pointing it to `main.js`:

```
// main.js

const electron = require('electron');
const app = electron.app;
const BrowserWindow = electron.BrowserWindow;

const path = require('path');
const url = require('url');

let mainWindow; // Keep this reference so the window doesn't close

function createWindow() {
  mainWindow = new BrowserWindow({width: 800, height: 800});
  mainWindow.loadURL(url.format({
    pathname: path.join(__dirname, 'index.html'),
    protocol: 'file:',
    slashes: true
  }));
  mainWindow.webContents.openDevTools();
  mainWindow.on('closed', () => {
    mainWindow = null;
  });
}

app.on('ready', createWindow);

app.on('window-all-closed', () => {
  app.quit();
});
```

You can imagine that Node is running the file, even though the executable that's running it is actually Electron (which has Node and V8 inside, of course). Note how the code can require familiar Node modules like `path` and `url` as well as some new ones, such as `electron`. The code in `main.js` creates a special Electron browser window that's 800 pixels wide and 800 pixels high, and navigates it to `index.html`:

```
<!DOCTYPE html>
<html>
  <head>
    <meta charset="UTF-8">
    <title>Hello, files</title>
  </head>
  <body>
    <p>
      <input type="button" value="Reload the app after changing the code"
onClick="window.location.reload()"/>
    </p>
    <div id="app">
      <p>{{ location }}</p>
      <button @click="up">..</button>
      <listing v-for="file in files" v-bind:key="file.id" v-
bind:item="file"></listing>
      <p><img v-bind:src="image"/></p>
    </div>
    <script src="https://unpkg.com/vue"></script>
    <script>
      require('./renderer.js')
    </script>
  </body>
</html>
```

This also looks quite familiar from what we'd expect on the web. We'll talk about Vue later in this chapter; right now, note the reload `button` at the top of the page and the `script` tag at the end.

The button is useful when developing. Instead of restarting the Electron process at the command line, you can just make a change to this page or the JavaScript it brings in and see the results from hitting the **Reload** button. Electron doesn't display Chromium's default browser toolbar, where the **Reload** button lives, but **View**, **Reload** is available on the menu bar on macOS, and it's even easier to put a **Reload** button right in the page.

To understand the `script` tag at the end, it's best to first get a basic understanding of Electron's process architecture.

Electron processes

Built from Chromium, Electron inherited Chromium's (and Chrome's) one-process-per-tab architecture. With Electron running our app, there is only one "tab": the window on your screen, but there are still two processes. The *main* process represents the underlying browser, which you started from the command line, at which point it read `package.json`, and then ran `main.js`. Electron's main process can create new `BrowserWindow` objects, and deal with events that affect the overall lifecycle of the desktop app, from startup to shutdown.

On the page Electron opens, however, a different process, the *renderer* process, runs the JavaScript there. Only a renderer process is able to perform GUI-related tasks, like manipulating the DOM.

Node is available in both processes. If a module expects the DOM to be present, it may not work in the main process, however. For instance, jQuery fails to load in Electron's main process, but works fine in a renderer process, while Handlebars works fine in both.

In instances where the code in one Electron process needs to perform an action or get an answer from some code in the other process, the solution is Node's standard inter-process communication tools, described later in `Chapter 7`, *Using Multiple Processes*. Additionally, Electron conveniently wraps some of these in its own API.

The renderer process

So far, we've seen Electron start, run `main.js`, and open `index.html`. In summary, here's how the whole thing works:

Electron's *main* process does the following:

- reads `package.json`, which tells it to then
- run `main.js`

This causes Electron to start a *renderer* process to do this:

- parse `index.html`, which then
- runs `renderer.js`

Let's take a look at the code there:

```
// renderer.js

const Promise = require("bluebird");
const fs = Promise.promisifyAll(require("fs"));
const path = require("path");

Vue.component('listing', {
  props: ['item'],
  template: '<div @click="clicked(item.name)">{{ item.name }}</div>',
  methods: {
    clicked(n) {
      go(path.format({ dir: app.location, base: n }));
    }
  }
});

var app = new Vue({
  el: '#app',
  data: {
    location: process.cwd(),
    files: [],
    image: null
  },
  methods: {
    up() {
      go(path.dirname(this.location));
    }
  }
});

function go(p) {

  if (p.endsWith(".bmp") || p.endsWith(".png") || p.endsWith(".gif") ||
p.endsWith(".jpg")) {

    // Image
    app.image = "file://" + p; // Show it

  } else {
```

```
    // Non-image
    app.image = null;

    // See if it's a directory or not
    fs.lstatAsync(p).then((stat) => {

      if (stat.isDirectory()) {

        // Directory, list its contents
        app.location = p;
        fs.readdirAsync(app.location).then((files) => {
          var a = [];
          for (var i = 0; i < files.length; i++)
            a.push({ id: i, name: files[i] });
          app.files = a;
        }).catch((e) => {
          console.log(e.stack);
        });
      } else {
        // Non-directory, don't go there at all
      }
    }).catch((e) => {
      console.log(e.stack);
    });
  }
}

go(app.location);
```

First, this code brings in the bluebird promise library, setting it to `Promise`. The call to `Promise.promisifyAll()` creates functions like `fs.lstatAsync()`, the promisified version of `fs.lstat()`.

Our app's core logic is factored into a single function named `go()`, which gets passed an absolute filesystem path the user wants the app to take a look at. If the path is to an image, the app shows it on the page. If the path is to a directory, the app lists the folder's contents.

To perform this logic, the preceding code first simply looks for a common image file extension. If not present, an asynchronous step looks at the disk with `fs.lstatAsync()` to then be able to call `stat.isDirectory()`. If it is a directory, another promisified call, `fs.readdirAsync()`, gets the directory listing.

Here's a picture of our simple Electron-powered file browser in action:

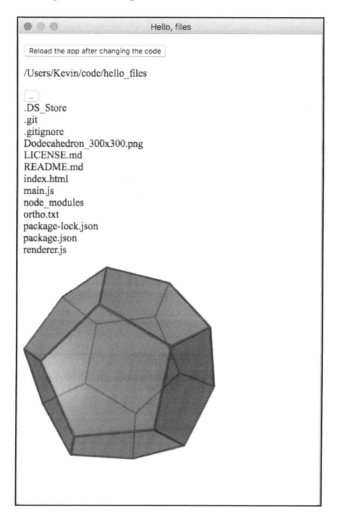

Vue.js

Our app's user experience is powered by *Vue.js*, a frontend JavaScript framework for building and easily changing the contents of a web page. Like React, Vue lets you template components, put them on the page, and change them when the data underneath changes.

React uses JSX to combine HTML tags with JavaScript code. This requires a preprocessor like *Babel* to transpile the JSX portions into ES6 JavaScript. In a typical React stack, *webpack* manages a build process that includes Babel, converting and combining your development files into files you'll run, test, and eventually deploy. The webpack dev server shows your site as you code it, even automatically refreshing as you change your code.

Vue, however, doesn't require a transpilation step. You can use it with webpack, but you can also use it with just a script tag, like this one in our app's `index.html`:

```
<script src="https://unpkg.com/vue"></script>
```

This flexibility makes it easy to get started with Vue, makes Vue easy to get running in Electron, and is why we've picked it for this example app.

Back on the `index.html` page, take a look at these lines:

```
<div id="app">
  <p>{{ location }}</p>
  <button @click="up">..</button>
  <listing v-for="file in files" v-bind:key="file.id" v-
bind:item="file"></listing&gt;
  <p><img v-bind:src="image"/></p>
</div>
<script src="https://unpkg.com/vue"></script>
```

Also, in the `renderer.js` script, take a look at this part:

```
var app = new Vue({
  el: '#app',
  data: {
    location: process.cwd(),
    files: [],
    image: null
  },
  methods: {
    up() {
      go(path.dirname(this.location));
    }
  }
});
```

In the page, `<div id="app">` identifies `div` as our app, and in the script, `var app = new Vue({})`; creates the new JavaScript object that connects to and controls the *app* `div`. The data object inside `app` defines values that appear in the div and thus on the page. For example, `app.location`, which through some clever internal linking with `this` reaches into the `data` object above, is shown on the page where `{{ location }}` appears. Vue even watches for changes to `data.location`—set that to a new value and the page will update automatically. With this ability, Vue is said to be *reactive*.

Browse around your local disk with the file browser we just built, and imagine all the desktop apps you can now create with Node and Electron.

> Earlier, this chapter asked, "What is Electron?" and composed different answers imagining different stakeholders and considering different perspectives.
>
> Electron gets JavaScript one step closer to Kris Kowal's goal for the language, which you may remember from Chapter 1, *Understanding the Node Environment*, is no less than "world domination", meaning able to run everywhere and do anything. Also, taking JavaScript's place in the last few decades of computing into consideration, it achieves this with some wry irony.
>
> Brendan Eich created JavaScript to script small tasks within web pages running on browsers on personal computers in the 1990s, which had just recently gained bitmapped displays and graphical operating systems. There, JavaScript was tightly contained within the sandbox of the browser tab. The sandbox enforced strict security requirements, and limited it from, among other things, looking at some files. Close to the user and close to the screen, JavaScript could validate form data, and change CSS on the fly. In this first stage of life, most days, JavaScript animated some text.
>
> Node took JavaScript to the server, distancing it from the graphical screen, but freeing it from the confines of the browser. There, JavaScript became a competent and complete systems language, accessing files and sockets to perform useful and powerful tasks. In this second stage of life, most days, JavaScript migrated a database.

Electron takes JavaScript back to the client. Like a wandering feudal warrior returning to his home village after years of exile, (and, of course, distant and elite training) JavaScript returns with ES6 features and npm modules it developed in the harsh wasteland of the server, being used and developed alongside formidable partners (and oftentimes foes) like C++ and Java. Back on the desktop and armed with Electron, it can use these abilities outside of the restricted confines of the browser. In this third stage of life, JavaScript really can do anything.

Summary

In this chapter, we saw how Node's API is a comprehensive map to native filesystem bindings, exposing a full range of functionality to the developer while requiring very little code or complexity. Additionally, we saw how files are easily wrapped into `Stream` objects, and how this consistency with the rest of Node's design simplifies interactions between different types of I/O, such as between network data and files. Using Electron, we built a file browser that runs as a cross-platform native application, opening up a whole new world for Node developers.

We've also learned something about how to build servers with Node that can accommodate regular client expectations, easily implementing file uploading and resource caching. Having covered the key features of Node, it is time to use these techniques in building larger applications able to handle many thousands of clients.

5

Managing Many Simultaneous Client Connections

"If everyone helps to hold up the sky, then one person does not become tired."

– Tshi Proverb

Maintaining a high level of throughput while managing thousands of simultaneous client transactions in the unpredictable and *bursty* environment of networked software is one expectation developers have for their Node implementations. Given a history of failed and unpopular solutions, the problem of concurrency has even been assigned its own numeronym: *"The C10K problem"*. How should network software confidently serving 10,000 simultaneous clients be designed?

The question of how to best build high concurrency systems has provoked much theory over the last several decades, with the debate mostly between two alternatives, threads and events:

> *"Threading allows programmers to write straight-line code and rely on the operating system to overlap computation and I/O by transparently switching across threads. The alternative, events, allows programmers to manage concurrency explicitly by structuring code as a single-threaded handler that reacts to events (such as non-blocking I/O completions, application-specific messages, or timer events)."*
>
> *– "A Design Framework for Highly Concurrent Systems" (Welsh, Gribble, Brewer & Culler, 2000), p. 2.*

Two important points are made in the preceding quote:

- Developers prefer to write structured code (straight line; single threaded) that hides the complexity of multiple simultaneous operations where possible
- I/O efficiency is a primary consideration of high-concurrency applications

Until very recently, programming languages and related frameworks were not (necessarily) optimized for software executing across nodes in a distributed network, or even across processors. Algorithms are expected to be deterministic; data written to a database is expected to be immediately available for reading. In this age of eventually consistent databases and asynchronous control flow, developers can no longer expect to know the precise state of an application at any given point of time; a sometimes mind-bending challenge for the architects of highly concurrent systems.

As we learned in `Chapter 2`, *Understanding Asynchronous Event-Driven Programming*, Node's design attempts to combine the advantages of both threads and events, serving all clients on a single thread (an event loop wrapping a JavaScript runtime) while delegating the blocking work (I/O) to an optimized thread pool that informs the main thread of state changes via an event notification system.

Think clearly about how the following HTTP server implementation, running on a single CPU, is responding to each client request by wrapping a callback function in the context of the request and pushing that execution context onto a stack that is constantly emptied and rebuilt within a single thread bound to an event loop:

```
require('http').createServer((req, res) => {
  res.writeHead(200, {'Content-Type': 'text/plain'});
  res.end('Hello client from ${req.connection.remoteAddress}`);
  console.log(req);
}).listen(8000);
```

Schematically, it is this:

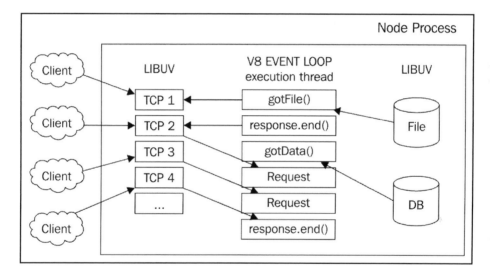

On the other hand, a server like Apache spins up a thread for each client request:

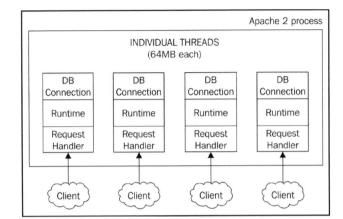

These two approaches are very different. The claim implicit in Node's design is this: it is easier to reason about highly concurrent software when program flow is organized along a single thread, and that decreasing I/O latency increases the number of simultaneous clients that can be supported even in a single-threaded execution model. The second claim will be tested later, but for now, let's see how easy it can be to build basic processes that naturally scale.

We will demonstrate how to track and manage the relationships between concurrent processes using Node, in particular, those servicing multiple clients simultaneously. Our goal is to set up a basic understanding of how state should be modeled within a Node server or other processes. How is it that a large online social network serves you customized information tailored by your friendships or interests? How is your shopping cart maintained over several shopping sessions, without disappearing, even containing suggestions based on your history of purchases? How can a single client interact with other clients?

Understanding concurrency

We would all agree that there are unexpected events in the world, and that many of them occur at exactly the same time. It is also clear that the state of any given system may be composed of any number of substates, where the full consequence of even minor state changes are difficult to predict—the power of a butterfly's wings being enough to tip a much larger system into an alternate state. Also, we also know that the volume and shape of a system, over time, changes in ways difficult to predict.

In his PHD thesis "*Foundations of Actor Semantics*", written in 1981, William Clinger proposed that his work was:

> "*...motivated by the prospect of highly parallel computing machines consisting of dozens, hundreds or even thousands of independent microprocessors, each with its own local memory and communications processor, communicating via a high-performance communications network.*"

As it turns out, Clinger was on to something. Concurrency is a property of systems composed of many simultaneously executing operations, and the network software we are now building resembles the one he envisioned, only much larger, where *hundreds or even thousands* is the lower bound, not the higher.

Node makes concurrency accessible, while simultaneously scaling across multiple cores, multiple processes, and multiple machines. It is important to note that Node places as much importance on the simplicity and consistency of programs as it does on being the fastest solution, embracing and enforcing non-blocking I/O in an effort to deliver high concurrency through well-designed and predictable interfaces. This is what Dahl meant when he said, "Node's goal is to provide an easy way to build scalable network programs".

Happily, it also turns out that Node is very fast.

Concurrency is not parallelism

A problem can be solved by dividing it into smaller problems, spreading those smaller problems across a pool of available people or workers to work on in parallel, and delivering the parallel results concurrently.

Multiple processes each solving one part of a single mathematical problem simultaneously is an example of parallelism.

Rob Pike, general wizard hacker and co-inventor of Google's Go programming language, defines concurrency in this way:

> "*Concurrency is a way to structure a thing so that you can, maybe, use parallelism to do a better job. But parallelism is not the goal of concurrency; concurrency's goal is a good structure.*"

Successful high-concurrency application development frameworks provide a simple and expressive vocabulary for describing such systems.

Node's design suggests that achieving its primary goal—to provide an easy way to build scalable network programs—includes simplifying how the execution order of coexisting processes is structured and composed. Node helps a developer struggling with a program within which many things are happening at once (such as serving many concurrent clients) to better organize his or her code.

This is not to say that Node is designed to concede efficiency in order to maintain simple interfaces—far from it. Instead, the idea is to move responsibility for implementing efficient parallel processing away from the developer and into the core design of the system, leaving the developer free to structure concurrency through a simple and predictable callback system, safe from deadlocks and other traps.

Node's bracing simplicity comes at a good time, as social and community networks grow alongside the world's data. Systems are being scaled to sizes that few would have predicted. It is a good time for new thinking, such as how to describe and design these systems, and the way they make requests of, and respond to, each other.

Routing requests

HTTP is a data transfer protocol built upon a request/response model. Using this protocol, many of us communicate our current status to friends, buy presents for family, or discuss a project over email with colleagues. A staggering number of people have come to depend on this foundational internet protocol.

Typically, a browser client will issue an HTTP GET request to a server. This server then returns the requested resource, often represented as an HTML document. HTTP is stateless, which simply means that each request or response maintains no information on previous requests or responses—with each back and forward movement through web pages, the entire browser state is destroyed and rebuilt from scratch.

Servers route state change requests from clients, ultimately causing new state representations to be returned, which clients (often browsers) redraw or report. When the WWW was first conceived, this model made sense. For the most part, this new network was understood as a distributed filesystem, accessible by anyone with a web browser, where a specific resource (such as a newspaper article) could be requested from a file-serving computer (a server) located somewhere on the network (at an Internet Protocol or IP address) via an HTTP request (such as GET) by simply typing in an URL (for example, `http://www.example.org/articles/april/showers.html`). A user requests a page and that page appears, perhaps containing (hyper) links to related pages.

However, since a stateless protocol does not maintain context information, it was nearly impossible for the operator of a server to develop a more interesting relationship with a visitor across a series of requests, or for a visitor to dynamically aggregate multiple responses into a single view.

Additionally, the expressiveness of requests was limited both by the protocol itself and by the lack of server content rich enough to usefully support a more descriptive vocabulary. For the most part, requests were as blunt as pointing a finger at an object of desire—*get that for me*. Consider the parts of a typical URL:

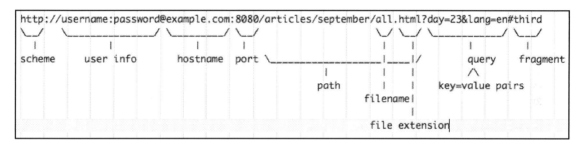

We can see how much client work is involved in describing a simple resource location, with query parameters and resource targets an awkward afterthought, becoming nearly unusable once more than a few resource descriptors are used. While this was workable in a time of simple documents in well-understood and invariant hierarchies, the demands and complexities of modern networked software have rendered the original concept unworkable and in need of improvement.

The clumsiness of passing around increasingly complex key/value pairs to maintain user state began to frustrate the ambitions of this new medium. Very quickly, it became obvious to developers that a growing reliance on the internet as the utility communication layer of the world's information, software, and commerce required a more refined approach.

Over time, these limitations have been overcome through a combination of improvements to the HTTP protocol, the introduction of JavaScript to the browser, technologies such as browser cookies and the attendant innovation from developers building products and services exploiting these advances.

Nevertheless, the HTTP protocol itself continues to be dominated by the same motifs of individual file-like resources existing at a distinct and permanent path and identified by an often non-descriptive name.

What actually exists on many servers now is a complex software specifying network interfaces to data models. Communicating with these types of networked applications involves getting and setting the state of that data model, both in general and as it applies in particular to the client making a request.

Clients deploying a real-time solution both set and get resource state representations on a server. Application servers must report a client's state in relation to multiple processes (databases, files, rules engines, calculation engines, and so on) on each request, and often unilaterally on application state changes (for example, a user losing access permission). Clients are often not browsers, but other servers. How should they communicate?

Understanding routes

Routes map URLs to actions. Rather than constructing an application interface in terms of URL paths to specific files that contain some logic, designing with routes involves assigning a specific function to a distinct combination of a URL path and request method. For example, a web service that accepts requests for lists of cities might be called in this manner:

```
GET /services/cities.php?country=usa&state=ohio
```

When your server receives this request, it would pass the URL information to a PHP process that will execute the application logic in `cities.php`, such as reading the query, parsing out the country and state, calling a database, building a response, and returning it. Node has the great benefit of being able to function both as the server and the application environment. The server can field requests directly. Then, it makes more sense to use URLs as simple statements of intent:

```
GET /listCities/usa/ohio
```

In a Node server, we might use something like the following code to handle these requests for cities:

```
let app = http.createServer((request, response) => {
  let url = request.url;
  let method = request.method;
  if (method === "GET") {
    if (url === "/listCities/usa/ohio") {
      database.call("usa","ohio", (err, data) => {
        response.writeHead(200, {'Content-Type': 'application/json' });
        // Return list of cities in Ohio, USA
        response.end(JSON.stringify(data));
      });
    }
```

```
        if (url === "/listCities/usa/arizona") { ... }
        if (url === "/listCities/canada/ontario") { ... }
    }
})
```

One good thing and one bad jump out:

- URL handling is clearly organized in one place
- The code is impossibly repetitive

Writing out every possible route won't work. We'll keep the organization, but need to create variables in routes, preferring to define a general route expression like this:

```
/listCities/:country/:state
```

The method `listCities` can accept `country` and `state` *variable* arguments, identified with a colon (`:`) prefix. Within our server, we would need to convert this symbolic expression into a regular expression. In this case, the `RegExp` `/^\/listCities\/([^\/\.]+)\/([^\/\.]+)\/?$/` could be used to extract ordered values from our example URL into a value map similar to:

```
{ country: "usa", state: "ohio" }
```

By treating requests as expressions, our server design has become a little saner, nicely routing any country/state combination to a common handler function:

```
if (request.method === "GET") {
  let match =
request.url.match(/^\/listCities\/([^\/\.]+)\/([^\/\.]+)\/?$/);
  if (match) {
    database.call(match[1],match[2],function(err, data) {...}
  }
}
```

This form of request routing has *won the argument* in the Node community, being the default behavior of various frameworks and tools. In fact, this way of thinking about routing requests has gained acceptance in many other development environments, such as Ruby on Rails. As a result, most web application frameworks for Node have been developed around routing.

The most popular web application framework for Node is T.J. Holowaychuk's Express framework, and we'll be using this framework frequently in this book when designing routing servers. You can install it via `npm` by running `npm install express`.

Using Express to route requests

Express simplifies the complexity of defining route-matching routines. Our example might be written in the following way using Express:

```
const express = require('express');
let app = express();
app.get('/listCities/:country/:state', (request, response) => {
  let country = request.params.country;
  let state = request.params.state;
  response.end(`You asked for country: ${country}and state: ${state}`);
});
app.listen(8080);

GET /listCities/usa/ohio
// You asked for country: usa and state: ohio
GET /didnt/define/this
// Cannot GET /didnt/define/this
GET /listCities // note missing arguments
// Cannot GET /listCities
```

Instantiating Express delivers a fully-formed web server wrapped in an easy-to-use application development API. Our cities service is clearly defined and its variables stated, expecting to be called via GET (one might also use app.post(...) or app.put(...), or any other standard HTTP method).

Express also introduces the idea of chaining request-handling routines, which in Express are understood as middleware. In our example, we are calling a single function in order to handle a cities request. What if, prior to calling our database, we want to check that the user is authenticated? We might add an authenticate() method prior to our main service method:

```
let authenticate = (request, response, next) => {
  if (validUser) {
    next();
  } else {
    response.end("INVALID USER!");
  }
}
app.get('/listCities/:country/:state', authenticate, (request, response) =>
{ ... });
```

Middleware can be chained, in other words, simplifying the creation of complex execution chains, nicely following the Rule of Modularity. Many types of middleware for handling favicons, logging, uploads, static file requests, and so on have already been developed. To learn more, visit: `https://expressjs.com/`.

Having established the proper way for Node servers to be configured for routing requests, we can now begin a discussion on how to identify the client making the request, assigning that client a unique session ID, and managing that session through time.

Using Redis for tracking client state

For some of the applications and examples in this chapter, we will be using **Redis**, an in-memory Key/Value (KV) database developed by *Salvatore Sanfilippo*. More information on Redis can be found at: `http://redis.io`. A well-known competitor to Redis is **Memcached** (`http://memcached.org`).

In general, any server that must maintain the session state of many clients will need a high-speed data layer with near-instantaneous read/write performance, as request validation and user state transformations can occur multiple times on each request. Traditional file-backed relational databases tend to be slower at this task than in-memory KV databases. We're going to use Redis for tracking the client state.

Redis is a single-threaded data store that runs in memory. It is very fast, and focused on implementing several data structures, such as hashes and lists and sets, and performing operations on those (such as set intersections and list pushing and popping). Instructions for installing Redis can be found here: `https://redis.io/topics/quickstart`.

To interact with Redis:

```
$ redis-cli
```

Notably, Amazon's ElastiCache service enables Redis "in the cloud" as an in-memory cache, with automatic scaling and redundancy at: `https://aws.amazon.com/elasticache/`.

Redis supports a standard interface for expected actions, such as getting or setting key/value pairs. To `get` the value stored at a key, first start the Redis CLI:

```
$ redis-cli
redis> get somerandomkey
(nil)
```

Redis will return (nil) when a key does not exist. Let's set a key:

```
redis> set somerandomkey "who am I?"
redis> get somerandomkey
"who am I?"
```

To use Redis within a Node environment, we will need some sort of binding. We will be using Matt Ranney's node_redis module. Install it with npm using the following command line:

```
$ npm install redis
```

To set a value in Redis and get it back again, we can now do this in Node:

```
let redis = require("redis");
let client = redis.createClient();
client.set("userId", "jack", (err) => {
  client.get("userId", (err, data) => {
    console.log(data); // "jack"
  });
});
```

Storing user data

Managing many users means at least tracking their user information, some stored long term (for example, address, purchase history, and contact list) and some session data stored for a short time (time since login, last game score, and most recent answer).

Normally, we would create a secure interface or similar, allowing administrators to create user accounts. It will be clear to the reader how to create such an interface by the end of this chapter. For the examples that follow, we'll only need to create one user, to act as a volunteer. Let's create Jack:

```
redis> hset jack password "beanstalk"
redis> hset jack fullname "Jack Spratt"
```

This will create a key in Redis—Jack—containing a hash resembling:

```
{
  "password": "beanstalk",
  "fullname": "Jack Spratt"
}
```

If we wanted to create a hash and add several KV pairs all at once, we could achieve the preceding with the `hmset` command:

```
redis> hmset jack password "beanstalk" fullname "Jack Spratt"
```

Now, `Jack` exists:

```
redis> hgetall jack
  1) "password"
  2) "beanstalk"
  3) "fullname"
  4) "Jack Spratt"
```

We can use the following command to fetch the value stored for a specific field in Jack's account:

```
redis> hget jack password // "beanstalk"
```

Handling sessions

How does a server know if the current client request is part of a chain of previous requests? Web applications engage with clients through long transactional chains—the shopping cart containing items to buy will still be there even if a shopper navigates away to do some comparison-shopping. We will call this a session, which may contain any number of KV pairs, such as a username, product list, or the user's login history.

How are sessions started, ended, and tracked? There are many ways to attack this problem, depending on many factors existing in different ways on different architectures. In particular, if more than one server is being used to handle clients, how is session data shared between them?

We will use cookies to store session IDs for clients, while building a simple long-polling server. Keep in mind that as applications grow in complexity, this simple system will need to be extended. As well, long-polling as a technology is giving ground to the more powerful socket techniques we will explore in our discussions around building real-time systems. However, the key issues faced when holding many connected clients simultaneously on a server, and tracking their sessions, should be demonstrated.

Cookies and client state

Netscape provided the preliminary specification for cookies in 1997:

> *According to* `https://web.archive.org/web/20070805052634/http://wp.`
> `netscape.com/newsref/std/cookie_spec.html`, *"Cookies are a general mechanism*
> *which server side connections (such as CGI scripts) can use to both store and retrieve*
> *information on the client side of the connection. The addition of a simple, persistent, client-*
> *side state significantly extends the capabilities of Web-based client/server applications. A*
> *server, when returning an HTTP object to a client, may also send a piece of state*
> *information which the client will store. Included in that state object is a description of the*
> *range of URLs for which that state is valid. Any future HTTP requests made by the client*
> *which fall in that range will include a transmittal of the current value of the state object*
> *from the client back to the server. The state object is called a cookie, for no compelling*
> *reason."*

Here, we have one of the first attempts to *fix* the stateless nature of HTTP, specifically, the maintenance of session state. It was such a good attempt, which still remains a fundamental part of the web.

We've already seen how to read and set the cookie header with Node. Express makes the process a little easier:

```
const express = require('express');
const cookieParser = require('cookie-parser');
const app = express();

app.use(cookieParser());

app.get('/mycookie', (request, response) => {
    response.end(request.cookies.node_cookie);
});

app.get('/', (request, response) => {
    response.cookie('node_cookie', parseInt(Math.random() * 10e10));
    response.end("Cookie set");
});

app.listen(8000);
```

Note the `use` method, which allows us to turn on the cookie handling middleware for Express. Here, we see that whenever a client hits our server, this client is assigned a random number as a cookie. By navigating to `/mycookie`, this client can see the cookie.

A simple poll

Next, let's create a concurrent environment, one with many simultaneously connected clients. We'll use a long-polling server to do this, broadcasting to all connected clients via `stdin`. Additionally, each client will be assigned a unique session ID, used to identify the client's `http.serverResponse` object, which we will push data to.

Long polling is a technique whereby a server holds on to a client connection until there is data available to send. When data is ultimately sent to the client, the client reconnects to the server and the process continues. It was designed as an improvement on short polling, which is the inefficient technique of blindly checking with a server for new information every few seconds or so, hoping for new data. Long polling only requires a reconnection following a tangible delivery of data to the client.

We'll use two routes. The first route is described using a forward slash (/), a root domain request. Calls to this path will return some HTML forming the client UI. The second route is `/poll`, which the client will use to reconnect with the server following the receipt of some data.

The client UI is extremely simple: its sole purpose is to make an XML HTTP request (XHR) to a server (which will hold that request until some data arrives), repeating this step immediately following the receipt of some data. Our UI will display a list of messages received within an unordered list. For the XHR bit we will use the jQuery library. Any similar library can be used, and building a pure JavaScript implementation is not difficult.

HTML:

```
<ul id="results"></ul>
```

JavaScript:

```
function longPoll() {
  $.get('http://localhost:2112/poll', (data) => {
    $('<li>' + data + '</li>').appendTo('#results');
    longPoll();
  });
}
longPoll();
```

In the client code above you should see how this will work. A client makes a GET call to **/poll**, and will wait until data is received. Once data is received it is added to the client display and another **/poll** call is made. In this way the client holds a long connection to the server, and reconnects only after receiving data.

The server is also simple, mainly responsible for setting session IDs and holding on to concurrent client connections until such time as data is available, which is broadcast to all connected clients. Data is made available through a redis pub/sub mechanism. These connections are indexed via session IDs, maintained using cookies:

```
const fs = require('fs');
const express = require('express');
const cookieParser = require('cookie-parser');
const redis = require("redis");
const receiver = redis.createClient();
const publisher = redis.createClient();
const app = express();

app.use(cookieParser());

let connections = {};

app.get('/poll', (request, response) => {
   let id = request.cookies.node_poll_id;
   if(!id) {
      return;
   }
   connections[id] = response;
});

app.get('/', (request, response) => {
    fs.readFile('./poll_client.html', (err, data) => {
       response.cookie('node_poll_id', Math.random().toString(36).substr(2,
9));
        response.writeHead(200, {'Content-Type': 'text/html'});
        response.end(data);
    });
});

app.listen(2112);

receiver.subscribe("stdin_message");
receiver.on("message", (channel, message) => {
   let conn;
   for(conn in connections) {
      connections[conn].end(message);
   }
```

```
        console.log(`Received message: ${message} on channel: ${channel}`);
});

process.stdin.on('readable', function() {
    let msg = this.read();
    msg && publisher.publish('stdin_message', msg.toString());
});
```

Run this server on the command line, and connect to the server via a browser (**http://localhost:2112**). A page with the text "Results:" will be displayed. Return to the command line and enter some text—this message should immediately appear in your browser. As you keep typing on the command line, your message will be routed to connected clients. You can try this as well with multiple clients -- note that you should use different browsers, incognito mode, or other ways to distinguish each client.

While this is a toy server used for demonstration (you probably shouldn't use long polling -- better options are presented in `Chapter 6`, *Creating Real-Time Applications*), ultimately it should be seen how one might use some business logic to update state, and then have those state change events caught and then broadcast to listening clients using a mechanism like Redis pub/sub.

Authenticating connections

In conjunction with establishing client session objects, a Node server often demands authentication credentials. The theory and practice of web security is extensive. We want to simplify our understanding into two main authentication scenarios:

- When the wire protocol is HTTPS
- When it is HTTP

The first is naturally secure, and the second is not. For the first, we will learn how to implement Basic authentication in Node, and for the second, a challenge-response system will be described.

Basic authentication

As mentioned, Basic authentication sends plain text over the wire containing a username/password combination, using standard HTTP headers. It is a simple and well-known protocol. Any server sending the correct headers will cause any browser to display a login dialog, like the following one:

Nonetheless, this method remains insecure, sending non-encrypted data in plain text over the wire. For the sake of simplicity, we will demonstrate this authentication method on an HTTP server, but it must be stressed that in real-world usage the server must be communicating via a secure protocol, such as HTTPS.

Let's implement this authentication protocol with Node. Employing the user database developed earlier in Redis, we validate submitted credentials by checking user objects for matching passwords, handling failures and successes:

```
http.createServer(function(req, res) {

    let auth = req.headers['authorization'];
    if(!auth) {
        res.writeHead(401, {'WWW-Authenticate': 'Basic realm="Secure
Area"'});
        return res.end('<html><body>Please enter some
credentials.</body></html>');
    }

    let tmp = auth.split(' ');
    let buf = Buffer.from(tmp[1], 'base64');
    let plain_auth = buf.toString();
    let creds = plain_auth.split(':');
    let username = creds[0];
```

```
    // Find this user record
    client.get(username, function(err, data) {
        if(err || !data) {
            res.writeHead(401, {'WWW-Authenticate': 'Basic realm="Secure
Area"'});
            return res.end('<html><body>You are not
authorized.</body></html>');
        }
        res.statusCode = 200;
        res.end('<html><body>Welcome!</body></html>');
    });
}).listen(8080);
```

By sending a `401` status and the `'authorization'` header on a new client connection, a dialog like the one previous screenshot will be created via this code:

```
    res.writeHead(401, {'WWW-Authenticate': 'Basic realm="Secure Area"'});
    return res.end('<html><body>Please enter some
credentials.</body></html>');
```

In this way, a straightforward login system can be designed. As browsers will naturally prompt users requesting access to a protected domain, even the login dialog is taken care of.

Handshaking

Another authentication method to consider in situations where an HTTPS connection cannot be established is a challenge-response system:

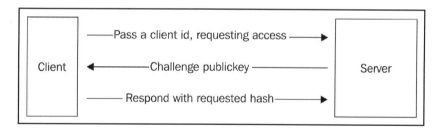

In this scenario, a client asks a server for access for a specific user, username, ID, or similar. Typically, this data would be sent via a login form. Let's mock up a challenge/response scenario, using for our example the user we created earlier—Jack.

The general design and purpose of a challenge/response system aims to avoid sending any password data in plain text over the wire. So, we will need to decide on an encryption strategy that both the client and the server share. For our example, let's use the SHA256 algorithm. Node's crypto library contains all of the tools necessary for creating this type of hash. The client likely does not, so we must provide one. We'll use the one developed by Chris Veness, which can be downloaded from the following link: `https://github.com/chrisveness/crypto/blob/master/sha256.js`.

To initiate this login, the client will need to send an authentication request for the user Jack:

`GET /authenticate/jack`

In response, the client should receive a server-generated public key—the challenge. The client must now form a string of Jack's password prefixed by this key. Create a SHA256 hash from it, and pass the resulting hash to `/login/`. The server will have also created the same SHA256 hash—if the two match, the client is authenticated:

```
<script src="sha256.js"></script>
<script>
$.get("/authenticate/jack", (publicKey) => {
    if (publicKey === "no data") {
    return alert("Cannot log in.");
  }
  // Expect to receive a challenge: the client should be able to derive a
SHA456 hash
  // String in this format: publicKey + password. Return that string.
  let response = Sha256.hash(publicKey + "beanstalk");
  $.get("/login/" + response, (verdict) => {
    if (verdict === "failed") {
      return alert("No Dice! Not logged in.");
    }
    alert("You're in!");
  });
});
</script>
```

The server itself is very simple, composed of the two mentioned authentication routes. We can see in the following code how, upon receipt of a username (jack), the server will first check for an existing user hash in Redis, breaking the handshake if no such data is found. If a record exists we create a new, random public key, compose the relevant SHA256 hash, and return this challenge value to the client. Additionally, we set this hash as a key in Redis, with its value being the sent username:

```
const crypto = require('crypto');
const fs = require('fs');
const express = require('express');
const redis = require("redis");

let app = express();
let client = redis.createClient();

app.get('/authenticate/:username', (request, response) => {
  let publicKey = Math.random();
  let username = request.params.username; // This is always "jack"
  // ... get jack's data from redis
  client.hgetall(username, (err, data) => {
    if (err || !data) {
      return response.end("no data");
    }
    // Creating the challenge hash
    let challenge = crypto.createHash('sha256').update(publicKey +
data.password).digest('hex');
    // Store challenge for later match
    client.set(challenge, username);
    response.end(challenge);
  });
});
app.get('/login/:response', (request, response) => {
  let challengehash = request.params.response;
  client.exists(challengehash, (err, exists) => {
    if (err || !exists) {
    return response.end("failed");
    }
  });
  client.del(challengehash, () => {
    response.end("OK");
  });
});
```

In the /login/ route handler, we can see how a check is made if the response exists as a key in Redis and, if found, we immediately delete the key. This is necessary for several reasons, not least of which is preventing others to send the same response and gain access. We also generally don't want these now useless we want keys to pile up. This presents a problem: what if a client never responds to the challenge? As the key cleanup only happens when a /login/ attempt is made, this key will never be removed.

Unlike most KV data stores, Redis introduces the idea of **key expiry**, where a set operation can specify a **Time To Live** (**TTL**) for a key. For example, here, we use the setex command to set a key userId to value 183 and specify that this key should expire in one second:

```
client.setex("doomed", 10, "story", (err) => { ... });
```

This feature offers an excellent solution to our problem. By replacing the client.set(challenge, username); line with the following line:

```
client.setex(challenge, 5, username);
```

We ensure that, no matter what, this key will disappear in 5 seconds. Doing things this way also functions as a light security measure, leaving a very short window for a response to remain valid, and being naturally suspicious of delayed responses.

Using JSON Web Tokens for authentication

A basic authentication system might require a client to send a username and password on each request. To initiate a token-based authenticated session a client sends credentials just once, receives a token in exchange, and then sends only that token on subsequent requests, gaining any access that token provides. Incessantly passing around sensitive credentials is no longer required.

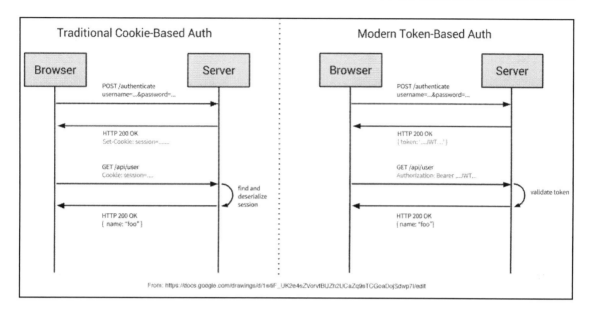

One particular advantage of JWTs is that servers are no longer responsible for maintaining access to a common database of credentials, as only the issuing authority need validate an initial sign-in. There is no need to maintain a session store when using JWTs. The issued token (think of it as an access card) can therefore be used within any domain (or server) that recognizes and accepts it. In terms of performance, the cost of a request is now the cost of decrypting a hash versus the cost of making a database call to validate credentials. We also avoid the problems one can face using cookies on mobile devices, cross-domain issues (cookies are domain-bound), certain types of request forgery attacks, and so on.

The `express-jwt` module can be useful if you want to integrate with Express: `https://github.com/auth0/express-jwt`.

Let's look at the structure of a JWT, then build a simple example demonstrating how to issue, validate, and otherwise use JWTs to manage sessions.

A JWT token has the following format:

```
<base64-encoded header>.<base64-encoded claims>.<base64-encoded signature>
```

Each segment is described in JSON format. A **header** simply describes the token -- its type and encryption algorithm. Consider this example:

```
{
  "typ":"JWT",
  "alg":"HS256"
}
```

Here, we declare that this is a JWT token, encrypted using HMAC SHA-256. See `https://nodejs.org/api/crypto.html` for more information about encryption, and how to perform encryption with Node. The JWT specification itself can be found at: `https://tools.ietf.org/html/rfc7519`.

The **claims** segment outlines security and other constraints that are should be checked by any service receiving the JWT. Check the specification for a full accounting. Typically, a JWT claims manifest will want to indicate when the JWT was issued, who issued it, when it expires, who the subject of the JWT is, and who should accept the JWT:

```
{
  "iss": "http://blogengine.com",
  "aud": ["http://blogsearch.com", "http://blogstorage"],
  "sub": "blogengine:uniqueuserid",
  "iat": "1415918312",
  "exp": "1416523112",
  "sessionData": "<some data encrypted with secret>"
}
```

The `iat` (issued-at) and `exp` (expires) claims are both set to numeric values indicating the number of seconds since the Unix epoch. The `iss` (issuer) should be a URL describing the issuer of the JWT. Any service that receives a JWT must inspect the `aud` (audience), and that service must reject the JWT if it does not appear in the audience list. The `sub` (subject) of the JWT identifies the subject of the JWT, such as the user of an application—a unique value that is never reassigned, such as the name of the issuing service and a unique user ID.

Finally, some sort of useful data is attached, using any key/value pairing you'd like. Here let's call the token data sessionData. Note that we need to encrypt this data—the signature segment of a JWT prevents tampering with session data, but JWTs are not themselves encrypted (though you can always encrypt the entire token itself).

The last step is to create a signature, which, as mentioned, prevents tampering—a JWT validator is specifically checking for mismatches between the signature and the packet received.

What follows is a scaffold server and client example demonstrating how to implement a JWT-driven authentication system. Rather than implementing the various signing and validation steps "by hand", we'll use the `jwt-simple` package. Feel free to browse the `/jwt` folder in your code bundle, which contains the full code we'll be unpacking as we move ahead.

To ask for a token, we will use the following client code:

```
function send(route, formData, cb) {
  if(!(formData instanceof FormData)) {
    cb = formData;
    formData = new FormData();
  }
  let caller = new XMLHttpRequest();
  caller.onload = function() {
    cb(JSON.parse(this.responseText));
  };
  caller.open("POST", route);
  token && caller.setRequestHeader('Authorization', 'Bearer ' + token);
  caller.send(formData);
}
```

And when we have received a `username` and `password` in some way:

```
formData = new FormData();
formData.append("username", "sandro");
formData.append("password", 'abcdefg');

send("/login", formData, function(response) {
  token = response.token;
  console.log('Set token: ' + token);
});
```

We'll implement the server code next. For now, note that we have a send method that expects at some point to have a global token set for it to pass along when making requests. The initial `/login` is where we ask for that token.

Using Express, we create the following server and `/login` route:

```
const jwt = require('jwt-simple');
const app = express();
app.set('jwtSecret', 'shhhhhhhhh');

...

app.post('/login', auth, function(req, res) {
    let nowSeconds     = Math.floor(Date.now()/1000);
```

```
    let plus7Days  = nowSeconds + (60 * 60 * 24 * 7);
    let token = jwt.encode({
        "iss"  : "http://blogengine.com",
        "aud"  : ["http://blogsearch.com", "http://blogstorage"],
        "sub"  : "blogengine:uniqueuserid",
        "iat"  : nowSeconds,
        "exp"  : plus7Days,
        "sessionData" : encrypt(JSON.stringify({
            "department" : "sales"
        }))
    }, app.get('jwtSecret'));
    res.send({
        token : token
    })
})
```

Note that we store our `jwtsecret` on the app server. This is the key that is used when signing tokens. When a login attempt is made the server will return the result of `jwt.encode`, which encodes the JWT claims discussed earlier. That's it. From now on, any client that mentions this token to the correct audience will be allowed to interact with any services those audience members provide for a period expiring 7 days from the date of issue. These services will implement something like the following:

```
app.post('/tokendata', function(req, res) {
    let </span>token = req.get('Authorization').replace('Bearer ', '');
    let decoded = jwt.decode(token, app.get('jwtSecret'));
    decoded.sessionData = JSON.parse(decrypt(decoded.sessionData));
    let now = Math.floor(Date.now()/1000);
    if(now > decoded.exp) {
        return res.end(JSON.stringify({
            error : "Token expired"
        }));
    }
    res.send(decoded)
});
```

Here, we are simply fetching the **Authorization** header (stripping out **Bearer**) and decoding via `jwt.decode`. A service must at least check for token expiry, which we do here by comparing the current number of seconds since the Epoch to the token's expiry time. Using this simple framework you can create an easily scalable authentication/session system using a secure standard. No longer required to maintain a connection to a common credentials database, individual services (deployed perhaps as microservices) can use JWTs to validate requests, incurring little CPU, latency, or memory cost.

Summary

Node provides a set of tools that help in the design and maintenance of large-scale network applications facing the C10K problem. In this chapter, we've taken our first steps into creating network applications with many simultaneous clients, tracking their session information and their credentials. This exploration into concurrency has demonstrated some techniques for routing, tracking, and responding to clients. We've touched on some simple techniques to use when scaling, such as the implementation of intra-process messaging via a publish/subscribe system built using a Redis database. We also touched on various authentication mechanisms, from basic authentication to token-based authentication with JSON Web Tokens.

We are now ready to go deeper into the design of real-time software—the logical next step after achieving high concurrency and low latency using Node. We will extend the ideas outlined during our discussion of long polling and place them in the context of more robust problems and solutions.

Further reading

Concurrency and parallelism are rich concepts that have enjoyed rigorous study and debate. When an application architecture is designed to favor threads, events, or some hybrid, it is likely that the architects are opinionated about both concepts. You are encouraged to dip a toe into the theory and read the following articles. A clear understanding of precisely what the debate is about will provide an objective framework that can be used to qualify a decision to choose (or not choose) Node:

- Some numbers: `http://citeseerx.ist.psu.edu/viewdoc/download?doi=10.1.1.154.7354rep=rep1type=pdf`
- Threads are a bad idea: `https://web.stanford.edu/~ouster/cgi-bin/papers/threads.pdf`
- Events are a bad idea: `https://people.eecs.berkeley.edu/~brewer/papers/threads-hotos-2003.pdf`
- How about together? : `https://www.cis.upenn.edu/~stevez/papers/LZ06b.pdf`
- The science: `http://courses.cs.vt.edu/cs5204/fall09-kafura/Presentations/Threads-VS-Events.pdf`

6
Creating Real-Time Applications

"Nothing endures but change."

– Heraclitus

What is real-time software? A list of friends gets updated the instant one joins or exits. Traffic updates automatically stream into the smartphones of drivers looking for the best route home. The sports page of an online newspaper immediately updates scoreboards and standings as points are scored in an actual game. Users of this type of software expect reactions to change to be communicated quickly, and this expectation demands a particular focus on reducing network latency from the software designer. Data I/O updates must occur along subsecond time frames.

Let's step back and consider the general characteristics of the Node environment and community that make it an excellent tool for creating these kinds of responsive network applications.

Some validation of Node's design, it may be argued, is found in the enormous community of open developers contributing enterprise-grade Node systems. Multicore, multiserver enterprise systems are being created using free software mostly written in JavaScript. Why are so many companies migrating toward Node when designing or updating their products? The following list enumerates the reasons why:

- Node offers the excellent npm package management system, which integrates easily with the Git version control system. A shallow learning curve helps even inexperienced developers safely store, modify, and distribute new modules, programs, and ideas. Developers can develop private modules on private Git repositories and distribute these repositories securely within a private network using npm. As a result, the community of Node users and developers has rapidly expanded, some members gaining great fame. *If you build it, they will come.*

- Node lifted the system-access barrier for a large group of skilled programmers, suddenly releasing pent-up talent into an empty volume, offering the ecosystem of opportunity that a popular new project in need of many improvements in infrastructure brings. The point is this: Node merged the opportunity of concurrency with native JavaScript events; its brilliantly designed API allowed users of a well-known programming paradigm to take advantage of high-concurrency I/O. *If you reward them, they will come.*

- Node lifted the network-access barrier for a large group of JavaScript developers whose work and ambition had begun to outgrow the tiny sandbox available to client developers. It should not be forgotten that the period of time extending from the introduction of JavaScript in 1995 to the present is now over 20 years. Nearly a generation of developers has struggled trying to implement new ideas for network applications within an event-driven development environment known for, even defined by, its limitations. Overnight, Node removed those limitations. *If you clear paths, they will come.*

- Node provides an easy way to build scalable network programs, where network I/O is no longer a bottleneck. The real shift is not from another popular system to Node—it is away from the idea that expensive and complex resources are needed to build and maintain efficient applications demanding burstable concurrency. If a resilient and scalable network architecture can be achieved cheaply, freed resources can be directed to solving other pressing software challenges, such as parallelizing data filtering, scaling massively multiplayer games, building real-time trading platforms or collaborative document editors, even implementing live code changes in hot systems. Confidence breeds progress. *If you make it easy, they will come.*

Node arrived at a time when those building dynamic web pages had begun to run up against the limitations of servers not equipped to smoothly field many small, simultaneous requests. The software architect must now solve some interesting problems: what are the rules of *real time*—will the user be satisfied with *soon*, or is *now* the only right response? And, what is the best way to design systems responsible for satisfying these user desires?

In this chapter, we will investigate three standard techniques available to developers to use when constructing real-time network applications: AJAX, WebSockets, and server-sent events (SSE). Our goals for this chapter are to learn the benefits and drawbacks of each of these techniques, and to implement each technique with Node. Remembering that we are aiming to achieve a consistent architecture reflecting the evented-streams design of Node, we will also consider how well each technique lends itself to representation as a readable, writable, or duplex stream.

We will close this chapter with the construction of a collaborative code editor, which should demonstrate the opportunities Node provides for those seeking to build real-time groupware. As you work your way through the examples, and build your own applications, these are some questions that are worth asking yourself:

- What is the volume of messages I expect to transact per second? How many simultaneously connected clients are expected at peak times and at off-peak times?
- What is the average size of the messages being transmitted?
- Can I accept occasional communication breakdowns or dropped messages if this concession buys me lower average latency?
- Do I really need bidirectional communication, or is one side responsible for nearly all message volume? Do I need a complicated communication interface at all?
- What sorts of networks will my application run within? Will there be proxy servers between a client and my Node server? Which protocols are supported?
- Do I need a complex solution or will simple and straightforward, even slightly slower, solutions bring other benefits in the long run?

Introducing AJAX

In 2005, Jesse James Garrett published an article in which he tried to condense the changes he had been seeing in the way that websites were being designed into a pattern. After studying this trend, Garrett proposed that dynamically updating pages represented a new wave of software, resembling desktop software, and he coined the acronym, *AJAX*, to describe the technological concept powering such rapid movement toward *web applications*. This was the diagram he used to demonstrate the general pattern:

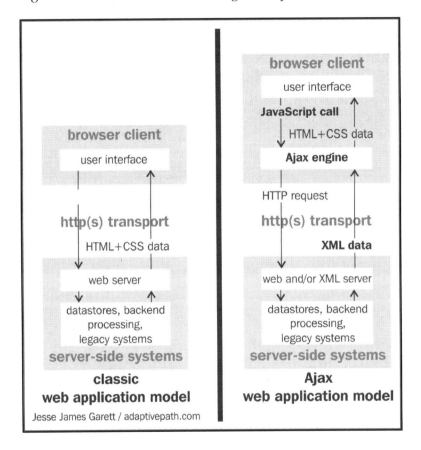

 The original article can be found at:
`http://adaptivepath.org/ideas/ajax-new-approach-web-applications/`.

The "*AJAX engine*" *Garrett's* diagram referred to had in fact existed in most common browsers by the year 2000, and even earlier in some. JavaScript implementations of the **XMLHttpRequest** (**XHR**) object in these browsers gave web pages the ability to request *chunks* of HTML or other data from servers. Partial updates could be dynamically applied to a web page, creating the opportunity for new kinds of user interfaces. For example, the latest pictures from an event could magically appear to a user, without that user actively requesting a page refresh, or clicking a **Next Picture** button.

More importantly, Garrett also understood how the synchronous, stateless world of the *old* internet was becoming an asynchronous, stateful one. The conversation between clients and servers was no longer being derailed by sudden amnesia and could continue usefully for longer periods of time, sharing increasingly useful information. Garret saw this as a shift to a new generation of network software.

Responding to calls

If changes can be introduced into a web application without requiring a complete reconstruction of state and state display, updating client information becomes cheaper. The client and server can talk more often, regularly exchanging information. Servers can recognize, remember, and respond immediately to client desires, aided by reactive interfaces gathering user actions and reflecting the impact of those actions within a UI in near real time.

With AJAX, the construction of a multiuser environment supporting real-time updates to each client's view on the overall application state involves regular polling of the server by clients checking for important updates:

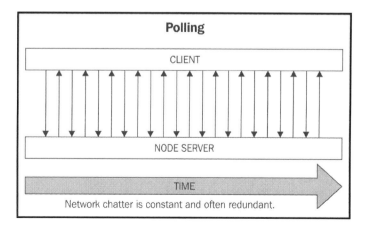

The significant drawback to this method of polling for state is that many of these requests will be fruitless. The client has become a broken record, constantly asking for status updates regardless of whether those updates are available or forthcoming. When an application spends time or energy performing unnecessary tasks, there should exist some clear benefit to the user or the provider (or both) offsetting this cost. Additionally, each futile call adds to the cost of building up then tearing down HTTP connections.

Such a system can only take snapshots of the state at periodic intervals, and as that polling interval may increase to several seconds in an effort to reduce redundant network chatter, our awareness of state changes can begin to appear dull, just a little behind the latest news. We saw a better solution in the previous chapter—long polling, the technique of letting a server hold on to a client connection until new data is available:

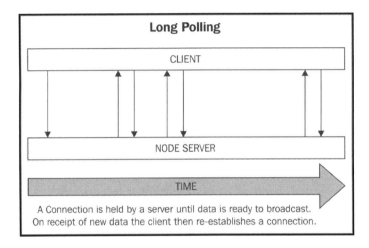

This improved AJAX technique does not fully escape the cost of building up and tearing down network connections, yet a significant reduction in the number of such costly operations is achieved. In general, AJAX fails to deliver a smooth, stream-like evented interface, requiring a great deal of attending services to persist state as connections are regularly broken and then reestablished.

Nevertheless, AJAX remains a real option for some applications, in particular simple applications where the ideal polling interval is fairly well known, each poll standing a good chance of gathering useful results. Let's use Node to build a server able to communicate with a stock reporting service, and build a polling client that periodically requests this server to check for changes and report them.

Creating a stock ticker

Ultimately, we will create an application that allows clients to pick a stock and watch for changes in the data points related to that stock, such as its price, and to highlight positive or negative changes:

To create the client, our work is minimal. We need to simply poll our server every few seconds or so, updating our interface to reflect any data changes. Let's use jQuery as our AJAX library provider. To fetch JSON from a server using jQuery, you will normally do something like this:

```
function fetch() {
  $.getJSON("/service", (data) => {
    // Do something with data
    updateDisplay(data);
    // Call again in 5 seconds
    setTimeout(fetch, 5000);
  });
}
fetch();
```

A Node server will receive this request for an update, perform some I/O (check a database, call an external service), and respond with data, which the client can use.

In our example, Node will be used to connect to the IEX Developer Platform (`https://iextrading.com/developer/`), which provides stock quotes for free.

We will construct a Node server that listens for clients requesting an update to the data for a given stock symbol, such as "IBM". The Node server will then create a YQL query for that stock symbol and execute that query via `http.get`, packaging the received data nicely for the calling client and sending it back.

This package will also be assigned a new `callIn` property, indicating the number of milliseconds the client should wait before calling again. This is a useful technique to remember, as our stock data server will have a much better idea of the traffic conditions and the update frequency than the client will. Instead of a client blindly checking on a fixed schedule, our server can recalibrate this frequency after each call, even demanding that the client stop calling!

As this design, particularly the visual design, can be done through any number of ways, we will simply look at the core functionality necessary for our client, contained within the following `fetch` method:

```
function fetch() {
  clearTimeout(caller);
  let symbol = $("#symbol").val();
  $.getJSON(`/?symbol=${symbol}`, function(data) {
    if(!data.callIn) {
      return;
    }
    caller = setTimeout(fetch, data.callIn);
    if(data.error) {
      return console.error(data.error);
    }
    let quote = data.quote;
    let keys = fetchNumericFields(quote);

    ...
    updateDisplay(symbol, quote, keys);
  });
}
```

Users on this page enter stock symbols into an input box with ID `#symbol`. This data is then fetched from our data service. In the preceding code, we see the service call being made via the `$.getJSON` jQuery method, the JSON data being received, and a `setTimeout` property being set using the `callIn` interval sent back by Node.

Our server is responsible for brokering the preceding client call with the data service. Assuming that we have a properly configured server that successfully receives stock symbols from clients, we need to open an HTTP connection to the service, read any response, and return this data:

```
https.get(query, res => {
 let data = "";
 res.on('readable', function() {
   let d;
   while(d = this.read()) {
     data += d.toString();
   }
 }).on('end', function() {
   let out = {};
   try {
     data = JSON.parse(data);
     out.quote = data;
     out.callIn = 5000;

     Object.keys(out.quote).forEach(k => {
       // Creating artificial change (random)
       // Normally, the data source would change regularly.
       v = out.quote[k];
       if(_.isFinite(v)) {
         out.quote[k] = +v + Math.round(Math.random());
       }
     })
   } catch(e) {
     out = {
       error: "Received empty data set",
       callIn: 10000
     };
   }
   response.writeHead(200, {
     "Content-type" : "application/json"
   });
   response.end(JSON.stringify(out));
 });
}).on('error', err => {
 response.writeHead(200, {
   "Content-type" : "application/json"
 });
 response.end(JSON.stringify({
   error: err.message,
   callIn: null
 }));
});
```

Here, we see a good example of why it is a good idea to let the server, the primary observer of state, modulate the frequency with which clients poll. If a successful data object is received, we set the poll interval (`callIn`) to about five seconds. Should an error occur, we increase that delay to 10 seconds. It is easy to see how we might do more, perhaps, throttling connections further if repeated errors occur. Given that, there will often be limits on the rate at which an application may make requests to an external service (such as limiting the number of calls that can be made in one hour); this is also a useful technique for ensuring that constant client polling doesn't exceed these rate limits.

AJAX is the original technique for creating real-time applications. It remains useful in some cases, but has been superseded by more efficient transports. As we leave this section, let's keep in mind some of the advantages and disadvantages of polling:

Pros	Cons
The theory and practice of REST is available, allowing more standardized communication	Making and breaking connections imposes a cost on network latency, especially if done very often
No need for any special protocol server, with polling easily implemented using a standard HTTP server	Clients must request data; servers are unable to unilaterally update clients as new data arrives
HTTP is well-known and consistently implemented	Even long polling doubles the network traffic needed to maintain a persistent connection
	Data is blindly pushed and pulled, rather than smoothly broadcast and listened for on channels

Let's move on now into a discussion of some newer protocols, in part designed to solve some of the issues we've found with AJAX: WebSockets and SSE.

Bidirectional communication with socket.io

We're already familiar with what sockets are. In particular, we know how to establish and manage TCP socket connections using Node, as well as how to pipe data through them bidirectionally or unidirectionally.

The W3C has proposed a socket API that allows browsers to communicate with a socket server over a persistent connection. socket.io is a library that facilitates the establishment of persistent socket connections for those developing with Node, providing both a Node-based socket server and an emulation layer for browsers that do not support the WebSocket API natively.

Let's first take a brief look at how the native WebSocket API is implemented, and how to build a socket server supporting this protocol using Node. We will then build a collaborative drawing application using socket.io with Node.

 The full specification for the WebSocket API can be found at: http://www.w3.org/TR/websockets/. Documentation and installation instructions for socket.io can be found at: https://socket.io/

Using the WebSocket API

Socket communication is efficient, only occurring when one of the parties has something useful to say:

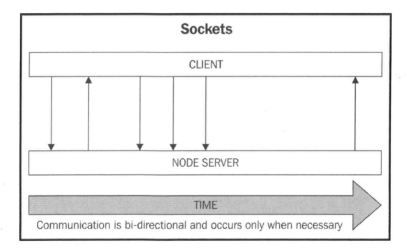

This lightweight model is an excellent choice for applications that require high-frequency message passing between a client and a server, such as found in multiplayer network games or chat rooms.

According to the W3C, the WebSocket API is intended *to "enable web applications to maintain bidirectional communications with server-side processes."* Assuming that we have established a socket server running at `localhost:8080`, we can connect to this server from a browser containing the following line of JavaScript:

```
let conn = new WebSocket("ws://localhost:8080", ['json', 'xml']);
```

`WebSocket` expects two arguments: an URL prefixed by the URI scheme `ws://`, and an optional subprotocol list, which can be an array or a single string of protocols that a server may implement.

 To establish a secure socket connection, use the `wss://` prefix. As with HTTPS servers, you'll need an SSL certificate.

Once a socket request is made, the connection events, open, close, error, and message can be handled by a browser:

```
<head>
  <title></title>
   <script>

      let conn = new WebSocket("ws://localhost:8080", 'json');
      conn.onopen = () => {
        conn.send('Hello from the client!');
      };
      conn.onerror = (error) => {
        console.log('Error! ' + error);
      };
      conn.onclose = () => {
        console.log("Server has closed the connection!");
      };
      conn.onmessage = (msg) => {
        console.log('Received: ' + msg.data);
      };
   </script>
</head>
```

For this example, we'll implement a `WebSocket` server in Node using the ws module at: `https://github.com/websockets/ws`. After installing ws using npm (`npm i ws`), establishing a Node socket server is straightforward:

```
let SocketServer = require('ws').Server;
  let wss = new SocketServer({port: 8080});
  wss.on('connection', ws => {
    ws.on('message', (message) => {
      console.log('received: %s', message);
    });
    ws.send("You've connected!");
  });
```

Here, we see how the server simply listens for the `connection` and `message` events from clients, responding as necessary. Should there be a need to terminate a connection (perhaps, if the client loses authorization), the server can simply emit a `close` event, which a client can listen for:

```
ws.close();
```

The general schematic for an application using the WebSocket API to create bidirectional communication therefore looks like this:

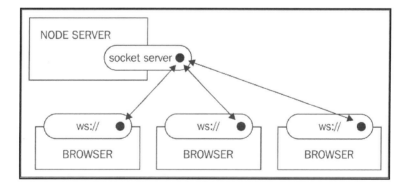

The native WebSocket browser implementation is used here to communicate with our custom Node socket server, which fields requests from the client as well as broadcasting new data or information to the client when necessary.

socket.io

As mentioned previously, socket.io aims to provide an emulation layer that will use the native WebSocket implementation in browsers that support it, reverting to other methods (such as long polling) to simulate the native API in legacy browsers that don't. This is an important fact to keep in mind: there are still some old browsers out there.

Nevertheless, socket.io does a very good job of hiding browser differences and remains a good choice when the control flow made available by sockets is a desirable model of communication for your application.

In the WebSocket implementation used in the preceding example (ws), it is clear that the socket server is independent of any specific client file. We wrote some JavaScript to establish a WebSocket connection on a client, independently running a socket server using Node. Unlike this native implementation, socket.io requires a custom client library to be installed on a server in addition to the socket.io server module:

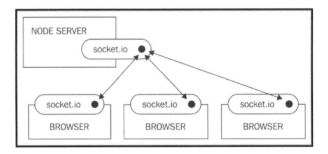

socket.io can be installed using the npm package manager:

```
$ npm install socket.io
```

Setting up a client/server socket pairing is straightforward.

On the server:

```
let io = require('socket.io').listen(8080);
io.sockets.on('connection', socket => {
  socket.emit('broadcast', { message: 'Hi!' });
  socket.on('clientmessage', data => {
    console.log("Client said" + data);
  });
});
```

On the client:

```
<script src="/socket.io/socket.io.js"></script>
 <script>
   let socket = io.connect('http://localhost:8080');
   socket.on('broadcast', data => {
     console.log(`Server sent: ${JSON.stringify(data)}`);
     socket.emit('clientmessage', { message: 'ohai!' });
   });
 </script>
```

We can see how both the client and the server are using the same file, `socket.io.js`. A server using `socket.io` handles the serving of the `socket.io.js` file to clients automatically when requested. It should also jump out how closely the `socket.io` API resembles a standard Node `EventEmitter` interface.

Drawing collaboratively

Let's create a collaborative drawing application using `socket.io` and Node. We want to create a blank canvas that will simultaneously display all the *pen work* being done by connected clients:

From the server end, there is very little to do. When a client updates coordinates by moving their mouse, the server simply broadcasts this change to all connected clients:

```
io.sockets.on('connection', socket => {
  let id = socket.id;

  socket.on('mousemove', data => {
    data.id = id;
    socket.broadcast.emit('moving', data);
  });
```

```
    socket.on('disconnect', () => {
      socket.broadcast.emit('clientdisconnect', id);
    });
  });
```

`socket.io` automatically generates a unique ID for each socket connection. We will pass this ID along whenever new draw events occur, allowing the receiving clients to track how many users are connected. Similarly, when a client disconnects, all other clients are instructed to remove their references to this client. Later, we will see how this ID is used within the application UI to maintain a pointer representing all connected clients.

This is an excellent example of just how simple it is to create multiuser network applications using Node and the packages created by the Node community. Let's break down what this server is doing.

Because we will need to deliver the HTML file that clients will use to draw, half of the server setup involves creating a static file server. For convenience, we'll use the node-static package at: `https://github.com/cloudhead/node-static`. Our implementation will serve an `index.html` file to any client who connects.

Our `socket.io` implementation expects to receive `mousemove` events from clients, and its only task is to send to all connected clients these new coordinates, which it does by emitting a moving event through its `broadcast` method. As one client changes the canvas state by drawing a line, all clients will receive the information necessary to update their view of the canvas state in real time.

With the communication layer built, we now must create client views. As mentioned, each client will load an `index.html` file containing the necessary canvas element, and the JavaScript necessary to listen for moving events, as well the `socket.io` emitter broadcasting client draw events to our server:

```
<head>
    <style type="text/css">
    /* CSS styling for the pointers and canvas */
    </style>
    <script src="/socket.io/socket.io.js"></script>
    <script src="/script.js"></script>
</head>
<body>
    <div id="pointers"></div>
    <canvas id="canvas" width="2000" height="1000"></canvas>
</body>
```

A `pointers` element is created to hold visible representations for the cursors of all connected clients, which will update as connected clients move their pointers and/or draw something.

Within the `script.js` file, we first set up event listeners on the `canvas` element, watching for the combination of `mousedown` and `mousemove` events indicating a draw action. Note how we create a time buffer of 50 milliseconds, delaying the broadcast of each draw event, slightly reducing the resolution of drawings but avoiding an excessive number of network events:

```
let socket = io.connect("/");
let prev = {};
let canvas = document.getElementById('canvas');
let context = canvas.getContext('2d');
let pointerContainer = document.getElementById("pointers");

let pointer = document.createElement("div");
pointer.setAttribute("class", "pointer");

let drawing = false;
let clients = {};
let pointers = {};

function drawLine(fromx, fromy, tox, toy) {
  context.moveTo(fromx, fromy);
  context.lineTo(tox, toy);
  context.stroke();
}
function now() {
  return new Date().getTime();
}
let lastEmit = now();
canvas.onmouseup = canvas.onmousemove = canvas.onmousedown = function(e) {
  switch(e.type) {
    case "mouseup":
      drawing = false;
      break;
    case "mousemove":
      if(now() - lastEmit > 50) {
        socket.emit('mousemove', {
          'x' : e.pageX,
          'y' : e.pageY,
          'drawing' : drawing
        });
        lastEmit = now();
      }
```

```
        if(drawing) {
          drawLine(prev.x, prev.y, e.pageX, e.pageY);
          prev.x = e.pageX;
          prev.y = e.pageY;
        }
        break;
      case "mousedown":
        drawing = true;
        prev.x = e.pageX;
        prev.y = e.pageY;
        break;
      default:
        break;
    }
  };
```

Whenever a draw action occurs (a combination of a `mousedown` and a `mousemove` event), we draw the requested line on the client's machine, and then broadcast these new coordinates to our `socket.io` server via `socket.emit('mousemove', ...)`, remembering to pass along the `id` value of the drawing client. The server in turn will broadcast them via `socket.broadcast.emit('moving', data)`, allowing client listeners to draw equivalent lines on their `canvas` element:

```
socket.on('moving', data => {
  if (!clients.hasOwnProperty(data.id)) {
    pointers[data.id] = pointerContainer.appendChild(pointer.cloneNode());
  }
  pointers[data.id].style.left = data.x + "px";
  pointers[data.id].style.top = data.y + "px";

  if (data.drawing && clients[data.id]) {
    drawLine(clients[data.id].x, clients[data.id].y, data.x, data.y);
  }
  clients[data.id] = data;
  clients[data.id].updated = now();
});
```

Within this listener, a client will establish a new client pointer if the sent client ID has not been seen previously, and animate both the drawing of a line and the client pointer, creating the effect of multiple cursors drawing distinct lines within a single client view.

Recalling the `clientdisconnect` event we track on our server, we also enable clients to listen for these disconnects, removing references to lost clients from both the view (visual pointer) and our `clients` object:

```
socket.on("clientdisconnect", id => {
  delete clients[id];
  if (pointers[id]) {
    pointers[id].parentNode.removeChild(pointers[id]);
  }
});
```

`socket.io` is an excellent tool to consider when building interactive, multiuser environments where continuous rapid bidirectional data transfer is necessary. Now, take a look at the pros and cons of `socket.io`:

Pros	Cons
Rapid bidirectional communication essential to real-time games, collaborative editing tools, and other applications	The number of allowed persistent socket connections can be limited on the server side or anywhere in between
Lower overhead than standard HTTP protocol requests, lowering the price of sending a package across the network	Many proxies and reverse proxies are known to confound socket implementations, leading to lost clients
The evented, streaming nature of sockets fits conceptually with the Node architecture—clients and servers are simply piping data back and forth through consistent interfaces	Requires a custom protocol server, and often a custom client library

> Another interesting project is SockJS, which implements socket servers in many different languages, including Node.js. Check out: `https://github.com/sockjs/sockjs-node`.

Listening for Server Sent Events

SSE are uncomplicated and specific. They are to be used when the majority of data transfer proceeds unidirectionally from a server to clients. A traditional and similar concept is the *push* technology. SSE pass text messages with simple formatting. Many types of applications passively receive brief status updates or data state changes. SSE are an excellent fit for these types of applications.

Like `WebSocket`, SSE also eliminate the redundant chatter of AJAX. Unlike `WebSocket`, an SSE connection is only concerned with broadcasting data from servers to connected clients:

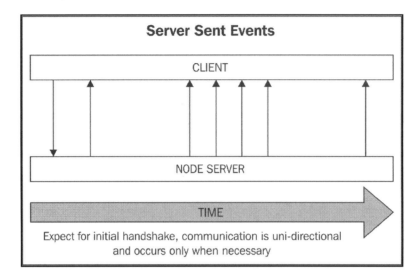

A client connects to a server supporting SSE by passing the `EventSource` constructor a path:

```
let eventSource = new EventSource('/login');
```

This instance of `EventSource` will now emit subscribable data events whenever new data is received from the server.

Using the EventSource API

The way in which `EventSource` instances emit subscribable data events whenever new data is received from the server is like the way `Readable` streams emit data events in Node, as we can see in this example client:

```
<script>
  let eventSource = new EventSource('/login');
  eventSource.addEventListener('message', (broadcast) => {
    console.log("got message: " + broadcast);
  });
  eventSource.addEventListener('open', () => {
    console.log("connection opened");
  });
  eventSource.addEventListener('error', () => {
```

```
        console.log("connection error/closed");
    });
  </script>
```

An EventSource instance emits three default events:

- open: When a connection is successfully opened, this event will fire
- message: The handler assigned to this event will receive an object whose data property contains the broadcast message
- error: This fires whenever a server error occurs, or the server disconnects or otherwise severs its connection with this client

Forming part of the standard HTTP protocol, a server responsive to SSE requests requires minimal configuration. The following server will accept EventSource bindings and broadcast the current date to the bound client every second:

```
const http = require("http");
const url = require("url");
http.createServer((request, response) => {
  let parsedURL = url.parse(request.url, true);
  let pathname = parsedURL.pathname;
  let args = pathname.split("/");
  let method = args[1];
  if (method === "login") {
    response.writeHead(200, {
      "Content-Type": "text/event-stream",
      "Cache-Control": "no-cache",
      "Connection": "keep-alive"
    });
    response.write(":" + Array(2049).join(" ") + "\n");
    response.write("retry: 2000\n");
    response.on("close", () => {
      console.log("client disconnected");
    });
    setInterval(() => {
      response.write("data: " + new Date() + "\n\n");
    }, 1000);
    return;
  }
}).listen(8080);
```

This server listens for requests and selects those made on the path /login, which it interprets as a request for an EventSource binding. Establishing an EventSource connection is simply a matter of responding to the request with a Content-Type header of text/event-stream. Additionally, we indicate that the client's Cache-Control behavior should be set to no-cache, as we expect a lot of original material on this channel.

From the point of connection, the response object of this client will remain an open pipe that messages can be sent through using write. Let's look at the next two lines:

```
response.write(":" + Array(2049).join(" ") + "\n");
response.write("retry: 2000\n");
```

 This first write is adjusting for an XHR implementation feature in some browsers, which ultimately requires all SSE streams to be prefixed by a 2-KB padding. This write action need happen only once, and has no relevance to subsequent messages.

One of the advantages of SSE is that clients will automatically try to reconnect with the server, should that connection be severed. The number of milliseconds before retrying will vary from client to client, and can be controlled using the retry field, which we use here to set a two-millisecond retry interval.

Finally, we listen for the client's close event, which fires when a client disconnects, and begins broadcasting the time on a one-second interval:

```
setInterval(() => {
  response.write("data: " + new Date() + "\n\n");
}, 1000);
```

A website might bind to this time server and display the current server time:

```
<html>
  <head>
    <script>
      let ev = new EventSource('/login');
      ev.addEventListener("message", broadcast => {
        document.getElementById("clock").innerHTML = broadcast.data;
      });
    </script>
  </head>
  <body>
    <div id="clock"></div>
  </body>
</html>
```

Because the connection is one way, any number of services can be set up as publishers very easily, with clients binding individually to these services via new EventSource instances. Server monitoring, for example, could be achieved easily by modifying the preceding server so that it periodically sends the value of process.memoryUsage(). As an exercise, use SSE to reimplement the stocks service we covered earlier in the section on AJAX.

The EventSource stream protocol

Once a server has established a client connection, it may now send new messages across this persistent connection at any time. These messages consist of one or more lines of text, demarcated by one or several of the following four fields:

- event: This is an event type. Messages sent without this field will trigger the client's general EventSource event handler for any message. If set to a string such as *latestscore*, the client's message handler will not be called, with handling being delegated to a handler bound using EventSource.addEventListener('latestscore'...).
- data: This is the message being sent. This is always of the String type, though it can usefully transport objects passed through JSON.stringify().
- id: If set, this value will appear as the lastEventID property of the sent message object. This can be useful for ordering, sorting, and other operations on the client.
- retry: The reconnection interval, in milliseconds.

Sending messages involves composing strings containing relevant field names and ending with newlines. These are all valid messages:

```
response.write("id:" + (++message_counter) + "\n");
response.write("data: I'm a message\n\n");
response.write("retry: 10000\n\n");
response.write("id:" + (++message_counter) + "\n");
response.write("event: stock\n");
response.write("data: " + JSON.stringify({price: 100, change: -2}) +
"\n\n");
response.write("event: stock\n");
response.write("data: " + stock.price + "\n");
response.write("data: " + stock.change + "\n");
response.write("data: " + stock.symbol + "\n\n");
response.write("data: Hello World\n\n");
```

We can see that multiple data fields can be set as well. An important thing to note is the double newline ("\n\n") to be sent after the final data field. Previous fields should just use a single newline.

The default EventSource client events (open, message, and close) are sufficient for modeling most application interfaces. All broadcasts from the server are caught within the solitary message handler, which takes responsibility for routing the message or otherwise updating the client, in the same way that event delegation would work when working with events in the DOM using JavaScript.

This system may not be ideal in cases where many unique message identifiers are needed, overwhelming a single handling function. We can use the event field of SSE messages to create custom event names that can be individually bound by a client, neatly separating concerns.

For example, if two special events actionA and actionB are being broadcast, our server would structure them like this:

```
event: actionA\n
data: Message A here\n\n

event: actionB\n
data: Message B here\n\n
```

Our client would bind to them in the normal way, as shown in the following code snippet:

```
ev.addEventListener("actionA", (broadcast) => {
    console.log(broadcast.data);
});
ev.addEventListener("actionB", (broadcast) => {
    console.log(broadcast.data);
});
```

In cases where a single message handling function is becoming too long or too complex, consider uniquely named messages and handlers.

Asking questions and getting answers

What if we wanted to create an interface to interests? Let's build an application enabling any number of people to ask and/or answer questions. Our users will join the community server, see a list of open questions and answers to those questions, and get real-time updates whenever a new question or answer is added. There are two key activities to model:

- Each client must be notified whenever another client asks a question or posts an answer
- A client can ask questions or supply answers

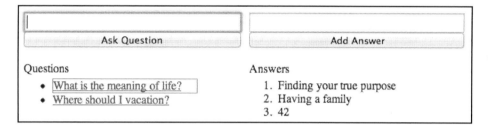

Where would the greatest amount of change happen in a large group of simultaneous contributors to this community?

Any individual client can potentially ask a few questions or provide a few answers. Clients will also select questions and have the answers displayed to them. We will need to satisfy merely a handful of client-to-server requests, such as when sending a new question or answer to the server. Most of the work will be in satisfying client requests with data (a list of answers to a question) and broadcasting application state changes to all connected clients (new question added; new answer given). The one-to-many relationship existing for clients within such collaborative applications implies that a single client broadcast may create a number of server broadcasts equal to the number of connected clients—1 to 10,000 or more. SSE are a great fit here, so let's get started.

The three main operations for this application are as follows:

- Asking a question
- Answering a question
- Selecting a question

Either of these actions will change the application state. As this state must be reflected across all clients, we will store the state of our application on our server—all questions, answers, and the relationships of clients to these data objects. We will also need to uniquely identify each client. Normally, one would use a database to persist some of this information, but for our purposes, we will simply store this data in our Node server:

```
let clients = {};
let clientQMap = {};
let questions = {};
let answers    = {};

function removeClient(id) {
  if(id) {
    delete clients[id];
    delete clientQMap[id];
  }
}
```

In addition to the `questions` and `answers` storage objects, we will also need to store client objects themselves—clients are assigned a unique ID that can be used to look up information (such as the client's socket) when broadcasts are made.

We only want to broadcast answer data to clients that have expressed an interest in the specific question—as client UIs are only displaying answers for a single question, we, of course, would not broadcast answers to clients indiscriminately. For this reason, we keep a `clientQMap` object, which maps a question to all clients listening to that question, by the ID.

The `removeClient` method is straightforward: when a client disconnects, the method removes its data from the pool. We'll see this again later.

With this setup in place, we next need to build our server to respond the `/login` path, which is used by `EventSource` to grab a connection. This service is responsible for configuring a proper event-stream for clients, storing this `Response` object for later use, and assigning the user a unique identifier, which will be used on future client requests to identify the client and fetch that client's communication socket:

```
http.createServer((request, response) => {
  let parsedURL = url.parse(request.url, true);
  let pathname = parsedURL.pathname;
  let args = pathname.split("/");
  //  Lose initial null value
  args.shift();
  let method = args.shift();
  let parameter = decodeURIComponent(args[0]);
```

```
    let sseUserId = request.headers['_sse_user_id_'];
    if (method === "login") {
      response.writeHead(200, {
        "Content-Type": "text/event-stream",
        "Cache-Control": "no-cache"
    });
    response.write(":" + Array(2049).join(" ") + "\n"); // 2kB
    response.write("retry: 2000\n");
    removeClient(sseUserId);
    // A very simple id system. You'll need something more secure.
    sseUserId = (USER_ID++).toString(36);
    clients[sseUserId] = response;
    broadcast(sseUserId, {
      type : "login",
      userId : sseUserId
    });
    broadcast(sseUserId, {
      type : "questions",
      questions : questions
    });
    response.on("close", () => {
      removeClient(sseUserId);
    });

    // To keep the conn alive we send a "heartbeat" every 10 seconds.
    // https://bugzilla.mozilla.org/show_bug.cgi?id=444328
    setInterval(() => {
      broadcast(sseUserId, new Date().getTime(), "ping");
    }, 10000);
    return;
}).listen(8080);
```

After establishing request parameters, our servers check the request for a `_sse_user_id_`
header, which is the unique string that is assigned to a user within `/login` on the initial
`EventSource` bind:

```
sseUserId = (USER_ID++).toString(36);
clients[sseUserId] = response;
```

This ID is then sent to the client via an immediate broadcast, an opportunity we use to send along the current batch of questions:

```
broadcast(sseUserId, sseUserId, "login");
```

The client is now responsible for passing along this ID whenever it makes a call. By listening for the /login event and storing the ID that is passed, a client can self-identify when making HTTP calls:

```
evSource.addEventListener('login', broadcast => {
  USER_ID = JSON.parse(broadcast.data);
});
let xhr = new XMLHttpRequest();
xhr.open("POST", "/...");
xhr.setRequestHeader('_sse_user_id_', USER_ID);
...
```

Recall that we have just created a unidirectional event-stream from our server to our client. This channel is used to communicate with clients—not response.end() or similar. The broadcast method, referenced in /login, accomplishes this task of broadcasting stream events, as shown in the following code:

```
let broadcast = function(toId, msg, eventName) {
  if (toId === "*") {
    for (let p in clients) {
      broadcast(p, msg);
    }
    return;
  }
  let clientSocket = clients[toId];
  if (!clientSocket) {
    return;
  }
  eventName && clientSocket.write(`event: ${eventName}\n`);
  clientSocket.write(`id: ${++UNIQUE_ID}\n`);
  clientSocket.write(`data: ${JSON.stringify(msg)}\n\n`);
}
```

Scan this code from the bottom up. Note how the primary purpose of broadcast is to take a client ID, look up that client's event stream, and write to it, accepting a custom event name if needed. However, as we will regularly broadcast to all connected clients, we allow for a special * flag to indicate mass broadcast.

Everything is now set up, requiring only the definition of services for the three main operations for this application: adding new questions and answers, and remembering the question each client is following.

When questions are asked, we ensure that the question is unique, add it to our `question` collection, and tell everyone the new question list:

```
if (method === "askquestion") {
  // Already asked?
  if (questions[parameter]) {
    return response.end();
  }
  questions[parameter] = sseUserId;
  broadcast("*", {
    type : "questions",
    questions : questions
  });
  return response.end();
}
```

Handling answers is nearly identical, except that here we want to broadcast new answers only to clients asking the right questions:

```
if (method === "addanswer") {
    ...
  answers[curUserQuestion] = answers[curUserQuestion] || [];
  answers[curUserQuestion].push(parameter);
  for (var id in clientQMap) {
    if (clientQMap[id] === curUserQuestion) {
      broadcast(id, {
        type : "answers",
        question : curUserQuestion,
        answers : answers[curUserQuestion]
      });
    }
  }
  return response.end();
}
```

Finally, we store changes to the client's interests by updating `clientQMap`:

```
if (method === "selectquestion") {
  if (parameter && questions[parameter]) {
    clientQMap[sseUserId] = parameter;
    broadcast(sseUserId, {
      type : "answers",
      question : parameter,
```

```
      answers : answers[parameter] ? answers[parameter] : []
    });
  }
  return response.end();
}
```

While we won't go too deeply into the client-side HTML and JavaScript necessary to render this interface, we will look at how some of the core events would be handled.

Assuming a UI rendered in HTML, which lists answers on one side and questions on the other, containing forms for adding new questions and answers, as well as for selecting questions to follow, our client code is very lightweight and easy to follow. After negotiating the initial /login handshake with our server, this client need simply send new data via HTTP when submitted. The handling of server responses is neatly encapsulated into three events, making for easy-to-follow event stream handling:

```
let USER_ID = null;
let evSource = new EventSource('/login');
let answerContainer = document.getElementById('answers');
let questionContainer = document.getElementById('questions');

let showAnswer = (answers) => {
  answerContainer.innerHTML = "";
  let x = 0;
  for (; x < answers.length; x++) {
    let li = document.createElement('li');
    li.appendChild(document.createTextNode(answers[x]));
    answerContainer.appendChild(li);
  }
}

let showQuestion = (questions) => {
  questionContainer.innerHTML = "";
  for (let q in questions) {
    //... show questions, similar to #showAnswer
  }
}

evSource.addEventListener('message', (broadcast) => {
  let data = JSON.parse(broadcast.data);
  switch (data.type) {
    case "questions":
      showQuestion(data.questions);
    break;
    case "answers":
      showAnswer(data.answers);
    break;
```

```
      case "notification":
        alert(data.message);
      break;
      default:
        throw "Received unknown message type";
      break;
    }
  });

  evSource.addEventListener('login', (broadcast) => {
    USER_ID = JSON.parse(broadcast.data);
  });
```

This interface needs only to wait for new question and answer data, and display it in lists. Three callbacks are enough to keep this client up to date, regardless of how many different clients update the application's state.

Pros	Cons
Lightweight: By using the native HTTP protocol, an SSE server can be created with a couple of simple headers	Inconsistent browser support requires a custom library for client-to-server communication, where unsupported browsers will normally long poll
Able to send data to a client unilaterally, without requiring matching client calls	One way only: Does not bring its advantages to cases where bidirectional communication is needed
Automatic reconnection of dropped connections, making SSE a reliable network binding	Server must send a "heartbeat" every 10 seconds or so in order to keep the connection alive
Simple, easily customizable, and an easy-to-understand messaging format	

 EventSource is not supported by all browsers (in particular, IE). An excellent emulation library for SSE can be found at: https://github.com/Yaffle/EventSource.

Building a collaborative document editing application

Now that we've examined various techniques to consider when building a collaborative application, let's put together a collaborative code editor using **Operational transformation (OT)**.

For our discussion here, OT will be understood as a technology that allows many people to edit the same document concurrently—collaborative document editing. Google described their (now defunct) Wave project in the following way:

> *As* https://svn.apache.org/repos/asf/incubator/wave/whitepapers/operational-transform/operational-transform.html *says, "Collaborative document editing means multiple editors are able to edit a shared document at the same time. It is live and concurrent when a user can see the changes another person is making, keystroke by keystroke. Google Wave offers live concurrent editing of rich text documents.".*

One of the engineers involved in the Wave project was Joseph Gentle, and Mr. Gentle was kind enough to write a module bringing OT technology to the Node community, named **ShareJS**, which later became **ShareDB**, the OT backend for the Derby web framework (http://derbyjs.com/). We are going to use this module to create an application that allows anyone to create a new collaboratively editable document.

 This example liberally borrows from the many examples contained in the ShareDB GitHub repository. To delve deeper into the possibilities of ShareDB, visit: https://github.com/share/sharedb.

To begin with, we will need a code editor to bind our OT layer to. For this project, we will use the excellent Quill editor, which can be cloned from: https://github.com/quilljs/quill. Quill is especially suited to working with ShareDB, as it is designed to represent documents as a sequence of changesets represented in JSON (https://github.com/ottypes/rich-text), which can be mapped to the OT types that ShareDB understands. While out of scope for this section, it might benefit the reader to dig into how OT works, especially with these two libraries.

Being a collaborative, real-time application, we will use the **ws** socket server to manage communication between clients and the database, and **Express** to manage serving static files, such as index.html.

In your code bundle for this chapter, there will be a sharedb folder. To install and try it out, run the following commands:

```
npm i
npm run build
npm start
// Now navigate to localhost:8080 and start editing.
// Open another browser to localhost:8080 to see collaboration in action!
```

The two main files there will be client.js and server.js. The client.js file will be bundled using **Browserify**, generating the JavaScript the client will use. Let's look at the client.js file:

```
const sharedb = require('sharedb/lib/client');
const richText = require('rich-text');
const Quill = require('quill');

sharedb.types.register(richText.type);

const socket = new WebSocket('ws://' + window.location.host);
const connection = new sharedb.Connection(socket);

window.disconnect = () => connection.close();
window.connect = () => connection.bindToSocket(new WebSocket('ws://' +
window.location.host));

// 0: Name of collection
// 1: ID of document
let doc = connection.get('examples', 'richtext');

doc.subscribe(err => {
  if(err) {
    throw err;
  }
  let quill = new Quill('#editor', {
    theme: 'snow'
  });
  quill.setContents(doc.data);
  // ... explained below
});
```

The header of this file simply instantiates ShareDB, setting its document type to rich-text, and providing the instance with a communication socket to the server. For the purposes of this demonstration, we're going to operate on a single collection examples and the one file richtext. This collection/document pairing is how you work with documents in ShareDB, and is reflected in the server.js file we'll be looking at shortly. In a more advanced implementation, you will likely need to create some sort of collection/document management layer, linking those collections to certain users, adding user accounts, permissions, and so forth.

Once we've established a subscription to the server, we bind a new Quill instance to the #editor element, set its contents (quill.setContents) to whatever the server returns as the current document, declaring that we'd like to use the snow theme, whose css we've included in index.html:

```html
<!DOCTYPE html>
<html lang="en">
<head>
  ...
  <link href="quill.snow.css" rel="stylesheet">
</head>
<body>
  <div id="editor"></div>
  <script src="dist/bundle.js"></script>
</body>
</html>
```

All that is left to do is create the Node server exposing the functionality of OT to the client. To do this, we will need to accept OT changes (deltas) from the server and apply those changes to the Quill editor, and report changes to the server as a user uses the Quill editor:

```js
doc.subscribe(err => {
  ...
  quill.setContents(doc.data);
  quill.on('text-change', (delta, oldDelta, source) => {
    ...
    doc.submitOp(delta, {
      source: quill
    });
  });
  doc.on('op', (op, source) => {
    ...
    quill.updateContents(op);
  });
}
```

We're now set up to update the document database whenever there is a `text-change` in the Quill editor, and to `updateContents` of any connected client editor whenever there is a new `op` on the shared document.

The server implementation largely reflects the client implementation:

```
const http = require('http');
const express = require('express');
const ShareDB = require('sharedb');
const richText = require('rich-text');
const WebSocket = require('ws');
const WebSocketJSONStream = require('websocket-json-stream');

ShareDB.types.register(richText.type);

const app = express();
app.use(express.static('static'));
app.use(express.static('node_modules/quill/dist'));

const backend = new ShareDB();
const connection = backend.connect();

// 0: Name of collection
// 1: ID of document
let doc = connection.get('examples', 'richtext');

doc.fetch(err => {
  if (err) {
    throw err;
  }
  if (doc.type === null) {
    return doc.create([
      {insert: 'Say Something!'}
    ], 'rich-text', startServer);
  }
  startServer();
});

function startServer() {
  const server = http.createServer(app);
  const wss = new WebSocket.Server({server: server});
  wss.on('connection', (ws, req) => {
    backend.listen(new WebSocketJSONStream(ws));
  });
  server.listen(8080, () => console.log('Editor now live on
http://localhost:8080'));
}
```

We require all of the libraries, making a note of the websocket-json-stream requirement, a library that creates a JSON object stream across the socket, needed to represent the JSON changesets we will be working with.

We then establish the collection/document setup our client expects, creating the document with some dummy text, "Say something!" if the document does not exist. The only thing left to do is to bind the ShareDB backend to this bidirectional JSON Object stream:

```
backend.listen(new WebSocketJSONStream(ws))
```

This server can now be used to share document state across all clients requesting identically named documents, facilitating collaborative editing.

Summary

In this chapter, we've gone over three of the major strategies employed when building real-time applications: AJAX, WebSocket, and SSE. We've shown that non-trivial collaborative applications can be developed with very little code using Node. We've also seen how some of these strategies enable the modeling of client/server communication as an evented data stream interface. We've considered the pros and cons of these various techniques, and we've gone through some clear examples of the best places to use each one.

Additionally, we've shown how client identifiers and state data can be built and managed within a Node server, so that state changes can be safely encapsulated in a central location and broadcast out to many connected clients safely and predictably. Demonstrating the quality of the modules being developed with the Node community, we created a collaborative code editing system through the use of operational transformation.

In the next chapter, we will be looking at how to coordinate the efforts of multiple Node processes running simultaneously. Through examples, we will learn how to achieve parallel processing with Node, from spawning many child processes running Unix programs to creating clusters of load-balancing Node socket servers.

7

Using Multiple Processes

"It is a very sad thing that nowadays there is so little useless information."

– Oscar Wilde

The importance of I/O efficiency is not lost on those witnessing the rapidly increasing volume of data being produced within a growing number of applications. User-generated content (blogs, videos, tweets, and posts) is becoming the premier type of internet content, and this trend has moved in tandem with the rise of social software, where mapping the intersections between content generates an exponential rise in yet another level of data.

A number of data silos, such as Google, Facebook, and hundreds of others, expose their data to the public through an API, often for free. These networks each gather astounding volumes of content, opinions, relationships, and so forth from their users, data further augmented by market research and various types of traffic and usage analysis. Most of these APIs are two-way, gathering and storing data uploaded by their members as well as serving that data.

Node has arrived during this period of data expansion. In this chapter, we will investigate how Node addresses this need for sorting, merging, searching, and otherwise manipulating large amounts of data. Fine-tuning your software so that it can process large amounts of data safely and inexpensively is critical when building fast and scalable network applications.

We will deal with specific scaling issues in the next chapter. In this chapter, we will study some best practices when designing systems where multiple Node processes work together on large volumes of data.

As part of that discussion, we will be investigating strategies for parallelism when building data-heavy applications, focusing on how to take advantage of multiple CPU environments, use multiple workers, and leverage the OS itself to achieve the efficiency of parallelism. The process of assembling applications out of these contained and efficient processing units will be demonstrated by example.

As noted in `Chapter 5`, *Managing Many Simultaneous Client Connections*, concurrency is not the same as parallelism. The goal of concurrency is good structure for programs, where modeling the complexities inherent in juggling multiple simultaneous processes is simplified. The goal of parallelism is to increase application performance by sharing parts of a task or computation across many workers. It is useful to recall *Clinger's* vision of "...dozens, hundreds or even thousands of independent microprocessors, each with its own local memory and communications processor, communicating via a high-performance communications network."

We've already discussed how Node helps us reason about non-deterministic control flow. Let's also recall how Node's designers follow the **Rule Of Modularity**, which encourages us to write simple parts connected by clean interfaces. This rule leads to a preference for simple networked processes communicating with each other using a common protocol. An associated rule is the **Rule of Simplicity**, stated as follows:

> *As* `https://en.wikipedia.org/wiki/Unix_philosophy` *says, "developers should design for simplicity by looking for ways to break up program systems into small, straightforward cooperating pieces. This rule aims to discourage developers' affection for writing "intricate and beautiful complexities" that are bug prone programs in reality."*

It is good to keep this rule in mind as we proceed through this chapter. To tame expanding data volume, we can build enormous, complex, and powerful monoliths in the hope that they will remain big and powerful enough. Alternatively, we can build small and useful units of processing that can be combined into a single processing team of any size, not unlike the way that supercomputers can be built out of many thousands or millions of cheap commodity processors.

A process viewer will be useful while working through this chapter. A good one for Unix systems is **htop**, which can be downloaded from: `http://hisham.hm/htop/`. This tool provides, among other things, a view into CPU and memory usage; here, we see how load is spread across all eight cores:

```
1  [|||||||                         15.0%]   5  [|||||||                          15.1%]
2  [|||||||                         15.8%]   6  [|||||||||||                      24.2%]
3  [|||||||                         15.7%]   7  [|||||||                          15.0%]
4  [|||||||                         14.4%]   8  [|||||||                          13.8%]
Mem[|||||||||||||||||||||||||| 1106/15946MB]   Tasks: 57, 30 thr; 1 running
Swp[                               0/2047MB]   Load average: 0.02 0.07 0.01
                                               Uptime: 240 days(!), 22:13:41

  PID USER     PRI  NI  VIRT   RES   SHR S CPU% MEM%   TIME+  Command
 5844 root      20   0  110M  1920  1220 R  2.0  0.0  0:00.34 htop
```

Let's get started by looking into threads and processes.

Node's single-threaded model

Taken in its entirety, the Node environment usefully demonstrates both the efficiency of multithreaded parallelism and an expressive syntax amenable to applications featuring high concurrency. Using Node does not constrain the developer, the developer's access to system resources, or the types of applications the developer might like to build.

Nevertheless, a surprising number of persistent criticisms of Node are based on this misunderstanding. As we'll see, the belief that Node is not multithreaded and is, therefore, slow, or not ready for prime time, simply misses the point. JavaScript is single-threaded; the Node stack is not. JavaScript represents the language used to coordinate the execution of several multithreaded C++ processes, even the bespoke C++ add-ons created by you, the developer. Node provides JavaScript, run through V8, primarily as a tool for modeling concurrency. That, additionally, where one can write an entire application using just JavaScript is simply another benefit of the platform. You are never stuck with JavaScript—you may write the bulk of your application in C++ if that is your choice.

In this chapter, we will attempt to dismantle these misunderstandings, clearing the way for optimistic development with Node. In particular, we will study techniques for spreading effort across cores, processes, and threads. For now, this section will attempt to clarify how much a single thread is capable of (hint: it's usually all you need).

The benefits of single-threaded programming

You will be hard-pressed to find any significant number of professional software engineers working on enterprise-grade software willing to deny that multithreaded software development is painful. However, why is it so hard to do well?

It is not that multithreaded programming is difficult per se—the difficultly lies in the complexity of thread synchronization. It is very difficult to build high concurrency using the thread model, especially models in which the state is shared. Anticipating every way that an action taken in one thread might affect all the others is nearly impossible once an application grows beyond the most basic of shapes. Entanglements and collisions multiply rapidly, sometimes corrupting shared memory, sometimes creating bugs nearly impossible to track down.

Node's designers chose to recognize the speed and parallelization advantages of threads without demanding that developers did the same. In particular, Node's designers wanted to save developers from managing the difficulties that accompany threaded systems:

- Shared memory and the locking behavior leads to systems that are very difficult to reason about as they grow in complexity.
- Communication between tasks requires the implementation of a wide range of synchronization primitives, such as mutexes and semaphores, condition variables, and so forth. An already challenging environment requires highly complex tools, expanding the level of expertise necessary to complete even relatively simple systems.
- Race conditions and deadlocks are common pitfalls in these sorts of systems. Contemporaneous read and write operations within a shared program space lead to problems of sequencing, where two threads may be in an unpredictable *race* for the right to influence a state, event, or other key system characteristic.
- As maintaining dependable boundaries between threads and their states is so difficult, ensuring that a library (what for Node would be a *module*) is thread-safe consumes a great deal of developer time. Can I know that this library will not destroy some part of my application? Guaranteeing thread safety requires great diligence on the part of a library's developer and these guarantees may be conditional; for example, a library may be thread-safe when reading, but not when writing.

The primary argument for single-threading is that control flow is difficult in concurrent environments, and especially so when memory access or code execution order is unpredictable:

- Instead of concerning themselves with arbitrary locking and other collisions, developers can focus on constructing execution chains whose ordering is predictable.

- As parallelization is accomplished through the use of multiple processes, each with an individual and distinct memory space, communication between processes remains uncomplicated—via the Rule of Simplicity, we achieve not only simple and bug-free components, but easier interoperability as well.
- As state is not (arbitrarily) shared between individual Node processes; a single process is automatically protected from surprise visits from other processes bent on memory reallocation or resource monopolization. Communication is through clear channels using basic protocols, all of which make it very difficult to write programs that make unpredictable changes across processes.
- Thread-safety is one less concern for developers to waste time worrying about. As single-threaded concurrency obviates the collisions present in multithreaded concurrency, development can proceed more quickly, on surer ground. In the following diagram, we see on the left how sharing state across threads requires diligent management to guard against collisions while on the right, a "share-nothing" architecture avoids collisions and blocking actions:

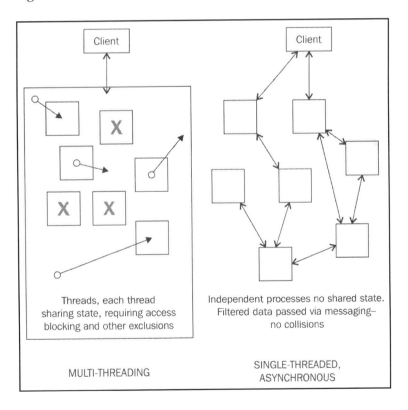

A single thread efficiently managed by an event loop brings stability, maintainability, readability, and resilience to Node programs. The big news is that Node continues to deliver the speed and power of multithreading to its developers—the brilliance of Node's design makes such power transparent, reflecting one part of Node's stated aim of bringing the most power to the most people with the least difficulty.

In the following diagram, the differences between two single-threaded models and a multithreaded model are shown:

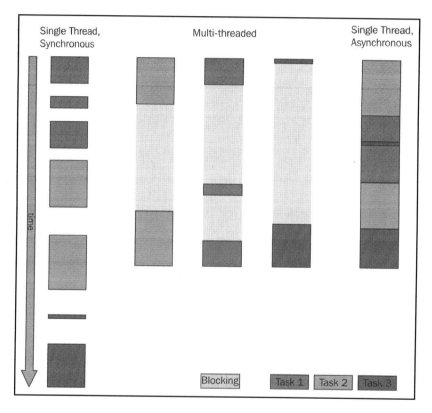

There is no escape from blocking operations—reading from a file, for example, will always take some time. A single-threaded synchronous model forces each task to wait for others to finish prior to starting, consuming more time. Several tasks can be started in parallel using threads, even at different times, where total execution time is no longer than that taken by the longest running thread. When using threads, the developer becomes responsible for synchronizing the activity of each individual thread, using locks or other scheduling tools. This can become very complex when the number of threads increases, and in this complexity live very subtle and hard-to-find bugs.

Rather than having the developer struggle with this complexity, Node itself manages I/O threads. You need not micromanage I/O threading; one simply designs an application to establish data availability points (callbacks) and the instructions to be executed once the said data is available. Threads provide the same efficiency under the hood, and yet their management is exposed to the developer through an easily comprehensible interface.

Multithreading is already native and transparent

Node's I/O thread pool executes within the OS scope, and its work is distributed across cores (just as any other job scheduled by the OS would be similarly distributed). When you are running Node, you are already taking advantage of its multithreaded execution.

In the upcoming discussion of child processes and the Cluster module, we will see this style of parallelism—of multiple parallel processes—in action. We will see how Node is not denied the full power of an OS.

As we saw earlier, when discussing Node's core architecture, the V8 thread in which one executes JavaScript programs is bound to `libuv`, which functions as the main, system-level, I/O event dispatcher. In this capacity, `libuv` handles the timers, filesystem calls, network calls, and other I/O operations requested by the relevant JavaScript process or module commands, such as `fs.readFile` and `http.createServer`. Therefore, the main V8 event loop is best understood as a control-flow programming interface, supported and powered by the highly-efficient, multithreaded, system delegate `libuv`.

Bert Belder, one of Node's core contributors, is also one of the core contributors to `libuv`. In fact, Node's development has provoked a simultaneous increase in `libuv` development, a feedback loop that has only improved the speed and stability of both the projects. It has merged and replaced the `libeo` and `libev` libraries that formed the original core of Node's stack.

Consider another of Raymond's rules, the **Rule of Separation**: "Separate policy from mechanism; separate interfaces from engines." The engine that powers Node's asynchronous, event-driven style of programming is `libuv`; the interface to that engine is V8's JavaScript runtime. Continuing with Raymond, look at this:

> *"One way to effect that separation is, for example, to write your application as a library of C service routines that are driven by an embedded scripting language, with the application flow of control written in the scripting language rather than C."*

The ability to orchestrate hyper-efficient parallel OS processes within the abstraction of a single predictable thread exists by design, not as a concession.

It concludes a pragmatic analysis of how the application development process can be improved, and it is certainly not a limitation on what is possible.

 A detailed unpacking of **libuv** can be found at: https://github.com/nikhilm/uvbook. **Burt Belder** also gives an in-depth talk on how **libuv**, and Node, works under the hood at: https://www.youtube.com/watch?v=PNa9OMajw9w.

Creating child processes

Software development is no longer the realm of monolithic programs. Applications running on networks cannot forego interoperability. Modern applications are distributed and decoupled. We now build applications that connect users with resources distributed across the internet. Many users are accessing shared resources simultaneously. A complex system is easier to understand if the whole is understood as a collection of interfaces to programs that solve one or a few clearly defined, related problems. In such a system, it is expected (and desirable) that processes do not sit idle.

An early criticism of Node was that it did not have multicore awareness, that is, if a Node server were running on a machine with several cores, it would not be able to take advantage of this extra horsepower. Within this seemingly reasonable criticism hid an unjustified bias based on a straw man: a program that is unable to explicitly allocate memory and execution *threads* in order to implement parallelization cannot handle enterprise-grade problems.

This criticism is a persistent one. It is also not true.

While a single Node process runs on a single core, any number of Node processes can be *spun up* through use of the child_process module. Basic usage of this module is straightforward: we fetch a ChildProcess object and listen for data events. This example will call the ls Unix command, listing the current directory:

```
const spawn = require('child_process').spawn;
let ls = spawn('ls', ['-lh', '.']);
ls.stdout.on('readable', function() {
    let d = this.read();
    d && console.log(d.toString());
});
ls.on('close', code => {
    console.log(`child process exited with code: ${code}`);
});
```

Here, we spawn the `ls` process (list directory), and read from the resulting `readable`
Stream, receiving something like this:

```
-rw-r--r-- 1 root root 43 Jul 9 19:44 index.html
 -rw-rw-r-- 1 root root 278 Jul 15 16:36 child_example.js
 -rw-r--r-- 1 root root 1.2K Jul 14 19:08 server.js
 child process exited with code 0
```

Any number of child processes can be spawned in this way. It is important to note here that
when a child process is spawned, or otherwise created, the OS itself assigns the
responsibility for that process to a given CPU. Node is not responsible for how an OS
allocates resources. The upshot is that on a machine with eight cores, it is likely that
spawning eight processes will result in each being allocated to independent processors. In
other words, child processes are automatically spread by the OS across CPUs, putting the
lie to claims that Node cannot take full advantage of multicore environments.

Each new Node process (child) is allocated 10 MB of memory, and
represents a new V8 instance that will take at least 30 milliseconds to start
up. While it is unlikely that you will be spawning many thousands of
these processes, understanding how to query and set OS limits on user-
created processes is beneficial; htop or top will report the number of
processes currently running, or you can use `ps aux | wc -l` from the
command line. The `ulimit` Unix command (`https://ss64.com/bash/`
`ulimit.html`) provides important information on user limits on an OS.
Passing `ulimit`, the –u argument will show the maximum number of user
processes that can be spawned. Changing the limit is accomplished by
passing it as an argument: `ulimit -u 8192`.

The `child_process` module represents a class exposing four main methods: `spawn`, `fork`,
`exec`, and `execFile`. These methods return a `ChildProcess` object that extends
`EventEmitter`, exposing an interface to child events and a few functions that are helpful in
managing child processes. We'll take a look at its main methods and follow up with a
discussion of the common `ChildProcess` interface.

Spawning processes

This powerful command allows a Node program to start and interact with processes spawned via system commands. In the preceding example, we used spawn to call a native OS process, `ls`, passing the `lh` and `.` arguments to that command. In this way, any process can be started just as one might start it via a command line. The method takes three arguments:

- **command**: A command to be executed by the OS shell
- **arguments (optional)**: These are command-line arguments, sent as an array
- **options**: An optional map of settings for spawn

The options for `spawn` allow its behavior to be carefully customized:

- `cwd` (String): By default, the command will understand its current working directory to be the same as that of the Node process calling spawn. Change that setting using this directive.
- `env` (Object): This is used to pass environment variables to a child process. For instance, consider spawning a child with an environment object, such as the following:

```
{
  name: "Sandro",
  role: "admin"
}
```

The child process environment will have access to these values:

- `detached` (Boolean): When a parent spawns a child, both processes form a group, and the parent is normally the leader of that group. To make a child the group leader, use detached. This will allow the child to continue running even after the parent exits. This is because the parent will wait for the child to exit by default. You can call `child.unref()` to tell the parent's event loop that it should not count the child reference, and exit if no other work exists.
- `uid` (Number): Set the `uid` (user identity) directive for the child process, in terms of standard system permissions, such as a UID that has execute privileges on the child process.
- `gid` (Number): Set the `gid` (group identity) directive for the child process, in terms of standard system permissions, such as a GID that has execute privileges on the child process.

- `stdio` (String or Array): Child processes have file descriptors, the first three being the `process.stdin`, `process.stdout` and `process.stderr` standard I/O descriptors, in order (fds = 0,1,2). This directive allows those descriptors to be redefined, inherited, and so forth.

Consider the output of the following child process program:

```
process.stdout.write(Buffer.from("Hello!"));
```

Here, a parent would listen on `child.stdout`. Instead, if we want a child to inherit its parent's `stdio`, such that when the child writes to `process.stdout`, what is emitted is piped through to the parent's `process.stdout`, we would pass the relevant parent file descriptors to the child, overriding its own:

```
spawn("node", ['./reader.js', './afile.txt'], {
  stdio: [process.stdin, process.stdout, process.stderr]
});
```

In this case, the child's output would pipe straight through to the parent's standard output channel. Also, see fork, as follows, for more information on this kind of pattern.

Each of the three (or more) file descriptors can take one of six values:

- **pipe**: This creates a pipe between the child and the parent. As the first three child file descriptors are already exposed to the parent (`child.stdin`, `child.stdout`, and `child.stderr`), this is only necessary in more complex child implementations.
- **ipc**: This creates an IPC channel for passing messages between a child and parent. A child process may have a maximum of one IPC file descriptor. Once this connection is established, the parent may communicate with the child via `child.send`. If the child sends JSON messages through this file descriptor, those emissions can be caught using `child.on("message")`. If running a Node program as a child, it is likely a better choice to use `ChildProcess.fork`, which has this messaging channel built in.
- **ignore**: The file descriptors 0-2 will have `/dev/null` attached to them. For others, the referenced file descriptor will not be set on the child.

- **A stream object**: This allows the parent to share a stream with the child. For demonstration purposes, given a child that will write the same content to any provided `WritableStream`, we can do something like this:

```
let writer = fs.createWriteStream('./a.out');
writer.on('open', () => {
  let cp = spawn("node", ['./reader.js'], {
    stdio: [null, writer, null]
  });
});
```

The child will now fetch its content and pipe it to whichever output stream it has been sent:

```
fs.createReadStream('cached.data').pipe(process.stdout);
```

- **An integer**: A file descriptor ID.
- **null and undefined**: These are the default values. For file descriptors 0-2 (`stdin`, `stdout`, and `stderr`), a pipe is created; others default to `ignore`.

In addition to passing `stdio` settings as an array, certain common groupings can be implemented by passing one of these shortcut string values:

- `'ignore'` = `['ignore', 'ignore', 'ignore']`
- `'pipe'` = `['pipe', 'pipe', 'pipe']`
- `'inherit'` = `[process.stdin, process.stdout, process.stderr]`
- `[0,1,2]`

We have shown some examples of using `spawn` to run Node programs as child processes. While this is a perfectly valid usage (and a good way to try out the API options), `spawn` is primarily for running system commands. Refer to the discussion of `fork`, as follows, for more information on running Node processes as children.

It should be noted that the ability to spawn any system process means that one can use Node to run other application environments installed on the OS. If one had the popular PHP language installed, the following would be possible:

```
const spawn = require('child_process').spawn;
let php = spawn("php", ['-r', 'print "Hello from PHP!";']);
php.stdout.on('readable', () => {
  let d;
  while (d = this.read()) {
    console.log(d.toString());
  }
});
// Hello from PHP!
```

Running a more interesting, larger program would be just as easy.

Apart from the ease with which one might run Java or Ruby or other programs through Node using this technique, asynchronously, we also have a good answer to a persistent criticism of Node here: JavaScript is not as fast as other languages for crunching numbers, or doing other CPU-heavy tasks. This is true, in the sense that Node is primarily optimized for I/O efficiency and helping with the management of high-concurrency applications, and JavaScript is an interpreted language without a strong focus on heavy computation.

However, using `spawn`, one can very easily pass off massive computations and long-running routines on analytics engines or calculation engines to separate processes in other environments. Node's simple event loop will be sure to notify the main application when those operations are done, seamlessly integrating the resultant data. In the meantime, the main application is free to keep serving clients.

Forking processes

Like `spawn`, `fork` starts a child process, but is designed for running Node programs with the added benefit of having a communication channel built in. Rather than passing a system command to `fork` as its first argument, one passes the path to a Node program. As with `spawn`, command-line options can be sent as a second argument, accessible via `process.argv` in the forked child process.

An optional options object can be passed as its third argument, with the following parameters:

- cwd (String): By default, the command will understand its current working directory to be the same as that of the Node process calling fork. Change that setting using this directive.
- env (Object): This is used to pass environment variables to a child process. Refer to spawn.
- encoding (String): This sets the encoding of the communication channel.
- execPath (String): This is the executable used to create the child process.
- silent (Boolean): By default, a forked child will have its stdio associated with the parent's (child.stdout is identical to parent.stdout, for example). Setting this option to true disables this behavior.

An important difference between fork and spawn is that the former's child process does not automatically exit when it is finished. Such a child must explicitly exit when it is done, easily accomplished via process.exit().

In the following example, we create a child that emits an incrementing number every tenth of a second, which its parent then dumps to the system console. First, let's look at the child program:

```
let cnt = 0;
setInterval(() => {
  process.stdout.write(" -> " + cnt++);
}, 100);
```

Again, this will simply write a steadily increasing number. Remembering that with fork, a child will inherit the stdio of its parent, we only need to create the child in order to get output in a Terminal running the parent process:

```
var fork = require('child_process').fork;
fork('./emitter.js');
// -> 0 -> 1 -> 2 -> 3 -> 4 -> 5 -> 6 -> 7 -> 8 -> 9 -> 10 ...
```

 The silent option can be demonstrated here; fork('./emitter.js', [], { silent: true }); turns off any output to the Terminal.

Creating multiple, parallel processes is easy. Let's multiply the number of children created:

```
fork('./emitter.js');
fork('./emitter.js');
fork('./emitter.js');
// 0 -> 0 -> 0 -> 1 -> 1 -> 1 -> 2 -> 2 -> 2 -> 3 -> 3 -> 3 -> 4 ...
```

It should be clear at this point that by using `fork`, we are creating many parallel execution contexts, spread across all machine cores.

This is straightforward enough, but the `fork` built-in communication channel provides makes communicating with forked children even easier, and cleaner. Consider the following file, which spawns a child process and communicates with it:

```
// parent.js
const fork = require('child_process').fork;
let cp = fork('./child.js');
cp.on('message', msgobj => {
    console.log(`Parent got message: ${msgobj.text}`);
});
cp.send({
    text: 'I love you'
});
```

We see that there is a communication channel now available, through which the parent can send messages, as well as receiving messages from the child process, given below:

```
// child.js
process.on('message', msgobj => {
    console.log('Child got message:', msgobj.text);
    process.send({
        text: `${msgobj.text} too`
    });
});
```

By executing the parent script, we will see the following in our console:

```
Child got message: I love you
Parent got message: I love you too
```

We'll go a little deeper into this important concept of cross-process communication shortly.

Buffering process output

In cases where the complete buffered output of a child process is sufficient, with no need to manage data through events, child_process offers the exec method. The method takes three arguments:

- **command:** A command-line string. Unlike spawn and fork, which pass arguments to a command via an array, this first argument accepts a full command string, such as ps aux | grep node.
- **options:** This is an optional argument:
    - cwd (String): This sets the working directory for the command process.
    - env (Object): This is a map of key-value pairs that will be exposed to the child process.
    - encoding (String): This is the encoding of the child's data stream. The default value is 'utf8'.
    - timeout (Number): This specifies the milliseconds to wait for the process to complete, at which point the child process will be sent the killSignal.maxBuffer value.
    - killSignal.maxBuffer (Number): This is the maximum number of bytes allowed on stdout or stderr. When this number is exceeded, the process is killed. This default is 200 KB.
    - killSignal (String): The child process receives this signal after a timeout. This default is SIGTERM.
- **callback:** This receives three arguments: an Error object, if any, stdout (a Buffer object containing the result), stderr (a Buffer object containing error data, if any). If the process was killed, Error.signal will contain the kill signal.

When you want the buffering behavior of exec but are targeting a Node file, use execFile. Importantly, execFile does not spawn a new subshell, which makes it slightly less expensive to run.

Communicating with your child

All instances of the `ChildProcess` object extend `EventEmitter`, exposing events useful for managing child data connections. Additionally, `ChildProcess` objects expose some useful methods for interacting with children directly. Let's go through those now, beginning with attributes and methods:

- `child.connected`: When a child is disconnected from its parent via `child.disconnect()`, this flag will be set to `false`.
- `child.stdin`: This is a `WritableStream` corresponding to the child's standard in.
- `child.stdout`: This is a `ReadableStream` corresponding to the child's standard out.
- `child.stderr`: This is a `ReadableStream` corresponding to the child's standard error.
- `child.pid`: This is an integer representing the process ID (PID) assigned to the child process.
- `child.kill`: This tries to terminate a child process, sending it an optional signal. If no signal is specified, the default is `SIGTERM` (for more about signals, visit: `https://en.wikipedia.org/wiki/Signal_(IPC)`). While the method name sounds terminal, it is not guaranteed to kill a process—it only sends a signal to a process. Dangerously, if `kill` is attempted on a process that has already exited, it is possible that another process that has been newly assigned the PID of the dead process will receive the signal, with indeterminable consequences. This method should fire a `close` event, which the signal used to close the process.
- `child.disconnect()`: This command severs the IPC connection between the child and its parent. The child will then die gracefully, as it has no IPC channel to keep it alive. You may also call `process.disconnect()` from within the child itself. Once a child has disconnected, the `connected` flag on that child reference will be set to `false`.

Sending messages to children

As we saw in our discussion of `fork`, and when using the `ipc` option on `spawn`, child processes can be sent messages via `child.send`, with the message passed as the first argument. A TCP server, or socket handle, can be passed along with the message as a second argument. In this way, a TCP server can spread requests across multiple child processes. For example, the following server distributes socket handling across a number of child processes equaling the total number of CPUs available. Each forked child is given a unique ID, which it reports when started. Whenever the TCP server receives a socket, that socket is passed as a handle to a random child process:

```
// tcpparent.js
const fork = require('child_process').fork;
const net = require('net');
let children = [];
require('os').cpus().forEach((f, idx) => {
  children.push(fork('./tcpchild.js', [idx]));
});
net.createServer((socket) => {
  let rand = Math.floor(Math.random() * children.length);
  children[rand].send(null, socket);
}).listen(8080)
```

That child process then sends a unique response, demonstrating that socket handling is being distributed:

```
// tcpchild.js
let id = process.argv[2];
process.on('message', (n, socket) => {
  socket.write(`child ${id} was your server today.\r\n`);
  socket.end();
});
```

Start the parent server in a Terminal window. In another window, run `telnet 127.0.0.1 8080`. You should see something similar to the following output, with a random child ID being displayed on each connection (assuming that there exist multiple cores):

```
Trying 127.0.0.1...
...
child 3 was your server today.
Connection closed by foreign host.
```

Hit that endpoint a few more times. You should see that your requests are being serviced by different child processes.

Parsing a file using multiple processes

One of the tasks many developers will take on is the building of a logfile processor. A logfile can be very large and many megabytes long. Any single program working on a very large file can easily run into memory problems or simply run much too slowly. It makes sense to process a large file in pieces. We'll build a simple log processor that breaks up a big file into pieces and assigns one to each of several child workers, running them in parallel.

The entire code for this example can be found in the `logproc` folder of the code bundle. We will focus on the main routines:

- Determining the number of lines in the logfile
- Breaking those up into equal chunks
- Creating one child for each chunk and passing it parse instructions
- Assembling and displaying the results

To get the word count of our file, we use the `wc` command with `child.exec`, as shown in the following code:

```
child.exec(`wc -l ${filename}`, function(e, fL) {
  fileLength = parseInt(fL.replace(filename, ""));

  let fileRanges = [];
  let oStart = 1;
  let oEnd = fileChunkLength;

  while(oStart < fileLength) {
    fileRanges.push({
      offsetStart: oStart,
      offsetEnd: oEnd
    })
    oStart = oEnd + 1;
    oEnd = Math.min(oStart + fileChunkLength, fileLength);
  }
  ...
}
```

Let's say that we use `fileChunkLength` of 500,000 lines. This means four child processes are to be created, and each will be told to process a range of 500,000 lines in our file, such as 1 to 500,000:

```
let w = child.fork('bin/worker');
w.send({
  file: filename,
  offsetStart: range.offsetStart,
  offsetEnd: range.offsetEnd
});
w.on('message', chunkData => {
  // pass results data on to a reducer.
});
```

Each of these workers will themselves use a child process to grab their allotted chunk, employing `sed`, the native Stream Editor for Unix:

```
process.on('message', (m) => {
  let filename = m.file;
  let sed = `sed -n '${m.offsetStart},${m.offsetEnd}p' ${filename}`;
  let reader = require('child_process').exec(sed, {maxBuffer: 1024e6},
(err, data, stderr) => {

    // Split the file chunk into lines and process it.
    //
    data = data.split("\n");
    ...

  })
})
```

Here, we are executing the `sed -n '500001,1000001p' logfile.txt` command, which plucks the given range of lines and returns them for processing. Once we're done processing the columns of data (adding them up, and so forth), this child will return its data to the master (as described earlier) and the data results will be written to a file, otherwise manipulated, or sent to `stdout`, as shown in the following output:

```
++++++++++++++++++++++++++++++++++++++++++++++++++++++++++++++++++++++++++++
+ FILE: ./short.log      CPUS: 8 +
++++++++++++++++++++++++++++++++++++++++++++++++++++++++++++++++++++++++++++
++++++++++++++++++++++++++++++++++++++++Stats++++++++++++++++++++++++++++++++
++++++++++++++++++++++++++++++++++++++++++++++++++++++++++++++++++++++++++++
Operation took: 1.076 seconds
Log start: December 28th 2011, 6:03:26 am
Log end: December 28th 2011, 6:28:29 am
Total Seconds: 1503.478
Total Datapoints: 2000000
Throughput: 1330.249/second
Outliers under (0): 0 (%0.000)
Outliers over (10): 1112268 (%55.613)
++++++++++++++++++++++++++++++++++++++++++++++++++++++++++++++++++++++++++++
+++++++++++++++++++++++++Distribution (Milliseconds : Count)++++++++++++++++
++++++++++++++++++++++++++++++++++++++++++++++++++++++++++++++++++++++++++++
+ 0 :      0                  (%0.000)
+ 1 :      0                  (%0.000)
+ 2 :      0                  (%0.000)
+ 3 :      0                  (%0.000)
+ 4 :      666                (%0.033)
+ 5 :      4520               (%0.226)
+ 6 :      18514              (%0.926)
+ 7 :      47180              (%2.359)
+ 8 :      90920              (%4.546)
+ 9 :      182262             (%9.113)
+ 10 :     543670             (%27.184)
++++++++++++++++++++++++++++++++++++++++++++++++++++++++++++++++++++++++++++
++++++++++++++++++++++++++++++++Percentiles++++++++++++++++++++++++++++++++++
++++++++++++++++++++++++++++++++++++++++++++++++++++++++++++++++++++++++++++
+ 0 :      0.000              (100.000)
+ 1 :      0.000              (100.000)
+ 2 :      0.000              (100.000)
+ 3 :      0.000              (100.000)
+ 4 :      0.033              (99.967)
+ 5 :      0.259              (99.741)
+ 6 :      1.185              (98.815)
+ 7 :      3.544              (96.456)
+ 8 :      8.090              (91.910)
+ 9 :      17.203             (82.797)
+ 10 :     44.387             (55.613)
++++++++++++++++++++++++++++++++++++++++++++++++++++++++++++++++++++++++++++
```

The full file for this example is much longer, but all that extra code is merely formatting and other detail—the Node child process management we have described suffices to create a parallelized system for number crunching that will process many millions of lines of code in seconds. By using more processes spread across more cores, the log parsing speed can be reduced even further.

View the README.MD file in the /logproc folder in your code bundle to experiment with this example.

Using the cluster module

As we saw when processing large logfiles, the pattern of a master parent controller for many child processes is just right for vertical scaling in Node. In response to this, the Node API has been augmented by a cluster module, which formalizes this pattern and helps make its achievement easier. Continuing with Node's core purpose of helping make scalable network software easier to build, the particular goal of cluster is to facilitate the sharing of network ports among many children.

For example, the following code creates a cluster of worker processes all sharing the same HTTP connection:

```
const cluster = require('cluster');
const http = require('http');
const numCPUs = require('os').cpus().length;

if(cluster.isMaster) {
    for(let i = 0; i < numCPUs; i++) {
        cluster.fork();
    }
}

if(cluster.isWorker) {
    http.createServer((req, res) => {
        res.writeHead(200);
        res.end(`Hello from ${cluster.worker.id}`);
    }).listen(8080);
}
```

We'll dig into the details shortly. For now, note that cluster.fork has taken zero arguments. What does fork without a command or file argument do? Within a cluster, the default action is to fork the current program. We see during cluster.isMaster, the action is to fork children (one for each available CPU). When this program is reexecuted in a forking context, cluster.isWorker will be true and a new HTTP server *running on a shared port* is started. Multiple processes are sharing the load for a single server.

Start and connect to this server with a browser. You will see something like `Hello from 8`, the integer corresponding to the unique `cluster.worker.id` value of the worker that assigned responsibility for handling your request. Balancing across all workers is handled automatically, such that refreshing your browser a few times will result in different worker IDs being displayed.

Later on, we'll go through an example of sharing a socket server across a cluster. For now, we'll lay out the cluster API, which breaks down into two sections: the methods, attributes, and events available to the cluster master, and those available to the child. As workers in this context are defined using fork, the documentation for that method of `child_process` can be applied here as well:

- `cluster.isMaster`: This is the Boolean value indicating whether the process is a master.
- `cluster.isWorker`: This is the Boolean value indicating whether the process was forked from a master.
- `cluster.worker`: This will bear a reference to the current worker object, only available to a child process.
- `cluster.workers`: This is a hash containing references to all active worker objects, keyed by the worker ID. Use this to loop through all worker objects. This only exists within the master process.
- `cluster.setupMaster([settings])`: This is a convenient way of passing a map of default arguments to be used when a child is forked. If all children will fork the same file (as is often the case), you will save time by setting it here. The available defaults are as follows:
    - `exec` (String): This is the file path to the process file, defaulting to `__filename`.
    - `args` (Array): This contains Strings sent as arguments to the child process. The default is to fetch arguments with `process.argv.slice(2)`.
    - `silent` (Boolean): This specifies whether or not to send output to the master's stdio, defaulting to false.
- `cluster.fork([env])`: This creates a new worker process. Only the master process may call this method. To expose a map of key-value pairs to the child's process environment, send an object to `env`.
- `cluster.disconnect([callback])`: This is used to terminate all workers in a cluster. Once all the workers have died gracefully, the cluster process will itself terminate if it has no further events to wait on. To be notified when all children have expired, pass `callback`.

Cluster events

The cluster object emits several events, listed as follows:

- fork: This is fired when the master tries to fork a new child. This is not the same as online. This receives a worker object.
- online: This is fired when the master receives notification that a child is fully bound. This differs from the fork event and receives a worker object.
- listening: When the worker performs an action that requires a listen() call (such as starting an HTTP server), this event will be fired in the master. The event emits two arguments: a worker object, and the address object containing the address, port, and addressType values of the connection.
- disconnect: This is called whenever a child disconnects, which can happen either through process exit events or after calling child.kill(). This will fire prior to the exit event—they are not the same. This receives a worker object.
- exit: Whenever a child dies, this event is emitted. The event receives three arguments: a worker object, the exit code number, and the signal string, such as SIGNUP, which caused the process to be killed.
- setup: This is called after cluster.setupMaster has executed.

Worker object properties

Workers have the following attributes and methods:

- worker.id: This is the unique ID assigned to a worker, also representing the worker's key in the cluster.workers index.
- worker.process: This specifies a ChildProcess object referencing a worker.
- worker.suicide: The workers that have recently had kill or disconnect called on them will have their suicide attribute set to true.
- worker.send(message, [sendHandle]): Refer to child_process.fork(), which is previously mentioned.
- worker.kill([signal]): This kills a worker. The master can check this worker's suicide property in order to determine whether the death was intentional or accidental. The default signal value that is sent is SIGTERM.

- `worker.disconnect()`: This instructs a worker to disconnect. Importantly, the existing connections to the worker are not immediately terminated (as with `kill`), but are allowed to exit normally prior to the worker fully disconnecting. This is because the existing connections may stay in existence for a very long time. It is a good pattern to regularly check whether the worker has actually disconnected, perhaps using timeouts.

Worker events

Workers also emit events, such as the ones mentioned in the following list:

- `message`: Refer to `child_process.fork`
- `online`: This is identical to `cluster.online`, except that the check is against only the specified worker
- `listening`: This is identical to `cluster.listening`, except that the check is against only the specified worker
- `disconnect`: This is identical to `cluster.disconnect`, except that the check is against only the specified worker
- `exit`: Refer to the `exit` event for `child_process`
- `setup`: This is called after `cluster.setupMaster` has executed

Now, using what we now know about the `cluster` module, let's implement a real-time tool for analyzing the streams of data emitted by many users simultaneously interacting with an application.

Using PM2 to manage multiple processes

PM2 is designed to be an enterprise-level process manager. As discussed elsewhere, Node runs within a Unix process, and its child process and cluster modules are used to spawn further processes, typically when scaling an application across multiple cores. PM2 can be used to instrument deployment and monitoring of your Node processes, both via the command line and programmatically. PM2 spares the developer the complexity of configuring clustering boilerplate, handles restarts automatically, and provides advanced logging and monitoring tools out of the box.

Install PM2 globally: `npm install pm2 -g`

The most straightforward way to use PM2 is as a simple process runner. The following program will increment and log a value every second:

```
// script.js
let count = 1;
function loop() {
  console.log(count++);
  setTimeout(loop, 1000);
}
loop();
```

Here, we fork a new process from `script.js`, running it in the background *forever*, until we stop it. This is a great way to run a daemonized process:

```
pm2 start script.js
// [PM2] Process script.js launched
```

Once the script launches, you should see something like this in your terminal:

The meaning of most of the values should be clear, such as the amount of memory your process is using, whether or not it is online, how long it has been up, and so forth (the mode and watching fields will be explained shortly). The process will continue to run until it is stopped or deleted.

To set a custom name for your process when you start it, pass the `--name` argument to PM2: `pm2 start script.js --name 'myProcessName'`.

This overview of all running PM2 processes can be brought up at any time via the command `pm2 list`.

PM2 offers other straightforward commands:

- `pm2 stop <app_name | id | all>`: Stop a process by name, id or stop all processes. A stopped process remains in the process list, and can be later restarted.
- `pm2 restart <app_name | id | all>`: Restart a process. The number of process restarts is displayed under restarted in all process lists. To automatically restart a process when it reaches some maximum memory limit (say, 15M) use the command `pm2 start script.js --max-memory-restart 15M`.
- `pm2 delete <app_name | id | all>`: Deletes a process. This process cannot be restarted. pm2 delete all deletes all PM2 processes.
- `pm2 info <app_name | id >`: Provides detailed info on a process.

You will be using `pm2 info <processname>` often. Ensure that `script.js` is running as a PM2 process using `PM2 list`, then inspect that process info with `pm2 info script`:

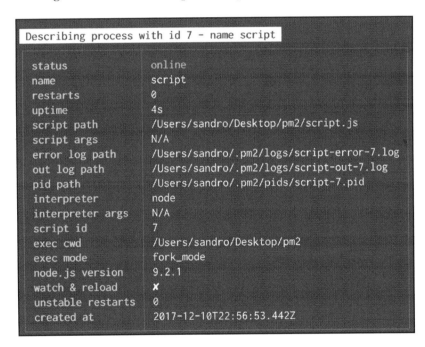

```
Describing process with id 7 - name script

status               online
name                 script
restarts             0
uptime               4s
script path          /Users/sandro/Desktop/pm2/script.js
script args          N/A
error log path       /Users/sandro/.pm2/logs/script-error-7.log
out log path         /Users/sandro/.pm2/logs/script-out-7.log
pid path             /Users/sandro/.pm2/pids/script-7.pid
interpreter          node
interpreter args     N/A
script id            7
exec cwd             /Users/sandro/Desktop/pm2
exec mode            fork_mode
node.js version      9.2.1
watch & reload       ✗
unstable restarts    0
created at           2017-12-10T22:56:53.442Z
```

Note the paths given for error and other logs. Remember that our script increments an integer by one every second and logs that count. If you `cat /path/to/script/out/log` your terminal will show what has been written to the out log, which should be a list of incrementing numbers. Errors are similarly written to a log. Furthermore, you can stream the output logs in real time with `pm2 logs`:

```
/Users/sandro/.pm2/logs/script-error-7.log last 15 lines:
/Users/sandro/.pm2/logs/script-out-7.log last 15 lines:
7|script   | 182
7|script   | 183
7|script   | 184
7|script   | 185
7|script   | 186
7|script   | 187
7|script   | 188
7|script   | 189
7|script   | 190
7|script   | 191
7|script   | 192
7|script   | 193
7|script   | 194
7|script   | 195
7|script   | 196
```

To clear all logs, use `pm2 flush`.

You can also use PM2 programmatically. To replicate the steps we took to run `scripts.js` with PM2, first create the following script, `programmatic.js`:

```js
const pm2 = require('pm2');

pm2.connect(err => {
    pm2.start('script.js', {
        name: 'programmed script runner',
        scriptArgs: [
            'first',
            'second',
            'third'
        ],
        execMode : 'fork_mode'
    }, (err, proc) => {
        if(err) {
            throw new Error(err);
        }
    });
});
```

This script will use the pm2 module to run `script.js` as a process. Go ahead and run it with `node programmatic.js`. Executing a `pm2 list` should show that programmed script runner is alive:

App name	id	mode	pid	status	restart	uptime	cpu	mem	user	watching
programmed script runner	8	fork	13352	online	0	5s	0%	33.0 MB	sandro	disabled

To make sure, try `pm2 logs` -- you should see numbers being incremented, just as before. You can read about the full set of programmatic options here: http://pm2.keymetrics.io/docs/usage/pm2-api/.

Monitoring

PM2 makes process monitoring easy. To view real-time statistics on CPU and memory usage for your processes, simply enter the command `pm2 monit`:

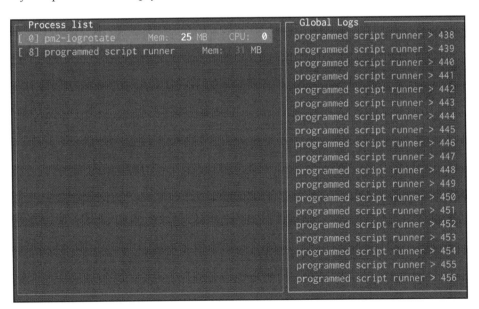

Pretty nice, right? On a production server where your Node app is managed via PM2, you can use this interface to get a quick look into an application's state, including memory usage and a running log.

PM2 also makes it easy to create web-based monitoring interfaces – it's as simple as running pm2 web. This command will start a monitored process listening on port 9615 -- running pm2 list will now list a process named pm2-http-interface. Run the web command and then navigate to localhost:9615 in your browser. You will see a detailed snapshot of your processes, OS, and so forth, as a JSON object:

```
...
"monit": {
  "loadavg": [ 1.89892578125, 1.91162109375, 1.896484375 ],
  "total_mem": 17179869184, "free_mem": 8377733120,
...
{
  "pid": 13352,
  "name": "programmed script runner",
  "pm2_env": {
    "instance_var": "NODE_APP_INSTANCE",
    "exec_mode": "fork_mode",
...
  "pm_id": 8, // our script.js process "monit": {
  "memory": 19619840, "cpu": 0
...
```

Creating a web-based UI that polls your server every few seconds, fetches process information, and then graphs it is made much simpler due to this built-in feature of PM2. PM2 also has an option to set a watcher on all managed scripts, such that any changes on the watched script will cause an automatic process restart. This is very useful when developing.

As a demonstration, let's create a simple HTTP server and run it through PM2:

```
// server.js
const http = require('http');
http.createServer((req, resp) => {
    if(req.url === "/") {
        resp.writeHead(200, {
            'content-type' : 'text/plain'
        });
        return resp.end("Hello World");
    }
    resp.end();
}).listen(8080);
```

This server will echo "Hello World" whenever localhost:8080 is hit. Now, lets use a PM2 process file to do more involved configuration.

Process files

Go ahead and kill all running PM2 processes with pm2 delete all. Then, create the following process.json file:

```
// process.json
{
  "apps" : [{
    "name" : "server",
    "script" : "./server.js",
    "watch" : true,
    "env": {
      "NODE_ENV": "development"
    },
    "instances" : 4,
    "exec_mode" : "cluster"
  }]
}
```

We're going to use this deployment definition to start our application on PM2. Note that apps is an array, which means you can list several different applications with different configurations and start them all at once. We'll explain the fields in a second, but for now, execute this manifest with pm2 start process.json. You should see something like this:

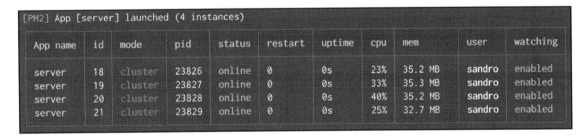

[PM2] App [server] launched (4 instances)										
App name	id	mode	pid	status	restart	uptime	cpu	mem	user	watching
server	18	cluster	23826	online	0	0s	23%	35.2 MB	sandro	enabled
server	19	cluster	23827	online	0	0s	33%	35.3 MB	sandro	enabled
server	20	cluster	23828	online	0	0s	40%	35.2 MB	sandro	enabled
server	21	cluster	23829	online	0	0s	25%	32.7 MB	sandro	enabled

It was that easy to deploy a multiprocess (clustered) application. PM2 will automatically balance load across your instances, set to 4 CPUs in the manifest via the instances attribute, with exec_mode of *cluster* (default mode is "fork"). In production, you would likely want to balance across the maximum number of cores, which you can flag simply by setting instances to 0. Additionally, you see that we've set environment variables via env: you can create a *dev* and a *prod* (and maybe even a *stage*) configuration for your server, set API keys and passwords, and other environment variables here.

Open a browser and visit `localhost:8080` to see that the server is running. Note that we set `watch` to `true` in our JSON manifest. This tells PM2 to automatically restart the application, across all cores, whenever any files are changed in your repository. Test it by changing the "Hello" message from your server to something else. If you then reload `localhost:8080`, you will see the new message, indicating that the servers have been restarted. If you list running PM2 processes, you will see the number of restarts:

App name	id	mode	pid	status	restart	uptime	cpu	mem	user	watching
server	18	cluster	23951	online	1	7s	0%	36.0 MB	sandro	enabled
server	19	cluster	23952	online	1	7s	0%	36.1 MB	sandro	enabled
server	20	cluster	23955	online	1	7s	0%	36.0 MB	sandro	enabled
server	21	cluster	23956	online	1	7s	0%	36.0 MB	sandro	enabled

Try it a few times. The restarts are stable, fast, and automatic.

You can also target specific files for the watcher:

```
{
  "apps" : [{
    ...
    "watch": [
      "tests/*.test",
      "app"
    ],
    "ignore_watch": [
      "**/*.log"
    ],
    "watch_options": {
      "followSymlinks": false
    },
    ...
  }]
}
```

Here, we tell PM2 to watch only `.test` files in `/test`, and the `/app` directory, ignoring changes in any .log files. Under the hood PM2 uses Chokidar (`https://github.com/paulmillr/chokidar#api`) to watch for file changes, so you can further configure the watcher by setting Chokidar options on `watch_options`. Note that you can use glob expressions (and regular expressions) in these settings.

You can read the full list of options for PM2 process files here: `http://pm2.keymetrics.io/docs/usage/application-declaration/`.

Some to note:

- `max_restarts`: The number of unstable restarts PM2 allows before stopping completely.
- `min_uptime`: The minimum time an app is given to start before being considered unstable and triggering a restart.
- `autorestart`: Whether to restart at all on a crash.
- `node_args`: Pass command-line arguments to the Node process itself. For example: `node_args: "--harmony"` is equivalent to `node --harmony server.js`.
- `max_memory_restart`: Restart occurs when memory usage breaks this threshold.
- `restart_delay`: Particularly in `watch` scenarios, you might want to delay restarts on file changes, waiting a bit for further edits before reacting.

Live development of your server applications just got easier, thanks to PM2.

Real-time activity updates of multiple worker results

Using what we've learned, we will construct a multiprocess system to track the behavior of all visitors to a sample web page. This will be composed of two main segments: a WebSocket-powered client library, which will broadcast each time a user moves a mouse, and an administration interface visualizing user interaction as well as when a user connects and disconnects from the system. Our goal is to show how a more complex system might be designed (such as one that tracks and graphs every click, swipe, or other interactions a user might make).

The final administration interface will show activity graphs for several users and resemble this:

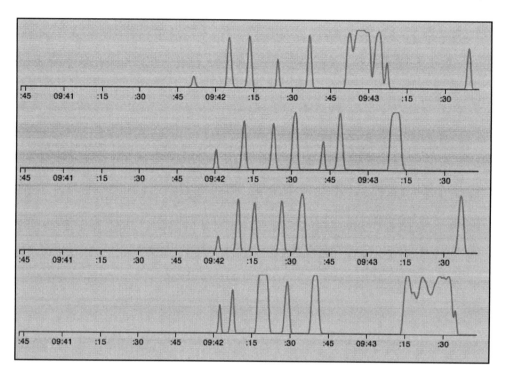

As this system will be tracking the X and Y positions of each mouse motion made by all users, we will spread this continuous stream of data across all available machine cores using `cluster`, with each worker in the cluster sharing the burden of carrying the large amounts of socket data being fed into a single, shared port. Go ahead and visit the code bundle for this chapter, and follow the README.MD instructions in the /watcher folder.

A good place to start is in designing the mock client page, which is responsible solely for catching all mouse movement events and broadcasting them, through a WebSocket, to our clustered socket server. We are using the native WebSocket implementation; you may want to use a library to handle older browsers (such as Socket.IO):

```
<head>
  <script>
    let connection = new WebSocket('ws://127.0.0.1:8081', ['json']);
      connection.onopen = () => {
        let userId = 'user' + Math.floor(Math.random()*10e10);
        document.onmousemove = e => {
          connection.send(JSON.stringify({id: userId, x: e.x, y: e.y}));
```

```
      }
    };
  </script>
</head>
```

Here, we need to simply turn on the basic `mousemove` tracking, which will broadcast the position of a user's mouse on each movement to our socket. Additionally, we send along a unique user ID, as a tracking client identity will be important to us later on. Note that in a production environment, you will want to implement a more intelligent unique ID generator, likely though a server-side authentication module.

In order for this information to reach other clients, a centralized socket server must be set up. As mentioned, we will want this socket server to be clustered. Clustered child processes, each duplicates of the following program, will handle mouse data sent by clients:

```
const SServer = require('ws').Server;
let socketServer = new SServer({port: 8081});
socketServer.on('connection', socket => {
  let lastMessage = null;
  function kill() => {
    if (lastMessage) {
      process.send({kill: lastMessage.id});
    }
  }
  socket.on('message', message => {
    lastMessage = JSON.parse(message);
    process.send(lastMessage);
  });
  socket.on('close', kill);
  socket.on('error', kill);
});
```

 In this demonstration, we are using *Einar Otto Stangvik's* very fast and well-designed socket server library, `ws`, which is hosted on GitHub at: `https://github.com/websockets/ws`

Thankfully, our code remains very simple. We have a socket server listening for messages (remember that the client is sending an object with mouse *X* and *Y* as well as a user ID). Finally, when data is received (the `message` event), we parse the received JSON into an object and pass that back to our cluster master via `process.send`.

Note as well how we store the last message (`lastMessage`), done for bookkeeping reasons, as when a connection terminates, we will need to pass along the last user ID seen on this connection to administrators.

The pieces to catch client data broadcasts are now set up. Once this data is received, how is it passed to the administration interface previously pictured?

We've designed this system with scaling in mind, and we want to decouple the collection of data from the systems that broadcast data. Our cluster of socket servers can accept a constant flow of data from many thousands of clients, and should be optimized for doing just that. In other words, the cluster should delegate the responsibility for broadcasting mouse activity data to another system, even to other servers.

In the next chapter, we will look at more advanced scaling and messaging tools, such as message queues and UDP broadcasting. For our purposes here, we will simply create an HTTP server responsible for managing connections from administrators and broadcasting mouse activity updates to them. We will use SSE for this, as the data flow needs to only be one-way, from server to client.

The HTTP server will implement a very basic validation system for administrator logins, holding on to successful connections in a way that will allow our socket cluster to broadcast mouse activity updates to all. It will also serve as a basic static file server, sending both the client and administration HTML when requested, though we will focus only on how it handles two routes: `admin/adminname`; and `/receive/adminname`. Once the server is understood, we will go into how our socket cluster connects to it.

The first route—`/admin/adminname`—is mostly responsible for validating administrator login, also ensuring that this is not a duplicate login. Once that identity is established, we can send back an HTML page to the administration interface. The specific client code used to draw the graphs previously pictured won't be discussed here. What we do need is an SSE connection to our server such that the interface's graphing tools receive real-time updates of mouse activity. Some JavaScript on the returned administrator's page establishes such a connection:

```
let ev = new EventSource('/receive/adminname');
ev.addEventListener("open", () => {
  console.log("Connection opened");
});
ev.addEventListener("message", data => {
  //  Do something with mouse data, like graph it.
}
```

On our server, we implement the `/receive/adminname` route:

```
if (method === "receive") {
  // Unknown admin; reject
  if (!admins[adminId]) {
    return response.end();
  }
  response.writeHead(200, {
    "Content-Type": "text/event-stream",
    "Cache-Control": "no-cache",
    "Connection": "keep-alive"
  });
  response.write(":" + Array(2049).join(" ") + "\n");
  response.write("retry: 2000\n");
  response.on("close", () => {
    admins[adminId] = {};
  });
  setInterval(() => {
    response.write("data: PING\n\n");
  }, 15000);
  admins[adminId].socket = response;
  return;
}
```

The main purpose of this route is to establish an SSE connection and store the administrator's connection, so that we can later broadcast to it.

We will now add the pieces that will pass mouse activity data along to a visualization interface. Scaling this subsystem across cores using the cluster module is our next step. The cluster master now simply needs to wait for mouse data from its socket-serving children, as described earlier.

We will use the same ideas presented in the earlier discussion of cluster, simply forking the preceding socket server code across all the available CPUs:

```
if (cluster.isMaster) {
  let i;
  for (i = 0; i < numCPUs; i++) {
    cluster.fork();
  }
  cluster.on('exit', (worker, code, signal) => {
    console.log(`worker ${worker.process.pid} died`);
  })

  // Set up socket worker listeners
  Object.keys(cluster.workers).forEach(id => {
    cluster.workers[id].on('message', msg => {
```

```
    let a;
    for (a in admins) {
      if (admins[a].socket) {
        admins[a].socket.write(`data: ${JSON.stringify(msg)}\n\n`);
      }
    }
  });
});
```

Mouse activity data pipes into a cluster worker through a socket and is broadcasted via `process.send` to the cluster master described earlier. On each worker message, we run through all connected administrators and send mouse data to their visualization interfaces using SSE. The administrators can now watch for the arrival and exit of clients as well as their individual level of activity.

To test the system, first log in as the default admin with `http://localhost:2112/admin/adminname`. You should see a turquoise background, empty for now since there are no connected clients. Next, create some clients by opening one or more browser windows and navigating to `http://localhost:2112`, where you will see a blank screen. Move your mouse around on this screen however you'd like. If you return to the admin interface you'll see that your mouse movements (one or many clients) are being tracked and graphed.

Summary

This is the first chapter where we've really begun to test Node's scalability goal. Having considered the various arguments for and against different ways of thinking about concurrency and parallelism, we arrived at an understanding of how Node has successfully maintained the advantages of threading and parallel processing while wrapping all that complexity within a concurrency model that is both easy to reason about and robust.

Having gone deeper into how processes work, and in particular, how child processes can communicate with each other, even spawn further children, we looked at some use cases. An example of how to combine native Unix command processes seamlessly with custom Node processes led us to a performant and straightforward technique for processing large files. The cluster module was then applied to the problem of how to share responsibility for handling a busy socket between multiple workers, this ability to share socket handles between processes demonstrating a powerful aspect of Node's design. And we learned about a production-grade process runner, PM2, and how it makes managing both single processes and clusters easier.

Having seen how Node applications might be scaled vertically, we can now look into horizontal scaling across many systems and servers. In the next chapter, we'll learn how to connect Node with third-party services, such as Amazon and Twilio, set up multiple Node servers behind proxies, and more.

8

Scaling Your Application

"Evolution is a process of constant branching and expansion."

- Stephen Jay Gould

Scalability and performance are not the same things:

"The terms "performance" and "scalability" are commonly used interchangeably, but the two are distinct: performance measures the speed with which a single request can be executed, while scalability measures the ability of a request to maintain its performance under increasing load. For example, the performance of a request may be reported as generating a valid response within three seconds, but the scalability of the request measures the request's ability to maintain that three-second response time as the user load increases."

- Steven Haines, "Pro Java EE 5"

In the last chapter, we looked at how Node clusters might be used to increase the performance of an application. Through the use of clusters of processes and workers, we learned how to efficiently deliver results in the face of many simultaneous requests. We learned to scale Node *vertically*, keeping the same footprint (a single server) and increasing throughput by piling on the power of the available CPUs.

In this chapter, we will focus on *horizontal* scalability; the idea is that an application composed of self-sufficient and independent units (servers) can be scaled by adding more units without altering the application's code.

We want to create an architecture within which any number of optimized and encapsulated Node-powered servers can be added or subtracted in response to changing demands, dynamically scaling without ever requiring a system rewrite. We want to share work across different systems, pushing requests to the OS, to another server, to a third-party service, while coordinating those I/O operations intelligently using Node's evented approach to concurrency.

Through architectural parallelism, our systems can manage increased data volume more efficiently. Specialized systems can be isolated when necessary, even independently scaled or otherwise clustered.

Node is particularly well-suited to handle two key aspects of horizontally-scaled architectures.

Firstly, Node enforces non-blocking I/O, such that the seizing up of any one unit will not cause a cascade of locking that brings down an entire application. As no single I/O operation will block the entire system, integrating third-party services can be done with confidence, encouraging a decoupled architecture.

Secondly, Node places great importance on supporting as many fast network communication protocols as possible. Whether through a shared database, a shared filesystem, or a message queue, Node's efficient network and `Stream` layers allow many servers to synchronize their efforts in balancing load. Being able to efficiently manage shared socket connections, for instance, helps when scaling out a cluster of servers as much as it does a cluster of processes.

In this chapter, we will look at how to balance traffic between many servers running Node, how these distinct servers can communicate, and how these clusters can bind to and benefit from specialized cloud services.

When to scale?

The theory around application scaling is a complex and interesting topic that continues to be refined and expanded. A comprehensive discussion of the topic will require several books, curated for different environments and needs. For our purposes, we will simply learn how to recognize when scaling up (or even scaling down) is necessary.

Having a flexible architecture that can add and subtract resources as needed is essential to a resilient scaling strategy. A vertical scaling solution does not always suffice (simply adding memory or CPUs will not deliver the necessary improvements). When should horizontal scaling be considered?

 It is essential that you are able to monitor your servers. One simple but useful way to check the CPU and memory usage commanded by Node processes running on a server is to use the Unix `ps` (*process status*) command, for example, `ps aux | grep node`. A more robust solution is to install an interactive process manager, such as HTOP (`http://hisham.hm/htop/`) for Unix systems, or Process Explorer for Windows-based systems (`https://docs.microsoft.com/en-us/sysinternals/downloads/process-explorer`).

Network latency

When network response times are exceeding some threshold, such as each request taking several seconds, it is likely that the system has gone well past a stable state.

While the easiest way to discover this problem is to wait for customer complaints about slow websites, it is better to create controlled stress tests against an equivalent application environment or server.

AB (Apache Bench) is a simple and straightforward way to do blunt stress tests against a server. This tool can be configured in many ways, but the kind of test you would do for measuring the network response times for your server is generally straightforward.

For example, let's test the response times for this simple Node server:

```
http.createServer(function(request, response) {
    response.writeHeader(200, {"Content-Type": "text/plain"});
    response.write("Hello World");
    response.end();
}).listen(2112)
```

Here's how one might test running 10,000 requests against that server, with a concurrency of 100 (the number of simultaneous requests):

```
ab -n 10000 -c 100 http://yourserver.com/
```

If all goes well, you will receive a report similar to this:

```
Concurrency Level:      100
Time taken for tests:   9.658 seconds
Complete requests:      10000
Failed requests:        0
Write errors:           0
Total transferred:      1120000 bytes
HTML transferred:       110000 bytes
Requests per second:    1035.42 [#/sec] (mean)
Time per request:       96.579 [ms] (mean)
Time per request:       0.966 [ms] (mean, across all concurrent
requests)
Transfer rate:          113.25 [Kbytes/sec] received
Connection Times (ms)
              min  mean[+/-sd] median   max
Connect:        0    0   0.4      0       6
Processing:    54   96  11.7     90     136
Waiting:       53   96  11.7     89     136
Total:         54   96  11.6     90     136
Percentage of the requests served within a certain time (ms)
  50%      90
  66%      98
     . . .
  99%     133
 100%     136 (longest request)
```

There is a lot of useful information contained in this report. In particular, one should be looking for failed requests and the percentage of long-running requests.

Much more sophisticated testing systems exist, but ab is a good quick-and-dirty snapshot of performance. Get in the habit of creating testing environments that mirror your production systems and test them.

 Running ab on the same server running the Node process you are testing will, of course, impact the test speeds. The test runner itself uses a lot of server resources, so your results will be misleading. Full documentation for ab can be found at: https://httpd.apache.org/docs/2.4/programs/ab.html.

Hot CPUs

When CPU usage begins to nudge maximums, start to think about increasing the number of units processing client requests. Remember that while adding one new CPU to a single-CPU machine will bring immediate and enormous improvements, adding another CPU to a 32-core machine will not necessarily bring an equal improvement. Slowdowns are not always about slow calculations.

As mentioned earlier, `htop` is a great way to get a quick overview of your server's performance. As it visualizes the load being put on each core in real time, it is a great way to get an idea of what is happening. Additionally, the load average of your server is nicely summarized with three values. This is a happy server:

```
Load average: 0.00 0.01 0.00
```

What do these values mean? What is a "good" or a "bad" load average?

All three numbers are measuring CPU usage, presenting measurements taken at one, five, and fifteen-minute intervals. Generally, it can be expected that short-term load will be higher than long-term load. If, on an average, your server is not overly stressed over time, it is likely that clients are having a good experience.

On a single-core machine, load average should remain between 0.00 and 1.00. Any request will take *some* time—the question is whether the request is taking *more time than necessary*—and whether there are delays due to excessive load.

If a CPU can be thought of as a pipe, a measurement of 0.00 means that there is no excessive friction, or delay, in pushing through a drop of water. A measurement of 1.00 indicates that our pipe is at its capacity; water is flowing smoothly, but any additional attempts to push water through will be faced with delays, or backpressure. This translates into latency on the network, with new requests joining an ever-growing queue.

A multicore machine simply multiplies the measurement boundary. A machine with four cores is at its capacity when load average reaches 4.00.

How you choose to react to load averages depends on the specifics of an application. It is not unusual for servers running mathematical models to see their CPU averages hit maximum capacity; in such cases, you want *all* available resources dedicated to performing calculations. A file server running at capacity, on the other hand, is likely worth investigating.

Generally, a load average above 0.60 should be investigated. Things are not urgent, but there may be a problem around the corner. A server that regularly reaches 1.00 after all known optimizations have been made is a clear candidate for scaling, as of course is any server exceeding that average.

Node also offers native process information via the os module:

```
const os = require('os');
// Load average, as an Array
console.log(os.loadavg());
// Total and free memory
console.log(os.totalmem());
console.log(os.freemem());
// Information about CPUs, as an Array
console.log(os.cpus());
```

Socket usage

When the number of persistent socket connections begins to grow past the capacity of any single Node server, however optimized, it will be necessary to think about spreading out the servers handling user sockets. Using socket.io, it is possible to check the number of connected clients at any time using the following command:

```
io.sockets.clients()
```

In general, it is best to track web socket connection counts within the application, via some sort of tracking/logging system.

Many file descriptors

When the number of file descriptors opened in an OS hovers close to its limit, it is likely that an excessive number of Node processes are active, files are open, or other file descriptors (such as sockets or named pipes) are in play. If these high numbers are not due to bugs or a bad design, it is time to add a new server.

Checking the number of open file descriptors of any kind can be accomplished using lsof:

```
# lsof | wc -l      // 1345
```

Data creep

When the amount of data being managed by a single database server begins to exceed many millions of rows or many gigabytes of memory, it is time to think about scaling. Here, you might choose to simply dedicate a single server to your database, begin to share databases, or even move into a managed cloud storage solution earlier rather than later. Recovering from a data layer failure is rarely a quick fix, and in general, it is dangerous to have a single point of failure for something as important as *all of your data*.

If you're using Redis, the `info` command will provide most of the data you will need, to make these decisions. Consider the following example:

```
redis> info
# Clients
connected_clients:1
blocked_clients:0
# Memory
used_memory:17683488
used_memory_human:16.86M
used_memory_rss:165900288
used_memory_peak:226730192
used_memory_peak_human:216.23M
used_memory_lua:31744
mem_fragmentation_ratio:9.38
# CPU
used_cpu_sys:13998.77
used_cpu_user:21498.45
used_cpu_sys_children:1.60
used_cpu_user_children:7.19
...
```

More information on `INFO` can be found at: `https://redis.io/commands/INFO`.

For MongoDB, you might use the `db.stats()` command:

```
> db.stats(1024)
{     "collections" : 3,
    "objects" : 5,
    "avgObjSize" : 39.2,
    "dataSize" : 0,
    "storageSize" : 12,
    "numExtents" : 3,
    "indexes" : 1,
    "indexSize" : 7,
    "fileSize" : 196608,
    "nsSizeMB" : 16,
    ...
    "ok" : 1 }
```

Passing the argument `1024` flags `stats` to display all values in kilobytes.

> More information can be found at: `https://docs.mongodb.com/v3.4/reference/method/db.stats/`

Tools for monitoring servers

There are several tools available for monitoring servers, but few designed specifically for Node. One strong candidate is **N|Solid** (`https://nodesource.com/products/nsolid`), a company staffed by many key contributors to Node's core. This cloud service is easily integrated with a Node app, offering a useful dashboard visualizing CPU usage, average response times, and more.

Other good monitoring tools to consider are listed in the following:

- **Nagios**: `https://www.nagios.org`
- **Munin**: `http://munin-monitoring.org/`
- **Monit**: `https://mmonit.com/`
- **NewRelic**: `https://newrelic.com/nodejs`
- **Keymetrics**: `https://keymetrics.io/`

Running multiple Node servers

It is easy to purchase several servers and then to run some Node processes on them. However, how can those distinct servers be coordinated such that they form part of a single application? One aspect of this problem concerns clustering multiple identical servers around a single entry point. How can client connections be shared across a pool of servers?

Horizontal scaling is the process of splitting up your architecture into network-distinct nodes and coordinating them. *Cloud computing* relates here, and simply means locating some of the functionality an application running on a server somewhere on a remote server, running somewhere else. Without a single point of failure (so the theory goes) the general system is more robust. The *parking lot problem* is another consideration that Walmart likely faces—during shopping holidays, you will need many thousands of parking spots, but during the rest of the year, this investment in empty space is hard to justify. In terms of servers, the ability to dynamically scale both up and down argues against building fixed vertical silos. Adding hardware to a running server is also a more complicated process than spinning up and seamlessly linking another virtual machine to your application.

File serving speeds are, of course, not the only reason you might use a proxy server like NGINX. It is often true that network topology characteristics make a reverse proxy the better choice, especially when the centralization of common services, such as compression, makes sense. The point is simply that Node should not be excluded solely due to outdated biases about its ability to efficiently serve files.

Forward and reverse proxies

A **proxy** is someone or something acting on behalf of another.

A **forward proxy** normally works on behalf of clients in a private network, brokering requests to an outside network, such as retrieving data from the internet. Earlier in this book, we looked at how one might set up a proxy server using Node, where the Node server functioned as an intermediary, forwarding requests from clients to other network servers, usually via the internet.

Early web providers such as AOL functioned in the following way:

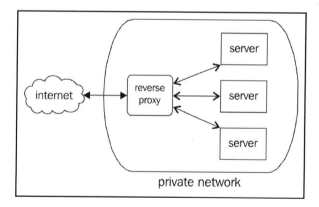

Network administrators use forward proxies when they must restrict access to the outside world, that is, the internet. If network users are downloading malware from somebadwebsite.com via an email attachment, the administrator can block access to that location. Restrictions on access to social networking sites might be imposed on an office network. Some countries even restrict access to public websites in this way.

A **reverse proxy**, not surprisingly, works in the opposite way, accepting requests from a public network and servicing those requests within a private network the client has little much visibility into. Direct access to servers by clients is first delegated to a reverse proxy:

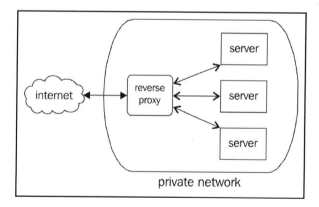

This is the type of proxy we might use to balance requests from clients across many Node servers. Client X does not communicate with any given server directly. A broker Y is the point of first contact, able to direct X to a server that is under less load, or that is located closer to X, or is in some other way the best server for X to access at this time.

We will now take a look at how to implement reverse proxies when scaling Node, discussing implementations that use **NGINX** (pronounced as **Engine X**), a popular choice when load balancing Node servers, and those using native Node modules.

Using the http-proxy module

For many years, it was recommended that a web server (such as NGINX) be placed in front of Node servers. The claim was that mature web servers handle static file transfers more efficiently. While this may have been true for earlier Node versions (which also suffered from the bugs that new technologies face), it is no longer necessarily true in terms of pure speed. More importantly, using **Content Delivery Networks** (**CDN**) and other *edge* services the static files your application might need will already be cached—your server won't be serving these files, to begin with.

Node is designed to facilitate the creation of network software, so it comes as no surprise that several proxying modules have been developed. A popular production-grade Node proxy is **http-proxy**. Let's take a look at how we would use it to balance requests to different Node servers.

The entirety of our routing stack will be provided by Node. One Node server will be running our proxy, listening on port 80. We'll cover the following three scenarios:

- Running multiple Node servers on separate ports on the same machine
- Using one box as a pure router, proxying to external URLs
- Creating a basic round-robin load balancer

As an initial example, let's look at how to use this module to redirect requests:

```
let httpProxy = require('http-proxy');
let proxy = httpProxy.createServer({
target: {
  host: 'www.example.com',
  port: 80
}
}).listen(80);
```

By starting this server on port 80 of our local machine, we are able redirect the user to another URL.

To run several distinct Node servers, each responding to a different URL, on a single machine, one simply has to define a router:

```
let httpProxy = httpProxy.createServer({
  router: {
    'www.mywebsite.com' : '127.0.0.1:8001',
    'www.myothersite.com' : '127.0.0.1:8002',
  }
});
httpProxy.listen(80);
```

For each of your distinct websites, you can now point your DNS name servers (via ANAME or CNAME records) to the same endpoint (wherever this Node program is running), and they will resolve to different Node servers. This is handy when you want to run several websites but don't want to create a new physical server for each one. Another strategy is to handle different paths within the same website on different Node servers:

```
let httpProxy = httpProxy.createServer({
  router: {
    'www.mywebsite.com/friends': '127.0.0.1:8001',
    'www.mywebsite.com/foes': '127.0.0.1:8002',
  }
});
httpProxy.listen(80);
```

This allows specialized functionality in your application to be handled by uniquely configured servers.

Setting up a load balancer is also straightforward. As we'll see later with NGINX's **upstream** directive, we simply provide a list of servers to be balanced:

```
const httpProxy = require('http-proxy');
let addresses = [
  { host: 'one.example.com', port: 80 },
  { host: 'two.example.com', port: 80 }
];
httpProxy.createServer((req, res, proxy) => {
  let target = addresses.shift();
  proxy.proxyRequest(req, res, target);
  addresses.push(target);
}).listen(80);
```

In this example, we treat servers equally, cycling through them in order. After the selected server is proxied, it is returned to the *rear* of the list.

It should be clear that this example can be easily extended to accommodate other directives, such as NGINX's **weight**.

 The `redbird` module is an extremely advanced reverse proxy built on top of **http-proxy**. Among other things, it has built-in support for automatic SSL certificate generation and HTTP/2 support. Learn more at: `https://github.com/OptimalBits/redbird`.

Deploying a NGINX load balancer on Digital Ocean

As Node is so efficient, most websites or applications can accommodate all of their scaling needs in the vertical dimension. Node can handle enormous levels of traffic using only a few CPUs and an unexceptional volume of memory.

NGINX is a very popular high-performance web server that is often used as a proxy server. There is some serendipity in the fact that NGINX is a popular choice with Node developers, given its design:

> As mentioned on `http://www.linuxjournal.com/magazine/nginx-high-performance-web-server-and-reverse-proxy`, *"NGINX is able to serve more requests per second with [fewer] resources because of its architecture. It consists of a master process, which delegates work to one or more worker processes. Each worker handles multiple requests in an event-driven or asynchronous manner using special functionality from the Linux kernel (epoll/select/poll). This allows NGINX to handle a large number of concurrent requests quickly with very little overhead."*

NGINX also makes load balancing very easy. In the following examples, we will see how proxying through NGINX comes with load balancing *out of the box*.

Digital Ocean is a cloud hosting provider that is inexpensive and easy to set up. We will build an NGINX load balancer on this service.

To sign up, visit: `https://www.digitalocean.com`. The basic package (at the time of this writing) incurs a five dollar fee, but promotion codes are regularly made available; a simple web search should result in a usable code. Create and verify an account to get started.

Digital Ocean packages are described as droplets, with certain characteristics—amount of storage space, transfer limits, and so on. A basic package is sufficient for our needs. Also, you will indicate a hosting region as well as the OS to install in your droplet (in this example, we'll use the latest version of Ubuntu). Create a droplet, and check your email for login instructions. You're done!

You will receive full login information for your instance. You can now open a Terminal and SSH into your box using those login credentials.

On your initial login, you might want to update your packages. For Ubuntu, you would run `apt-get update` and `apt-get upgrade`. Other package managers have similar commands (such as `yum update` for RHEL/CentOs).

Before we begin to install, let's change our root password and create a non-root user (it is unsafe to expose root to external logins and software installs). To change your root password, type `passwd` and follow the instructions in your Terminal. To create a new user, enter `adduser <new user name>` (for example, `adduser john`). Follow the instructions.

One more step: we want to give some administrative privileges to our new user, as we'll be installing software as that user. In Unix parlance, you want to give `sudo` access to this new user. Instructions on how to do this are easy to find for whichever OS you've chosen. Essentially, you will want to change the `/etc/sudoers` file. Remember to do this using a command such as `lvisudo`; do not edit the sudoers file by hand! You may also want to restrict root logins and do other SSH access management at this point.

After successfully executing `sudo -i` in your Terminal, you will be able to enter commands without prefixing each one with `sudo`. The following examples assume that you've done this.

We'll now create a NGINX load balancer frontend for two Node servers. This means we will create three droplets: one for the balancer, and an additional two droplets to serve as Node servers. At the end, we will end up with an architecture that looks something like this:

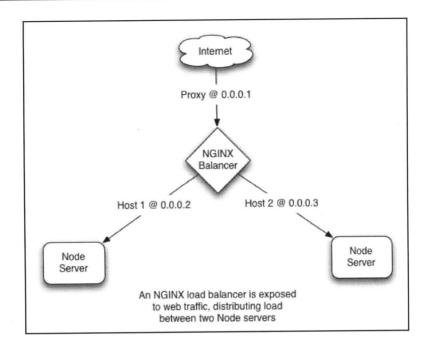

An NGINX load balancer is exposed
to web traffic, distributing load
between two Node servers

Installing and configuring NGINX

Let's install NGINX and Node/npm. If you're still logged in as root, log out and
reauthenticate as the new user you've just created. To install NGINX (on Ubuntu), simply
type this:

```
apt-get install nginx
```

Most other Unix package managers will have NGINX installers.

To start NGINX, use this:

```
service nginx start
```

Full documentation for NGINX can be found at: `https://www.nginx.com/ resources/wiki/start/`.

You should now be able to point your browser to the IP you were assigned (check your inbox if you've forgotten) and see something like this:

Welcome to nginx!

If you see this page, the nginx web server is successfully installed and working. Further configuration is required.

For online documentation and support please refer to nginx.org. Commercial support is available at nginx.com.

Thank you for using nginx.

Now, let's set up the two servers that NGINX will balance.

Create an additional two droplets in Digital Ocean. You will *not* install NGINX on these severs. Configure permissions on these servers as we did earlier, and install Node in both droplets. An easy way to manage your Node installation is using *Tim Caswell's* **NVM** (Node Version Manager). NVM is essentially a bash script that provides a set of command-line tools facilitating Node version management, allowing you to easily switch between versions. To install it, run the following command in your Terminal:

```
curl https://raw.githubusercontent.com/creationix/nvm/v7.10.1/install.sh |
sh
```

Now, install your preferred Node version:

```
nvm install 9.2.0
```

You might want to add a command to your `.bashrc` or `.profile` file to ensure that a certain node version is used each time you start a shell:

```
nvm use 9.2.0
```

To test our system, we need to set up Node servers on both of these machines. Create the following program file on each server, changing ** to something unique on each (such as *one* and *two*):

```
const http = require('http');
http.createServer((req, res) => {
  res.writeHead(200, {
    "Content-Type" : "text/html"
  });
  res.write('HOST **');
  res.end();
}).listen(8080)
```

Start this file on each server (`node serverfile.js`). Each server will now answer on port 8080. You should now be able to reach this server by pointing a browser to each droplet's IP:8080. Once you have two servers responding with distinct messages, we can set up the NGINX load balancer.

Load balancing across servers is straightforward with NGINX. You need simply indicate, in the NGINX configuration script, which upstream servers should be balanced. The two Node servers we've just created will be the upstream servers. NGINX will be configured to balance requests to each:

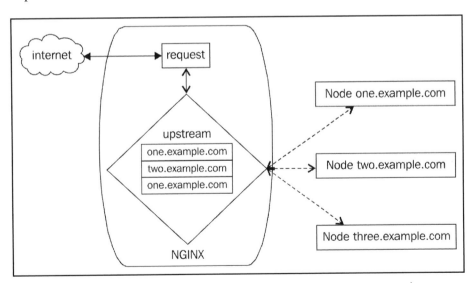

Each request will be handled first by NGINX, which will check its *upstream* configuration, and based on how it is configured, will (reverse) proxy requests to upstream servers that will actually handle the request.

You will find the default NGINX server configuration file on your balancer droplet at `/etc/nginx/sites-available/default`.

In production, you'll likely want to create a custom directory and configuration file, but for our purposes, we'll simply modify the default configuration file (you might want to make a backup before you start modifying it).

At the top of the NGINX configuration file, we want to define some *upstream* servers that will be candidates for redirection. This is simply a map with the `lb-servers` arbitrary key, to be referenced in the server definition that follows:

```
upstream lb_servers {
  server first.node.server.ip;
  server second.node.server.ip;
}
```

Now that we've established the candidate map, we need to configure NGINX such that it will forward requests in a balanced way to each of the members of lb-servers:

```
server {
    listen 80 default_server;
    listen [::]:80 default_server ipv6only=on;

    #root /usr/share/nginx/html;
    #index index.html index.htm;

    # Make site accessible from http://localhost/
    server_name localhost;

    location / {
        proxy_pass http://lb-servers; # Load balance mapped servers
        proxy_http_version 1.1;
        proxy_set_header Upgrade $http_upgrade;
        proxy_set_header Connection 'upgrade';
        proxy_set_header Host $host;
        proxy_cache_bypass $http_upgrade;
    }
... more configuration options not specifically relevant to our purposes
}
```

The key line is this one:

```
proxy_pass http://lb-servers
```

Note how the name `lb-servers` matches the name of our upstream definition. This should make what is happening clear: an NGINX server listening on port `80` will pass the request on to a server definition as contained in lb-servers. If the upstream definition has only one server in it, that server gets all the traffic. If several servers are defined, NGINX attempts to distribute traffic evenly among them.

It is also possible to balance load across several *local servers* using the same technique. One would simple run different Node servers on different ports, such as `server 127.0.0.1:8001` and `server 127.0.0.1:8002`.

Go ahead and change the NGINX configuration (consulting the `nginx.config` file in the code bundle for this book if you get stuck). Once you've changed it, restart NGINX with the following command:

```
service nginx restart
```

Alternatively, if you prefer, use this:

```
service nginx stop
service nginx start
```

Assuming that the other two droplets running Node servers are active, you should now be able to point your browser to your NGINX-enabled droplet and see messages from those servers!

As we will likely want more precise control over how traffic is distributed across our upstream servers, there are further directives that can be applied to upstream server definitions.

NGINX balances load using a weighted round-robin algorithm. In order to control the relative weighting of traffic distribution, we use the weight directive:

```
upstream lb-servers {
    server first.node.server.ip weight=10;
    server second.node.server.ip weight=20;
}
```

This definition tells NGINX to distribute twice as much load to the second server as to the first. Servers with more memory or CPUs might be favored, for example. Another way to use this system is to create an A/B testing scenario, where one server containing a proposed new design receives some small fraction of total traffic, such that metrics on the testing server (sales, downloads, engagement length, and so forth) can be compared against the wider average.

Three other useful directives are available, which work together to manage connection failures:

- `max_fails`: The number of times communication with a server fails prior to marking that server as inoperative. The period of time within which these failures must occur is defined by `fail_timeout`.
- `fail_timeout`: The time slice during which `max_fails` must occur, indicating that a server is inoperative. This number also indicates the amount of time after a server is marked inoperative that NGINX will again attempt to reach the flagged server.

Consider this example:

```
upstream lb-servers {
    server first.node.server.ip weight=10 max_fails=2
fail_timeout=20s;
    server second.node.server.ip weight=20 max_fails=10
fail_timeout=5m;
}
```

- `backup`: A server marked with this directive will only be called when and if *all* the other listed servers are unavailable.

Additionally, there are some directives for the upstream definition that add some control over how clients are directed to upstream servers:

- `least_conn`: Pass a request to the server with the least connections. This provides a slightly smarter balancing, taking into consideration server load as well as weighting.
- `ip_hash`: The idea here is to create a hash of each connecting IP, and to ensure that requests from a given client are always passed to the same server.

Another commonly used tool for balancing Node servers is the dedicated load balancer HAProxy, available at: http://www.haproxy.org.

Message queues – RabbitMQ

One of the best ways to ensure that distributed servers maintain a dependable communication channel is to bundle the complexity of remote procedure calls into a distinct unit-a messaging queue. When one process wishes to send a message to another process, the message can simply be placed on this queue-like a to-do list for your application, with the queue service doing the work of ensuring that messages get delivered as well as delivering any important replies back to the original sender.

There are a few enterprise-grade message queues available, many of them deploying **AMQP (Advanced Message Queueing Protocol)**. We will focus on a very stable and well-known implementation—RabbitMQ.

To install RabbitMQ in your environment, follow the instructions found at: https://www.rabbitmq.com/download.html.

Once installed, you will start the RabbitMQ server with this command:

```
service rabbitmq-server start
```

To interact with RabbitMQ using Node, we will use the node-amqp module created by *Theo Schlossnagle*:

```
npm install amqp
```

To use a message queue, one must first create a consumer—a binding to RabbitMQ that will listen for messages published to the queue. The most basic consumer will listen for all messages:

```
const amqp = require('amqp');
const consumer = amqp.createConnection({ host: 'localhost', port: 5672 });
consumer.on('error', err => {
console.log(err);
});
consumer.on('ready', () => {
let exchange = consumer.exchange('node-topic-exchange', {type: "topic"});
```

```
consumer.queue('node-topic-queue', q => {
q.bind(exchange, '#');
q.subscribe(message => {    // Messages are buffers
console.log(message.data.toString('utf8'));
});
exchange.publish("some-topic", "Hello!");
});
});
```

We are now listening for messages from the RabbitMQ server bound to port 5672.

Once this consumer establishes a connection, it will establish the name of the queue it will listen to, and should bind to an exchange. In this example, we create a topic exchange (the default), giving it a unique name. We also indicate that we would like to listen for *all* messages via #. All that is left to do is subscribe to the queue, receiving a message object. We will learn more about the message object as we progress. For now, note the important data property, containing sent messages.

Now that we have established a consumer, let's publish a message to the exchange. If all goes well, we will see the sent message appear in our console:

```
consumer.on('ready', function() {
  // ...
  exchange.publish("some-topic", "Hello!");
});
// Hello!
```

We have already learned enough to implement useful scaling tools. If we have a number of distributed Node processes, even on different physical servers, each can reliably send messages to one another via RabbitMQ. Each process simply needs to implement an **exchange queue subscriber** to receive messages, and an **exchange publisher** to send messages.

Types of exchanges

RabbitMQ provides three types of exchanges: **direct**, **fanout**, and **topic**. The differences appear in the way each type of exchange processes **routing keys**—the first argument sent to exchange.publish.

A direct exchange matches routing keys directly. A queue binding like the following one matches *only* messages sent to 'room-1':

```
queue.bind(exchange, 'room-1');
```

As no parsing is necessary, direct exchanges are able to process more messages than topic exchanges in a set period of time.

A fanout exchange is indiscriminate; it routes messages to all the queues bound to it, ignoring routing keys. This type of exchange is used for wide broadcasts.

A topic exchange matches routing keys based on the wildcards # and *. Unlike other types, routing keys for topic exchanges *must* be composed of words separated by dots, `"animals.dogs.poodle"`, for example. A # matches zero or more words; it will match every message (as we saw in the previous example), just like a fanout exchange. The other wildcard is *, and this matches *exactly* one word.

Direct and fanout exchanges can be implemented using nearly the same code as the given topic exchange example, requiring only that the exchange type be changed, and bind operations be aware of how they will be associated with routing keys (fanout subscribers receive all messages, regardless of the key; for direct, the routing key must match directly).

This last example should drive home how topic exchanges work. We will create three queues with different matching rules, filtering the messages each queue receives from the exchange:

```
consumer.on('ready', function() {
  // When all 3 queues are ready, publish.
  let cnt = 3;
  let queueReady = function() {
    if(--cnt > 0) {
      return;
    }
    exchange.publish("animals.dogs.poodles", "Poodle!");
    exchange.publish("animals.dogs.dachshund", "Dachshund!");
    exchange.publish("animals.cats.shorthaired", "Shorthaired Cat!");
    exchange.publish("animals.dogs.shorthaired", "Shorthaired Dog!");
    exchange.publish("animals.misc", "Misc!");
  }
  let exchange = consumer.exchange('topical', {type: "topic"});
  consumer.queue('queue-1', q => {
    q.bind(exchange, 'animals.*.shorthaired');
    q.subscribe(message => {
      console.log(`animals.*.shorthaired ->
${message.data.toString('utf8')}`);
    });
    queueReady();
  });
  consumer.queue('queue-2', q => {
    q.bind(exchange, '#');
    q.subscribe(function(message) {
```

```
        console.log('# -> ' + message.data.toString('utf8'));
      });
      queueReady();
    });
    consumer.queue('queue-3', q => {
      q.bind(exchange, '*.cats.*');
      q.subscribe(message => {
        console.log(`*.cats.* -> ${message.data.toString('utf8')}`);
      });
      queueReady();
    });
  });

  //    # -> Poodle!
  //    animals.*.shorthaired -> Shorthaired Cat!
  //    *.cats.* -> Shorthaired Cat!
  //    # -> Dachshund!
  //    # -> Shorthaired Cat!
  //    animals.*.shorthaired -> Shorthaired Dog!
  //    # -> Shorthaired Dog!
  //    # -> Misc!
```

The `node-amqp` module contains further methods for controlling connections, queues, and exchanges; in particular, it contains methods for removing queues from exchanges, and subscribers from queues. Generally, changing the makeup of a running queue on the fly can lead to unexpected errors, so use these with caution.

 To learn more about the AMQP (and the options available when setting up with `node-amqp`), visit: `http://www.rabbitmq.com/tutorials/amqp-concepts.html`.

Using Node's UDP module

UDP (User Datagram Protocol) is a lightweight core internet messaging protocol, enabling servers to pass around concise **datagrams**. UDP was designed with a minimum of protocol overhead, forgoing delivery, ordering, and duplication prevention mechanisms in favor of ensuring high performance. UDP is a good choice when perfect reliability is not required and high-speed transmission is, such as what is found in networked video games and videoconferencing applications.

This is not to say that UDP is normally unreliable. In most applications, it delivers messages with high probability. It is simply not suitable when *perfect* reliability is needed, such as in a banking application. It is an excellent candidate for monitoring and logging applications, and for non-critical messaging services.

Creating a UDP server with Node is straightforward:

```
const dgram = require("dgram");
let socket = dgram.createSocket("udp4");
socket.on("message", (msg, info) => {
  console.log("socket got: " + msg + " from " +
  info.address + ":" + info.port);
});
socket.bind(41234);
socket.on("listening", () => {
  console.log("Listening for datagrams.");
});
```

The `bind` command takes three arguments, which are as follows:

- **port**: The `Integer` port number.
- **address**: This is an optional address. If this is not specified, the OS will try to listen on all addresses (which is often what you want). You might also try using `0.0.0.0` explicitly.
- **callback**: This is an optional callback, which receives no arguments.

This socket will now emit a `message` event whenever it receives a datagram via the `41234` port. The event callback receives the message itself as a first parameter, and a map of packet information as the second:

- **address**: The originating IP
- **family**: One of IPv4 or IPv6
- **port**: The originating port
- **size**: The size of the message in bytes

This map is similar to the map returned when calling `socket.address()`.

In addition to the message and listening events, a UDP socket also emits a **close** and **error** event, the latter receiving an `Error` object whenever an error occurs. To close a UDP socket (and trigger the close event), use `server.close()`.

Sending a message is even easier:

```
let client = dgram.createSocket("udp4");
let message = Buffer.from('UDP says Hello!', 'utf8');
client.send(message, 0, message.length, 41234, "localhost", (err, bytes) =>
client.close());
```

The `send` method takes the `client.send(buffer, offset, length, port, host, callback)` form:

- `buffer`: A Buffer containing the datagram to be sent.
- `offset`: An Integer indicating the position in buffer where the datagram begins.
- `length`: The number of bytes in a datagram. In combination with **offset**, this value identifies the full datagram within buffer.
- `port`: An Integer identifying the destination port.
- `address`: A String indicating the destination IP for the datagram.
- `callback`: An optional callback function, called after the send has taken place.

 The size of a datagram cannot exceed 65507 bytes, which is equal to 2^{16-1} (65535) bytes, minus the 8 bytes used by the UDP header minus the 20 bytes used by the IP header.

We now have another candidate for inter-process messaging. It will be rather easy to set up a monitoring server for our node application, listening on a UDP socket for program updates and stats sent from other processes. The protocol speed is fast enough for real-time systems, and any packet loss or other UDP hiccups will be insignificant taken as a percentage of total volume over time.

Taking the idea of broadcasting further, we can also use the `dgram` module to create a multicast server. A **multicast** is simply a one-to-many server broadcast. We can broadcast to a range of IPs that have been permanently reserved as multicast addresses:

As can be found on
http://www.iana.org/assignments/multicast-addresses/multicast-addresses
.xhtml, *"Host Extensions for IP Multicasting [RFC1112] specifies the extensions required of a host implementation of the Internet Protocol (IP) to support multicasting. The multicast addresses are in the range 224.0.0.0 through 239.255.255.255."*

Additionally, the range between `224.0.0.0` and `224.0.0.255` is further reserved for special routing protocols. Also, certain port numbers are allocated for use by UDP (and TCP), a list of which can be found at: `https://en.wikipedia.org/wiki/List_of_TCP_and_UDP_port_numbers`.

The upshot of all this fascinating information is the knowledge that there is a block of IPs and ports reserved for UDP and/or multicasting, and we will use some of them to implement multicasting over UDP with Node.

UDP multicasting with Node

The only difference between setting up a multicasting UDP server and a *standard* one is binding to a special UDP port for sending, and indicating that we'd like to listen to *all* available network adapters. Our multicasting server initialization looks like the following code snippet:

```
let socket = dgram.createSocket('udp4');
let multicastAddress = '230.1.2.3';
let multicastPort = 5554;
socket.bind(multicastPort);
socket.on("listening", function() {
    this.setMulticastTTL(64);
    this.addMembership(multicastAddress);
});
```

Once we've decided on a multicast port and an address and have bound, we catch the `listenng` event and configure our server. The most important command is `socket.addMembership`, which tells the kernel to join the multicast group at `multicastAddress`. Other UDP sockets can now subscribe to the multicast group at this address.

Datagrams hop through networks just like any network packet. The `setMulticastTTL` method is used to set the maximum number of hops (Time To Live) a datagram is allowed to make before it is abandoned, and not delivered. The acceptable range is 0-255, with the default being one (1) on most systems. This is not normally a setting one needs to worry about, but it is available when precise limits make sense, such as when packets are cheap and hops are costly.

 If you'd like to also allow listening on the local interface, use `socket.setBroadcast(true)` and `socket.setMulticastLoopback(true)`. This is normally not necessary.

We will eventually use this server to broadcast messages to all UDP listeners on `multicastAddress`. For now, let's create two clients that will listen for multicasts:

```
dgram.createSocket('udp4').on('message', (message, remote) => {
  console.log(`Client1 received message ${message} from
${remote.address}:${remote.port}`);
}).bind(multicastPort, multicastAddress);

dgram.createSocket('udp4').on('message', (message, remote) => {
  console.log(`Client2 received message ${message} from
${remote.address}:${remote.port}`);
}).bind(multicastPort, multicastAddress);
```

We now have two clients listening to the same multicast port. All that is left to do is the multicasting. In this example, we will use `setTimeout` to send a counter value every second:

```
let cnt = 1;
let sender;
(sender = function() {
  let msg = Buffer.from(`This is message #${cnt}`);
  socket.send(
    msg,
    0,
    msg.length,
    multicastPort,
    multicastAddress
  );
  ++cnt;
  setTimeout(sender, 1000);
})();
```

The counter values will produce something like the following:

```
Client2 received message This is message #1 from 67.40.141.16:5554
Client1 received message This is message #1 from 67.40.141.16:5554
Client2 received message This is message #2 from 67.40.141.16:5554
Client1 received message This is message #2 from 67.40.141.16:5554
Client2 received message This is message #3 from 67.40.141.16:5554
...
```

We have two clients listening to broadcasts from a specific group. Let's add another client, listening on a different group, let's say at multicast address 230.3.2.1:

```
dgram.createSocket('udp4').on('message', (message, remote) =>{
  console.log(`Client3 received message ${message} from
${remote.address}:${remote.port}`);
}).bind(multicastPort, '230.3.2.1');
```

As our server currently broadcasts messages to a different address, we will need to change our server configuration and add this new address with another addMembership call:

```
socket.on("listening", function() {
  this.addMembership(multicastAddress);
  this.addMembership('230.3.2.1');
});
```

We can now send to *both* addresses:

```
(sender = function() {
  socket.send(
      ...
      multicastAddress
  );
  socket.send(
      ...
      '230.3.2.1'
  );
  // ...
})();
```

Nothing stops the client from broadcasting to others in the group, or even members of another group:

```
dgram.createSocket('udp4').on('message', (message, remote) => {
  let msg = Buffer.from('Calling original group!', 'utf8');
  // 230.1.2.3 is the multicast address
  socket.send(msg, 0, msg.length, multicastPort, '230.1.2.3');
}).bind(multicastPort, '230.3.2.1');
```

Any node process that has an address on our network interface can now listen on a UDP multicast address for messages, providing a fast and elegant inter-process communication system.

Using Amazon Web Services in your application

As a few thousand users become a few million users, as databases scale to terabytes of data, the cost and complexity of maintaining an application begins to overwhelm teams with insufficient experience, funding, and/or time. When faced with rapid growth, it is sometimes useful to delegate responsibilities for one or more aspects of your application to cloud-based service providers. **AWS(Amazon Web Services)** is just such a suite of cloud-computing services, offered by `amazon.com`.

You will need an AWS account in order to use these examples. All the services we will explore are free or nearly free for low-volume development uses. To create an account on AWS, visit the following link: `https://aws.amazon.com/`. Once you have created an account, you will be able to manage all of your services via the AWS console: `https://aws.amazon.com/console/`

In this section we will learn how to use three popular AWS services:

- For storing documents and files we will connect with Amazon **S3 (Simple Storage Service)**
- Amazon's Key/Value database, **DynamoDB**
- To manage a large volume of e-mail, we will leverage Amazon's **SES (Simple Email Service)**

To access these services we will use the AWS SDK for Node, which can be found at the following link: `https://github.com/aws/aws-sdk-js`

To install the module run the following command:

```
npm install aws-sdk
```

Full documentation for the `aws-sdk` module can be found at: `https://docs.aws.amazon.com/AWSJavaScriptSDK/latest/index.html`.

Authenticating

Developers registered with AWS are assigned two identifiers:

- A public **Access Key ID** (a 20-character, alphanumeric sequence).
- A **Secret Access Key** (a 40-character sequence). It is very important to keep your Secret Key private.

Amazon also provides developers with the ability to identify the region with which to communicate, such as "us-east-1". This allows developers to target the closest servers (regional endpoint) for their requests.

The regional endpoint and both authentication keys are necessary to make requests.

 For a breakdown of regional endpoints, visit: https://docs.aws.amazon.com/general/latest/gr/rande.html.

As we will be using the same credentials in each of the following examples, let's create a single config.json file that is reused:

```
{
  "accessKeyId" : "your-key",
  "secretAccessKey" : "your-secret",
  "region" : "us-east-1",
  "apiVersions" : {
    "s3" : "2006-03-01",
    "ses" : "2010-12-01",
    "dynamodb" : "2012-08-10"
  }
}
```

We also configure the specific API versions we will use for services. Should Amazon's services API change, this will ensure that our code will continue to work.

An AWS session can now be initialized with just two lines of code. Assume that these two lines exist prior to any of the example code that follows:

```
const AWS = require('aws-sdk');
AWS.config.loadFromPath('./config.json');
```

Errors

When experimenting with these services, it is likely that error codes will appear on occasion. Due to their complexity, and the nature of cloud computing, these services can sometimes emit surprising or unexpected errors. For example, because S3 can only promise eventual consistency in some regions and situations, attempting to read a key that has just been written to may not always succeed. We will be exploring the complete list of error codes for each service, and they can be found at the following locations:

- **S3:** `https://docs.aws.amazon.com/AmazonS3/latest/API/ErrorResponses.html`

- **DynamoDB:** `http://docs.aws.amazon.com/amazondynamodb/latest/developerguide/Programming.Errors.html`

- **SES:** `https://docs.aws.amazon.com/ses/latest/DeveloperGuide/api-error-codes.html` and `https://docs.aws.amazon.com/ses/latest/DeveloperGuide/smtp-response-codes.html`

As it will be difficult in the beginning to predict where errors might arise, it is important to employ the `domain` module or other error-checking code as you proceed.

Additionally, a subtle but fundamental aspect of Amazon's security and consistency model is the strict synchronization of its web server time and time as understood by a server making requests. A discrepancy of 15 minutes is the maximum allowed. While this seems like a long time, in fact time drift is very common. When developing watch out for 403: Forbidden errors that resemble one of the following:

- `SignatureDoesNotMatch`: This error means that the signature has expired

- `RequestTimeTooSkewed`: The difference between the request time and the current time is too large

If such errors are encountered, the internal time of the server making requests may have drifted. If so, that server's time will need to be synchronized. On Unix, one can use the **NTP(Network Time Protocol)** to achieve synchrony. One solution is to use the following commands:

```
rdate 129.6.15.28
ntpdate 129.6.15.28
```

 For more information on NTP and time synchronization, visit: `http://www.pool.ntp.org/en/use.html`.

Let's start using AWS services, beginning with the distributed file service, S3.

Using S3 to store files

S3 can be used to store any file one expects to be able to store on a filesystem. Most commonly, it is used to store media files such as images and videos. S3 is an excellent document storage system as well, especially well-suited for storing small JSON objects or similar data objects.

Also, S3 objects are accessible via HTTP, which makes retrieval very natural, and REST methods such as PUT/DELETE/UPDATE are supported. S3 works very much like one would expect a typical file server to work, is spread across servers that span the globe, and offers storage capacity that is, for all practical purposes, limitless.

S3 uses the concept of a **bucket** as a sort of corollary to *hard drive*. Each S3 account can contain 100 buckets (this is a hard limit), with no limits on the number of files contained in each bucket.

Working with buckets

Creating a bucket is easy:

```
const AWS = require('aws-sdk'); // You should change this to something
unique. AWS bucket names must// be unique and are shared across ALL USER
namespaces.
const bucketName = 'nodejs-book';AWS.config.loadFromPath('../config.json');
const S3 = new AWS.S3();
S3.createBucket({
 Bucket: bucketName
}, (err, data) => {
if(err) {  throw err; }
console.log(data);
});
```

We will receive a data map containing the `Location` bucket, and a `RequestId`:

```
{
Location: '/masteringnodejs.examples'
}
```

It is likely that many different operations will be made against a bucket. As a convenience, the `aws-sdk` allows a bucket name to be automatically defined in the parameter list for all further operations:

```
let S3 = new AWS.S3({
   params: { Bucket: 'nodejs-book' }
});
S3.createBucket((err, data) => { // ... });
```

Use `listBuckets` to fetch an array of the existing buckets:

```
S3.listBuckets((err, data) => {
   console.log(data.Buckets);
});
//    [ { Name: 'nodejs-book',
//        CreationDate: Mon Jul 15 2013 22:17:08 GMT-0500 (CDT) },
//        ...
//    ]
```

 Bucket names are global to all S3 users. No single user of S3 can use a bucket name that another user has claimed. If I have a bucket named `foo`, no other S3 user can ever use that bucket name. This is a gotcha that many miss.

Working with objects

Let's add a document to the `nodejs-book` bucket on S3:

```
const AWS = require('aws-sdk');AWS.config.loadFromPath('../config.json');
const S3 = new AWS.S3({
 params: {  Bucket: 'nodejs-book' }
});
let body = JSON.stringify({ foo: "bar" });
let s3Obj = {
 Key: 'demos/putObject/first.json',
 Body: body,
 ServerSideEncryption: "AES256",
 ContentType: "application/json",
 ContentLength: body.length,
 ACL: "private"};
S3.putObject(s3Obj, (err, data) => {
 if(err) {  throw err; }
   console.log(data);
});
```

If the PUT is successful, its callback will receive an object similar to the following:

```
{ ETag: '"9bb58f26192e4ba00f01e2e7b136bbd8"',
ServerSideEncryption: 'AES256'}
```

You are encouraged to consult the SDK documentation and experiment with all the parameters that `putObject` accepts. Here, we focus on the only two required fields, and a few useful and common ones:

- `Key`: A name to uniquely identify your file within this bucket.
- `Body`: A Buffer, String, or Stream comprising the file body.
- `ServerSideEncryption`: Whether to encrypt the file within S3. The only current option is AES256 (which is a good one!).
- `ContentType`: Standard MIME type.
- `ContentLength`: A String indicating the destination IP for the datagram.
- `ACL`: Canned access permissions, such as `private` or `public-read-write`. Consult the S3 documentation.

It is a good idea to have the `Key` object resemble a filesystem path, helping with sorting and retrieval later on. In fact, Amazon's S3 console reflects this pattern in its UI:

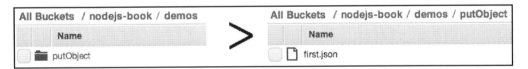

Let's stream an image up to S3:

```
fs.stat("./testimage.jpg", (err, stat) => {
 let s3Obj = {
  Key    : 'demos/putObject/testimage.jpg',
  Body   : fs.createReadStream("./testimage.jpg"),
  ContentLength : stat.size,
  ContentType  : "image/jpeg",
  ACL    : "public-read"
};
  S3.putObject(s3Obj, (err, data) => {  if(err) {    throw err;  }
console.log(data);
});
});
```

As we gave this image `public-read` permissions, it will be accessible at: `https://s3.` `amazonaws.com/nodejs-book/demos/putObject/testimage.jpg`.

Fetching an object from S3 and streaming it onto a local filesystem is even easier:

```
let outFile = fs.createWriteStream('./fetchedfile.jpg');
S3.getObject({
  Key : 'demos/putObject/testimage.jpg'
}).createReadStream().pipe(outFile);
```

Alternatively, we can catch data events on the HTTP chunked transfer:

```
S3.getObject({
  Key : 'demos/putObject/testfile.jpg'
})
.on('httpData', chunk => outFile.write(chunk))
.on('httpDone', () => outFile.end())
.send();
```

To delete an object, do this:

```
S3.deleteObject({
  Bucket : 'nodejs-book',
  Key : 'demos/putObject/optimism.jpg'
}, (err, data) => { // ... });
```

To delete multiple objects, pass an Array (to a maximum of 1,000 objects):

```
S3.deleteObjects({
  Bucket : 'nodejs-book',
  Delete : {
    Objects : [{
      Key : 'demos/putObject/first.json'
    }, {
      Key : 'demos/putObject/testimage2.jpg'
    }]
  }
}, (err, data) => { // ... });
```

Using AWS with a Node server

Putting together what we know about Node servers, streaming file data through pipes, and HTTP, it should be clear how to mount S3 as a filesystem in just a few lines of code:

```
http.createServer(function(request, response) {
  let requestedFile = request.url.substring(1);
  S3.headObject({
    Key : requestedFile
  }, (err, data) => {
    // 404, etc.
    if(err) {
      response.writeHead(err.statusCode);
      return response.end(err.name);
    }
    response.writeHead(200, {
      "Last-Modified" : data.LastModified,
      "Content-Length" : data.ContentLength,
      "Content-Type" : data.ContentType,
      "ETag" : data.ETag
    });
    S3.getObject({
      Key : requestedFile
    }).createReadStream().pipe(response);
  });
}).listen(8080);
```

A standard Node HTTP server receives a request URL. We first attempt a HEAD operation using the `aws-sdk` method `headObject`, accomplishing two things:

- We'll determine whther the file is available
- We will have the header information necessary to build a response

After handling any non-200 status code errors, we only need to set our response headers and stream the file back to the requester, as previously demonstrated.

Such a system can also operate as a **fail-safe**, in both directions; should S3, or the file, be unavailable, we might bind to another filesystem, streaming from there. Conversely, if our preferred local filesystem fails, we might fall through to our backup S3 filesystem.

Refer to the `amazon/s3-redirect.js` file in the code bundle available at the Packt website for an example of using 302 redirects to similarly mount an AWS filesystem.

S3 is a powerful data storage system with even more advanced features than those we've covered, such as object versioning, download payment management, and setting up objects as torrent files. With its support for streams, the `aws-sdk` module makes it easy for Node developers to work with S3 as if it was a local filesystem.

Getting and setting data with DynamoDB

DynamoDB (DDB) is a NoSQL database providing very high throughput and predictability that can be easily scaled. DDB is designed for **data-intensive** applications, performing massive map/reduce and other analytical queries with low latency and reliably. That being said, it is also an excellent database solution for general web applications.

The whitepaper announcing DynamoDB was highly influential, sparking a real interest in NoSQL databases, and inspiring many, including **Apache Cassandra**. The paper deals with advanced concepts, but rewards careful study; it is available at: `http://www.allthingsdistributed.com/files/amazon-dynamo-sosp2007.pdf`.

A Dynamo database is a collection of tables, which is a collection of items, which are a collection of attributes. Each item in a table (or row, if you prefer) must have a primary key, functioning as an index for the table. Each item can have any number of attributes (up to a limit of 65 KB) in addition to the primary key.

This is an item with five attributes, one attribute serving as the primary key (`Id`):

```
{
    Id = 123
    Date = "1375314738466"
    UserId = "DD9DDD8892"
    Cart = [ "song1", "song2" ]
    Action = "buy"
}
```

Let's create a table with both a primary and a secondary key:

```
const AWS = require('aws-sdk');
AWS.config.loadFromPath('../config.json');
let db = new AWS.DynamoDB();
db.createTable({
  TableName: 'purchases',
  AttributeDefinitions : [{
    AttributeName : "Id", AttributeType : "N"
  }, {
    AttributeName : "Date", AttributeType : "N"
```

```
  }],
  KeySchema: [{
    AttributeName: 'Id',  KeyType: 'HASH'
  }, {
    AttributeName: 'Date',  KeyType: 'RANGE'
  }],
  ProvisionedThroughput: {
    ReadCapacityUnits: 2,
    WriteCapacityUnits: 2
  }
}, (err, data) => console.log(util.inspect(data)));
```

The callback will receive an object similar to this:

```
{
  TableDescription: {
    AttributeDefinitions: [ // identical to what was sent],
    CreationDateTime: 1375315748.029,
    ItemCount: 0,
    KeySchema: [ // identical to what was sent ],
    ProvisionedThroughput: {
      NumberOfDecreasesToday: 0,
      ReadCapacityUnits: 2,
      WriteCapacityUnits: 2
    },
    TableName: 'purchases',
    TableSizeBytes: 0,
    TableStatus: 'CREATING'
  }
}
```

Table creation/deletion is not immediate; you are essentially queueing up the creation of a table (note `TableStatus`). At some point in the (near) future, the table will exist. As DDB table definitions cannot be changed without deleting the table and rebuilding it, in practice, this delay is not something that should impact your application—build once, and then work with items.

DDB tables must be given a schema indicating the item attributes that will function as keys, defined by `KeySchema`. Each attribute in `KeySchema` can be either a `RANGE` or a `HASH`. There must be one such index; there can be at most two. Each added item must contain any defined keys, with as many additional attributes as desired.

Each item in `KeySchema` must be matched in count by the items in `AttributeDefinitions`. In `AttributeDefinitions`, each attribute can be either a number ("N") or a string ("S"). When adding or modifying attributes, it is always necessary to identify attributes by its type as well as by the name.

To add an item, use the following:

```
db.putItem({
  TableName : "purchases",
  Item : {
    Id : {"N": "123"},
    Date : {"N": "1375314738466"},
    UserId : {"S" : "DD9DDD8892"},
    Cart : {"SS" : [ "song1", "song2" ]},
    Action : {"S" : "buy"}
  }
}, () => { // ... });
```

In addition to our primary and (optional) secondary keys, we want to add other attributes to our item. Each must be given one of the following types:

- S: A String
- N: A Number
- B: A Base64-encoded string
- SS: An Array of Strings (String set)
- NS: An Array of Numbers (Number set)
- BS: An Array of Base64-encoded strings (Base64 set)

 All items will need to have the same number of columns; again, dynamic schemas are *not* a feature of DDB.

Assume that we've created a table that looks like the following table:

Id	Date	Action	Cart	UserId
123	1375314738466	buy	{ "song1", "song2" }	DD9DDD8892
124	1375314738467	buy	{ "song2", "song4" }	DD9EDD8892
125	1375314738468	buy	{ "song12", "song6" }	DD9EDD8890

Now, let's perform some search operations.

Searching the database

There are two types of search operations available: **query** and **scan**. A scan on a table with a single primary key will, without exception, search every item in a table, returning those matching your search criteria. This can be very slow on anything but small databases. A query is a direct key lookup. We'll look at queries first. Note that in this example, we will assume that this table has only one primary key.

To fetch the `Action` and `Cart` attributes for item `124`, we use the following code:

```
db.getItem({
  TableName : "purchases",
  Key : {
    Id : { "N" : "124" }
  },
  AttributesToGet : ["Action", "Cart"]
}, (err, res) => console.log(util.inspect(res, { depth: 10 })));
```

This will return the following:

```
{
  Item: {
    Action: { S: 'buy' },
      Cart: { SS: [ 'song2', 'song4' ] }
  }
}
```

To select all attributes, simply omit the `AttributesToGet` definition.

A scan is more expensive, but allows more involved searches. The usefulness of secondary keys is particularly pronounced when doing scans, allowing us to avoid the overhead of scanning the entire table. In our first example of scan, we will work as if there is only a primary key. Then, we will show how to filter the scan using the secondary key.

To get all the records whose `Cart` attribute contains `song2`, use the following code:

```
db.scan({
  TableName : "purchases",
  ScanFilter : {
    "Cart": {
      "AttributeValueList" : [{
        "S":"song2"
      }],
      "ComparisonOperator" : "CONTAINS"
    },
  }
```

```
}, (err, res) => {
  console.log(util.inspect(res, {
    depth: 10
  }));
});
```

This will return all attribute values for items with Id 123 and 124.

Let's now use our secondary key to filter this further:

```
db.scan({
  TableName : "purchases",
  ScanFilter : {
    "Date": {
      "AttributeValueList" : [{
        "N" : "1375314738467"
      }],
      "ComparisonOperator" : "EQ"
    },
    "Cart": {
      "AttributeValueList" : [{
        "S" : "song2"
      }],
      "ComparisonOperator" : "CONTAINS"
    },
  }
}, (err, res) => {
  console.log(util.inspect(res, {depth: 10}));
});
```

This new filter limits results to item 124.

Sending mail via SES

Amazon describes the problems SES is designed to solve in this way:

> *"Building large-scale email solutions to send marketing and transactional messages is often a complex and costly challenge for businesses. To optimize the percentage of emails that are successfully delivered, businesses must deal with hassles such as email server management, network configuration, and meeting rigorous Internet Service Provider (ISP) standards for email content."*

Apart from the typical network scaling problems inherent in growing any system, providing email services is made particularly difficult due to the prevalence of spam. It is very hard to send a large number of unsolicited emails without ending up blacklisted, even when the recipients are amenable to receiving them. Spam control systems are automated; your service must be listed in the *whitelists*, which is used by various email providers and spam trackers in order to avoid having a low percentage of your emails end up somewhere other than your customer's inbox. A mail service must have a good reputation with the right people or it becomes nearly useless.

Amazon's SES service has the necessary reputation, providing application developers with cloud-based e-mail service which is reliable and able to handle a nearly infinite volume of e-mail. In this section we will learn how SES can be used by a Node application as a reliable mail delivery service.

 Ensure that you have SES access by visiting your developer console. When you first sign up with SES, you will be given *Sandbox* access. When in this mode, you are limited to using only Amazon's mailbox simulator, or sending email to address you have verified (such as one's own). You may request production access, but for our purposes, you will only need to verify an email address to test with.

As the cost of using a service such as SES will increase as your mail volume increases, you might want to periodically check your quotas:

```
let ses = new AWS.SES();
ses.getSendQuota((err, data) => {
  console.log(err, data);
});
```

To send a message, do this:

```
ses.sendEmail({
  Source : "spasquali@gmail.com",
  Destination : {
    ToAddresses : [ "spasquali@gmail.com" ]
  },
  Message : {
    Subject: { Data : "NodeJS and AWS SES" },
    Body : {
      Text : { Data : "It worked!" }
    }
  }
}, (err, resp) => console.log(resp));
```

The callback will receive something like the following output:

```
RequestId: '623144c0-fa5b-11e2-8e49-f73ce5ee2612'

MessageId: '0000014037f1a167-587a626e-ca1f-4440-a4b0-81756301bc28-000000'
```

Multiple recipients, HTML body contents, and all the other features one would expect from a mail service are available.

Using Twilio to create an SMS bot on Heroku

We are going to be building an application that works as a customer service application, whereby customer service agents can field SMS requests from customers and respond to them. There will be two parts to the system.

- Part 1 : A client application, running on your local machine, which spins up a React-powered web interface that displays incoming SMS messages, indicates the sentiment of the message (is the customer angry? Happy?) and allows you to respond to the message. Note that even though this server is running on a local machine, it could just as well be deployed to Heroku, or somewhere else -- the goal is to demonstrate how many servers in different locations can intelligently communicate with each other.
- Part 2 : A *switchboard* that fields messages arriving via the Twilio SMS gateway, processes them, and distributes messages across any number of client servers -- if you have 10 customer service representatives connected to the switchboard using the client application, messages the switchboard receives will be spread across these clients evenly. This second application will be deployed on Heroku.

You will first need to get an account on **Heroku**, a cloud server provider similar to Digital Ocean: http://www.heroku.com

Heroku provides free accounts, so you will be able to build out the following application without any cost to you.

Once you have your account, log in and download the Heroku CLI for your system: https://devcenter.heroku.com/articles/getting-started-with-nodejs#set-up. Follow the steps on that page to log in to the command line toolbelt for Heroku.

Make sure you have Git installed (https://git-scm.com/book/en/v2/Getting-Started-Installing-Git).

Create a directory on your local file system, and clone the following two repositories into that folder:

- `https://github.com/sandro-pasquali/thankyou`
- `https://github.com/sandro-pasquali/switchboard`

The *thankyou* repository is the client application. You will now deploy the *switchboard* repository to Heroku.

Using your Terminal navigate to the *switchboard* repository and deploy a copy to Heroku:

> **`heroku create`**

You should see something like the following displayed in your Terminal:

```
Creating app... done, ● fast-dawn-19254
https://fast-dawn-19254.herokuapp.com/ | https://git.heroku.com/fast-dawn-19254.git
```

Heroku has established a Git endpoint on your server. Now, run the following command:

> **`git remote`**

You will see a list of two elements returned: *heroku* and *origin*. These are the two remote branches that your local *switchboard* repository is tracking, the one on Heroku and the one you originally cloned from.

The next step is to push your local repository into the Heroku repository:

> **`git push heroku master`**

You should see a lot of installation instructions. When everything completes successfully navigate to your application URL. You should see that there is an *Application Error*. Heroku provides complete logs for your application. Let's access them now to discover what went wrong:

> **`heroku logs`**

To keep a running tail of log activity on your Heroku server, use:
> `heroku logs --tail`

You should see several errors around the absence of environment variables, especially for Twilio. The application expects these to be set in the application environment, and they haven't been. Let's do that now.

Using Twilio webhooks to receive and send SMS messages

The switchboard application ultimately provides a single service—to set up a REST-enabled endpoint that Twilio can call with SMS messages received on the number you've registered. It stores a log of those messages on a per-phone-number basis in LevelDB (a very fast key/value storage library), broadcasting new messages to clients connected to the switchboard.

The logical flow of the entire application will look like this:

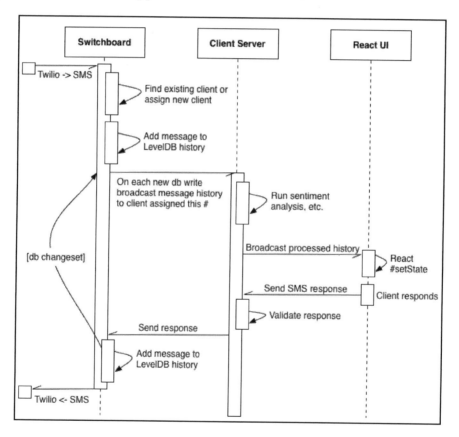

We can see that the logic of our application begins with an SMS from Twilio, and supports responses from clients. This is the basic pattern for constructing a *NoUI*, or pure SMS application. This pattern is growing in popularity, often seen in the form of chat bots, AI-enabled assistants, and so on. We'll dig deeper into the application soon.

Right now, we need to enable the Twilio bridge.

To start, you will need to create a test account on Twilio to get some API variables. Go to `https://www.twilio.com` and sign up for a test account. Ensure that you set up a test phone number; we'll be sending SMS messages to that number.

Once you've done that, grab your Twilio API keys from the account Dashboard, your phone number, and your phone number SID. Now you'll need to add that information to the environment variables for Heroku, along with some other keys. Go to your Heroku dashboard, find your instance, click on it, and navigate to **Settings | Reveal Config Vars**:

This is where you add key/value pairs to `process.env` in your running Node process. Add the following key/value pairs:

- `TWILIO_AUTH_TOKEN` / <your auth token>
- `TWILIO_SID` / <your sid>
- `TWILIO_PHONE_NUMBER_SID` / <your phone # sid>
- `TWILIO_DEFAULT_FROM` / <your assigned phone number>
- `SOCK_PORT` / 8080
- `URL` / <your server URL (with no trailing slash)

Once you've saved these new environment variables, your application will automatically restart on Heroku. Try your application URL again. If everything is working, you should see a message like **Switchboard is active**.

You can quickly load your application into a browser from the command line with > `heroku open`.

While we will not be using the shell, you can log in to your Heroku box via your Terminal with `> heroku run bash`.

To communicate with Twilio, we'll be using the official Node library at: `https://github.com/twilio/twilio-node`. The important code can be found in the `router/sms/` folder of the switchboard repository. This module will allow us to register a webhook to receive messages, and to respond to those messages.

Now, let's build the switchboard.

The switchboard

The switchboard will have a single responsibility—to communicate with Twilio. Since we're using webhooks, we'll need to create a server that can catch POST data from Twilio. For the web server, we'll use the `restify` package (`http://www.restify.com`). This is a very fast Node server implementation that is designed specifically for fast, high-load REST-based APIs. Since the switchboard is solely focused on handling incoming messages from Twilio, and its outbound traffic is through WebSockets, there is no need for a *higher-level* server like Express, which is designed to facilitate the presentation of views through templates, sessions, and so forth.

Let's look at the code instantiating a restify server that accepts POST messages from Twilio containing SMS message data, and the socket server to bind clients to the switchboard:

```
// router/index.js
const restify = require('restify');
const SServer = require("ws").Server;
const server = restify.createServer({
  // additional configuration can be done here
});
server.use(restify.plugins.acceptParser(server.acceptable));
server.use(restify.plugins.bodyParser());

function responder(req, res) {
   res.send(200, 'Switchboard is active');
}
server.get('/', responder);

// process.env.PORT is set by heroku (add it yourself if hosting elsewhere)
server.listen(process.env.PORT, () => {});

// Get the LevelDB interface, and its readable stream
```

```
require('./Db')((db, dbApi) => {

  // Configure the sms webhook routing
  require('./sms')(server, dbApi);
  // Configure a leveldb datastream listener which has the job
  // of informing clients of data changes.
  require('./dataStream.js')(db, Clients);
  // Configure the socket listener for client connections
  let wss = new SServer(server);

  wss.on("connection", clientConn => {
    clientConn.on("close", () => {
      // remove clients, close the connection
    });
    clientConn.on("message", payload => {
      // ...more on this later
    });

    // Say something nice to clients when they connect
    clientConn.send(JSON.stringify({
      type: 'alert',
      text: 'How can I help you?'
    }));
  });
});
```

With very little code, we've set up a web server and extended it with a socket server (using the excellent ws module, which you can grab at: https://github.com/websockets/ws). You are encouraged to look at the code in the switchboard repository, where the details of how client connections are managed should be easy to follow. In particular, investigate the router/Db/index.js file, where a levelDB connection is established and an API for storing message histories (api.addToNumberHistory) is defined. For our purposes, note the server.get method, which establishes a handler for GET requests used simply as a *ping* service should we need to check whether the switchboard is available. We'll add the important webhook route next.

The Twilio webhook code is presented with the following line:

```
// router/sms/index.js
require('./sms')(server, dbApi);
```

The code in that file looks like this:

```
const env = process.env;
const twilioAPI = require('twilio')(env.TWILIO_SID, env.TWILIO_AUTH_TOKEN);
module.exports = (server, dbApi) => {
  let smsUrl = env.URL + '/smswebhook';
  twilioAPI.incomingPhoneNumbers(env.TWILIO_PHONE_NUMBER_SID).update({
    smsUrl: smsUrl
  });
  server.post('/smswebhook', (req, res) => {
    let dat = req.body;
    let meta = {
      message : dat.Body,
      received : Date.now(),
      fromCountry : dat.FromCountry,
      phoneNumber : dat.From
    };
    dbApi
    .addToNumberHistory(dat.From, meta)
    .then(newVal => console.log('Received message from', dat.From))
    .catch(err => console.log("levelERRR:", err));
    res.end();
  });
};
```

Given that we're connecting to and using a global SMS gateway, the code is surprisingly simple. After instantiating an instance of the Twilio API using the environment variables we set earlier on Heroku, we can conveniently use this API to programmatically establish a webhook, avoiding the manual process of logging into a Twilio dashboard:

```
let smsUrl = `${env.URL}/smswebhook`;
twilioAPI.incomingPhoneNumbers(env.TWILIO_PHONE_NUMBER_SID).update({
  smsUrl: smsUrl
});
```

More importantly, this technique allows us to dynamically reconfigure the Twilio endpoint Twilio; it is always nice to be able to *hot swap* handlers should naming, or something else, change.

The body that Twilio POSTs and we will be receiving looks something like this:

```
{
  ToCountry: 'US',
  ToState: 'NY',
  SmsMessageSid: 'xxxxxx',
  NumMedia: '0',
  ToCity: 'SOUTH RICHMOND HILL',
  FromZip: '11575',
  SmsSid: 'xxxxxx',
  FromState: 'NY',
  SmsStatus: 'received',
  FromCity: 'SOUTH RICHMOND HILL',
  Body: 'Hi! This is a test message!',
  FromCountry: 'US',
  To: '+5555554444',
  ToZip: '11244',
  NumSegments: '1',
  MessageSid: 'xxxxxx',
  AccountSid: 'xxxxxx',
  From: '+555555555',
  ApiVersion: '2010-04-01'
}
```

In the hook handler, we grab the key info—the number of the sender and the message—storing them in `levelDB` via the `api.addToNumberHistory` method (which returns a Promise). Now we are ready to inform a client of the message. How do we do that?

Clients are connected via a websocket. We can, after writing to the DB, simply send the message to the client in the same function body. However, now our code is starting to become complex, taking on two responsibilities (receiving and sending) rather than just one (receiving). It may seem like a small matter, but this is the sort of place where feature creep appears—maybe next we add logging in this function, and so on. Also, if we are responsible for notifying clients of new messages, we'll also be required to confirm that a database write was successful; this is often not clear cut, false positives not being out of the ordinary.

Instead of doing that, let's create a notification system that broadcasts changesets. Whenever a new message is written to the DB—a confirmed write—announce that update event, and register an event handler. In our intial server code, this functionality is bound using the following line:

```
require('./dataStream.js')(db, Clients);
```

The code to catch changesets and broadcast them uses *Domenic Tarr's* `level-live-stream`
package:

```
module.exports = (db, Clients) => {
  const dbStream = require('level-live-stream')(db);

  // When a new write has been successfully written...
  dbStream.on('data', data => {
    let number = data.key;
    let val = data.value;
    // Find any clients that are listening on this number
    let boundClient = Clients.withNumber(number);
    // Send the current history to this client
    if(boundClient) {
      try {
        return boundClient.send(JSON.stringify({
          type: 'update',
          list: val
        }));
      } catch(e) {
        Clients.delete(boundClient);
      }
    }
    // Try to find an available client to handle this number
    let waitingClient = Clients.nextAvailable();

    if(waitingClient) {
      // This client is no longer `available`. Assign client a number.
      // Then send number history.
      Clients.set(waitingClient, number);
      waitingClient.send(JSON.stringify({
        type: 'update',
        list: val
      }));
    }
    // TODO: handle situations without available clients
  });
};
```

Using `level-live-stream`, we are able to concentrate our logic on the right event—a confirmed write to the database—leaving this *microservice* responsible solely for finding an available client and sending them the updated message history. Note that the way clients are stored and referenced in this example is not at all definitive. You might want to continue with the *do one thing well* philosophy and create another small service solely responsible for brokering connections. For example, we might remove all the client code from this example and create another service exposing a `getNextAvailableClient` method. This type of compositional strategy orchestrating microservices will be discussed further in the next chapter.

We can now receive, store, and broadcast incoming SMS messages. There is only one bit of functionality left—sending client responses back to Twilio, continuing the SMS conversation. The composition of these responses is performed by the *thankyou* application we'll be discussing next. Ultimately, however, those responses are directed by the switchboard (recall the preceding sequence diagram), and the following is the very short code that you can use to send SMS messages through the Twilio gateway:

```
// router/sms/sendResponse.js
const Twilio = require('twilio');
const twilioAPI = new Twilio(process.env.TWILIO_SID,
process.env.TWILIO_AUTH_TOKEN);
module.exports = (number, message) => twilioAPI.messages.create({
  to: number,
  from: process.env.TWILIO_DEFAULT_FROM,
  body: message
});
```

You should recall an *on message* listener for the websocket registered in our base server code, which uses the preceding functionality to respond to callers. We can now expand that listener:

```
// router/index.js
...
clientConn.on("message", payload => {
  try {
    payload = JSON.parse(payload);
  } catch(e) {
    return;
  }
  switch(payload.type) {
    case 'available':
      Client.set(clientConn, 'available');
    break;
    case 'response':
      let number = Clients.get(clientConn);
```

```
      // Add to message history when bound client
      // sends valid message to a known number.
      if(/^\+?[0-9]*$/.test(number)) {
        dbApi.addToNumberHistory(number, {
          message : payload.message,
          received : Date.now(),
          phoneNumber : number
        })
        .then(() => require('./sms/sendResponse.js')(number,
payload.message))
        .catch(err => console.log("response send error:", err));
      }
      break;
  }
});
```

We see `addToNumberHistory` here again since responses are of course part of the conversation history. Once the outgoing message is added to the database record, send it along via Twilio. Did you note something? That's only one of the things we have to do. The other is send the updated message history *back to the client* so that this response can appear in their view of the history. Typically, this is done using some client JavaScript that, when the client types a response and clicks on *send*, it optimistically updates the client state in the hope the message makes it to the switchboard. What does it not, though?

We see how the changeset approach helps here. If the client message fails to reach the switchboard or otherwise fails, the `levelDB` will never be updated and the client's history state will not be out of sync with the canonical history represented by the data layer. While this may not matter so much in a trivial application like this one, it will matter if you're building transactional software.

Now, let's walk through the other half of the application—the *thankyou* client.

The ThankYou interface

To recap, we want to create a system whereby a switchboard receives SMS messages and passes them along to *service representatives* running a conversational interface on their local laptop or similar. This client is defined in the `thankyou` repository, and will look like this:

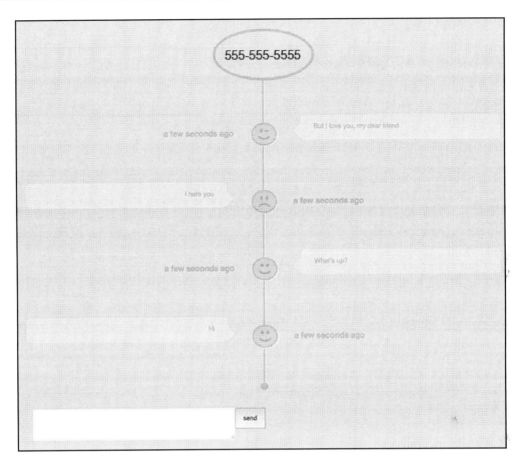

Here, we see the message history the switchboard manages, and the interface for sending back responses. Importantly, there are icons indicating the sentiment (the winking happiness, the sad anger), of the messages as well as their timestamp in a human readable format (*a few seconds ago*). The goal for thankyou will be to catch incoming (and outgoing) messages, run sentiment analysis on the message stream, and display the results. We'll use React to build the UI.

React requires a build system, and we're using **Browserify**, **Gulp**, and **BrowserSync**. How those technologies work is beyond the scope of this chapter. Go over the contents of gulpfile.js and the /source directory of the thankyou repository. There are many online tutorials for these popular technologies.

As we are serving a real UI, for this project, we will use Express to build our Node server. Still, the server is very simple. It is only responsible for serving the single view just pictured, which is contained in a single `index.html` file:

```
// /source/views/index.html

<!DOCTYPE html>
<html>
<head>
    <title>Untitled</title>
    <link rel="stylesheet" type="text/css" href="css/app.css">
</head&gt;
<body>

<div id="main"></div>
<div id="page_controls">
    <span id="message-composer"></span>
</div>

<script src="https://code.jquery.com/jquery-3.2.1.min.js"
integrity="sha256-hwg4gsxgFZhOsEEamdOYGBf13FyQuiTwlAQgxVSNgt4="
crossorigin="anonymous"></script>
<script src="js/socketConnector.js"></script>
<script src="js/components.js"></script>
<script src="js/app.js"></script>
</body>
</html>
```

React components are bundled by the build system into `components.js`; JavaScript files are similarly bundled into `app.js`, as stylesheets are into `app.css`. The jQuery DOM manipulation library is used for simple element effects and for managing the message composer. As mentioned, we won't be going deep into client JavaScript. It will be useful to take a brief look at the React component used to construct the timeline, as this component is ultimately what will be receiving new messages from the switchboard.

This is the main UI component powering `thankyou`:

```
// source/jsx/MessageComposer.jsx
export class Timeline extends React.Component {
  constructor(props) {
    super(props);
    this.state = {
      phone : '',
      messages: []
    };
  }
```

```
    componentDidMount() {
      ws.onmessage = mOb => {
        let data = JSON.parse(mOb.data);
        if(data.messages && data.phone) {
          return this.setState(data);
        }
      }
    }
    render() {
      return <div>
        <MessageHistory history={this.state} />
      </div>
    }
}

export class MessageHistory extends React.Component {
  constructor(props) {
    super(props);
  }
  render() {
    let history = this.props.history;
      return <div id="timeline_container">
        <div className="history_header">
          <figure>{history.phone}</figure>
        </div>
          <ul>
            { history.messages.map(function(it) {
                return <li className="message_event" key={it.received}>
                  <div className={"event_icn icon-emo-" +
it.sentiment}></div>
                  <div className="event_content">
                    <p>{it.message}</p>
                  </div>
                  <div className="event_date">
                    {it.date}
                  </div>
                </li>
            }) }
          </ul>
      </div>;
    }
}

render(
  <Timeline />, document.getElementById('main')
);
```

Even if you don't know React, you should be able to see that the `MessageHistory` component extends the `Timeline` component. The `Timeline` component is responsible for maintaining the application state, or in our case, the current message history.

This is the key UI code in `MessageHistory`:

```
{ history.messages.map(function(it) {
    return <li className="message_event" key={it.received}>
        <div className={"event_icn icon-emo-" + it.sentiment}></div>
        <div className="event_content">
            <p>{it.message}</p>
        </div>
        <div className="event_date">
            {it.date}
        </div>
    </li>
}) }
```

You may recall the message history that switchboard works with:

```
dbApi.addToNumberHistory(number, {
  message : payload.message,
  received : Date.now(),
  phoneNumber : number
})
```

This is the section in the `MessageHistory` where that data is rendered into UI views. We won't go too much farther into the UI code, but you should note a property that switchboard did not generate: `it.sentiment`. Keep that in mind that as we go over how thankyou communicates data with switchboard.

Since the switchboard receives and sends messages over WebSockets, `Timeline` has such a reference:

```
ws.onmessage = mOb => {
  let data = JSON.parse(mOb.data);
  if(data.messages && data.phone) {
    return this.setState(data);
  }
}
```

The socket code was included in our `index.html` file:

```
<script src="js/socketConnector.js"></script>
```

Also, it looks like this:

```
let ws = new WebSocket('ws://' + host + ':8080');
ws.sendMessage = function(command, msg) {
  this.send(JSON.stringify({
    command : command || '',
    message : msg || ''
  }));
};
```

This code puts the ws reference in the browser global scope on the client (window.ws). While generally not the best practice, for our simple UI, this makes it easy for React components to grab the same socket reference. This reference is also used in the MessageComposer component, which accepts responses from the client:

```
// source/jsx/MessageComposer.jsx
export class MessageComposer extends React.Component {
  constructor(props) {
    super(props);
  }
  sendMessage(ev) {
    // Get message; clear input; exit if
    let input = document.getElementById('composer');
    let msg = input.value;

    input.value = '';

    if(msg.trim() === '') {
      return;
    }

    ws.sendMessage('response', msg);
  }
  render() {
    return <span>
      <textarea id="composer"></textarea><button
onClick={this.sendMessage}>send</button>
    </span>
  }
}

render(
  <MessageComposer />, document.getElementById('message-composer')
);
```

This component renders a text area, into which responses can be composed and sent, via socket, to the switchboard.

Now, let's look at how the client server communicates with the client UI, brokering communication with the switchboard.

The client server is defined in `router/index.js`:

```
const http = require('http');
const express = require('express');
const bodyParser = require('body-parser');

let defaultPort = 8080;
let app = express();

app.use(bodyParser.json());
app.use(bodyParser.urlencoded({
  extended: true
}));
app.use(express.static('./public'));

let server = http.createServer(app);
server.listen(process.env.PORT || defaultPort);

console.log('HTTP server listening on', process.env.PORT || defaultPort);

// The client is connected to a local socket server, which sends
client->LocalSS->customer messages.
// The local SS is connected to switchboard, receiving
SMS->switchboard->LocalSS->client messages.
require('./bindSocketServer.js')(server);
```

This is a standard Express setup. Note the following line:

```
require('./bindSocketServer.js')(server);
```

This is the main broker logic. Recalling the application sequence diagram, here is where switchboard messages are received and passed along, through another socket, to the UI and ultimately, the React renderer. Similarly, the server listens for messages from the UI and passes those along to the switchboard:

```
// router/bindSocketServer.js
const WebSocket = require('ws');
const SServer = WebSocket.Server;

let arrayToStream = require('./transformers/arrayToStream.js');
let timeTransformer = require('./transformers/time.js');
let sentimentTransformer = require('./transformers/sentiment.js');
let accumulator = require('./transformers/accumulator.js');
```

```
const sbUrl = process.env.SWITCHBOARD_URL;

module.exports = server => {
  // Bind the local socket server, which communicates
  // with web clients.
  (new SServer({
    server: server
  })).on('connection', localClientSS => {
    let keepalive;
    // A remote SMS gateway
    let switchboard = new WebSocket(sbUrl);
    // ... boilerplate ping/pong functionality

    // handle
    switchboard.onmessage = event => {
      let data = event.data;
      try {
        data = JSON.parse(data);
      } catch(e) {
        return console.log(`Unable to process data: ${data}`);
      }
      // switchboard sent an update
      if(data.type === 'update') {
        // Transform messages into expected format for UI.
        arrayToStream(data.list.reverse())
        .pipe(timeTransformer({
          format: "%s ago"
        }))
        .pipe(sentimentTransformer('message'))
        .pipe(accumulator((err, messages) => {
          if(err) {
            return console.log(err);
          }
          localClientSS.sendMessage({
            messages: messages,
            phone: messages[0].phoneNumber
          })
        }));
      }
    };

    // Need to configure handlers so we can bidirectionally
    // communicate with client UI (snd/rcv messages)
    localClientSS.sendMessage = obj => {
      localClientSS.send(JSON.stringify(obj));
    };

    // Client UI is responding
```

```
          localClientSS.on('message', payload => {
            try {
              payload = JSON.parse(payload);
            } catch(e) {
              return;
            }
            switch(payload.command) {
              case 'response':
                switchboard.send(JSON.stringify({
                  type: 'response',
                  message : payload.message
                }));
                break;
              default:
                // do nothing
                break;
            }
          });

          // ... handle socket close, etc.
      };
```

This should make sense now, given the *switchboard* design. Starting at the bottom, we see that when the client socket server `localClientSS` receives a message, it validates and passes the message along to the *switchboard*, where it will be added to the message history for the phone number this client is handling. More interesting is the code to receive messages from the switchboard, which performs sentiment analysis and converts timestamps into human readable sentences.

To perform these transformations, the payload received from the *switchboard* (an Array in JSON format) is converted into an object stream using the `arrayToStream.js` module. Streams are covered in Chapter 3, *Streaming Data Across Nodes and Clients*; we're simply creating a `Readable` Stream that pipes each element in the array as a distinct object. The real fun begins when we apply transformations. Let's look at the code to do sentiment analysis (which processes the `'message'` property of the history object), using the `through2` module (`https://github.com/rvagg/through2`) to simplify the creation and design of a transform stream, and of course, the sentiment module (`https://github.com/thisandagain/sentiment`) to gauge the mood of the message:

```
// router/transformers/sentiment.js
const through2 = require('through2');
const sentiment = require('sentiment');

module.exports = targProp => {
  if(typeof targProp !== 'string') {
```

```
      targProp = 'sentiment';
  }

  return through2.obj(function(chunk, enc, callback) {
    // Add #sentiment property
    let score = sentiment(chunk[targProp]).score;
    // Negative sentiments
    if(score < 0) {
      chunk.sentiment = score < -4 ? 'devil' : 'unhappy';
    }
    // Positive sentiments
    else if(score >= 0) {
      chunk.sentiment = score > 4 ? 'wink' : 'happy';
    }
    this.push(chunk);
    callback()
  });
};
```

The functionality is straightforward; for each object in the history array sent from the switchboard, determine the sentiment score for the message. Negative scores are *bad*, along the range from very bad (*devil*) to *unhappy*. We similarly score positive sentiments along a range from very good (*wink*) to *happy*. A new `sentiment` property is added to the message object, and as we saw earlier when considering the `MessageHistory` component, this will set which icon the message receives in the UI.

> If you want to continue development of this application on your own, you should fork the repositories onto your own GitHub account, and repeat the process with these personal repositories. This will allow you to push changes and otherwise modify the application to suit your own needs.

The coordination of *switchboard* and *thankyou* should give you some ideas on how to use services, sockets, REST endpoints, and third-party APIs to distribute functionality, helping you scale through adding (or removing) components, across the stack. By using transform streams, you can apply "on the fly" stream data transformations without blocking, managing data models on your servers, and leaving layout to the UI itself.

Summary

Big data applications have placed significant responsibility on developers of network applications to prepare for scale. Node has offered help in creating a network-friendly application development environment that can easily connect to other devices on a network, such as cloud services and, in particular, other Node servers.

In this chapter, we learned some good strategies for scaling Node servers, from analyzing CPU usage to communicating across processes. With our new knowledge of message queues and UDP, we can build networks of Node servers scaling horizontally, letting us handle more and more traffic by simply replicating the existing nodes. Having investigated load balancing and proxying with both Node and NGINX, we can confidently add capacity to our applications. When matched with the cloud services provided by Digital Ocean, AWS, and Twilio, we can attempt enterprise-scale development, data storage, and broadcast at a low cost and without adding much complexity to our application.

As our applications grow, we will need to maintain continuous awareness of how each part as well as the whole is behaving. As we keep adding new components and functionality, some local, some through the cloud, some maybe even written in another language, how do we, as developers, intelligently track and plan additions and other changes? In the next chapter, we will learn about microservices, a way of developing one application out of many, small, cooperating horizontally-distributed network services.

9
Microservices

Let everyone sweep in front of his own door, and the whole world will be clean.

– Goethe

As software has grown more complex, it has become impossible for any one person, or even a single team, to maintain total awareness of an entire architecture. The rise of the internet promoted the concepts of *frontend* (a browser on one computer processing JavaScript, CSS, HTML) and *backend* (another computer running a database and an HTTP server) unified on a single server to deliver one product—the *web page*. A user might click on a button, a call is made to a server, that server might check a database, and will ultimately deliver an HTML page.

The pace has picked up. The modern user expects powerful and highly-interactive mobile apps to entertain them or drive their business, at a low cost, with regular updates. Now, one person can create an app that gains millions of users within months. To scale from one person to a company supporting millions of concurrent users in a few months—even a few years—requires efficient teams and engineering management.

Today's network-based applications are composed of several independent subsystems that must cooperate to fulfil the business or other requirements of the larger system. For example, many web applications will present browser-based interfaces composed of one or several libraries and/or UI frameworks translating user actions against JavaScript controllers running on phones, microcontrollers, and laptops, into formalized network requests issued across several web protocols, ultimately communicating with any number of servers executing units of business logic programmed in different languages, all sharing one or several databases, maybe across several data centers, themselves initiating and coordinating even longer chains of requests to a cloud API or other servers, and so on.

Software of any complexity is today rarely contained on one machine or within a single code base. In this chapter, we will look into the recently popular technique of composing distributed architectures out of independent actors, each in the form of a small, delineated, hot-reloadable service, or microservices. Microservices allow you to rewire, rewrite, reuse, and redeploy modular parts of your application, making change easier.

Why microservices?

Building larger systems out of smaller, dedicated units is not a new idea. Object-oriented programming follows the same principle. Unix is built this way. Architectures facilitating composable networked software (CORBA, WebObjects, NetBeans) are decades-old ideas. What is new is the scale of profits networked software generates. Customers across nearly every business sector require new software and new features, and software developers are constantly delivering and/or refining those features in response to changing market conditions. Microservices are really a management idea whose goal is to decrease the time it takes to reflect changing business/customer needs in code. The goal is to reduce the cost of change.

As there is no absolute *right way* to build software, every language design is biased toward one or a few key principles, in particular, principles guiding how a system should scale, which normally affects how it is deployed. Some of the key principles informing the Node community—modular systems composed of small programs that do one thing well, event-driven, I/O focused, network focused—align closely with those underpinning microservices:

1. A system should be broken out into many small services where each does one thing, and no more. This helps with clarity.
2. The code powering services should be short and simple. A common guideline in the Node community is to limit programs to somewhere near 100 lines of code. This helps with maintainability.

3. No service should depend on the existence of another service—or even know of the existence of other services. Services are decoupled. This helps with scalability, clarity, and maintainability.

4. Data models should be decentralized, with a common (but not required) microservice pattern being each service maintaining its own database or similar model. Services are stateless. This reinforces (3).

5. Independent services are easy to replicate (or cull). Scaling (in both directions) is a natural feature of microservice architectures as new *nodes* can be added or removed as necessary. This also enables easy experimentation, where prototype services can be tested, new features can be tested or deployed temporarily, and so forth.

6. Independent, stateless, services can be replaced or upgraded (or downgraded) independently, regardless of the state of any system they form a part of. This opens the possibility of more focused, discreet deployments and refactors.

7. Failure is unavoidable, so systems should be designed to fail gracefully. Localize points of failure (1, 2), isolate failure (3, 4), and implement recovery mechanisms (easier when error boundaries are clearly defined, small, and non-critical), promoting robustness by reducing the scope of unreliability.

8. Testing is essential to any non-trivial system. Unambiguous and simple stateless services are easy to test. A key aspect of testing is simulation—the *stubbing* or *mocking* of services in order to test service interoperability. Clearly delineated services are also easy to simulate, and can, therefore, be intelligently composed into testable systems.

The idea is simple: smaller services are easy to reason about individually, encouraging correctness of specification (little or no grey area) and clarity of API (constrained sets of outputs follow constrained sets of inputs). Being stateless and decoupled, services promote system composability, helping with scaling and maintainability, making them easier to deploy. Also, very precise, discrete monitoring of these sorts of systems is possible.

With that rough sketch in mind, let's go back in time and survey some foundational architectural patterns such as "3-Tier" architectures, and how their character led to the idea of a *microservice*. Bringing that progression up to the present, we'll then take a look at how the incredible scale of modern networked applications has forced a reimagining of the classic client->server->database setup, a new world often best composed with microservices.

When building web-based APIs using microservices, it will be useful to have tools that give you precise control over handling calls, headers, POST bodies, responses and so on, especially when debugging. I recommend installing **Postman** (https://www.getpostman.com/), and an extension for your browser that "prettifies" JSON objects. For Chrome, a good one is **JSON Formatter** (https://chrome.google.com/webstore/detail/json-formatter/bcjindcccaagfpapjjmafapmmgkkhgoa?hl=en).

From 3-Tiers to 4-Tiers

To understand how microservices can improve your Node application, you must understand the problems they are designed to solve, and how those problems were solved previously. It is important to know *where* a microservice-oriented architecture might apply, and *why* such a change will help you. Let's look at how multitiered, distributed network architectures have developed over time.

Monoliths

This is a monolith:

It is big, of one piece, and grows vertically. It would probably be difficult to reshape, or otherwise modify without great effort, great danger, and great cost. When someone describes an architecture as *monolithic*, they are using the preceding metaphor to suggest something very large and immovable and so massive as to discourage those attempting to improve it or to survey its total constituent parts in a comprehensive way.

Consider a simple application, like a *to-do* list. A list manager requires functionality to create, add, delete, and otherwise change lists. The code for that application might resemble this pseudo-code:

```
let orm = require('some-orm');

module.exports = {
  create: list  => orm.createList(list),
  add: (list, item) => List(list).insert(new Item(item)),
  delete: (list, item) => List(list).delete(item)
};
```

This example shows monolithic design thinking. The data is on the same machine as the UI controllers as the process logic, functionality resides within the same context (the enclosing Node module), the same file, and the same OS process. You need not be pro-microservices to understand that as you add user accounts, drafts, and media attachments, sharing, multi-device synchronization, and other features to your to-do app, the original singular, monolithic repository for all application logic has grown too dense, and will need to be broken up into pieces.

What if you broke each of those functions off into an independent process, running in its own memory space, so pure and unattached to any other process that it can be updated, shut down, duplicated, deployed, tested, or even replaced with no impact on any other part of the system? Microservices come out of that kind of thinking.

It is perfectly okay to construct your software using standard OO, or a list of functions or structures all in one file or a small collection of files, and to expect your software to be running on a single machine. That architectural model probably works for most people; on modern hardware, a single-core machine running a simple Node server can likely handle several thousand concurrent users performing non-trivial, database-driven tasks. It is perfectly okay to scale a growing application by adding more cores or more memory to scale an architecture vertically. It's also okay to scale an architecture by standing up several already vertically-scaled servers and balancing the load between them. That strategy is still used by some billion-dollar companies.

It is okay to build a monolith *if it's the right choice for your needs*. At other times, microservices will be the right choice. You may not need to use decentralized data sources; you might have no need to *hot-reload* your services when they change. The widely used database MYSQL is commonly scaled vertically. When limits are being pushed, one simply adds more processing cores, memory, and storage space to your database server, or creates multiple copies of the same database and balances requests between them. This sort of monolithic architecture is easy to reason about and is typically resilient.

What are the advantages of vertically scaled architectures (monoliths)?:

- **Testing and debugging**: What happens in the application begins and ends with the application itself, independent of random network effects. This can be helpful when testing and debugging.

- **Strong consistency**: A persistent local database connection can help guarantee transactional integrity, including rollbacks. Distributed databases, especially those being accessed concurrently by many thousands of clients, are much more difficult to keep synchronized, and are typically described as *eventually consistent*, which may be a problem, especially if you're a bank.

- **Simplicity**: A well-designed application with, for example, a single REST API locally bounded within the same logical space as a single database can be easily described, and is predictable. Often, an individual can understand the entire system and even run it singlehandedly! This is a non-trivial advantage, especially in terms of the increased velocity of employee onboarding, and the opportunity for individual entrepreneurship.

- **Linear scaling**: If you can, hypothetically, double your capacity by doubling memory on a single machine, that is a very easy upgrade. At some point, this solution won't suffice, but that point is probably much farther out than you might think. It is relatively easy to predict the cost of increased load and the steps needed to scale the system.

A few companies, or developers, will encounter scales absolutely requiring a distributed architecture. Some smart data object design and componentized UI related through a single database, well-designed and maintained, can be enough for a very long time, or even forever. In many ways, the popular Ruby on Rails framework continues to champion the monolith and the value of integrated systems, a position strongly argued for by its creator *David Heinemeier Hansson* at: `http://rubyonrails.org/doctrine/#integrated-systems`.

From monoliths to 3-Tiered architectures

You might say with some precision that few people are truly building monolithic applications anymore. What people call *monolith* nowadays is typically a 3-Tiered application, which concretizes the following conceptual layers:

- **Presentation tier**: Interfaces for clients to request, view, and modify information. Typically communicates with the Application tier.
- **Application tier:** Logic to connect the Presentation and Data tiers
- **Data-tier**: Where information is persisted and organized

A Node developer will likely recognize applications composed of a client framework such as React (Presentation), *served* by an application layer built using Express, communicating with a MongoDB database via some sort of connector, such as Mongoose. These are the **LAMP** stacks, the **MEAN** stacks. System architects have known for a long time that the separation of an application into distinct systems is a smart strategy. In many ways, this architecture reflects the **Model View Controller** (**MVC**) model, where M=Data, V=Presentation, and C=Application.

How did this architecture come about?

Firstly, it was recognized that there are very clearly distinct parts of systems that should be understood separately. A browser-based UI has nothing to do with your database or with your web server. It may, through various layers of abstraction, come to *reflect* your database structure (the display of profiles linked by interests, for example), but that characteristic of your system is ultimately a design decision, not a necessary condition. Maintaining and updating your database independent of your layout grid or interactive components just makes sense. Unfortunately, these distinct things can end up entangled, through lazy design or the vicissitudes of fast-paced business environments, and for other reasons.

Secondly, rapid, continuous deployment and integration is much more difficult when changing one part of one of the tiers ultimately requires retesting the entire system. Integration tests must either touch on real systems or create artificial simulations, neither of which are dependable, and both of which can lead to destructive results. Similarly, deployments are holistic—each part, even if conceptually distinct, is in reality intimately bound with the others, where the integrity of each must be validated by validating the integrity of the whole. Enormous test suites reflect the enormity and density of the application designs they attempt to cover.

The focus on having exactly three tiers makes elasticity difficult. New data models, functions, services, even UIs that might be *one-off* additions (a completely independent login system from Facebook, for instance) must be linked across the three tiers, and its integration with many or all the existing data models, functions, business logic, UIs must be done carefully (and somewhat artificially) both initially and on every change. As new caching mechanisms (CDNs) and API-driven development has taken hold, the artificiality of the 3-tier system has begun to frustrate developers.

Service-Oriented Architectures

The idea of microservices is largely a refinement and recontextualization of the ideas around **Service-Oriented Architectures (SOA)**, which Wikipedia defines this way:

> *"A [SOA] is a style of software design where services are provided to the other components by application components, through a communication protocol over a network. ... A service is a discrete unit of functionality that can be accessed remotely and acted upon and updated independently, such as retrieving a credit card statement online."*

An SOA makes a lot of sense when a distinct piece of functionality can be delineated. If you are running an online store, you'll probably want to separate the search functionality and the payments functionality from the signup system and the client UI server. We can see that the foundational idea here is to create functionality that is logically self-contained and accessible via a network—useful services that other system components (including services) can work with without colliding with each other.

Separating like functionality into individual services is a common adjustment to 3-Tier architectures, where the business logic on a server might delegate its responsibilities to a third-party API. For example, one might use an identity management service like **Auth0** to manage user accounts, rather than store them locally in a database. This means the business logic for logins functions as a proxy to an external service. Financial transactions, like sales, are often delegated to external providers, as are log collection and storage. For companies that might offer up their services as an API, the entirety of the API management might be delegated to a cloud service such as Swagger or Apiary.

Possibly as a result of architectural trend toward services, driven by third-party services managing once *on-site* functionality such as caching and other APIs, a new basket of ideas generally referred to as "4-Tier architecture" has attracted the attention of system architects.

4-Tiers and microservices

The last several years of modern distributed application development has led to somewhat of a consensus of patterns advantageous to scaling. Let's consider first what is generally meant by a "4-Tier Architecture", and then how microservices have come to define the design of these types of systems.

4-Tier architectures extend and expand 3-Tier architectures:

- **Tier 1:** The Data tier in a 3-Tier architecture is replaced by a **Services** tier. The thinking is straightforward: data is stored at such scale, in so many different ways, across so many different technologies, and changes so often in quality and type that the idea of a "single source of truth", like a single database, is no longer workable. Data is exposed through abstract interfaces whose internal design (calling a Redis database and/or pulling your inbox from Gmail and/or reading weather data from government databases) is a "black box" that need simply return data in the expected format.

- **Tier 2:** 4-Tier architectures introduce the concept of an **Aggregation** tier. Just as data is now broken into services (1), business logic is also being isolated into individual services. As we'll see later when discussing Lambda architectures, the distinction between the way you fetch data or call a *subroutine* has blurred into a general API driven model, where individual services with consistent interfaces generate protocol-aware data. This tier assembles and transforms data, augmenting and filtering aggregated source data into data modeled in structured, predictable ways. This is the layer that might have been called the *backend*, or the Application tier. This is where developers program the channels through which data flows as agreed upon (programmed) protocols. Generally, we want to produce structured data here.

- The remaining tiers are created by splitting the Presentation tier into two:

  - **Tier 3:** The **Delivery** Tier: This tier, aware of client profile (mobile, desktop, IOT, and so on), transforms data delivered by the Aggregation tier into client-specific formats. Cached data would be fetched here, via CDN or otherwise. Selection of ads to insert into a *webpage* might be done here. This tier is responsible for optimizing data received from the Aggregation tier for an individual user. This layer can often be fully automated.

  - **Tier 4:** The **Client** Tier: This tier customizes what is generally returned from the Delivery tier for the specific clients. This can be as simple as rendering a data stream for a mobile device (perhaps a responsive CSS structure or device specific native format) or the reflection of a personalized view (only images, or language translation). Here's where the same data source can be aligned with a specific business partnership, made to conform with an **SLA (Service Level Agreement)** or other business function.

The notable change is the splitting of the Presentation tier into two. Node often appears in the Delivery tier, querying the Aggregation tier on behalf of the Client, customizing the data response it receives for the Client.

In general, we have moved to an architecture where individual services are not expected to reflect the needs of the caller in any specific way, like a browser-focused templating engine in an Express server might have. Services need not share the same technology or programming language, or even the same OS version or kind. Architects instead declare a certain type of topology, with clearly defined communication points and protocols, generally distributed into: 1) data sources, 2) data aggregators, 3) data shapers, and 4) data displayers.

Deploying microservices

In this section, we'll consider several variations on microservices, looking at a few common ways in which developers are using microservices with Node. We'll start with **Seneca**, a microservices framework for Node. Then, we'll move on to developing cloud-based microservices using **Amazon Lambda**. From there, we will attempt to model a **Kubernetes** cluster out of **Docker** containers, exploring modern containerized microservice orchestration.

Microservices with Seneca

Seneca is a Node-based microservice construction kit that helps you organize your code into distinct actions triggered by patterns. Seneca applications are composed of services that can accept JSON messages and optionally return some JSON. Services register an interest in messages with certain characteristics. For example, a service might run whenever a JSON message displaying the `{ cmd: "doSomething" }` pattern is broadcast.

To start, let's create a service that responds to three patterns, one pattern returning "Hello!", and the other two different ways of saying "Goodbye!".

Create a `hellogoodbye.js` file containing the following code:

```javascript
// hellogoodbye.js
const seneca = require('seneca')({ log: 'silent' });
const clientHello = seneca.client(8080);
const clientGoodbye = seneca.client(8081);

seneca
.add({
role: 'hello',
cmd:'sayHello'
}, (args, done) => done(null, {message: "Hello!"}))
.listen(8082);

seneca
.add({
role: 'goodbye',
cmd:'sayGoodbye'
}, (args, done) => done(null, {message: "Goodbye"}))
.add({
role: 'goodbye',
cmd:'reallySayGoodbye'
}, (args, done) => done(null, {message: "Goodbye!!"}))
.listen(8083);

clientHello.act({
role: 'hello',
cmd: 'sayHello'
}, (err, result) => console.log(result.message));

clientGoodbye.act({
role: 'goodbye',
cmd: 'sayGoodbye'
}, (err, result) => console.log(result.message));

clientGoodbye.act({
role: 'goodbye',
cmd: 'reallySayGoodbye'
}, (err, result) => console.log(result.message));
```

Seneca works on the idea of service clients listening for certain command patterns, and routing to the right handler based on pattern matching. Our first job is to set up two Seneca service clients, listening on ports 8080 and 8081. Already, we can see how services are being organized into two groups, the "hello service" with one method, and the "goodbye service" with another. We now need to add actions to those services. To do that, we need to tell Seneca how to act when a service call matching a certain pattern is made, here defined using certain object keys. It is left open how to define your service objects, but the "cmd" and "role" pattern is common—it helps you create logical groups and a standard command call signature. We'll be using that pattern in the examples that follow.

Considering the preceding code, we see that when a JSON object is received with the cmd field set to sayHello and a role of hello, the service handler should return { message: "Hello!" }. The "goodbye" role methods are similarly defined. At the bottom of the file, you see how we can directly call those services via Node. It is easy to imagine how these service definitions can be broken out into several module exports in individual files, dynamically imported as needed, and otherwise used to compose applications in an organized way (a goal of microservice-based architectures).

To get rid of the log data being displayed, you can initialize your Seneca instance with require('seneca')({ log: 'silent' }).

As the Seneca service is listening on HTTP by default, you can achieve the same result by making a direct call over HTTP, operating against the /act route:

```
curl -d "{\"cmd\":\"sayHello\",\"role\":\"hello\"}"
http://localhost:8082/act
// {"message":"Hello!"}
```

This automatic HTTP interface gets us network-discoverable services for free, which is handy. We can already get a sense of the microservice pattern: simple, independent, small bits of functionality that communicate using standard network data patterns. Seneca gives us both a programmatic and networked interface for free, and that's a bonus.

Once you start creating a lot of services, it will become difficult to keep track of which service group operates out of which port. Service discovery is a difficult, new problem that microservice architectures introduce. Seneca solves this via its **mesh** plugin, which adds service discovery to your Seneca cluster. Let's create a simple calculator service to demonstrate. We'll create two services, each listening on a distinct port, one that performs addition and the other subtraction, as well as a base service to instantiate the mesh. Finally, we'll create a simple script that performs addition/subtraction operations using services whose location it need not know, via the mesh.

The code for this example is in the /seneca folder in your code bundle. To start, you will need to install two modules:

```
npm i seneca-balance-client seneca-mesh
```

Now, we create a base node that will enable the mesh:

```
// base.js
require('seneca')().use('mesh', {
  base: true
});
```

Once this node is started, other services will be automatically discovered once connected to the mesh.

The add service block looks like this:

```
// add.js
require('seneca')()
.add({
  role: 'calculator',
  cmd: 'add'
}, (args, done) => {
  let result = args.operands[0] + args.operands[1];
  done(null, {
    result : result
  })
})
.use('mesh', {
  pin: {
    role: 'calculator',
    cmd: 'add'
  }
})
.listen({
  host: 'localhost',
  port: 8080
});
```

(The **subtract** service looks exactly the same, changing only the math operator it uses, and of course its cmd will be "subtract").

Using the familiar role/cmd pattern, we attach the add command to the calculator group, similar to how we defined the "hello" service in our earlier example, with a handler to perform the addition operation.

We also instruct our service to `listen` for calls on localhost to a specific port, as we normally do. What is new is that we `use` the mesh network, using the `pin` attribute to indicate the role and cmd that this service will respond to, making it discoverable in the mesh.

Jump into the `/seneca` folder in your code bundle and start the following three files in separate terminals, in the following order: `base.js` -> `add.js` -> `subtract.js`. The logical units for our calculator are set up and running independently, which is the general goal of microservices. The last step is to interact with them, for which we'll use the following `calculator.js` file:

```
// calculator.js
require('seneca')({ log: 'silent' })
.use('mesh')
.ready(function() {

  let seneca = this;

  seneca.act({
    role: 'calculator',
    cmd: 'add',
    operands: [7,3]
  }, (err, op) => console.log(`Addition result -> ${op.result}`));

  seneca.act({
    role: 'calculator',
    cmd:'subtract',
    operands: [7,3]
  }, (err, op) => console.log(`Subtraction result -> ${op.result}`));
});
```

Apart from running our actions from within the `ready` handler for Seneca (a useful practice), and of course our `use` of `mesh`, the `seneca.act` statements look the same as the "hello" acts we used earlier, don't they? They are the same, except for one important detail: we are not using the `.listen(<port>)` method! There is no need to create new Seneca clients bound to certain ports as there were in the `hellogoodbye.js` example, because the mesh network services are autodiscovered. We can simply make calls without needing to know which port services exist on. Go ahead and run the preceding code. You should see the following result:

```
Addition result -> 10
Subtraction result -> 4
```

This allows great flexibility. By building out your calculator in this way, each operation can be isolated into its own service, and you can add or remove functionality as needed, without affecting the overall program. Should a service develop bugs, you can fix and replace it without stopping the general calculator application. If one operation requires more powerful hardware or more memory, you can shift it to its own server without stopping the calculator application or altering your application logic. It is easy to see how stringing together database, authentication, transaction, mapping, and other services can be more easily modeled, deployed, scaled, monitored, and maintained than if they were all coupled to a centralized service manager.

Serverless applications

The abstractions that emerge from the design of these distributed systems, largely built on microservices, suggest a natural next step. Why have servers in the traditional sense at all? Servers are big, powerful machines designed in the age of monoliths. If our thinking is in terms of small, resource sipping, independent actors indifferent to the world around them, shouldn't we be deploying microservices to "microservers"? This line of thought has led a revolutionary ideas: AWS Lamda.

AWS Lambda

The introduction of Amazon's AWS Lambda technology boostrapped the serverless movement we have today. Amazon describes Lambda like this:

> *"AWS Lambda lets you run code without provisioning or managing servers...With Lambda, you can run code for virtually any type of application or backend service - all with zero administration. Just upload your code and Lambda takes care of everything required to run and scale your code with high availability. You can set up your code to automatically trigger from other AWS services or call it directly from any web or mobile app."*

Lambda is a technology allowing you to create an infinitely scalable computation cloud composed out of microservices written in JavaScript. You no longer manage servers, only functions (Lambda functions). The cost of scaling is measured on *usage*, not *counts*. It costs more to call 1 Lambda service 10 times than to call each of 9 Lambda services once. Similarly, your services can sit idle, never being called, without incurring any charges.

Lambda functions are functional virtual machines. A Lambda function is essentially a containerized Node application which builds and deploys automatically, including security updates and further maintenance of the underlying services and infrastructure. You will never need to manage Lambda functions beyond writing the code they execute.

On the other hand, you trade off some of the flexibility developing on a server architecture provides. At the time of writing this, these are the limits for each Lambda function:

Resource	Limits
Memory allocation range	Minimum = 128 MB / Maximum = 1536 MB (with 64 MB increments). If the maximum memory use is exceeded, function invocation will be terminated.
Ephemeral disk capacity ("/tmp" space)	512 MB
Number of file descriptors	1,024
Number of processes and threads (combined total)	1,024
Maximum execution duration per request	300 seconds
Invoke request body payload size (RequestResponse/synrchronous invocation)	6 MB
Invoke request body payload size (Event/asynchronous invocation)	128 K

These limits need to be kept in mind when designing your application. Generally, Lambda functions should not depend on persistence, do one thing well, and do it quickly. These limits also imply that you cannot spin up a local database, or other in-process applications, within your Lambda function.

When it was released, Lambda was exclusively designed for Node; you wrote Lambda functions in JavaScript via the Node runtime. This fact is at least some indication of just how important Node is to modern application development. While other languages are now supported, Lambda continues to treat Node as a first-class citizen. In this section, we'll develop an application using the Lambda compute cloud.

While the process of setting up with Lambda is much easier now than it was when the project was first released, there is still a lot of automatic boilerplate you will need to build, and a lot of manual work to make changes. For this reason a number of very high quality Lambda-focused "serverless" frameworks have sprung up in the Node ecosystem. Some of the leading frameworks are listed below:

- **Serverless:** `https://github.com/serverless/serverless`
- **Apex:** `https://github.com/apex/apex`
- **Claudia:** `https://github.com/claudiajs/claudia`

For the following examples, we'll use `claudia`, which is well-designed, documented, and maintained, and is easy to use. The `claudia` developer puts it this way:

> *"...if you want to build simple services and run them with AWS Lambda, and you're looking for something low-overhead, easy to get started with, and you only want to use the Node.js runtime, Claudia is a good choice. If you want to export SDKs, need fine-grained control over the distribution, allocation or discovery of services, need support for different runtimes and so on, use one of the alternative tools."*

API Gateway is a fully-managed AWS service "that makes it easy for developers to create, publish, maintain, monitor, and secure APIs at any scale". We will now assemble a scalable web server out of Lambda-powered microservices using Claudia and AWS API Gateway.

Scaling with Claudia and API Gateway

To begin, you will need to create a developer account with Amazon Web Services (AWS) `https://aws.amazon.com`. This account setup is free. Additionally, most AWS services have very generous free usage tiers, within which limits you may use AWS while learning and developing without incurring any cost. With Lambda, the first one million requests per month are free.

Once you have a developer account, log in to your dashboard, and from the **Services** tab, select **IAM**. You will now add a user that we'll use for these examples. Claudia needs permission to communicate with your AWS account. You generally do not want to use your root account privileges in applications, which should be understood as "sub-users" of your account. AWS provides an **Identity and Access Management (IAM)** service to help with that. Let's create an AWS profile with IAM full access, Lambda full access, and API Gateway Administrator privileges.

From the side panel, select **Users** and click on **Add user:**

Set user details

You can add multiple users at once with the same access type and permissions. Learn more

User name*   claudia

⊕ **Add another user**

Select AWS access type

Select how these users will access AWS. Access keys and autogenerated passwords are provided in the last step. Learn more

Access type* ☑ **Programmatic access**
              Enables an **access key ID** and **secret access key** for the AWS API, CLI, SDK, and other development tools.

              ☐ **AWS Management Console access**
              Enables a **password** that allows users to sign-in to the AWS Management Console.

As indicated, create a new user `claudia`, affording this user programmatic access.

Once you're done, click on the **Next: Permissions** button. We now need to attach this IAM account to the **Lambda** and **API Gateway** services and give it administrative privileges:

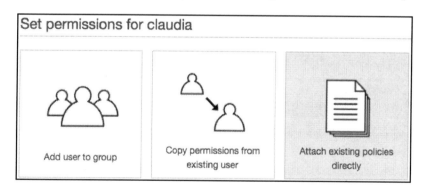

After selecting **Attach existing policies directly**, you will see a long checklist of options appear below. Select the following three permissions for the `claudia` user: **AdministratorAccess**, **AmazonAPIGatewayAdministrator**, and of course, **AWSLambdaFullAccess**.

After clicking on **Review**, you should see the following:

User details		
	User name	claudia
	AWS access type	Programmatic access - with an access key

Permissions summary

The following policies will be attached to the user shown above.

Type	Name
Managed policy	AdministratorAccess
Managed policy	AmazonAPIGatewayAdministrator
Managed policy	AWSLambdaFullAccess

Great. Click on **Create User** and copy the provided **Access key ID** and **Secret access key** (you'll need these later). You're now ready to start deploying Lambda functions using `claudia`.

Installing claudia and deploying a service

To begin installing the `claudia` module, type the following command:

```
npm install claudia -g
```

Now, you should store the credentials you just created for the `claudia` user. A good pattern here is to store an AWS configuration file in your home directory (on OSX, this would be `/Users/<yoursystemusername>`). Once you're in your home directory, create the `.aws/credentials` directory and file with your IAM user keys:

```
[claudia]
aws_access_key_id = YOUR_ACCESS_KEY
aws_secret_access_key = YOUR_ACCESS_SECRET
```

Here, we are indicating that `claudia` is the AWS profile name, targeting these IAM credentials. When we run our deployment, AWS will be informed of this profile and credentials.

Now, let's create a web-accessible HTTP endpoint that returns the string "Hello from AWS!".

Create a new directory and initialize an npm package with npm init, using any name that you'd like for the package. To work with AWS API Gateway, we'll also need to install an extension to claudia:

```
npm install claudia-api-builder
```

Next, add the following app.js file to this directory:

```
const ApiBuilder = require('claudia-api-builder');
const api = new ApiBuilder();

module.exports = api;

api.get('/hello', function () {
    return 'Hello from AWS!';
});
```

Using claudia ApiBuilder, we attach a Lambda function to handle a GET on the /hello route. Surprisingly, we're done! To deploy, enter the following into your terminal:

```
AWS_PROFILE=claudia claudia create --region us-east-1 --api-module app
```

The AWS_PROFILE environment variable is referencing the [claudia] profile identifier in our credentials file, and we are using the --region flag to establish the deployment region.

If everything goes right, your endpoint will be deployed, and information similar to the following will be returned:

```
{
  "lambda": {
    "role": "claudiaapi-executor",
    "name": "claudiaapi",
    "region": "us-east-1"
  },
  "api": {
    "id": "s8r80rsu22",
    "module": "app",
    "url": "https://s8r80rsu22.execute-api.us-east-1.amazonaws.com/latest"
  }
}
```

The returned URL points to our API gateway. Now, we need to add the name of our Lambda function, which was set as `'hello'` in the GET handler we defined earlier:

```
api.get('/hello', function () ...
```

Copy and paste the returned URL in your browser and add the name of your Lambda function:

`https://s8r80rsu22.execute-api.us-east-1.amazonaws.com/latest/hello`

You will see the following message:

Hello from AWS!

That was easy. Updating the function is just as easy. Return to the code and change the string message your function return's to something else, then run:

```
AWS_PROFILE=claudia claudia update
```

A JSON object will be returned on success, indicating code size and other useful information about your function. Go ahead and reload the endpoint in your browser and you will see the updated message. These are zero-downtime updates—your service never stops working while the new code is deployed. Here, we satisfy the key goal of creating "independent, stateless, services [that] can be replaced or upgraded (or downgraded) independently, regardless of the state of any system they form a part of."

You can now validate the existence of your Lambda function by returning to the AWS dashboard and visiting your Lambda services:

We can see the package name listed (`claudiaapi`) and the Node runtime we are using (the highest available version on AWS at the time of this writing). If you click on the function, you will see the management page for your Lambda function, including its code, and interfaces for managing maximum execution times and memory limits.

Change your handler function in `app.js` to the following:

```
api.get('/hello', function (request, context, callback) {
    return request;
});
```

You will see three new arguments are passed to the `handler`, `request`, `context`, and `callback`. The `context` argument contains useful information about the Lambda context for this call, such as the invocation ID, the name of the called function, and more. Usefully, `claudia` mirrors Lambda context in the passed `request` object at key `lambdaContext`. For this reason, when using `claudia`, you need to only work with the `request` argument, which simplifies things.

 To learn more about Lambda event contexts, refer to: `http://docs.aws.amazon.com/lambda/latest/dg/nodejs-prog-model-context.html`.

Now, update your Lambda function using `claudia update`, and check the URL. You should see a large amount of JSON data returned, the totality of the request event information available to you. For more on this data object, visit: `https://github.com/claudiajs/claudia-api-builder/blob/master/docs/api.md#the-request-object`.

 An interesting collection of serverless development information and links can be found at: `https://github.com/anaibol/awesome-serverless`.

Containerized microservices

The Amazon AWS infrastructure is able to create services like Lambda because their engineers no longer provision hardware (ie. new physical servers) when customers create another cloud function or API. Instead, they provision lightweight **VM (Virtual Machines)**. Nobody is lifting a big new metal box onto a rack when you sign up. Software is the new hardware.

Containers aim for the same general architectural idea and advantages that virtualized servers provide —to mass produce virtualized, independent, machines. The main difference is that while a VM provides its own OS (typically called a **Hypervisor**), a container requires a host OS to provide actual kernel services (such as a filesystem, other devices, and resource management and scheduling) as they do not need to carry around their own OS but operate parasitically on a host OS containers are very light, using fewer (host) resources and able to be started up much more quickly. In this section, we'll go over how any developer can use **Docker**, a leading container technology, to cheaply manufacture and manage many virtualized servers.

> This is a good StackOverflow discussion on the distinctions between virtual environments at: `https://stackoverflow.com/questions/16047306/how-is-docker-different-from-a-normal-virtual-machine`.

This image from the Docker website (`http://www.docker.com/`) gives some information on how, and why, the Docker team feels their technology fits into the future of application development:

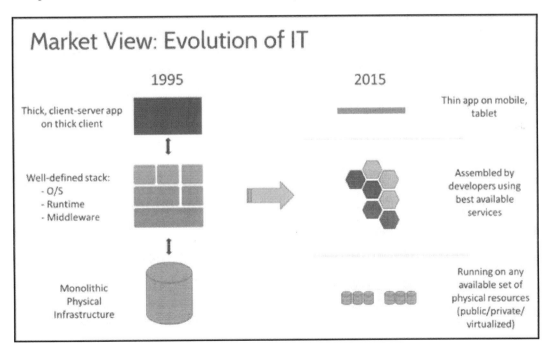

Recalling our discussion of 4-Tier architectures, here we can see that developers asked themselves a question: if my application is composed out of many independently developed, tested, deployed, and managed communicating services in the cloud running on their own infrastructure, couldn't we just do the same with our "local" services and give each its own isolated container so that those can be independently developed, tested, deployed, and so forth? Reducing the cost of implementing change is the goal of containerization, and of microservices. A container generating one localized, independent service with protected local memory that can be started and restarted quickly, tested individually, and fail quietly fits right into a microservices architecture:

- Clearly defined areas of responsibility
- Isolated dependencies and state
- Processes are disposable
- Lightweight and easy to start and replicate
- Graceful termination with zero application downtime
- Can be independently tested
- Can be independently monitored

Getting started with Docker

The Docker ecosystem has three main components. Here's what the documentation says:

- **Docker containers**. A Docker container holds everything that is needed for an application to run. Each container is created from a Docker image. Docker containers can be run, started, stopped, moved, and deleted. Each container is an isolated and secure application platform. You can consider Docker containers as the run portion of the Docker framework.
- **Docker images**. The Docker image is a template, for example, an Ubuntu operating system with Apache and your web application installed. Docker containers are launched from images. Docker provides a simple way to build new images or update the existing images. You can consider Docker images to be the build portion of the Docker framework.

- **Docker Registries**. Docker registries hold images. These are public (or private!) stores that you can upload or download images to and from. These images can be images you create yourself or you can also make use of images that others have previously created. You can consider Docker registries to be the share portion of the Docker framework. You create images of applications to be run in any number of isolated containers, sharing those images with others if you'd like. The most popular is **Docker Hub** (https://hub.docker.com/), but you can also operate your own.

The concept of composing Node applications out of many independent processes naturally aligns with the philosophy behind Docker. Docker containers are sandboxed, unable to without your knowledge execute instructions on their host. They can expose a port to their host OS, however, allowing many independent virtual containers to be linked together into a larger application.

 It will be a good idea to learn a little about how to find information about your OS, which ports are being used, by which processes, and so on. We've mentioned HTOP previously, and you should familiarize yourself with at least gathering network statistics—most OS's offer a `netstat` utility, useful to discover which ports are open and who is listening on them. For example, `netstat -an | grep -i "listen"`.

Download and install **Docker Community Edition** (https://www.docker.com/community-edition) or the **Docker Toolbox** (https://docs.docker.com/toolbox/overview/). A comparison between the two can be found at: https://docs.docker.com/docker-for-mac/docker-toolbox/. If you're using the toolbox, select the Docker Quickstart Terminal when prompted, which will spawn a terminal and install the necessary components on your system. The installation process might take while, so don't panic! When done, you should see something like the following in your terminal:

docker is configured to use the default machine with IP 192.158.59.101

Note that the name of the Docker machine is "default".

To get a sense of how images work, run the `docker run hello-world` command. You should see the machine pull an image and containerize it—full details of what is happening will be printed. If you now run the command docker images, you'll see something like this:

REPOSITORY	TAG	IMAGE ID	CREATED	SIZE
hello-world	latest	f2a91732366c	3 weeks ago	1.85kB

This command will tell you something about your Docker installation: `docker info`.

A Docker container runs an image of your application. You can create these images yourself, of course, but there does exist a large ecosystem of the existing images. Let's create our own image of a Node server running Express.

First, we'll need to build an application to run. Create a folder to put your application files into. Within that folder, create an `/app` folder; this is where we will put our server files. As with all Node applications, we'll need to create a `package.json` file. Enter the `/app` folder and `run npm init`, giving this package a name of "docker-example". Then, install Express with `npm i express`.

Now, create a simple Express server and save it to `app/index.js`:

```
// index.js
const express = require('express');
const port = 8087;
const app = express();
const message = `Service #${Date.now()} responding`;
app.get('/', (req, res) => {
    res.send(message);
});
app.listen(port, () => console.log(`Running on http://localhost:${port}`));
```

Go ahead and start the server:

```
> node app.js
// Running on http://localhost:8087
```

You can now point your browser to your host on port `8087` and see a unique message similar to `Service #1513534970093 responding` displayed. Great. There is a reason for creating a unique message (via `Date.now()`) that will make more sense later when we discuss scaling services. For now, let's build these files into a container using Docker.

Creating a Dockerfile

Our goal is to describe the environment this application executes within, now, so that Docker can reproduce that environment in a container. Also, we want to add the source files of our application to run in this newly virtualized environment. Docker can act as a builder, in other words, following the instructions you provide on how to build an image of your application.

To begin with, you should have a folder containing your application files. This is your source code repository, which your docker image will build within. As mentioned, a Dockerfile is a list of instructions for building an application. A Dockerfile describes a build process. What you will normally declare in a Dockerfile is the OS version the container will run, and any OS installations you might need done, such as Node.

Create a `Dockerfile` file (no extension):

```
# Dockerfile
FROM node:9
LABEL maintainer="your@email.com"
ENV NODE_ENV=development
WORKDIR /app
COPY ./app .
RUN npm i
EXPOSE 8087
CMD [ "npm", "start" ]
```

You see in the this file various directives, and there are several others you might use for more complex builds. We'll keep it simple to start. To go deeper into Dockerfiles, you can run through the full documentation at: `https://docs.docker.com/engine/reference/builder/`.

The `FROM` directive is used to set the base image you will build upon. We will be building upon `node:9`, an image containing the latest Node. More complex images are usually included here, typically built around common patterns. For example, this image implements the **MEAN (Mongo Express Angular Node)** stack: `https://hub.docker.com/r/meanjs/mean/`. `FROM` should be the very first directive in a Dockerfile.

You can set (optional) metadata for your image via `LABEL`. There can be multiple `LABEL` declarations. This is useful for version management, credits, and so forth. We also set some environment variables (`ENV`) for the Node process (exposed as you would expect in `process.env`).

We state our working directory (`WORKDIR`) for the application, and `COPY` all the local files on our machine into the filesystem of the container; the container is isolated and has no access to a filesystem outside of itself, so we need to build its filesystem from ours.

Now, we establish startup directives. `RUN npm i` to install `package.json`, `EXPOSE` the port our server runs on (`8087`) to the outside world (again, containers are isolated and cannot expose internal ports without permission), and run the command (`CMD`) `npm start`. You may set multiple `RUN` and `CMD` directives, whatever is necessary to start your application.

We're now ready to build and run a container.

Running containers

From within the directory containing your Dockerfile, run this command:

`docker build -t mastering-docker` . (note trailing dot).

Docker will now fetch all base dependencies and build your image according to your directives:

```
Sending build context to Docker daemon  18.43kB
Step 1/7 : FROM node:9
9: Pulling from library/node
f49cf87b52c1: Downloading [=====================>              ]  24.87MB/52.6MB
7b491c575b06: Download complete
b313b08bab3b: Downloading [==========================>         ]  23.89MB/43.25MB
51d6678c3f0e: Downloading [===>                                ]  8.641MB/135MB
da59faba155b: Waiting
7f84ea62c1fd: Waiting
1ae6c7e5e8c9: Waiting
7c07b0a5c6a6: Waiting
```

You just created your first Docker image! To see your image, use `docker images`:

REPOSITORY	TAG	IMAGE ID	CREATED	SIZE
mastering-docker	latest	9b804791a498	6 minutes ago	676MB
node	9	3d1823068e39	33 hours ago	676MB

Here, we see the image we created—`mastering-docker`—and the image our image was based on—`node:9`. Note how the colon is used to created tagged versions of images -- we are ultimately using the **node** image tagged **9**. More on versioning later.

The next step is to containerize and run the image. Use this command:

`docker run -p 8088:8087 -d mastering-docker`

If all goes well, you will be able to list your running Docker process with the `docker ps` command:

CONTAINER ID	IMAGE	COMMAND	CREATED	STATUS	PORTS	NAMES
db32761ce3da	mastering-docker	"npm start"	11 minutes ago	Up 11 minutes	0.0.0.0:8088->8087/tcp	keen_poincare

Recall the `EXPOSE 8087` directive? We needed to map the port our container exposed to the local OS network interface, which we flagged in the run command with `-p 8088:8087`, and which mapping we can see in the screenshot above under `PORTS`.

The −d flag indicates to Docker that we'd like to run the container in detached mode. This is probably what you want to do, running your container in the background. Without this flag, you will terminate the container when you terminate your terminal session.

You are now running a Node server in a container completely isolated from your local machine. Try it out by navigating a browser to `localhost:8088`. It's pretty great to be able to construct entirely isolated builds, with completely different operating systems, databases, software versions and so forth all on you local machine, knowing that you can take that exact same container and deploy it into a data center without changing a thing.

Here are some more useful commands:

- Delete a container: `docker rm <containerid>`
- Delete all containers: `docker rm $(docker ps -a -q)`
- Delete an image: `docker rmi <imageid>`
- Delete all images: `docker rmi $(docker images -q)`
- Stop or start a container: `docker stop (or start) <containerid>`

Orchestrating Containers with Kubernetes

A microservices-driven architecture is composed of independent services. We've just looked at how containers can be used to isolate distinct services. Now, the question is how to manage and coordinate these 10, 20, 100, 1,000 service containers? "By hand" doesn't seem like the right approach. **Kubernetes** automates container orchestration, helping you deal with questions of deployment and scaling and fleet health. Developed by Google, it is a mature technology used in Google's own incomprehensibly massive data centers to orchestrate millions of containers.

We'll install an application, **Minikube**, that runs a single-node Kubernetes cluster inside a VM on your local machine, so you can test develop a Kubernetes cluster locally before deploying. As the configuration of the cluster you do locally mirrors a "real" Kubernetes cluster, once you are satisfied, you can deploy your definitions to Kubernetes in production without any changes.

Creating a basic Kubernetes cluster

You'll need some sort of VM driver for Minikube, and by default, Minikube uses **VirtualBox**. You can find installation instructions at: `https://www.virtualbox.org/wiki/Downloads`. VirtualBox stands on its own as a free hypervisor, which is used to power other useful developer tools, like **Vagrant**.

Now, we'll install `kubectl` (think of it as "Kube Control"), the Kubernetes command-line interface. Follow the instructions at: `https://kubernetes.io/docs/tasks/tools/install-kubectl/`.

Finally, we install Minikube: `https://kubernetes.io/docs/tasks/tools/install-minikube/`.

Start the cluster up with `minikube start` (this can take a while, so be patient). The output is sufficiently descriptive: you will be starting a VM, getting an IP address, and building a Kubernetes cluster. The output should end with something like **Kubectl is now configured to use the cluster.** You can always check its status with `minikube status`:

```
minikube: Running
cluster: Running
kubectl: Correctly Configured: pointing to minikube-vm at 192.160.80.100
```

To see that kubectl is configured to communicate with Minikube, try `kubectl get nodes`, which should show that the Minkube machine '**minikube**' is '**Ready**'.

This VM is being run via VirtualBox. Open the Virtualbox Manager on your machine. You should see a machine named "minikube" listed. If you do, great; a Kubernetes cluster is running on your machine!

 You can test different Kubernetes versions with Minikube. To get available versions, run `minikube get-k8s-versions`. Once you have a version, start Minikube on that version with `minikube start --kubernetes-version v1.8.0`.

Now, we'll use Kubernetes to deploy the "hello world" server we earlier containerized with Docker. Usefully, Minikube manages its own Docker daemon and local repository. We'll use that to build what follows. First, link into Minikube's Docker with `eval $(minikube docker-env)`. When you want to return control back to your host Docker daemon, try `eval $(minikube docker-env -u)`.

Return to the folder containing our server and build our Docker image (note trailing dot):

```
docker build -t mastering-kube:v1 .
```

When that process has completed, you should see something like this displayed in your terminal:

```
Successfully built 754d44e83976
Successfully tagged mastering-kube:v1
```

One thing that you may have noted is the :v1 suffix on our image name. We saw that earlier when we declared Node in our Dockerfile (remember the FROM Node:9 directive)? If you run docker images, you'll see that tags are applied:

Later on, if we want to release a new version of mastering-kube, we can simply build with a new tag, which creates an independent image. This is what you should do over time to manage versioning of your container images.

Great, now let's start a container with that image and **deploy** it into our Kubernetes cluster:

```
kubectl run kubernetes-demo --image=mastering-kube:v1
```

Here, we declare a new deployment with the name kubernetes-demo that should import the mastering-kube image at version v1. If everything works, you should see **deployment "kubernetes-demo" created** in your terminal. You can list deployments with kubectl get deployments:

We've just deployed a single **Pod** into a Kubernetes cluster. Pods are the basic organizational unit of Kubernetes, and they are an abstract wrapper around containers. Pods may contain one or more containers. Kubernetes manages pods, and Pods manage their own containers. Each Pod receives its own IP address and is isolated from other pods, but containers within pods are not isolated from each other (they can all communicate via localhost, for example).

A Pod presents the abstraction of a single machine running somewhere (locally, on AWS, in a data center) and all the containers running on that single machine. In this way you can have a single Kubernetes cluster running Pods located in different locations in the cloud. Kubernetes is an abstraction across differently located machine hosts that lets you orchestrate their behavior indifferent to whether one is a VM hosted on AWS or a laptop in your office, in the same way that you might use an ORM to abstract away database details, leaving you free to change the technical makeup of a deployment without altering configuration files.

With the `kubectl get pods` command, you should now see something like this:

```
NAME                              READY   STATUS    RESTARTS   AGE
kubernetes-demo-c7cd8bf66-tbqpw   1/1     Running   0          36s
```

The final step is to expose this deployed pod as a service. Run this command:

```
kubectl expose deployment kubernetes-demo --port=8087 --type=LoadBalancer
```

If successful, you should see the message **service "kubernetes-demo" exposed**. To view services, use `kubectl get services`:

```
NAME              CLUSTER-IP      EXTERNAL-IP   PORT(S)    AGE
kubernetes        10.96.0.1       <none>        443/TCP    43m
kubernetes-demo   10.110.13.227                 8087/TCP   0s
```

Note how we have created a load-balanced type of deployment, exposing a Kubernetes service mapped to our **mastering-kube** service (container), accessible through the unique IP this deployed Pod will be assigned. Let's find that URL:

```
minikube service kubernetes-demo --url
```

You should get back a URL (note how Kubernetes is running its own DNS), and browsing to that URL, you should see something like this message:

```
Service #1513534970093 responding
```

Via Minikube, you can start your service in a browser in just one step: `minikube service kubernetes-demo`.

Great. However, the real magic with Kubernetes has to do with how deployments can be scaled and otherwise respond to network conditions.

Recalling that this deployment is load balanced, let's create multiple containers within the same pod sharing load (not unlike the way you might use Node's Cluster module to balance load). Run the following command:

```
kubectl scale deployment kubernetes-demo --replicas=4
```

You should get the message **deployment "kubernetes-demo" scaled**. Let's make sure that's true. Run `kubectl get pods` again. You should see that our deployment has autoscaled the number of pods that it balances:

NAME	READY	STATUS	RESTARTS	AGE
kubernetes-demo-c7cd8bf66-785fx	1/1	Running	0	2m
kubernetes-demo-c7cd8bf66-czh9g	1/1	Running	0	7m
kubernetes-demo-c7cd8bf66-d92ft	1/1	Running	0	2m
kubernetes-demo-c7cd8bf66-mkqtk	1/1	Running	0	2m

That was easy. Let's do a quick test to demonstrate that load is being balanced across more than one container. We'll use **AB (Apache Bench)** for a quick benchmarking and display of responses. Use the following command against our service URL (replace the URL for your local service):

```
ab -n 100 -c 10 -v 2 http://192.168.99.100:31769/
```

All that matters with the above is that we've simulated 100 calls to our server, which was done to check if it is responding as expected. We'll receive output similar to the following:

```
Service #1513614868094 responding
LOG: header received:
    HTTP/1.1 200 OK
X-Powered-By: Express
...
Connection: close

Service #1513614581591 responding
...

Service #1513614867927 responding
...
```

Remember that the server we've scaled across 4 containers has a constant message with a unique timestamp?:

```
// Per-server unique message
const message = `Service #${Date.now()} responding`;

app.get('/', (req, res) => {
```

```
        res.send(message);
    });
```

The variance in the responses `ab` returned proves that calls to one endpoint are being balanced across multiple servers/containers.

If you ever find Minikube in a strange or unbalanced state, just clear its home directory and reinstall. For example: `rm -rf ~/.minikube; minikube start`. You can also delete the Kubernetes cluster entirely with `minikube delete`.

While the command-line tools are extremely useful, you also have access to a dashboard for your Kubernetes cluster. You can start up a dashboard to monitor your cluster by typing `kubectl proxy` into your terminal. You'll see something similar to this displayed: **Starting to serve on 127.0.0.1:8001**. This points to the dashboard server. Open the `/ui` path on this server (`127.0.0.1:8001/ui`) in a browser. You should see a UI with your cluster fully described:

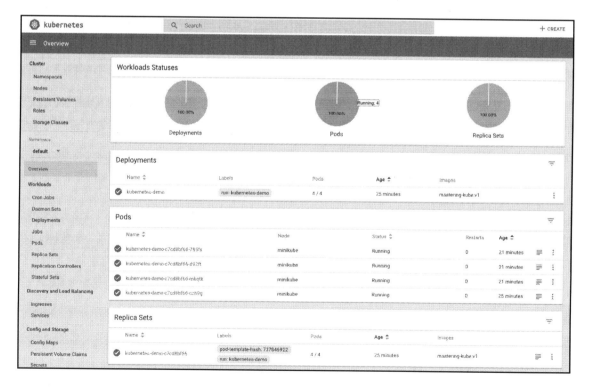

Here, we see all our pods, statuses, and so forth, in particular the 4/4 scaling of our Pod container. Later in the chapter, we'll go a little deeper into how you can use the dashboard to inspect your running clusters.

 Minikube provides a shortcut that will automatically open this dashboard: `minikube dashboard`.

Now, let's look at how to use **YAML (Yet Ain't Markup Language)** to create Pod declarations, avoiding the manual configuration we've been doing, and simplifying deployments later.

Declaring Pod deployments

In this section, we'll create one Pod with three containers, demonstrating both how managing configuration declarations using YAML files simplifies the deployment process, and how containers within the same Pod can communicate with each other.

In your code bundle, there will be a directory `/kubernetes` with this layout:

```
/kubernetes
    /rerouter
    /responder
    three-containers.yaml
```

Each directory defines a Docker container which defines an Express server which will become containers in this Pod. We will treat each of these as an individual service, and demonstrate how they might communicate with each other via `localhost`.

First, let's look at the YAML file:

```
apiVersion: v1
kind: Pod
metadata:
  name: three-containers
spec:
  restartPolicy: OnFailure
  volumes:
  - name: shared-data
    emptyDir: {}

  containers:
  - name: service-rerouter
```

```
    image: rerouter:v1
    volumeMounts:
    - name: shared-data
      mountPath: /app/public

  - name: service-responder
    image: responder:v1

  - name: service-os
    image: debian
    volumeMounts:
    - name: shared-data
      mountPath: /pod-data
    command: ["/bin/sh"]
    args: ["-c", "echo Another service wrote this! > /pod-data/index.html"]
```

This manifest is of a `kind` (`Pod`) with a specification (`spec`) defining three `containers`, with a shared `volume` (more on that in a second), and a `restartPolicy` indicating that containers should only be restarted if they exit with a failure code.

Volumes are used when containers need to share data. Within a container, data storage is ephemeral -- if your container is restarted, that data is lost. A shared volume is held external to the containers within a Pod, and therefore can persist data through container restarts and crashes. More importantly, many containers in a single Pod can write to and read from a shared volume, creating a shared data space. Our services will use this volume as a shared filesystem, and containers who wish to use it can add a mount path -- we'll see how that works in just a second. For more on volumes, visit: `https://kubernetes.io/docs/concepts/storage/volumes/`.

To begin, navigate into the `/rerouter` folder and build the docker image: `docker build -t rerouter:v1 .`. Note how in the above Pod manifest this image is listed:

```
    image: rerouter:v1
```

The `name` for this container is `service-rerouter`, and it provides an Express server handling two routes:

1. When the root route is called (/), it will look for an `index.html` file in the `/public` directory.

2. When /rerouter is called, it will redirect the user to another service in this Pod, the service listening on port 8086:

```
const express = require('express');
const port = 8087;
const app = express();

app.use(express.static('public'));

app.get('/rerouter', (req, res) => {
    res.redirect('http://localhost:8086/oneroute');
});

app.listen(port, () => console.log(`Running on http://localhost:${port}`));
```

If you look at the declaration for service-rerouter, you'll see that it has mounted to the shared volume on the path /app/public. Any container in this Pod can now write to the shared volume and what it writes will end up in this container's /public folder (making it available as a static file for serving). We create a container service that does just that:

```
- name: service-os
    image: debian
    volumeMounts:
    - name: shared-data
      mountPath: /pod-data
    command: ["/bin/sh"]
    args: ["-c", "echo Another service wrote this! > /pod-data/index.html"]
```

The service-os container will contain a Debian operating system, and will mount the shared volume at the path /pod-data. Now, any OS operation that writes to the filesystem will actually be writing to this shared volume. Using the system shell (/bin/sh), when this container starts up, it will echo an index.html file to the shared volume with the contents "Another service wrote this!". Since this container has nothing else to do after echoing, it will terminate. It is for this reason that we set our restart policy to only restart on failure -- we don't want this container to be endlessly restarted. This pattern of adding terminating "helper" services that contribute to the construction of Pod containers and then exit is a common one for Kubernetes deployments.

Recalling that `service-rerouter` also declared that its volume mounts `shared-data` on path `/app/public`, the `index.html` file generated by `service-os` will now appear in that folder, making it available for serving:

```
- name: service-rerouter
  image: rerouter:v1
  volumeMounts:
  - name: shared-data
    mountPath: /app/public
```

Go ahead and build the docker image for the application in folder `/responder` like you did for `/rerouter`. The `service-responder` container resolves a single route, `/oneroute`, returning a simple message:

```
const express = require('express');
const port = 8086;
const app = express();
app.get('/oneroute', (req, res) => {
    res.send('\nThe routing worked!\n\n');
});
app.listen(port, () => console.log(`Running on http://localhost:${port}`));
```

This container will be used to demonstrate how `service-rerouter` can redirect HTTP requests across the (shared) `localhost` Kubernetes has set up for this Pod. Since `service-responder` is bound on port 8086, `service-rerouter` (running on port 8087) can route to it via localhost:

```
// rerouter/app/index.js
res.redirect('http://localhost:8086/oneroute');
```

So, we have shown how containers within a Pod can share a common network and data volume. Assuming that you've successfully built the `rerouter:v1` and `responder:v1` Docker images, execute the Pod manifest with the following command:

```
kubectl create -f three-containers.yaml
```

You should see **pod "three-containers" created** displayed. Open up the dashboard with `minikube dashboard`. You should see the **three-containers** Pod:

Click on **three-containers** to bring up a description:

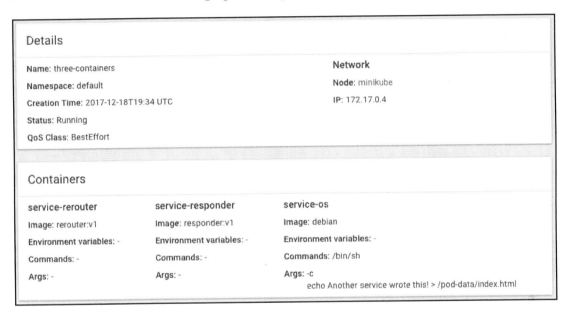

Great, everything is running. Now, let's verify that things are working by connecting to our containers.

Get a shell to `service-router`:

```
kubectl exec -it three-containers -c service-rerouter -- /bin/bash
```

Install **curl**:

```
apt-get install curl
```

Your working directory should have a `/public` folder. There should be an `index.html` file in there, created by the `service-os` container. Fetch that file's contents: `cat public/index.html`. If everything is working you should see the message "Another service wrote this!", which you'll recall is what the `service-os` service created, via the shared volume -- a `public/index.html` file that `service-rerouter` will serve.

Now, let's call the `/rerouter` route, which should redirect to the `service-responder` server on `localhost:8086/oneroute/` and receive its response "routing service works!":

```
curl -L http://localhost:8087/rerouter
```

This demonstrates how containers in the same Pod can communicate via localhost across port ranges, just as if their containing Pod was a single host machine.

 Mesos is another option for orchestration (`http://mesos.apache.org/`), as is CoreOS: `https://coreos.com/`

This just scratches the surface of how Docker and Kubernetes can be deployed to simplify scaling, especially on a microservice architecture. You can further orchestrate your entire fleet through declarative manifests for services and deployments. For example, it is easy to see how the Seneca microservices we designed earlier might fit into Pods. It should be clear that you are now able to abstract away the implementation details of individual servers and begin to think declaratively, simply describing your desired deployment topology (replicas, volumes, recovery behavior, and so on) and letting Kubernetes make that a reality, which is much nicer than imperatively micromanaging hundreds of thousands of services.

Summary

In this chapter, we did a deep dive into various architectural patterns, from monoliths to 4-Tier. In the process, we started to consider how we might start building highly dynamic applications out of microservices, exploring their general advantages in terms of scalability, flexibility, and maintainability. We took a look at the Seneca framework for microservices, whose pattern-based execution model is easy to construct against and follow, particularly when combined with the benefits of autodiscovered mesh services. Jumping into full distributed mode, we deployed serverless Lambda functions with Claudia, using API-Gateway to push a RESTful API into the AWS cloud, with always-on availability and nearly infinite scale at a low cost. With Docker and Kubernetes (with an assist from Minikube), we went deep into how to construct clusters of independent virtual machines, declaring and deploying Pods of containers that scale on demand.

In the next and final chapter of this book, we will study possibly the most important skill a software developer can develop: how to test and debug your code. Now that we have learned to separate the logical parts of our applications out into independent pieces, we can start to explore the advantages of such a design in terms of testing, both in abstract test harnesses and live code situations.

10

Testing Your Application

"When the terrain disagrees with the map, trust the terrain."

– Swiss Army Manual

Since Node is being built by a community fully committed to code sharing, where interoperability between modules is so important, it should come as no surprise that code testing tools and frameworks entered Node's ecosystem right after inception. Indeed, the normally parsimonious core Node team added the `assert` module early on, suggesting a recognition that testing is a fundamental part of the development process.

Testing is not solely a bug-detecting and defect-fixing process. Test-Driven Development, for example, insists on having tests precede the existence of any code! Testing, generally, is the process of making comparisons between the existing behavior and desired behavior in software, where new information is continuously fed back into the process. In this sense, testing involves modeling expectations and verifying that individual functions, composed units, and implementation paths satisfy the expectations of every stakeholder, both within and beyond the boundaries of an organization.

Testing is, therefore, also about managing risk. In this way, anomalies can be identified and quantified, while bumps in the terrain can now usefully inform our current understanding of the map such that the number of missteps (or defects) decline and our confidence rises. Testing helps us measure when we are done.

In this chapter, we will focus on some known and useful patterns for testing Node applications, investigating native Node tools for code integrity testing, general testing with the Mocha framework, and headless browser testing, the last allowing for the testing of browser-based JavaScript from within a Node environment. We'll also be looking at the other side of the testing coin—debugging—and combine the two.

As you move through this chapter, it might be useful to keep in mind that integrating the philosophy of testing into a project can be difficult to do well. Writing the right tests is more difficult than writing some tests. Testing the right things is more difficult than testing everything (full code coverage seldom means nothing can go wrong). A good testing strategy should be implemented as early as possible—something to consider as you embark on your next Node project.

Why testing is important

A good testing strategy builds confidence through the accumulation of proof and increasing clarity. Within a company, this might mean that some criteria for the execution of a business strategy have been satisfied, allowing for the release of a new service or product. The developers within a project team gain the pleasure of an automated judge that confirms or denies whether changes committed to a code base are sound. With a good testing framework, refactoring loses its danger; the "if you break it you own it" caveat that once placed negative pressure on developers with new ideas is no longer as ominous. Given a good version control system and test/release process, any breaking change can be rolled back without negative impact, freeing curiosity and experimentation.

Three common types of tests are: unit tests, functional tests, and integration tests. While our goal in this chapter is not to put forward a general theory about how to test applications, it will be useful to briefly summarize what unit, functional, and integration tests are, which members of a team are most interested in each, and how we might go about building up (or breaking up) a code base into testable units.

Unit tests

Unit tests concern themselves with units of system behavior. Each unit being tested should encapsulate a very small set of code paths, without entanglements. When a unit test fails, this should, ideally, indicate that an isolated part of the overall functionality is broken. If a program has a well-described set of unit tests, the purpose and expected behavior of an entire program should be easy to comprehend. A unit test applies a limited perspective to small parts of a system, unconcerned with how those parts may be wrapped up into larger functional blocks.

An example unit test might be described in this way; when the `123` value is passed to a `validate_phone_number()` method, the test should return false. There is no confusion about what this unit does, and a programmer can use it with confidence.

Unit tests are normally written and read by programmers. Class methods are good candidates for unit tests, as are other service endpoints whose input signatures are stable and well understood, with expected outputs that can be accurately validated. Generally, it is assumed that unit tests run quickly. If a unit test is taking a long time to execute, it is likely that the code under test is much more complex than it should be.

Unit tests are not concerned with how a function or method will receive its inputs, or how it will be used in general. A test for an `add` method shouldn't be concerned with whether the method will be used in a calculator or somewhere else, it should simply test whether the two integer inputs (3,4) will cause the unit to emit a correct result (7). A unit test is not interested in where it fits in the dependency tree. For this reason, unit tests will often *mock* or *stub* data sources, such as passing two sample integers to an `add` method. As long as the inputs are typical, they need not be actual. Additionally, good unit tests are reliable: unencumbered by external dependencies, they should remain valid, regardless of how the system around them changes.

Unit tests only confirm that a single entity works in isolation. Testing whether units can work well when combined is the purpose of functional testing.

Functional tests

Where unit tests concern themselves with specific behaviors, **functional tests** are designed to validate pieces of functionality. The ambiguity of the root word *function*, especially for programmers, can lead to confusion, where *unit tests* are called *functional tests*, and vice versa. A functional test combines many units into a body of functionality, such as *when a user enters a username and password and clicks on send, that user will be logged into the system*. We can easily see that this functional group will comprise of many unit tests, one for validating a username, one for handling a button click, and so on.

Functional tests are normally the concern of those responsible for some specific domain within an application. While programmers and developers will remain the ones to implement these tests, product managers or similar stakeholders will normally devise them (and complain when they fail). These tests for the most part check whether larger product specifications are being satisfied, rather than for technical correctness.

The example unit test for `validate_phone_number` given earlier might form part of a functional test with this description: when a user enters the wrong phone number, display a help message that describes the right format in that user's country. That an application bothers to help users who make mistakes with phone numbers is an abstract effort very different from simply validating a technical entity like a phone number. Functional tests might be thought of as abstract models of how well some collection of units work together to satisfy a product need.

As functional tests are made against combinations of many units, it is expected that, unlike an isolated unit test, executing them will involve mixing concerns from any number of external objects or systems. In the preceding login example, we see how a relatively simple functional test can cut across database, UI, security, and other application layers. As it is compositionally more complex, it's OK if functional tests take a little more time to run than unit tests. Functional tests are expected to change less often than unit tests, such that changes in functionality often represent major releases, as opposed to the minor changes unit test modifications usually indicate.

Note that, like unit tests, functional tests are themselves isolated from concerns about how the functional group under test, as a whole, relates to the rest of an application. For this reason, mock data may be used as a context for running functional tests, as the functional group itself is not concerned with its effect on general application state, which is the domain of integration tests.

Integration tests

Integration tests ensure that the entire system is correctly wired together, so that a user would feel that the application is working correctly. In this way, integration tests typically validate the expected functionality of an entire application, or one of a small set of significant product functionality.

The most important difference between integration and the other types of tests under discussion is that integration tests are to be executed within a realistic environment, on real databases with actual domain data, on servers, and other systems mirroring the target production environment. In this way, integration tests can easily break formerly passing unit and functional tests.

For example, a unit test for `validate_phone_number` may have given a pass to an input like `555-123-4567`, but during an integration test, it will fail to pass some real (and valid) system data like `555.123.4567`. Similarly, a functional test may successfully test the ability of an ideal system to open a help dialog, but when integrated with a new browser or other runtime, it is found that the expected functionality is not achieved. An application that runs well against a single local filesystem may fail when run against a distributed filesystem.

Due to this added complexity, system architects—the team members that are able to apply a higher-level perspective on what system correctness entails—normally design integration tests. These tests find errors in the wiring that isolated tests are not able to recognize. Not surprisingly, integration tests can often take a long time to run, typically designed to not only run simple scenarios but to imitate expected high-load, realistic environments.

Native Node testing and debugging tools

A preference for tested code has formed part of the Node community's ethos since its inception, reflected in the fact that most popular Node modules, even simple ones, are distributed with test suites. While browser-side development with JavaScript suffered for many years without usable testing tools, the relatively young Node distribution contains many. Perhaps because of this, many mature and easy-to-use third-party testing frameworks have been developed for Node. This leaves a developer no excuse for writing untested code! Let's look into some of the provided tools for debugging and testing Node programs.

Writing to the console

Console output is the most basic testing and debugging tool, providing a quick way to see what is happening at some point in a script. The globally accessible `console.log` is commonly used when debugging.

Node has enriched this standard output mechanism with more useful methods, such as `console.error(String, String...)`, which prints arguments to `stderr` rather than `stdout`, and `console.dir(Object)`, which runs `util.inspect` (refer to the following) on the provided object and writes results to `stdout`.

The following pattern is commonly seen when a developer wants to track how long a piece of code takes to execute:

```
let start = new Date().getTime();
for (x = 0; x < 1000; x++) {
  measureTheSpeedOfThisFunction();
}
console.log(new Date().getTime() - start);
// A time, in milliseconds
```

The `console.time` and `console.timeEnd` methods standardize this pattern:

```
console.time('Add 1000000 records');
let rec = [];
for (let i = 0; i < 1000000; i++) {
    rec.push(1);
}
console.timeEnd('Add 1000000 records');
//  > Add 1000000 records: 59ms
```

Ensure that you pass the same label to `timeEnd()` so that Node can find the measurement you started with `time()`. Node prints the stopwatch result to `stdout`. We will see other special console methods when discussing the assert module and performing stack traces later in this chapter.

Formatting console output

The preceding methods are all very useful when logging simple strings. More often, useful logging data may need to be formatted, either by composing several values into a single string, or by neatly displaying a complex data object. The `util.format` and `util.inspect` methods can be used to handle these cases.

The util.format(format, [arg, arg...]) method

This method allows a formatting string to be composed out of placeholders, each of which captures and displays the additional values passed. Consider the following example:

```
> util.format('%s:%s', 'foo','bar')
  'foo:bar'
```

Here, we see that the two placeholders (prefixed by %) are replaced in order by the passed arguments. Placeholders expect one of the following three types of values:

- %s: A string
- %d: A number, either an integer or a float
- %j: A JSON object

If a greater number of arguments than placeholders is sent, the extra arguments are converted to strings via util.inspect(), and concatenated to the end of the output, separated by spaces:

```
> util.format('%s:%s', 'foo', 'bar', 'baz');
  'foo:bar baz'
```

If no formatting string is sent, the arguments are simply converted to strings and concatenated, separated by a space.

The util.inspect(object, [options]) method

Use this method when a string representation of an object is desired. Through the setting of various options, the look of the output can be controlled:

- showHidden: Defaults to false. If true, the object's non-enumerable properties will be shown.
- depth: An object definition, such as a JSON object, can be deeply nested. By default, util.inspect only traverses two levels into the object. Use this option to increase (or decrease) that depth.
- colors: Allows the colorization of the output (check out the following code snippet).
- customInspect: If the object being processed has an inspect method defined, the output of that method will be used instead of Node's default stringification method (refer to the following code snippet). Defaults to true.

Setting a custom inspector:

```
const util = require('util');
let obj = function() {
    this.foo = 'bar';
};
obj.prototype.inspect = function() {
    return "CUSTOM INSPECTOR";
};
console.log(util.inspect(new obj));
// CUSTOM INSPECTOR
console.log(util.inspect(new obj, { customInspect: false }));
// { foo: 'bar' }
```

This can be very useful when logging complex objects, or objects whose values are so large as to make console output unreadable. If your shell is showing pretty colors in your terminal, `util.inspect` will too if color is set to true. You can even customize which colors, and how they are used. By default, the colors just indicate the data type.

Here are the defaults, as set in `util.inspect.styles`:

```
{
    number: 'yellow',
    boolean: 'yellow',
    string: 'green',
    date: 'magenta',
    regexp: 'red'
    null: 'bold',
    undefined: 'grey',
    special: 'cyan',
}
```

Node shows functions in cyan under the special category in the preceding code. These default color assignments may be swapped out with one of the supported ANSI color codes stored in the `util.inspect.colors` object: bold, italic, underline, inverse, white, grey, black, blue, cyan, green, magenta, red, and yellow. For example, to have the number values of objects displayed in green rather than the default of yellow, use the following code:

```
util.inspect.styles.number = "green";
console.log(util.inspect([1,2,4,5,6], {colors: true}));
// [1,2,3,4,5,6] Numbers are in green
```

The Node debugger

Most developers have used an IDE for development. A key feature of all good development environments is access to a debugger, which allows breakpoints to be set in a program in places where state or other aspects of the runtime need to be checked.

V8 comes with a powerful debugger (commonly seen powering the Google Chrome browser's developer tools panel), and this debugger is accessible to Node. It is invoked using the **inspect** directive:

```
> node inspect somescript.js
```

Simple step-through and inspection debugging can now be achieved within a node program. Consider the following program:

```
// debug-sample.js
setTimeout(() => {
  let dummyVar = 123;
  debugger;
  console.log('world');
}, 1000);
console.log('hello');
```

The `dummyVar` will make sense in a second. For now, note the `debugger` directive. Executing this program without that line runs the program as you would expect: print `hello`, wait a second, and then print `world`. With the debugger directive, running **inspect** produces this:

```
> node inspect debug-sample.js
< Debugger listening on ws://127.0.0.1:9229/b3f76643-9464-41d0-943a-
d4102450467e
< For help see https://nodejs.org/en/docs/inspector
< Debugger attached.
Break on start in debug-sample.js:1
> 1 (function (exports, require, module, __filename, __dirname) {
setTimeout(() => {
  2 let dummyVar = 123;
  3 debugger;
debug>
```

The debugger directive creates a break point, and once hit, Node gives us a CLI to the debugger itself, from within which we can execute some standard debugging commands:

- `cont` or `c`: Continue execution from the last break point, until the next break point

- `step` or `s`: Step in, that is, keep running until a new source line (or break point) is hit, then return control to debugger
- `next` or `n`: The same as `step`, but function calls made on the new source line are executed without stopping
- `out` or `o`: Step out, that is, execute the remainder of the current function and back out to the parent function
- `backtrace` or `bt`: Trace the steps to the current execution frame

- `setBreakpoint()` or `sb()`: Set a break point on the current line
- `setBreakpoint(Integer)` or `sb(Integer)`: Set a break point on the specified line
- `clearBreakpoint()` or `cb()`: Clear break point on the current line
- `clearBreakpoint(Integer)` or `cb(Integer)`: Clear a break point on the specified line
- `run`: If the debugger's script has terminated, this will start it again
- `restart`: Terminates and restarts the script
- `pause` or `p`: Pause running code
- `kill`: Kill the running script
- `quit`: Exit the debugger
- `version`: Display V8 version
- `scripts`: Lists all loaded scripts

To repeat the last debugger command, simply press *Enter* on your keyboard. Your carpal tunnels will thank you.

Returning to the script we are debugging: entering `cont` into the debugger will result in the following output:

```
. . .
debug> cont
< hello // A pause will now occur because of setTimeout
break in debug-sample.js:3
  1 (function (exports, require, module, __filename, __dirname) {
setTimeout(() => {
  2 let dummyVar = 123;
> 3 debugger;
  4 console.log('world');
  5 }, 1000);
debug>
```

We're now stopped at the **debugger** statement on line 3 (note the chevron). If you now, for example, type `next` (or n,) the debugger will step to the next instruction and stop at `console.log('world')`.

It is normally useful at a break point to do some state inspection, such as the value of variables. You can jump into the **repl** from the debugger in order to do that. Currently, we're paused at the `debugger` statement. What if we wanted to check the value of `dummyVar`?

```
debug> repl
Press Ctrl + C to leave debug repl
> dummyVar
123
```

As an experiment, run the script again, using `next` instead of `cont`, just before the execution of this final context. Keep hitting Enter (which repeats your last command) and try to follow the code that is being executed. After a few steps you'll notice that the `timers.js` script will be introduced into this execution context, and you'll see something like the following:

```
debug> next
break in timers.js:307
  305 threw = false;
  306 } finally {
 >307 if (timerAsyncId !== null) {
  308 if (!threw)
  309 emitAfter(timerAsyncId);
debug>
```

Run the `scripts` command in the debugger at this point, which lists currently loaded scripts. You will see something like this:

```
debug> scripts
* 39: timers.js <native>
71: debug-sample.js
```

Experiment with various methods of using the powerful V8 debugger to pause, inspect, and navigate within your Node program. Beyond common debugging needs, the debugger is great at showing you what Node does at a deep level when executing your code.

Later in this chapter, we'll return to a discussion of other debugging and testing techniques and tools available to the Node developer. For now, let's consider the `assert` module, and how to deploy this native testing framework provided with Node.

The assert module

Node's `assert` module is used for simple unit testing. In many cases, it suffices as a basic scaffolding for tests, or is used as the assertion library for testing frameworks (such as Mocha, as we'll see later). Usage is straightforward: we want to assert the truth of something, and throw an error if our assertion is not true. Consider this example:

```
> require('assert').equal(1,2,'Not equal!')
AssertionError [ERR_ASSERTION]: Not equal!
>
```

If the assertion were true (both values are equal), nothing would be returned:

```
> require('assert').equal(1,1,"Not equal!")
undefined
```

Following the UNIX Rule of Silence (when a program has nothing surprising, interesting, or useful to say, it should say nothing), assertions only return a value when the assertion fails. The value returned can be customized using an optional message argument, as seen in the preceding section.

The `assert` module API is composed of a set of comparison operations with identical call signatures: the actual value, the expected value, and an optional message to display when the comparison fails. Alternate methods functioning as shortcuts or handlers for special cases are also provided.

A distinction must be made between identity comparison (===) and equality comparison (==), the former often referred to as strict equality comparison (as is the case in the `assert` API). As JavaScript employs dynamic typing, when two values of different types are compared using the == equality operator, an attempt is made to coerce (or cast) one value into the other, a sort of common denominator operation. Take a look at this example:

```
1 == "1" // true
false == "0" // true
false == null // false
```

Note the more predictable results when identity comparison is used:

```
1 === "1" // false
false === "0" // false
false === null // false
```

The thing to remember is that the === operator does not perform type coercion prior to the comparison, while the equality operator compares after type coercion.

Equating strings and numerals makes JavaScript a forgiving language for newcomers to programming, and soon after, creates a bug the now more experienced programmer inadvertantly hid in a larger code base. Language authors such as *Brendan Eich* make decisions like these, and are seldom able to change behavior so fundamental later on, and they have to defend their decisions through unending arguments and controversy as programmers bash and laud their languages because of them.

Additionally, because objects may contain the same values but not be derived from the same constructor, the identity of two objects with the same values is distinct; identity requires that both operands refer to the same object:

```
let a = function(){};
let b = new a;
let c = new a;
let d = b;
console.log(a == function(){}) // false
console.log(b == c) // false
console.log(b == d) // true
console.log(b.constructor === c.constructor); // true
```

Finally, the concept of deep equality is used for object comparisons where identity need not be exact. Two objects are deeply equal if they both possess the same number of owned properties, the same prototype, the same set (though not necessarily the same order) of keys, and equivalent (not identical) values for each of their properties:

```
const assert = require('assert');
let a = [1,2,3];
let b = [1,2,3];
assert.deepEqual(a, b); // passes, so nothing is output
assert.strictEqual(a, b); // throws Assertion error
```

It is useful to test your assumptions about how values are understood in comparison to each other by designing some assertion tests. The results may surprise you.

Here are the functions in Node's assert module, organized into groups based on how you might use them:

```
equal              notEqual
strictEqual        notStrictEqual
deepEqual          notDeepEqual
deepStrictEqual    notDeepStrictEqual
ok
ifError
fail
throws             doesNotThrow
```

Using an assert function with equal in the name follows the same rules as the == operator, while strict equal is like using === instead. Additionally, choose a function with deep in the title, or not, to pick the desired behavior we explored earlier. The simplest function, `assert.ok`, can be all you need if you write the logic of equating yourself.

Node's asynchronous functions return an error object to your callback function. Give this object to `assert.ifError(e)` and if e is defined, `ifError` will throw it. Use `assert.fail()` when execution has reached a part of your code where it should never go. This is most useful when the exception is trapped by a `try/catch` block:

```js
// assertthrows.js
const assert = require('assert');
try {
    assert.fail(1,2,'Bad!','NOT EQ')
} catch(e) {
    console.log(e);
}
```

Running the preceding code produces the following output:

```
{ AssertionError [ERR_ASSERTION]: Bad!
    at Object.<anonymous>
(/Users/sandro/Desktop/clients/ME/writing/Mastering_V2/chapter_ten/code/ass
ertthrows.js:4:9)
    at Module._compile (module.js:660:30)
    ...
    at bootstrap_node.js:618:3
    generatedMessage: false,
      name: 'AssertionError [ERR_ASSERTION]',
    code: 'ERR_ASSERTION',
    actual: 1,
    expected: 2,
    operator: 'NOT EQ' }
```

A shortcut method for logging assertion results is available in the console API:

```
> repl
> console.assert(1 == 2, 'Nope!')
AssertionError [ERR_ASSERTION]: Nope!
```

Alternatively, you can confirm that functions always throw or never throw with `assert.throws` and `assert.doesNotThrow`.

For a more detailed explanation of how comparison is done in JavaScript, consult:https://developer.mozilla.org/en-US/docs/Web/JavaScript/Reference/Operators/Comparison_Operators

Node's assert module is strongly influenced by the CommonJS test specification, which can be found at: http://wiki.commonjs.org/wiki/Unit_Testing.

Sandboxing

In some instances, you might want to run a script within a separate and more limited context, isolated from the scope of your larger application. For these situations, Node provides the vm module, a sandbox environment consisting of a new V8 instance and a limited execution context for running script blocks:

```
const vm = require('vm');
let sandbox = {
    count: 2
};
let suspectCode = '++count;';
vm.runInNewContext(suspectCode, sandbox);
console.log(sandbox);
// { count: 3 }
```

Here, we see how a provided sandbox becomes the local execution scope for the provided script. The running script only operates within the provided sandbox object, and is denied access to even the standard Node globals, such as the running process, which we can demonstrate by changing the preceding code:

```
suspectCode = '++count; process.exit()';
vm.runInNewContext(suspectCode, sandbox);

// evalmachine.<anonymous>:1
// ++count; process.exit()
//            ^
//
// ReferenceError: process is not defined
// at evalmachine.<anonymous>:1:10
// at ContextifyScript.Script.runInContext (vm.js:59:29)
// ...
```

This module does not guarantee a perfectly safe *jail* within which completely untrusted code can be executed safely. If this is your need, consider running a separate process with proper system-level permissions. As vm spins up a new V8 instance, each invocation costs some milliseconds of startup time and about two megabytes of memory. Use vm only when it's worth this performance cost.

For the purpose of testing code, the vm module can be quite effective, in particular, in its ability to force code to run in a limited context. When performing a unit test, for example, one can create a special environment with mocked data simulating the environment within which the tested script will run. This can be better than creating an artificial call context with fake data. Additionally, this sandboxing will allow the execution context for new code to be better controlled, providing good protection against memory leaks and other unanticipated collisions that may bubble up while testing.

Distinguishing between local scope and execution context

Before covering further examples, we need to distinguish between the local scope of a process and its execution context. The distinction will help with understanding the difference between the two primary vm methods: vm.runInThisContext and vm.runInNewContext.

At any time, V8 might have a single, or more likely, several, execution contexts. These contexts act as separate containers, in which V8 can execute some more JavaScript. When using Chrome, you can think of these execution contexts as different tabs navigated to different websites.

The script on one site can't see or mess up the script on another site. The execution context of a Node process represents the runtime context within V8, including native Node methods and other global objects (process, console, setTimeout, and so on).

A script executed through vm.runInNewContext has no visibility into either scope; its context is limited to the sandbox object to which it was passed, as seen earlier.

A script executed through `vm.runInThisContext` has visibility into the global execution scope of your Node process, but not into the local scope. We can demonstrate this as follows:

```
const vm = require('vm');

global.x = 1; // global scope
let y = 1; // local scope

vm.runInThisContext('x = 2; y = 3');
console.log(x, y); // 2, 1 <- only global is changed

eval('x = 3; y = 4');
console.log(x, y); // 3, 4 <- eval changes x, y
```

Scripts are, therefore, run within contexts through `vm`.

It is often useful to precompile contexts and scripts, in particular, when each will be used repeatedly. Use `vm.createContext([sandbox])` to compile an execution context, and pass in a key/value map. In the next section, we'll look at how to apply these contexts to precompiled scripts.

Using compiled contexts

After receiving a string of JavaScript code, the V8 compiler will do its best to optimize the code into a compiled version that runs more efficiently. This compilation step must occur each time a `vm` context method receives code as a string. If your code doesn't change and is reused at least once, it is better to use `new vm.Script(code, [filename])` to compile it once and for all.

We can executed these compiled scripts in the contexts inherited from `runInThisContext` and `runInNewContext`. Here, we run a compiled script in both contexts, demonstrating how the x and y variables being incremented exist in fully isolated scopes:

```
const vm = require('vm');

global.x = 0;
global.y = 0;

let script = new vm.Script('++x, ++y;');
let emulation = vm.createContext({ x:0, y:0 });

for (let i = 0; i < 1000; i++) {
    script.runInThisContext(); // using global
```

```
        script.runInNewContext(emulation); // using own context
}

console.log(x, y); // 1000 1000
console.log(emulation.x, emulation.y); // 1000 1000
```

Had both scripts modified the same x and y in context, the outputs would have been 2000 2000 instead.

Note that if the `runInNewContext` script is not passed an emulation layer (sandbox), it will throw a `ReferenceError: x is not defined`, having access to neither the local nor global x and y values. Try it out.

Now that we know something about assertions and creating test contexts, let's write some real tests using some common testing frameworks and tools.

Testing with Mocha, Chai, and Sinon

One of the great benefits of writing tests for your code is that you will be forced to think through how what you've written works. A test that is difficult to write might indicate code that is difficult to understand.

On the other hand, comprehensive coverage with good tests helps others (and you) understand how an application works. In this section, we'll look at how to describe your tests using the test runner **Mocha**, using **Chai** as its assertion library, and **Sinon** when mocking is necessary to a test. We'll use **redis** to demonstrate how to create tests against a simulated dataset (rather than testing against production databases, which would, of course, be a bad idea). We'll use **npm** as a test script runner.

To start, set up the following folder structure:

```
/testing

/scripts

/spec
```

Now, initialize a `package.json` file with `npm init` within the `/testing` folder. You can just press *Enter* at the prompts, but when you are asked for a test command, enter the following:

```
mocha ./spec --require ./spec/helpers/chai.js --reporter spec
```

This sets up our project for importation of the modules we'll need. We'll discuss what Chai does later. For now, suffice it to say that in this test command, Mocha is being referred to a configuration file for dependency information.

Go ahead and install the needed libraries into this package:

```
npm install --save-dev mocha chai sinon redis
```

The /scripts folder will contain the JavaScript we'll be testing. The /spec folder will contain configuration and test files.

This will make more sense as we move ahead. For now, recognize that this assignation to npm's test attribute asserts that we will be using Mocha for testing, Mocha's test report will be of the spec type, and that tests will exist in the /spec directory. We are also requiring a configuration file for Chai, which will be explained as we move on. Importantly, this has now created a script declaration in npm that will allow you to run your test suite with the npm test command. Use that command whenever you need to run the Mocha tests we'll be developing in what follows.

Mocha

Mocha is a test runner that does not concern itself with test assertions themselves. Mocha is used to organize and run your tests, primarily through the use of the describe and it operators. Schematically, Mocha tests look like this:

```
describe("Test of Utility Class", function() {
  it("should return a date", function(){
   // Test date function somehow and assert success or failure
  });
  it("should return JSON", function() {
   // Test running some string through #parse
  });
});
```

As you can see, the Mocha harness leaves open how the tests are described and organized, and makes no assumptions about how test assertions are designed. It is an organizational harness for your tests, with the additional aim of producing human-readable test definitions.

You can set up tests that run synchronously, as described earlier, or asynchronously using the completion handler passed to all its callbacks:

```
describe("An asynchronous test", () => {
  it("Runs an async function", done => {
    // Run async test, and when finished call... done();
  });
});
```

Blocks can also be nested:

```
describe("Main block", () => {
  describe("Sub block", () => {
    it("Runs an async function", () => {
      // A test running in sub block
    });
  });
  it("Runs an async function", () => {
    // A test running in main block
  });
});
```

Finally, Mocha offers *hooks*, enabling you to run some code before and/or after tests:

- `beforeEach()` runs before each test in a describe block
- `afterEach()` runs after each test in a describe block
- `before()` runs code once prior to any test—prior to any run of `beforeEach`
- `after()` runs code once after all tests have run—after any run of `afterEach`

Usually, these are used to set up test contexts, such as creating some variables before tests and cleaning them up prior to some other tests. This simple collection of tools is expressive enough to handle most testing needs. Additionally, Mocha provides various test reporters that offer differently formatted results. We'll see those in action later as we build some realistic test scenarios.

Chai

As we saw earlier with Node's native assert module, at its base, testing involves asserting what we expect some chunk of code to do, executing that code, and checking whether our expectations were met. Chai is an assertion library that offers a more expressive syntax, offering three assertion styles: `expect`, `should`, and `assert`. We will use Chai to provide the assertions (tests) to be wrapped within Mocha `it` statements, favoring the `expect` style of assertion.

Note that while `Chai.assert` is modeled after the core Node assert syntax, Chai augments the object with additional methods.

To begin with, we will create a configuration file, `chai.js`:

```
let chai = require('chai');

chai.config.includeStack = true;
global.sinon = require('sinon');
global.expect = chai.expect;
global.AssertionError = chai.AssertionError;
global.Assertion = chai.Assertion;
```

Place this file in the `/spec/helpers` folder. This will tell Chai to display the full stack trace of any errors, and to expose the expect assertion style as a global. Similarly, Sinon is also exposed as a global (more on Sinon in the next section). This file will augment the Mocha test run context such that we can use these tools without having to redeclare them in each test file. The `expect` style of assertion reads like a sentence, with *sentences* composed from works like *to*, *be*, *is*, and more. Consider the following example:

```
expect('hello').to.be.a('string')
expect({ foo: 'bar' }).to.have.property('foo')
expect({ foo: 'bar' }).to.deep.equal({ foo: 'bar' });
expect(true).to.not.be.false
expect(1).to.not.be.true
expect(5).to.be.at.least(10) // fails
```

To explore the extensive list of *words* available when creating expect test chains, consult the full docs at: `http://chaijs.com/api/bdd/`. As stated earlier, Mocha does not have an opinion on how you create assertions. We will use `expect` to create assertions in the tests that follow.

Consider testing the capitalize function in the following object:

```
let Capitalizer = () => {
  this.capitalize = str => {
    return str.split('').map(char => {
      return char.toUpperCase();
    }).join('');
  };
};
```

We might do something like this:

```
describe('Testing Capitalization', () => {
  let capitalizer = new Capitalizer();
  it('capitalizes a string', () => {
    let result = capitalizer.capitalize('foobar');
    expect(result).to.be.a('string').and.equal('FOOBAR');
  });
});
```

This Chai assertion will be true, and Mocha will report the same. You will construct your entire test suite out of these blocks of descriptions and assertions.

Next, we'll look at how to add Sinon to our test process.

Sinon

Within a testing environment, you are typically emulating the realities of a production environment, as access to real users or data or other live systems is unsafe or otherwise undesirable. Being able to simulate environments is, therefore, an important part of testing. Also, you will often want to inspect more than just call results; you might want to test whether a given function is being called in the right context or with the right examples. Sinon is a tool that helps you simulate external services, emulate functions, track function calls, and so on.

 The **sinon-chai** module extends Chai with Sinon assertions at: `https://github.com/domenic/sinon-chai`.

The key Sinon technologies are spies, stubs, and mocks. Additionally, you can set fake timers, create fake servers, and more (visit: `http://sinonjs.org/`). This section focuses on the first three. Let's go over some examples of each.

Spies

From the Sinon documentation:

> *"A test spy is a function that records arguments, returns value, the value of this and exception thrown (if any) for all its calls. A test spy can be an anonymous function, or it can wrap an existing function."*

A spy gathers information on the function it is tracking. Take a look at this example:

```
const sinon = require('sinon');

let argA = "foo";
let argB = "bar";
let callback = sinon.spy();

callback(argA);
callback(argB);

console.log(
  callback.called,
  callback.callCount,
  callback.calledWith(argA),
  callback.calledWith(argB),
  callback.calledWith('baz')
);
```

This will log the following:

```
true
2
true
true
false
```

The spy was called twice; once with `foo`, once with `bar`, and never with `baz`. If you're writing a test of whether a certain function was called and/or testing the arguments it received, spies are a great testing tool for your case.

Let's suppose that we wanted to test whether our code properly connects to the pub/sub functionality of Redis:

```
const redis = require("redis");
const client1 = redis.createClient();
const client2 = redis.createClient();

// Testing this
function nowPublish(channel, msg) {
  client2.publish(channel, msg);
};
describe('Testing pub/sub', function() {
  before(function() {
    sinon.spy(client1, "subscribe");
  });
  after(function() {
    client1.subscribe.restore();
  });

  it('tests that #subscribe works', () => {
    client1.subscribe("channel");
    expect(client1.subscribe.calledOnce);
  });
  it('tests that #nowPublish works', done => {
    let callback = sinon.spy();
    client1.subscribe('channel', callback);
    client1.on('subscribe', () => {
      nowPublish('channel', 'message');
        expect(callback.calledWith('message'));
        expect(client1.subscribe.calledTwice);
        done();
    });
  });
});
```

In this example, we do more with spy and Mocha. We deploy spy to proxy the native subscribe method of client1, importantly setting up and tearing down the spy proxy (restoring the original functionality) within Mocha's before and after methods. The Chai assertions prove that both `subscribe` and `nowPublish` are functioning correctly, and are receiving the right arguments. More information on spies can be found at: `http://sinonjs.org/releases/v4.1.2/spies`.

Stubs

Test stubs are functions (spies) with preprogrammed behavior. They support the full test spy API in addition to methods that can be used to alter the stub's behavior. A stub, when used as a spy, can be wrapped around an existing function such that it can fake the behavior of that function (rather than simply recording function executions, as we saw earlier with spies).

Let's assume that you have some functionality in your application that makes calls to some HTTP endpoint. The code may be something like this:

```
http.get("http://www.example.org", res => {
  console.log(`Got status: ${res.statusCode}`);
}).on('error', e => {
  console.log(`Got error: ${e.message}`);
});
```

When successful, the call will log `Got status: 200`. Should the endpoint be unavailable, you'll see something like `Got error: getaddrinfo ENOTFOUND`.

It is likely that you will need to test the ability of your application to handle alternate status codes, and, of course, explicit errors. It may not be in your power to force the endpoint to emit these, yet you must prepare for them, should they occur. Stubs are useful here to create synthetic responses, so that your response handlers can be tested comprehensibly.

We can use stubs to emulate a response without actually calling the `http.get` method:

```
const http = require('http');
const sinon = require('sinon');

sinon.stub(http, 'get').yields({
  statusCode: 404
});

// This URL is never actually called
http.get("http://www.example.org", res => {
  console.log(`Got response: ${res.statusCode}`);
  http.get.restore();
})
```

This stub yields a simulated response by wrapping the original method, which is never called, resulting in a `404` being returned from a call that would normally return a status code of `200`. Importantly, note how we `restore` the stubbed method to its original state when done.

For example, the following *pseudo* code describes a module that makes HTTP calls, parses the response, and responds with `'handled'` if everything went okay, and `'not handled'` if the HTTP response was unexpected:

```
const http = require('http');
module.exports = function() => {
  this.makeCall = (url, cb) => {
    http.get(url, res => {
      cb(this.parseResponse(res));
    })
  }
  this.parseResponse = res => {
    if(!res.statusCode) {
      throw new Error('No status code present');
    }
    switch(res.statusCode) {
      case 200:
        return 'handled';
        break;
      case 404:
        return 'handled';
        break;
      default:
        return 'not handled'; break;
    }
  }
}
```

The following Mocha test ensures that the `Caller.parseReponse` method can handle all response codes we need handled, using stubs to simulate the entire expected response range:

```
let Caller = require('../scripts/Caller.js');
describe('Testing endpoint responses', function() {
  let caller = new Caller();
  function setTestForCode(code) {
    return done => {
      sinon.stub(caller, 'makeCall').yields(caller.parseResponse({
        statusCode: code
      }));
      caller.makeCall('anyURLWillDo', h => {
        expect(h).to.be.a('string').and.equal('handled');
        done();
      });
    }
  }
  afterEach(() => caller.makeCall.restore());
```

```
    it('Tests 200 handling', setTestForCode(200));
    it('Tests 404 handling', setTestForCode(404));
    it('Tests 403 handling', setTestForCode(403));
});
```

By proxying the original `makeCall` method, we can test `parseResponse` against a range of status codes without the difficulty of forcing remote network behavior. Noting that the preceding test should fail (there is no handler for `403` codes), the output of this test should look something like this:

```
1) Testing endpoint responses Tests 403 handling:

    AssertionError: expected 'not handled' to equal 'handled'
    + expected - actual

    +handled
    -not handled
```

The full API for stubs can be seen at: `http://sinonjs.org/releases/v4.1.2/stubs/`.

Mocks

Mocks (and mock expectations) are fake methods (like spies) with preprogrammed behavior (like stubs) as well as preprogrammed expectations. A mock will fail your test if it is not used as expected. Rather than checking expectations *after the fact*, mocks can be used to check whether the unit under test is being used correctly; they enforce implementation details.

In the following example, we check the number of times a specific function is called and that it is called with specific, expected arguments. Specifically, we again test the `capitalize` method of Utilities, this time using mocks:

```
const sinon = require('sinon');
let Capitalizer = require('../scripts/Capitalizer.js');
let capitalizer = new Capitalizer();

let arr = ['a','b','c','d','e'];
let mock = sinon.mock(capitalizer);

// Expectations
mock.expects("capitalize").exactly(5).withArgs.apply(sinon, arr);
// Reality
arr.map(capitalizer.capitalize);
```

```
// Verification
console.log(mock.verify());

// true
```

After setting up a mock on `utilities`, we map a five element array to `capitalize`, expecting `capitalize` to be called exactly five times, with the array's elements as arguments (using `apply` to spread the array into individual arguments). The well-named `mock.verify` is then checked to see whether our expectations were satisfied. As usual, when done, we unwrap the utilities object with `mock.restore`. You should see **true** logged to your terminal.

Now, remove one element from the tested array, frustrating expectations. When you run the test again, you should see the following near the top of the output:

```
ExpectationError: Expected capitalize([...]) 5 times (called 4 times)
```

This should clarify the type of test results that mocks are designed to produce.

 Note that mocked functions do not execute; `mock` overrides its target. In the preceding example, no array members are ever run through `capitalize`.

Let's revisit our earlier example testing Redis `pub`/`sub`, using mocks:

```
const redis = require("redis");
const client = redis.createClient();

describe('Mocking pub/sub', function() {
  let mock = sinon.mock(client);
  mock.expects('subscribe').withExactArgs('channel').once();
  it('tests that #subscribe is being called correctly', function() {
    client.subscribe('channel');
    expect(mock.verify()).to.be.true;
  });
});
```

Rather than checking for conclusions, here, we assert our expectation that the mocked `subscribe` method will receive the exact argument channel only once. Mocha expects `mock.verify` to return `true`. To make this test fail, add one more `client.subscribe('channel')` line, producing something like this:

```
ExpectationError: Unexpected call: subscribe(channel)
```

More information on how to use mocks can be found at: `http://sinonjs.org/releases/v4.1.2/mocks/`.

Headless testing with Nightmare and Puppeteer

One way to test whether a UI is working is to pay several people to interact with a website via a browser and report any errors they find. This can become a very expensive and, ultimately, unreliable process. Also, it requires putting potentially failing code into production in order to test it. It's better to test whether browser views are rendering correctly from within the testing process itself, prior to releasing anything *into the wild*.

A browser, stripped of its buttons and other controls, is at heart a program that validates and runs JavaScript, HTML, and CSS, and creates a view. That the validated HTML is rendered visually on your screen is simply a consequence of humans only being able to see with their eyes. A machine can interpret the logic of compiled code and see the results of interactions with that code without a visual component. Perhaps, because eyes are usually found in one's head, a browser run by machines on a server is typically referred to as a headless browser.

We'll look at two headless browser test automation libraries: **Nightmare** (`https://github.com/segmentio/nightmare`) and **Puppeteer** (`https://github.com/GoogleChrome/puppeteer`). Nightmare uses **Electron** as its browser environment, while Puppeteer uses headless **Chromium**. They both provide you with a scriptable environment around a browser context, enabling various operations on that *page*, such as grabbing a screenshot, filling out and submitting a form, or pulling some content from the page based on a CSS selector. In keeping with our earlier work, we'll also learn how to use Mocha and Chai to harness these headless browser tests.

Let's get familiar with both of these tools, and then look at how they can be integrated into your testing environment.

Nightmare

Nightmare exposes a very expressive API for working with web content. Let's jump right in with an example Mocha test that validates the document title of a web page:

```
const Nightmare = require('nightmare');

describe(`Nightmare`, function() {
  let nightmare;

  beforeEach(() => nightmare = Nightmare({
    show: false
  }));

  afterEach(function(done) {
    nightmare.end(done);
  });

  it(`Title should be 'Example Domain'`, function(done) {
    nightmare
    .goto('http://example.org')
    .title()
    .then(title => expect(title).to.equal(`Example Domain`))
    .then(() => done())
    .catch(done);
  });
});
```

Here, we use Mocha's `beforeEach` and `afterEach` to anticipate many test blocks, creating a fresh Nightmare instance for each, and automatically cleaning up those instances after each test has run via `nightmare.end`. You don't necessarily have to do this, but it is a useful *boilerplate*. Nightmare accepts a configuration object reflecting Electron's **BrowserWindow** options (`https://github.com/electron/electron/blob/master/docs/api/browser-window.md#new-browserwindowoptions`), and here, we use the `show` attribute, which makes the rendering instance visible—the view *pops up* on your screen so that you can watch the page being manipulated. Especially with tests where navigation and UI interactions are being made, it can be useful to see those manipulations in action. Go ahead and try it here and in the tests that follow.

This test is easy to read. Here, we simply head to a URL, fetch the title of that page, and run an assertion to test that we have the right title. Note that Nightmare is designed to natively work with Promises, and the `Promise` chain you see is built on Node-native Promises. If you'd like to use another `Promise` library, you can do that:

```
const bbNightmare = Nightmare({
  Promise: require('bluebird')
});

bbNightmare.goto(...)
```

Interacting with pages is the sine qua non of headless browser testing, letting you write UI tests that run automatically. For example, you might want to test your application's login page, or whether a search input returns the right results in the right order when submitted. Let's add another test to this suite, one where we search for the Nightmare home page on Yahoo and query the result page for the link text:

```
it('Yahoo search should find Nightmare homepage', done => {
    nightmare
    .goto('http://www.yahoo.com')
    .type('form[action*="/search"] [name=p]', 'nightmare.js')
    .click('form[action*="/search"] [type=submit]')
    .wait('#main')
    .evaluate(() => document.querySelector('#main .searchCenterMiddle
a').href)
    .then(result => expect(result).to.equal(`http://www.nightmarejs.org/`))
    .then(() => done())
    .catch(done);
})
```

You can see how this works. Find the search box on Yahoo's front page using a CSS selector, type `'nightmare.js'` into it and click on the **Submit** button to submit the form. Wait for a new element `#main` to show up, indicating that the result page has been rendered. We then create an `evaluate` block, which will execute within the browser scope. This is a good place to do custom DOM selections and manipulations. Here, we find the first link, and check whether it is the one we expected. This simple pattern can be easily modified to click links on your website to ensure that the links are working, for example, or indeed running several selectors over the resulting page to ensure that the right results were delivered.

In your tests, you may find repeating patterns. Imagine that extracting text from links targeted by selector is a common pattern in your tests. Nightmare allows you to turn these into custom actions. Let's create a custom `getLinkText` action on Nightmare, and use that in our tests instead. To start—and prior to instantiating Nightmare—define a new `action`:

```
Nightmare.action('getLinkText', function(selector, done) {
    // `this` is the nightmare instance
    this.evaluate_now(selector => {
        return document.querySelector(selector).href;
    }, done, selector)
});
```

Now, replace the original evaluate instruction with a call to our custom action:

```
...
.wait('#main')
.getLinkText('#main .searchCenterMiddle a') // Call action
...
```

We have simply transposed our original instructions to an action block, with a custom name and function signature, and called that from our test chain. While this example is contrived, it is easy to imagine much more complex actions, even a library of them your engineers might draw on as a sort of *programming language* for tests. Note that `evaluate_now`, not `evaluate`, is used in the action. Nightmare will queue `evaluate` instructions, and since our action has already been queued (as part of the original test chain), we want to evaluate the command right now, immediately in our action, not requeue it.

For more information on Nightmare, visit: `https://github.com/segmentio/nightmare#api`.

Puppeteer

Puppeteer is a shiny new Google project focused on creating a browser testing API using Chromium engine. The team is aggressively targeting the very latest Node versions, taking advantage of all the latest features of the Chromium engine (visit: `https://github.com/GoogleChrome/puppeteer/issues/316`). In particular, it is designed to encourage the use of async/await patterns when writing your tests.

Here's the document title example from earlier written using Puppeteer:

```
it(`Title should be 'Example Domain'`, async function() {
    let browser = await puppeteer.launch({
        headless: true
    });

    let page = await browser.newPage();
    await page.goto(`http://example.org`);
    let title = await page.title();
    await browser.close();

    expect(title).to.equal(`Example Domain`);
});
```

Note the `async` function wrapper. This pattern is very tight, and given how often tests must jump in and out of the browser context, `async/await` feels like a good fit here. We can also see how much the Puppeteer API was influenced by the Nightmare API. Like Nightmare, Puppeteer accepts a configuration object: `https://github.com/GoogleChrome/puppeteer/blob/master/docs/api.md#puppeteerlaunchoptions`. The equivalent of Nightmare's `show` is `headless`, which places Chrome into headless mode. It might be a good exercise to rewrite the preceding Nightmare Yahoo search example in Puppeteer. Full documentation is available at: `https://github.com/GoogleChrome/puppeteer/blob/master/docs/api.md`.

Here's a Mocha test using Puppeteer to read the NYTimes, intercept image rendering calls and cancel them, and then take a screenshot of the image-less page and write it to your local filesystem:

```
it(`Should create an imageless screenshot`, async function() {

    let savePath = './news.png';
    const browser = await puppeteer.launch({
        headless: true
    });

    const page = await browser.newPage();
    await page.setRequestInterception(true);
    page.on('request', request => {
        if (request.resourceType === 'image') {
            request.abort();
        }
        else {
            request.continue();
        }
    });
    await page.goto('http://www.nytimes.com');
```

```
await page.screenshot({
    path: savePath,
    fullPage: true
});
await browser.close();

expect(fs.existsSync(savePath)).to.equal(true);
});
```

To create a PDF, you can just swap out the `screenshot` section with the following:

```
savePath = './news.pdf';
await page.pdf({path: savePath});
```

It is not uncommon for developers to build test suites that take screenshots of the same page at various mobile device sizes, even running visual diffs to check whether your website is rendering correctly in all (for example, `https://github.com/mapbox/pixelmatch`). You might even create a service that selects fragments of several URLs and combines them into a single PDF report.

 Navalia is another new framework with an interesting approach to testing with the headless Chrome API; you can find it at: `https://github.com/joelgriffith/navalia`.

You should now have enough information to start implementing UI tests for your applications. Some hypermodern applications even involve running Chromium on AWS Lambda (refer to `Chapter 9`, *Microservices*), letting you *farm out* your testing work. Both Nightmare and Puppeteer are modern, well-maintained, and document projects that fit very nicely into the Node testing ecosystem.

Now, let's dig a little deeper into how to figure out just what is happening *behind the scenes* when a Node process is running, and how to be more surgical when testing and debugging.

Testing the terrain

Testing Node can also require a more scientific, experimental effort. For example, memory leaks are notoriously difficult bugs to track down. You will need powerful process profiling tools to take samples, test scenarios, and get a grip on just where the problem is coming from. If you are designing a log analysis and summarization tool that must crunch through gigabytes of data, you might want to test out various parsing algorithms and rank their CPU/memory usage. Whether testing the existing processes or being a software engineer, gathering information on resource usage is important. What we will look at in this section is how to take data snapshots of running processes, and how to draw useful information out of them.

Node already provides some process information natively. Basic tracking of how much memory your Node process is using is easy to fetch with `process.memoryUsage()`:

```
{
  rss: 23744512,
  heapTotal: 7708672,
  heapUsed: 5011728,
  external: 12021
}
```

You can build scripts to watch these numbers and, perhaps, emit warnings when memory allocation exceeds some predetermined threshold. There are many companies that provide such monitoring services, such as **Keymetrics** (`https://keymetrics.io`), the makers and maintainers of PM2. There are also modules like **node-report** (`https://github.com/nodejs/node-report`), which provide a great way to generate system reports whenever your process is terminated via process crash, system signal, or other reason. The great module **memeye** (`https://github.com/JerryC8080/Memeye`) makes it easy to create browser-based dashboards displaying this kind of system data.

 There are several native sources of information on Node processes. Visit the documentation at: `https://nodejs.org/api/process.html`.

Let's start by learning how to gather more extensive memory usage statistics, profile running processes, gather key data profiles on how V8 is performing, and so on in the next few sections.

Testing processes, memory, and CPU

There are native tools for Node, enabling you to profile running V8 processes. These are snapshots with summaries that capture statistics on how V8 treated the process when compiling, and the sorts of actions and decisions it made while it was selectively optimizing the *hot* code as it ran. This is a powerful debugging technique when trying to track down the reasons why, for example, a function is running slowly.

Any node process can have a a V8 log generated simply by passing the `--prof` (for profile) flag. Let's use an example to see how V8 process profiling works. Reading a large log file is a sufficiently non-trivial and common task that Node developers will come across. Let's create a log reader and check its performance.

Profiling processes

In your code bundle, there will be a `logreader.js` file under the `/profiling` directory for this chapter. This simply reads the `dummy.log` file also found in the code bundle. It's a good example of how to use a `stream.Transform` to process large files:

```
const fs = require('fs');
const stream = require('stream');
let lineReader = new stream.Transform({
    objectMode: true
});

lineReader._transform = function $transform(chunk, encoding, done) {
    let data = chunk.toString();
    if(this._lastLine) {
        data = this._lastLine + data;
    }
    let lines = data.split('\n');
    this._lastLine = lines.pop();
    lines.forEach(line => this.push(line));
    done();
};

lineReader._flush = function $flush(done) {
    if(this._lastLine) {
        this.push(this._lastLine);
    }
    this._lastLine = null;
    done();
};
```

```
lineReader.on('readable', function $reader() {
   let line;
   while(line = this.read()) {
      console.log(line);
   }
});

fs.createReadStream('./dummy.log').pipe(lineReader);
```

The important thing to note is that the main functions have been named, prefixed with $. This is a good practice generally—you should always name your functions, and the reason is specifically relevant to debugging. We want those names to show up in the reports we're about to generate.

To generate a v8 log, run this script using the --prof argument:

node --prof logreader.js

You should now see a V8 log file in the current working directory, named something like isolate-0x103000000-v8.log. Go ahead and take a look at it—the log is somewhat intimidating, but if you do a search for, say, $reader, you'll find instances of how V8 is recording its structuring of the call stack and compilation work. Regardless, this is clearly not meant for humans to read.

You can create a much more useful summary of this profile by running the following command against that log:

node --prof-process isolate-0x103000000-v8.log > profile

After a couple of seconds, the process will finish, and a new file, **profile**, will exist in the directory. Go ahead and open that. There is a lot of information, and doing a deep dive into what it all means is well beyond the scope of this chapter. Nevertheless, you should see that the summary neatly summarizes key V8 activity, measured with ticks (remember our discussion about the event loop in Chapter 2, *Understanding Asynchronous Event-Driven Programming*?). For example, consider this line:

```
8    50.0%    LazyCompile: *$reader /../profiling/logreader.js:26:43
```

Here, we can see that $reader consumed 8 ticks, was lazy compiled, and was optimized (*). If it had not been optimized, it would have been marked with a tilde(~). If you see that an unoptimized file was consuming a large number of ticks, you'll probably take a look and try to rewrite it in an optimal way. This can be a powerful way to "solve" slower parts of your application stack.

Dumping the heap

As we learned earlier, a heap is essentially a large allocation of memory, and in this specific case, it is the memory allocated to the V8 process. By examining where and how memory is being used, you can track down things such as memory leaks, or simply find out where the most memory is being used and make adjustments to your code, if needed.

The de-facto module for taking heap snapshots is `heapdump` (`https://github.com/bnoordhuis/node-heapdump`) by *Ben Noordhuis*, a core Node developer since the very beginning of the project.

Go ahead and install that module and create a new file with the following code:

```
// heapdumper.js
const path = require('path');
const heapdump = require('heapdump');

heapdump.writeSnapshot(path.join(__dirname, `${Date.now()}.heapsnapshot`));
```

Run that file. You will that a file is generated with a name like `1512180093208.heapsnapshot`. It's not a human-readable file, but it contains everything you need to reconstruct a view on heap usage. You just need the right visualization software. Thankfully, you can use the Chrome web browser to do just that.

Open up Chrome DevTools. Go to the **Memory** tab. You will see an option there to **Load** a heap snapshot:

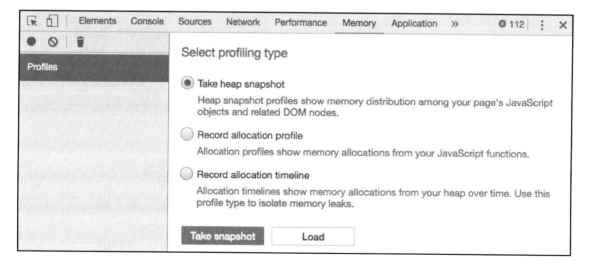

Load the file that you just created (note that it **must** have the `.heapsnapshot` extension).
Once loaded, click on the heap icon, and you'll see something like the following:

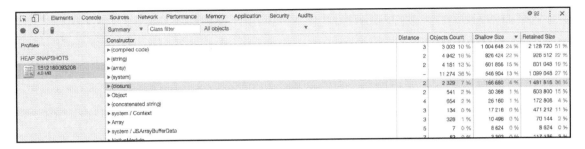

Click on **Summary** to activate the dropdown, and select **Statistics**. You'll now see
something like the following graph:

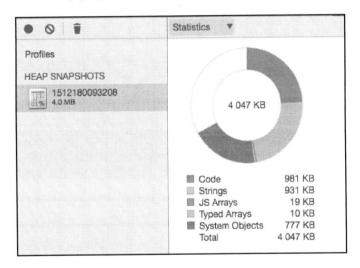

Becoming familiar with how to read heap dumps is a skill useful to any Node developer.
For a good intro on how to understand memory allocation, try: `https://developer.`
`chrome.com/devtools/docs/memory-analysis-101`. The source code to run Chrome
DevTools UI is open and free, `https://github.com/ChromeDevTools/devtools-frontend`,
as is the protocol itself. Think about how you might take periodic heap dumps of running
processes and test system health using DevTools, either as we've demonstrated or via a
custom build.

While we use Chrome in our demonstrations, other tools can *hook into* this protocol. Check out `https://nodejs.org/en/docs/inspector/` and `https://github.com/ChromeDevTools/awesome-chrome-devtools#chrome-devtools-protocol`.

The Chrome DevTools have even more functionalities useful to developers. Let's take a look at those now.

Connecting Node to Chrome DevTools

The Chrome Debugging Protocol was recently *integrated* with the Node core (`https://github.com/nodejs/node/pull/6792`), which means that you can now debug a running Node process using Chrome DevTools (and other tools). This includes being able to not only watch memory allocation but also to gather active feedback on CPU usage, along with directly debugging your live code—adding break points and inspecting current variable values, for instance. This is an essential debugging and testing tool for the professional Node developer. Let's dig into it.

For demonstration purposes, we'll create a quick server that performs some significant work:

```
// server.js
const Express = require('express');
let app = Express();

function $alloc() {
    Buffer.alloc(1e6, 'Z');
}

app.get('/', function $serverHandler(req, res) => {

    let d = 100;
    while(d--){ $alloc() }

    res.status(200).send(`I'm done`);
})

app.listen(8080);
```

Note the `$alloc` and `$serverHandler` named functions; these function names will be used to trace our process. Now, we'll start that server up, but with a special `--inspect` flag indicating to Node that we plan to inspect (debug) the process:

```
node --inspect server.js
```

You should see something like the following displayed:

```
Debugger listening on ws://127.0.0.1:9229/bc4d2b60-0d01-4a66-
ad49-2e990fa42f4e
For help see https://nodejs.org/en/docs/inspector
```

Looks like the debugger is active. To view it, open up a Chrome browser and enter the following:

```
chrome://inspect
```

You should see the process you've started listed. You can inspect that process or simply load up an active debugging screen by clicking on **Open dedicated DevTools for Node**, which will, from now on, attach to any Node process you start with `--inspect`.

CPU profiling

Open up another browser window and navigate to our test server at `localhost:8080`. You should see **I'm done** displayed (if not, go back and start up `server.js`, as instructed earlier). Keep that open; you'll be reloading this page shortly.

Click on **Memory** in the debugger UI, and you'll see the interface from earlier. This is the *standalone* version of the debugger we saw earlier.

Now, click on **Profiler**, which is the interface to debug CPU behavior (execution time in particular), and click on **Start**. Go back to your browser and reload the **I'm done** page a few times. Return to the debugger and click on **Stop**. You should see something like this:

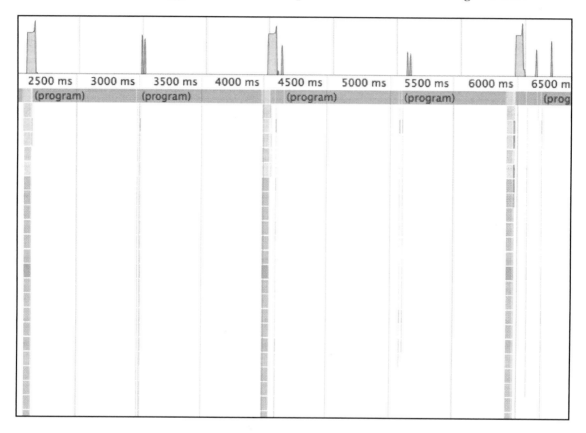

Note the three larger *blocks*, which were generated by three runs of our server handler. Using your mouse, select one of these blocks and zoom in:

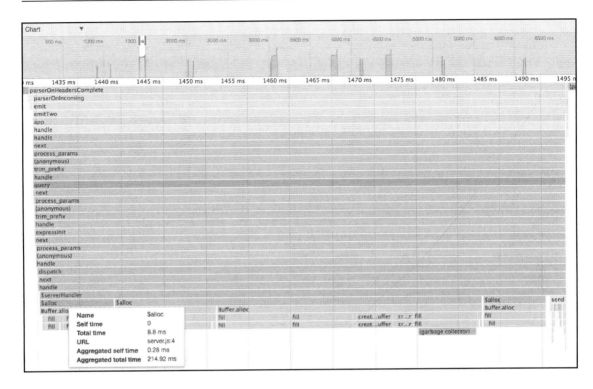

Here, we see a full breakdown of V8 activity engaged when handling our request. Remember $alloc? By mousing over its timeline, you can inspect the total CPU time it consumed. If we zoom in to the **send** section in the bottom-right, we can also see that it took our server **1.9 ms** to execute an HTTP response:

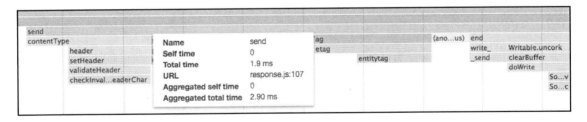

Play around with this interface. In addition to helping you find and debug the slower parts of your application, when developing tests, you can use this tool to create a mental map of what the expected behavior of a *normal* run is, and design health tests. For example, one of your tests might call a specific route handler and pass or fail based on some predetermined maximum execution time threshold. If these tests are *always on*, probing your live application periodically, they might even trigger automatic throttling behaviors, log entries, or the sending of urgent emails to your engineering team.

Live debugging

Perhaps, the most powerful feature of this interface is its ability to directly debug running code, and to test the state of live applications. Click on the **Sources** tab in the debugger. This is an interface to the actual *scripts* comprising the Node process. You should see the *mounted* version of our `server.js` file:

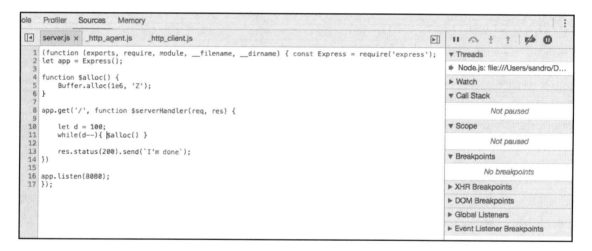

Fun fact: here, you can see how Node actually wraps your modules so that the global `exports`, `require`, `module`, `__filename`, and `__dirname` variables are available to you.

Let's set a break point on line 11. Just click on the number; you should see this:

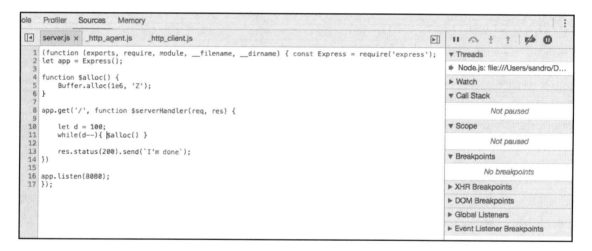

Recall our discussion about the Node debugger earlier? The same principles will apply here; we'll be able to use this interface to step through executing code, stopping execution periodically, and examining application state.

To demonstrate, let's cause this code to be executed in our server. Go back to your browser and reload `localhost:8080`, calling the route and ultimately hitting the break point you just set. The debugger interface should pop up, and will look something like this:

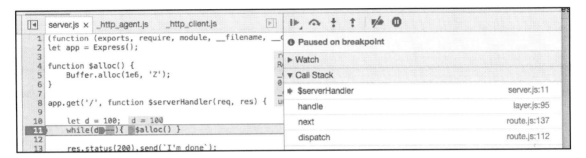

In addition to clearly indicating where we are (the line number, within the `$serverHandler` function), the interface is also usefully showing us the value of d in the current iteration of a `while` loop. Recall our Node debugger discussion earlier? The same principles apply here. If you hover over the debugging control icons on the right, you'll see that the second one is the *step over* function. We're in a loop; let's step to the next iteration. Go ahead and hit step over the loop several times. Did you note how the value of d is being updated while you step through this loop?

If you explore the interface on the right, you can dig very far into the current state of the program, with a full breakdown of all scope variables, globals being referenced, and so forth. By using the *step into* control, you can watch the progress of every single request through the execution stack, walking through the Node runtime as it executes. You will benefit from this exercise and understand your code (and how Node works) much more clearly. This will help you become a better test writer.

Usefully, there is a chrome plugin that makes interacting with inspected Node processes as simple as point and click; it's available at: `https://chrome.google.com/webstore/detail/nodejs-v8-inspector-manag/gnhhdgbaldcilmgcpfddgdbkhjohddkj`.

Mathias Buus has created an interesting tool, providing very useful debugging information for the rare but hair-pulling case of processes not ending when they are supposed to, and you can find it at: `https://github.com/mafintosh/why-is-node-running`.

Matteo Collina's excellent `loopbench` (`https://github.com/mcollina/loopbench`) and its packaged version for Node servers (`https://github.com/davidmarkclements/overload-protection`) can be used to not only provide testing and debugging information, but for the development of smart, self-regulating servers than will automatically shed (or redirect) loads when running too hot, a nice feature in a distributed application architecture of independent, networked nodes.

Summary

The Node community has embraced testing from the beginning, and many testing frameworks and native tools are made available to developers. In this chapter, we examined why testing is so important to modern software development as well as something about functional, unit, and integration testing, what they are, and how they can be used. With the vm module, we learned how to create special contexts for testing JavaScript programs, and picking up some techniques for sandboxing untrusted code along the way.

In addition, we learned how to work with the extensive set of Node testing and error-handling tools, from more expressive console logging to Mocha and mocking with Sinon, onto one line tracing and debugging heaps and live code. Finally, we learned about two different headless browser testing libraries, learning two ways in which such testing might be done in each, and how these virtual browsers can be integrated with other testing environments.

Now that you can test your code, go out and experiment with the power of Node.

A
Organizing Your Work into Modules

"Complexity must be grown from simple systems that already work."

– Kevin Kelly, "Out of Control"

Node's straightforward module management system encourages the development of code bases that grow and remain maintainable. The Node developer is blessed with a rich ecosystem of clearly defined packages with consistent interfaces that are easy to combine, delivered via npm. When developing solutions, the Node developer will find many pieces of the functionality they need ready-made, and can rapidly compose those open source modules into larger, but still consistent and predictable, systems. Node's simple and scalable module architecture has let the Node ecosystem grow rapidly.

In this chapter, we will cover the details of how Node understands modules and module paths, how modules are defined, how to use modules in the npm package repository, and how to create and share new npm modules. By following some simple rules, you will find it easy to shape the structure of your application, and help others work with what you've created.

Module and *package* will be used interchangeably to describe the file or collection of files compiled and returned by `require()`.

How to load and use modules

Before we begin, take a look at these three commands:

```
$ node --version
v8.1.2

$ npm --version
5.5.1

$ npm install npm@latest -g
```

To install Node, you likely navigated your favorite web browser to `https://nodejs.org/ en/`, downloaded the appropriate installer app for your operating system, and clicked through some **OK** buttons. When you did this, you also got npm. However, npm updates quite frequently, so even if you've updated Node recently, you may not have the latest version of npm.

Additionally, downloading and installing a new Node installer will update Node, but doesn't always update npm, so use `npm install npm@latest -g` to ensure that you've got the most recent version.

The Node designers believe that most modules should be developed in userland—by developers, for developers. As such, an effort is made to limit the growth of the standard library. At the time of writing this, Node's standard module library contains the following short list of modules:

Network and I/O	Strings and Buffers	Utilities
TTY UDP/Datagram HTTP HTTPS Net DNS TLS/SSL Readline FileSystem	Path Buffer Url StringDecoder QueryString	Utilities VM Readline Domain Console Assert
Encryption and Compression	**Environment**	**Events and Streams**
ZLIB Crypto PunyCode	Process OS Modules	Child Processes Cluster Events Stream

Modules are loaded via the global `require` statement, which accepts the module name or path as a single argument. As a Node developer, you are encouraged to augment the module ecosystem by creating new modules or new combinations of modules of your own, and share them with the world.

The module system itself is implemented in the require (`module`) module.

The module object

A Node module is simply a Javascript file. Reference functions (and anything else) that might be useful to outside code to exports, as follows:

```
// library1.js
function function1a() {
  return "hello from 1a";
}
exports.function1a = function1a;
```

We now have a module that can be required by another file. Back in our main app, let's use it:

```
// app.js
const library1 = require('./library1'); // Require it
const function1a = library1.function1a; // Unpack it
let s = function1a(); // Use it
console.log(s);
```

Note how it was not necessary to use the `.js` suffix. We'll discuss how Node resolves paths shortly.

Let's make our library a little bigger, growing it to three functions, as shown:

```
// library1.js
exports.function1a = () => "hello from 1a";
exports.function1b = () => "hello from 1b";
exports.function1c = () => "hello from 1c";

// app.js
const {function1a, function1b, function1c} = require('./library1'); //
Require and unpack
console.log(function1a());
console.log(function1b());
console.log(function1c());
```

Destructuring assignment, brought to JavaScript with ES6, is a great way to assign many functions exported by a required module to their local variables in a single line.

Modules, exports, and module.exports

As you inspect the code of Node modules you might see that some modules export their functionality using `module.exports`, while others simply use `exports`:

```
module.exports.foo = 'bar';
// vs...
exports.foo = 'bar';
```

Is there a difference? The short answer is no. You can for the most assign properties to either when building your code. Both methods given above will "do" the same thing -- the property 'foo' of the exported module will resolve to 'bar' in both cases.

The longer answer is that there is a subtle difference between them, having to do with how JavaScript references work. Consider how modules are wrapped in the first place:

```
// https://github.com/nodejs/node/blob/master/lib/module.js#L92
Module.wrap = function(script) {
    return Module.wrapper[0] + script + Module.wrapper[1];
};

Module.wrapper = [
    '(function (exports, require, module, __filename, __dirname) { ',
    '\n});'
];
```

When you create a module it is wrapped using the above code. That is how the "globals" of **__dirname** and of course **exports** are available to the **script** (content) being imported -- they are injected into your execution scope:

```
// https://github.com/nodejs/node/blob/master/lib/module.js#L625
var wrapper = Module.wrap(content);

var compiledWrapper = vm.runInThisContext(wrapper, {
    filename: filename,
    lineOffset: 0,
    displayErrors: true
});

...
result = compiledWrapper.call(this.exports, this.exports, require, this,
filename, dirname);
```

Recall the discussion on vm contexts in Chapter 10, *Testing Your Application*? The Module constructor itself demonstrates how exports is simply an empty object literal on the Module object:

```
// https://github.com/nodejs/node/blob/master/lib/module.js#L70
function Module(id, parent) {
    this.id = id;
    this.exports = {};
    this.parent = parent;
    updateChildren(parent, this, false);
    this.filename = null;
    this.loaded = false;
    this.children = [];
}
```

Wrapping up, we see that in the final compilation whatever module.exports contains is returned to require:

```
// https://github.com/nodejs/node/blob/master/lib/module.js#L500
var module = new Module(filename, parent);
...
Module._cache[filename] = module;
...
return module.exports;
```

To summarize and simplify, when you are creating a module you are essentially defining its exports in this context:

```
var module = { exports: {} };
var exports = module.exports;
// ...your code, which can apply to either
```

So exports is just a reference to module.exports, which is why setting **foo** on the exports object is the same as setting **foo** on module.exports. However, *if you set* exports *to something else* module.exports will **not** reflect that change:

```
function MyClass() {
    this.foo = 'bar';
}

// require('thismodule').foo will be 'bar'
module.exports = new MyClass();

// require('thismodule').foo will be undefined
exports = new MyClass();
```

As we saw above it is only `module.exports` that is returned; `exports` is never returned. If `exports` overwrites its own reference to `module.exports` that value never escapes the compilation context. To be safe, just use `module.exports`.

Node's core modules are also defined using the standard `module.exports` pattern. You can see an example of this by browsing the source code defining console: `https://github.com/nodejs/node/blob/master/lib/console.js`.

Modules and caching

Modules, once loaded, are cached. Modules are cached based on their resolved filename, resolved relative to the calling module. Subsequent calls to require (`./myModule`) will return the same (*cached*) object.

To demonstrate this, imagine that we've got three (poorly designed, in this case) modules, each of which require the other two:

```
// library1.js
console.log("library 1 -\\");
const {function2a, function2b, function2c} = require('./library2');
const {function3a, function3b, function3c} = require('./library3');
exports.function1a = () => "hello from 1a";
exports.function1b = () => "hello from 1b";
exports.function1c = () => "hello from 1c";
console.log("library 1 -/");

// library2.js
console.log("library 2 --\\");
const {function1a, function1b, function1c} = require('./library1');
const {function3a, function3b, function3c} = require('./library3');
exports.function2a = () => "hello from 2a";
exports.function2b = () => "hello from 2b";
exports.function2c = () => "hello from 2c";
console.log("library 2 --/");

// library3.js
console.log("library 3 ---\\");
const {function1a, function1b, function1c} = require('./library1');
const {function2a, function2b, function2c} = require('./library2');
exports.function3a = () => "hello from 3a";
exports.function3b = () => "hello from 3b";
exports.function3c = () => "hello from 3c";
console.log("library 3 ---/");
```

Without caching, requiring any of them will cause infinite loops. However, because Node doesn't rerun an already loaded (or currently being loaded) module, it all works:

```
$ node library1.js
library 1 -\
library 2 --\
library 3 ---\
library 3 ---/
library 2 --/
library 1 -/

$ node library2.js
library 2 --\
library 1 -\
library 3 ---\
library 3 ---/
library 1 -/
library 2 --/

$ node library3.js
library 3 ---\
library 1 -\
library 2 --\
library 2 --/
library 1 -/
library 3 ---/
```

Note, however, that accessing the same module via a different relative path (such as `../../myModule`) will return a different object; think of the cache being keyed by relative module paths.

A snapshot of the current cache can be fetched via `require('module')._cache`. Let's take a look:

```
// app.js
const u = require('util');
const m = require('module');
console.log(u.inspect(m._cache));
const library1 = require('./library1');
console.log("and again, after bringing in library1:")
console.log(u.inspect(m._cache));

{
  'C:\code\example\app.js': Module {
    id: '.',
    exports: {},
    parent: null,
```

```
    filename: 'C:\\code\\example\\app.js',
    loaded: false,
    children: [],
    paths:
    [ 'C:\\code\\example\\node_modules',
      'C:\\code\\node_modules',
      'C:\\node_modules' ]
  }
}
```

and again, after bringing in library1:

```
{
  'C:\code\example\app.js': Module {
    id: '.',
    exports: {},
    parent: null,
    filename: 'C:\\code\\example\\app.js',
    loaded: false,
    children: [ [Object] ],
    paths: [
      'C:\\code\\example\\node_modules',
      'C:\\code\\node_modules',
      'C:\\node_modules'
    ]
  },
  'C:\code\example\library1.js': Module {
    id: 'C:\\code\\example\\library1.js',
    exports: {
      function1a: [Function],
      function1b: [Function],
      function1c: [Function]
    },
    parent: Module {
      id: '.',
      exports: {},
      parent: null,
      filename: 'C:\\code\\example\\app.js',
      loaded: false,
      children: [Array],
      paths: [Array]
    },
    filename: 'C:\\code\\example\\library1.js',
    loaded: true,
    children: [],
    paths: [
      'C:\\code\\example\\node_modules',
      'C:\\code\\node_modules',
```

```
    'C:\\node_modules'
  ]
 }
}
```

The module object itself contains several useful readable properties:

- `module.filename`: The name of the file defining this module. You can see these paths in the preceding code block.
- `module.loaded`: Whether the module is in the process of loading. Boolean true if loaded. In the preceding code, library1 has finished loading (true), while app is still loading (false).
- `module.parent`: The module that required this one, if any. You can see how library1 knows that app required it.
- `module.children`: The modules required by this one, if any.

 You can determine whether a module is being executed directly via `node module.js` or via `require('./module.js')` by checking `require.main === module`, which will return true in the former case.

How Node handles module paths

As modular application composition is The Node Way, you will often see (and use) the require statement. You will have noticed that the argument passed to require can take many forms, such as the name of a core module or a file path.

The following pseudocode, taken from the Node documentation, is an ordered description of the steps taken when resolving module paths:

```
// require(X) from module at path Y
REQUIRE(X)
   1. If X is a core module,
      a. return the core module
      b. STOP
   2. If X begins with '/'
      a. set Y to be the filesystem root
   3. If X begins with './' or '/' or '../'
      a. LOAD_AS_FILE(Y + X)
      b. LOAD_AS_DIRECTORY(Y + X)
   4. LOAD_NODE_MODULES(X, dirname(Y))
   5. THROW "not found"
```

```
LOAD_AS_FILE(X)
  1. If X is a file, load X as JavaScript text. STOP
  2. If X.js is a file, load X.js as JavaScript text. STOP
  3. If X.json is a file, parse X.json to a JavaScript Object. STOP
  4. If X.node is a file, load X.node as binary addon. STOP
LOAD_INDEX(X)
  1. If X/index.js is a file, load X/index.js as JavaScript text. STOP
  2. If X/index.json is a file, parse X/index.json to a JavaScript Object.
STOP
  3. If X/index.node is a file, load X/index.node as a binary addon. STOP
LOAD_AS_DIRECTORY(X)
  1. If X/package.json is a file,
     a. Parse X/package.json, and look for "main" field.
     b. let M = X + ("main" field)
     c. LOAD_AS_FILE(M)
     d. LOAD_INDEX(M)
  2. LOAD_INDEX(X)
LOAD_NODE_MODULES(X, START)
  1. let DIRS=NODE_MODULES_PATHS(START)
  2. for each DIR in DIRS:
     a. LOAD_AS_FILE(DIR/X)
     b. LOAD_AS_DIRECTORY(DIR/X)
NODE_MODULES_PATHS(START)
  1. let PARTS = path split(START)
  2. let I = count of PARTS - 1
  3. let DIRS = []
  4. while I >= 0,
     a. if PARTS[I] = "node_modules" CONTINUE
     b. DIR = path join(PARTS[0 .. I] + "node_modules")
     c. DIRS = DIRS + DIR
     d. let I = I - 1
  5. return DIRS
```

File paths may be absolute or relative. Note that local relative paths will not be implicitly resolved and must be stated. For example, if you would like to require the `myModule.js` file from the current directory, it is necessary to at least prepend `./` to the filename; – `require('myModule.js')` will not work. Node will assume that you are referring to either a core module or a module found in the `./node_modules` folder. If neither exists, a `MODULE_NOT_FOUND` error will be thrown.

As seen in the preceding pseudocode, this `node_modules` lookup ascends a directory tree beginning from the resolved path of the calling module or file. For example, if the file at `/user/home/sandro/project.js` called `require('library.js')`, Node would seek in this order:

```
/user/home/sandro/node_modules/library.js
/user/home/node_modules/library.js
/user/node_modules/library.js
/node_modules/library.js
```

Organizing your files and/or modules into directories is always a good idea. Usefully, Node allows modules to be referenced through their containing folder in two ways. Given a directory, Node will first try to find a `package.json` file in that directory, alternatively seeking for an `index.js` file. We will discuss the use of `package.json` files in the next section. Here, we simply need to point out that if require is passed the `./myModule` directory, it will look for `./myModule/index.js`.

> If you've set the `NODE_PATH` environment variable, then Node will use that path information to do further searches if a requested module is not found via normal channels. For historical reasons, `$HOME/.node_modules`, `$HOME/.node_libraries`, and `$PREFIX/lib/node` will also be searched. `$HOME` represents a user's home directory, and `$PREFIX` will normally be the location Node was installed to.

Creating a package file

As mentioned when discussing how Node does path lookups, modules may be contained within a folder. If you are developing a program that will work well as a module for someone else to use, you should organize that module within its own folder, and create a `package.json` file within that folder.

As we've seen throughout the examples in this book, a `package.json` file describes a module, usefully documenting the module's name, version number, dependencies, and so forth. It must exist if you would like to publish your package via npm. In this section, we will outline only a few key properties of this file, and we will also provide more detail on some of the obscure ones.

Try $ `npm help json` to fetch detailed documentation for all available package.json fields, or visit: `https://docs.npmjs.com/files/package.json`.

A `package.json` file must conform to the JSON specification. Properties and values must be double-quoted, for example.

Easy init

You can create a package file by hand, or use the handy $ `npm init` command-line tool, which will ask some questions and generate a `package.json` file for you. Let's run through some of these:

- **name**: (Required) This string is what will be passed to `require()` in order to load your module. Make it short and descriptive, using only alphanumeric characters; this name will be used in URLs, command-line arguments, and folder names. Try to avoid using `js` or `node` in the name.
- **version**: (Required) npm uses semantic versioning, where these are all valid:
  - >=1.0.2 <2.1.2
  - 2.1.x
  - ~1.2

For more information on version numbers, visit: `https://docs.npmjs.com/misc/semver`.

- **description**: When people search `npmjs.org` for packages, this is what they will read. Make it short and descriptive.
- **entry point** (main): This is the file that should set `module.exports`; it defines where the module object definition resides.
- **keywords**: A comma-separated list of keywords that will help others find your module in the registry.
- **license**: Node is an open community that likes permissive licenses. *MIT* and *BSD* are good ones here.

You might also want to set the `private` field to `true` while you are developing your module. This ensures that npm will refuse to publish it, avoiding accidental releases of not-yet-good or time-sensitive code.

Adding scripts to package.json

Another advantage is that npm can also be used as a build tool. The `scripts` field in your package file allows you to set various build directives executed at some point following certain npm commands. For example, you might want to minify Javascript, or execute some other processes that build dependencies that your module will need whenever `npm install` is executed. The available directives are as listed:

- `prepublish, publish, postpublish`: Run by the `npm publish` command as well as on local `npm install` without any arguments.
- `prepublishOnly`: Run before published only on the `npm publish` command.
- `prepare`: Run before the package is published and on `npm install` without any arguments. Run after `prepublish`, but before `prepublishOnly`.
- `prepack`: Run before a tarball is packed via `npm pack` or `npm publish`, and when installing git dependencies.
- `postpack`: Run after a tarball has been generated and moved to its final location.
- `preinstall, install, postinstall`: Run by the `npm install` command.
- `preuninstall, uninstall, postuninstall`: Run by the `npm uninstall` command.
- `preversion, version, postversion`: Run by the `npm version` command.
- `preshrinkwrap, shrinkwrap, postshrinkwrap`: Run by the `npm shrinkwrap` command.
- `pretest, test, posttest`: Run by the `npm test` command.
- `prestop, stop, poststop`: Run by the `npm stop` command.
- `prestart, start, poststart`: Run by the `npm start` command.
- `prerestart, restart, postrestart`: Run by the `npm restart` command. Note that `npm restart` will run the `stop` and `start` scripts if no `restart` script is provided.

It should be clear that pre- commands will run before, and post- commands will run after their primary command (such as `publish`) is executed.

npm as a build system using custom scripts

You aren't limited to using only this predefined bag of default script commands. Extending the **scripts** collection in a package file with, for example, build instructions is a very common practice. Consider the following script definition:

```
"dev": "NODE_ENV=development node --inspect --expose-gc index.js"
```

When this command is run via `npm run dev` we start a hypothetical server in debug mode (**--inspect**), and expose the garbage collector so that we can track its impact on our application's performance.

This also implies that npm scripts can in many cases completely replace more complex build systems like **gulp** or **webpack**. For example you might want to use **Browserify** to bundle your application for deployment, and that build step is easy to describe in a script:

```
"scripts" : {
  "build:browserify" : "browserify -t [babelify --presets [react]]
src/js/index.js -o build/app.js"
}
```

After executing `npm run build:browserify` Browserify will process the file at **src/js/index.js**, running it through a transformer (**-t**) that can compile React code (**babelify**) and output (**-o**) the result to **build/app.js**.

Additionally, npm scripts are running on the host system in the context of npm, so you are able to execute system commands and address locally installed modules. Another build step you might implement is JavaScript minification, moving compiled files into a target folder:

```
"build:minify": "mkdir -p dist/js uglify src/js/**/*.js >
dist/js/script.min.js"
```

Here we use an OS command **mkdir** to create the target folder for compiled files, perform minification against all JavaScript files in a folder with the (locally installed) **uglify** module, and redirect the resulting minified script bundle to a single build file.

Now we can add a general build command to our scripts collection, and simply use `npm run build` whenever we need to deploy a new build:

```
"build": "npm run build:minify && npm run build:browserify"
```

Any number of steps can be chained in this manner. You might add tests, run a file watcher, and so forth.

For your next project consider using npm as a build system rather than complicating your stack with large and abstract systems that can be very hard to debug when they go wrong. The company **Mapbox**, for instance, uses npm scripts to manage a complex build/test pipeline: `https://github.com/mapbox/mapbox-gl-js/blob/master/package.json`.

Registering package dependencies

It is likely that a given module will itself depend on other modules. These dependencies are declared within a `package.json` file using four related properties:

- `dependencies`: The core dependencies of your module should reside here.
- `devDependencies`: You may depend on some modules, while developing your module, that are not necessary to those who will use it. Typically, test suites are included here. This will save some space for those using your module.
- `bundledDependencies`: Node is changing rapidly, as are npm packages. You may want to *lock* a certain bundle of dependencies into a single bundled file and have those published with your package, so that they will not change via the normal `npm update` process.
- `optionalDependencies`: Contains modules that are optional. If these modules cannot be found or installed, the build process will not stop (as it will with other dependency load failures). You can then check for this module's existence in your application code.

Dependencies are normally defined with a npm package name, followed by versioning information:

```
"dependencies" : {
  "express" : "3.3.5"
}
```

However, they can also point to a tarball:

```
"foo" : "http://foo.com/foo.tar.gz"
```

You can point to a GitHub repository:

```
"herder": "git://github.com/sandro-pasquali/herder.git#master"
```

They can even point to the shortcut:

```
"herder": "sandro-pasquali/herder"
```

These GitHub paths are also available to `npm install`, for example, `npm install sandro-pasquali/herder`.

Additionally, in cases where only those with proper authentication are able to install a module, the following format can be used to source secure repositories:

```
"dependencies": {
  "a-private-repo":
    "git+ssh://git@github.com:user/repo.git#master"
}
```

By properly organizing your dependencies by type, and intelligently sourcing those dependencies, build requirements should be easy to accommodate using Node's package system.

Publishing and managing NPM packages

When you install Node, npm is installed natively, and it functions as the primary package manager for the Node community. Let's learn how to set up an account on the npm repository, publish (and unpublish) modules, and work with GitHub as an alternative source target.

In order to publish to npm, you will need to create a user; `npm adduser` will trigger a series of prompts requesting your name, email, and password. You may then use this command on multiple machines to authorize the same user account.

 To reset your npm password, visit: `https://npmjs.org/forgot`.

Once you have authenticated with npm, you will be able to publish your packages using the `npm publish` command. The easiest path is to run this command from within your package folder. You may also target another folder for publishing (remembering that a `package.json` file must exist in that folder).

You may also publish a gzipped tar archive containing a properly configured package folder.

Note that if the `version` field of the current `package.json` file is lower or equal to that of the existing, published package, npm will complain and refuse to publish. You can override this using the `--force` argument with `publish`, but you probably want to update the version and republish.

To remove a package, use `npm unpublish <name>[@<version>]`. Note that once a package is published, other developers may come to depend on it. For this reason, you are strongly discouraged from removing packages that others are using. If you want to discourage the use of a version, use npm deprecate `<name>[@<version>] <message>`.

To further assist collaboration, npm allows multiple owners to be set for a package:

- `npm owner ls <package name>`: Lists the users with access to a module
- `npm owner add <user> <package name>`: The added owner will have full access, including the ability to modify the package and add other owners
- `npm owner rm <user> <package name>`: Removes an owner and immediately revokes all privileges

All owners have equal privileges—special access controls are unavailable, such as being able to give write but not delete access.

Global installs and binaries

Some Node modules are useful as command-line programs. Rather than requiring something like `$ node module.js` to run a program, we might want to simply type `$ module` on the console and have the program execute. In other words, we might want to treat a module as an executable file installed on the system PATH and therefore is accessible from anywhere. There are two ways to achieve this using npm.

The first and simplest way is to install a package using the `-g` (`global`) argument is as follows:

```
$ npm install -g module
```

If a package is intended as a command-line application that should be installed globally, it is a good idea to set the `preferGlobal` property of your `package.json` file to `true`. The module will still install locally, but users will be warned about its global intentions.

Another way to ensure global access is by setting a package's `bin` property:

```
"name": "aModule",
  "bin" : {
    "aModule" : "./path/to/program"
}
```

When this module is installed, `aModule` will be understood as a global CLI command. Any number of such programs may be mapped to `bin`. As a shortcut, a single program can be mapped, as shown:

```
"name": "aModule",
  "bin" : "./path/to/program"
```

In this case, the name of the package itself (`aModule`) will be understood as the active command.

Other repositories

Node modules are often stored in version control systems, allowing several developers to manage package code. For this reason, the `repository` field of `package.json` can be used to point developers to such a repository, should collaboration be desired. Consider the following example:

```
"repository" : {
  "type" : "git",
  "url" : "http://github.com/sandro-pasquali/herder.git"
}
"repository" : {
  "type" : "svn",
  "url" : "http://v8.googlecode.com/svn/trunk/"
}
```

Similarly, you might want to point users to where bug reports should be filed using the bugs field:

```
"bugs": {
  "url": "https://github.com/sandro-pasquali/herder/issues"
}
```

Lockfiles

Ultimately, npm install is a command that takes a `package.json` and builds a `node_modules` folder from it. However, does it always product the same one? The answer is sometimes, and we will cover the details in a bit.

If you've made a new project, or recently updated npm to version 5, you may have noticed a new file alongside the familiar `package.json`—`package-lock.json`.
Inside, the contents looks like this:

```
{
  "name": "app1",
  "version": "1.0.0",
  "lockfileVersion": 1,
  "dependencies": {
    "align-text": {
      "version": "0.1.4",
      "resolved":
"https://registry.npmjs.org/align-text/-/align-text-0.1.4.tgz",
      "integrity": "sha1-DNkKVhCT810KmSVsIrcGlDP60Rc=",
      "dev": true
    },
    "babel-core": {
      "version": "6.25.0",
      "resolved":
"https://registry.npmjs.org/babel-core/-/babel-core-6.25.0.tgz",
      "integrity": "sha1-fdQrBGPHQunVKW3rPsZ6kyLa1yk=",
      "dev": true,
      "dependencies": {
        "source-map": {
          "version": "0.5.6",
          "resolved":
"https://registry.npmjs.org/source-map/-/source-map-0.5.6.tgz",
          "integrity": "sha1-dc449SvwczxafwwRjYEzSiu19BI=",
          "dev": true
        }
      }
    }
  }
}
```

Parts will immediately be familiar. Here are the npm packages your project depends upon. Dependencies of dependencies are nested appropriately: `align-text` doesn't require anything, while `babel-core` needs `source-map`.

The real usefulness beyond `package.json` is delivered by the resolved and integrity fields. Here, you can see the exact file the npm downloaded and unzipped to create the corresponding folder within `npm_modules`, and, even more importantly, the cryptographically-secure hash digest of that file.

With `package-lock.json`, you can now get an exact and `reproducable node_modules` folder. Committed into source control, you can see when a dependant module version has changed right in a diff during a code review. Also, with hashes everywhere, you can be more certain that the code your application depends upon hasn't been tampered with.

`package-lock.json` is here; it's long, it's filled with hash values, but actually, you can ignore it. The file's appearance with npm 5 didn't change the behavior of commands such as npm install and npm update that you're used to. To explain how, and why, it's helpful to expose two common questions (or exclamations) that developers commonly have when encountering the file:

1. So this means my `node_modules` folder will be made from these hashes, right?
2. Why does my `package-lock.json` file keep changing?

The answers are (1) no, and (2) that's why.

When npm finds a newer version of a package, it'll download it and update your `node_modules` folder, just as earlier. With npm 5, it'll also update `package-lock.json`, with the new version number and the new hash.

Also, most of the time, this is what you want it to do. If there's a newer version of a package the project you're developing depends upon, you probably want npm install to give you the most recent one.

However, what if you want npm to not do this? What if you want it to get the modules with exactly these versions and exactly these hashes? The way to do this lies not in `package-lock.json`, but back in `package.json`, and deals with semantic version numbers. Take a look at these three:

- `1.2.3`
- `~1.2.3`
- `^1.2.3`

`1.2.3` means exactly that version, nothing earlier, and nothing later. `~1.2.3` matches that version, or anything more recent. The third example with the caret, `^1.2.3`, will bring in that version or something more recent, but stay in version 1. Caret is the default, and likely already written everywhere in your `package.json` files. It makes sense, as a change to the first number indicates a major version which might break compatibility with previous versions, in turn potentially breaking your preceding code.

 Far beyond these three common examples, there's a whole language of comparators, operators, identifiers, tags, and ranges possible with semantic versioning and supported by npm. Curious readers can check it out at: `https://docs.npmjs.com/misc/semver`. However, remember to keep it simple! Your current collaborators, and future self, will thank you.

So, npm is changing your `node_modules` folder, and `package-lock.json`, because you told it to, with `^` in `package.json`. You can remove all the carets to get npm to stick to the exact versions, but for the instances where you want to do that, there's a better way:

```
$ npm shrinkwrap
```

All npm's `shrinkwrap` command actually does is rename `package-lock.json` to `npm-shrinkwrap.json`. The significance comes in how npm uses the files later. When publishing to npm, `package-lock.json` stays behind, because it's likely changing as newer versions of the dependencies of what you're working on come out. On the other hand, `npm-shrinkwrap.json` is meant to get published with your module.

When npm acts on a project with a `npm-shrinkwrap.json` file, the `shrinkwrap` file and its exact versions and hashes, not `package.json` with its version ranges, determines how npm builds the `node_modules` folder. Like the cardboard box from a software store in a mall in the 1990s, you know that what's inside is unchanged from the factory by removing the plastic wrapping.

Creating Your Own C++ Add-ons

B

"If two (people) on the same job agree all the time, then one is useless. If they disagree all the time, then both are useless."

– *Darryl F. Zanuck*

A very common description of Node is this one: *NodeJS allows Javascript to be run on the server*. This is of course true; it is also misleading. The accomplishment of Node was in organizing and linking powerful C++ libraries in such a way that their efficiency could be harnessed without needing to comprehend their complexities, all accomplished by linking native C++ libraries, through V8, to the JavaScript-driven runtime that *is* Node. Node aimed to abstract away the complexity of multiuser, simultaneous multithreaded I/O management by wrapping that concurrency model into a single-threaded environment that was easy to understand, and already well understood by millions of web developers.

The point is simply this: when you are working with Node, you are ultimately working with C++ bindings to your OS, a language whose suitability is for enterprise-level software development that no one would seriously question.

This native bridge to C++ programs puts the lie to claims that Node is not enterprise-ready. These claims confuse what Javascript's role in the Node stack actually is. The bindings to Redis and other database drivers regularly used in Node programs are C bindings—fast, and near the *metal*. As we've seen, Node's simple process bindings (spawn, exec, and so on) facilitate a smooth integration of powerful system libraries with headless browsers and HTTP data streams. We are able to access the enormously powerful suite of native Unix programs as if they were part of the Node API itself. Also, of course, we can write our own add-ons.

Paraphrasing Professor *Keith Devlin's* description in "*Calculus: One of the Most Successful Technologies*" (https://www.youtube.com/watch?v=8ZLC0egL6pc), these are some features of successful consumer technologies:

- It should remove difficulty or drudgery from the process of completing a task.
- It should be easy to learn and use.
- It should be easier to learn and use than the popular method, if one exists.
- Once learned, it can be used without constant expert guidance. A user remains able to remember and/or derive most or all of the rules governing interactions with the technology through time.
- It should be possible to use it without knowing how it works.

Hopefully, as you think about the class of problems Node aims to solve, and the form of the solution it provides, the mentioned five features are easily seen in the technology Node represents. Node is fun to learn and use, with a consistent and predictable interface. Importantly, "*under the hood*" Node runs enormously powerful tools that the developer need only understand in terms of their API.

Wonderfully, Node, V8, libuv, and the other libraries composing the Node stack are open source, a significant fact that further distinguishes Node from many competitors. Not only can one contribute directly to the core libraries, one can *cut and paste* code blocks and other routines to use in one's own work. In fact, you should see your growth into a better Node developer as a chance to simultaneously become a better C++ programmer.

This is not a primer on C++, leaving you to pursue this study on your own. Don't be intimidated! The C-family of languages are designed using forms and idioms, not unlike what you are already used to using with JavaScript. The syntax and flow control should look very familiar. You should be able to understand the design and goals of the following examples with little effort, and can dip into C++ programming to resolve the meaning of the parts that aren't clear. Extending these examples iteratively is an excellent way to gently enter the world of C++ programming.

Hello World

Let's build our first add-on. In keeping with tradition, this add-on will result in a Node module that will print out "Hello World!" Even though this is a very simple example, it typifies the structure of all further C++ add-ons you will build. This allows you to incrementally experiment with new commands and structures, growing your knowledge in easy-to-understand steps.

For the steps that follow to work, you'll need a C/C++ compiler and Python 2.7 installed on your system. The tools to build native code on an operating system are specific to that operating system (and provided by the community or corporation that maintains or owns it). Here are instructions for some of the major operating systems:

- On macOS, for instance, Apple offers Xcode, an integrated development environment (IDE) that includes a compiler.
- For Windows, Microsoft's compiler comes with Visual Studio. There is also an npm package available for this purpose— `npm i -g windows-build-tools`.
- On Linux and elsewhere, **GCC, the GNU Compiler Collection**, is common. **GNU Make** and **Python** are also needed.

 C++ programmers might benefit from learning how V8 is embedded, from: `https://github.com/v8/v8/wiki/Embedder%27s-Guide`.

When compiling native code, there's usually another piece of software—the build automation tool. This tool directs the steps the compiler takes to turn your source code into a native binary. One of the first, for C, was Make. You can type into your compiler directly, of course, but Make lets you rerun the same set of commands, keeps a record of what those commands are, and transfer those commands to another developer. Make was developed in April 1976, and it has been in continuous use ever since.

Visual Studio and Xcode don't use a script-based tool like Make. Instead, they keep build steps and settings in binary files, and let developers edit them by clicking on checkboxes and entering text in graphical dialog boxes. This approach appeared friendlier, but can be more cumbersome and error-prone.

To make it easier, Google developed a tool called **GYP**, for **Generate Your Projects**. It's a meta-build system, taking information from you (in text format) and generating the build files the native compiler or IDE expects. Instead of opening up Visual Studio or Xcode and clicking around on menus and checkboxes, GYP will generate the required files for you. For any developer who has spent an evening (or several) hunting through settings to fix a broken native build, GYP is wonderful magic.

Google first created GYP to build Chrome and V8, but as an open source project, a community brought it to an ever-expanding list of new uses. To build native Node add-ons, the Node team creates and maintains `node-gyp`, which bundles Google's GYP. Use the mentioned commands to install `node-gyp` globally on your system, and verify that it's there by getting the version. You can find the installation instructions for `node-gyp` on the below mentioned link: `https://github.com/nodejs/node-gyp`

You may remember our discussion in the first chapter about the Unix design philosophy, and specifically, Doug McIlroy's directive to "*Write programs to handle text streams, because that is a universal interface.*"

For the task of compiler automation, Make followed this guideline in the 1970s, Apple and Microsoft broke the rule in the 1990s with their graphical IDEs and binary project files, and now in this decade, Google has restored it with GYP.

To understand where we're going, it may be helpful to take a look at what we'll have at the end. When we're done, we'll have a module definition folder with a handful of files in it. Here's the structure we'll create first:

```
/hello_module
   binding.gyp
   hello.cc
   index.js
```

The `/hello_module` module folder contains a C++ file (`hello.cc`), the *instruction* file for GYP (`binding.gyp`), and a convenience *wrapper* (`index.js`), whose purpose will be made clear shortly.

Create a file named `hello.cc` with these contents:

```
#include <node.h>

namespace hello_module {

    using v8::FunctionCallbackInfo;
    using v8::Isolate;
    using v8::Local;
    using v8::Object;
    using v8::String;
    using v8::Value;

    // Our first native function
    void sayHello(const FunctionCallbackInfo<Value>& args) {
      Isolate* isolate = args.GetIsolate();
      args.GetReturnValue().Set(String::NewFromUtf8(isolate, "Hello Node
from native code!"));
    }

    // The initialization function for our module
    void init(Local<Object> exports) {
      NODE_SET_METHOD(exports, "sayHello", sayHello);
    }

    // Export the initialization function
    NODE_MODULE(NODE_GYP_MODULE_NAME, init)
}
```

After including Node's C header, defining a namespace for our code, and declaring various parts of V8 that we'll need to use, there are three parts. The `void sayHello` function is the native function we will export. Below that, `init` is a required initialization function that sets up the exports for the Node module that this will all become (here, the function name `"sayHello"`, bound to its C++ counterpart), and `NODE_MODULE()` is a C++ macro that actually exports the module that GYP was configured to export. As it's a macro, there's no semicolon at the end of that line.

You are embedding C++ code into the V8 runtime, so that Javascript can be bound into the relevant scope. V8 must scope all the new allocations made in your code, and so, you'll need to wrap the code you write, extending V8. To this end, you'll see several instances of the `Handle<Value>` syntax, wrapping C++ code in the examples that follow. Comparing these wrappers to what will be defined in the initialization function pushed out to `NODE_MODULE` should make it clear how Node is being bound to C++ methods via the V8 bridge.

To learn more about how V8 embeds C++ code, check out: `https://github.com/v8/v8/wiki/Getting%20Started%20with%20Embedding`.

Along with `hello.cc`, create `binding.gyp` with this code inside:

```
{
  "targets": [
    {
      "target_name": "hello",
      "sources": [ "hello.cc" ]
    }
  ]
}
```

In cases where you've got more than one source file to compile, simply add more filenames to the sources array.

This manifest tells GYP that we want to see `hello.cc` turned into compiled binary code in a file named `hello.node` (`target_name`) in the `/Release` folder. We now have the C++ file and the compilation instructions we need to compile our first native add-on!

Run the following command in the `/hello_module` folder:

```
$ node-gyp configure
```

Essentially, `configure` generates a Makefile, and the `build` command runs it. After you run the `configure` command, you can take a look inside the `/build` folder that GYP created to familiarize yourself; they're all text files that you can inspect. On a Mac with Xcode installed, it'll contain a handful of files, including a 300 line Makefile. If successful, the output from the `configure` command should look something like this:

```
$ node-gyp configure
  gyp info it worked if it ends with ok
```

```
gyp info using node-gyp@3.6.2
gyp info using node@8.7.0 | darwin | x64
gyp info spawn /usr/bin/python
gyp info spawn args [ '/usr/local/lib/node_modules/node-
gyp/gyp/gyp_main.py',
gyp info spawn args    'binding.gyp',
gyp info spawn args    '-f',
gyp info spawn args    'make',
gyp info spawn args    '-I',


...

gyp info spawn args    '--generator-output',
gyp info spawn args    'build',
gyp info spawn args    '-Goutput_dir=.' ]
gyp info ok
```

Next, try the `build` command, which runs this Makefile. The output looks like this:

```
$ node-gyp build
gyp info it worked if it ends with ok
gyp info using node-gyp@3.6.2
gyp info using node@8.7.0 | darwin | x64
gyp info spawn make
gyp info spawn args [ 'BUILDTYPE=Release', '-C', 'build' ]
    CXX(target) Release/obj.target/hello_native/hello.o
    SOLINK_MODULE(target) Release/hello_native.node
gyp info ok
```

Now, you'll see a new `/build/Release` folder containing (among other things) the binary `hello.node` file.

> To remove the `/build` folder, you can run `node-gyp clean`. As a build shortcut, you can use `node-gyp configure build` (one line) to configure and build in one step, or simply `node-gyp rebuild`, which runs `clean configure build` for you in one go. Further command-line options can be found at: `https://github.com/nodejs/node-gyp#command-options`.

Now, always staying in the `/hello_module` folder, create the following `index.js` file:

```
// index.js
module.exports = require('./build/Release/hello');
```

This file will function as the exporter for this module. Depending on how you write your C++ code, you might use this opportunity to craft your module's native interface into a Node-specific API. For now, let's just export the `hello` function directly, saving the developer the trouble of following our build folder structure when using `require`.

To complete the "modularization", create a `package.json` file for this module, and set the "entry point" value to `index.js`:

Now, let's demonstrate how to use this module in your code. Jump up a directory and create a file that will require the module we've just created. Consider the following example:

```
const {sayHello} = require('./hello_module');
console.log(sayHello())
```

Using destructuring, we pull the `sayHello` function from the object our module returns. Now, execute that code:

```
$ node hello.js
Hello Node from native code!
```

You are now both a C++ programmer and a Node extender!

Note how we're using the same familiar `require` statement, but in a subtly powerful way. Instead of bringing in a Node module coded in more JavaScript, it detects and loads our newly-minted native add-on.

A calculator

Of course, one would never bother to write an add-on to simply echo back strings. It is more likely that you will want to expose an API or interface to your Node programs. Let's create a simple calculator, with two methods: add and subtract. In this example, we will demonstrate how to pass arguments from Javascript to methods within an add-on, and to send any results back.

The complete code for this example will be found in your code bundle. The meat of the program can be seen in this snippet, where we define an interface for our two methods, each one expecting to receive two numbers as arguments:

```
#include <node.h>

namespace calculator_module {

  using v8::Exception;
  using v8::FunctionCallbackInfo;
  using v8::Isolate;
  using v8::Local;
  using v8::Number;
  using v8::Object;
  using v8::String;
  using v8::Value;
  void Add(const FunctionCallbackInfo<Value>& args) {
    Isolate* isolate = args.GetIsolate();
    // Check argument arity
    if (args.Length() < 2) {
      isolate->ThrowException(Exception::TypeError(
        String::NewFromUtf8(isolate, "Must send two argument to #add")));
      return;
    }
    // Check argument types
    if (!args[0]->IsNumber() || !args[1]->IsNumber()) {
      isolate->ThrowException(Exception::TypeError(
        String::NewFromUtf8(isolate, "#add only accepts numbers")));
      return;
    }
    // The actual calculation now
    double value = args[0]->NumberValue() + args[1]->NumberValue();
    Local<Number> num = Number::New(isolate, value);
    // Set the return value (using the passed in
FunctionCallbackInfo<Value>&)
    args.GetReturnValue().Set(num);
  }
  void Subtract(const FunctionCallbackInfo<Value>& args) {
    Isolate* isolate = args.GetIsolate();
    if (args.Length() < 2) {
      isolate->ThrowException(Exception::TypeError(
        String::NewFromUtf8(isolate, "Must send two argument to
#subtract")));
      return;
    }
    if (!args[0]->IsNumber() || !args[1]->IsNumber()) {
      isolate->ThrowException(Exception::TypeError(
```

```
          String::NewFromUtf8(isolate, "#subtract only accepts numbers")));
       return;
     }
     double value = args[0]->NumberValue() - args[1]->NumberValue();
     Local<Number> num = Number::New(isolate, value);
     args.GetReturnValue().Set(num);
   }
   void Init(Local<Object> exports) {
     NODE_SET_METHOD(exports, "add", Add);
     NODE_SET_METHOD(exports, "subtract", Subtract);
   }
   NODE_MODULE(NODE_GYP_MODULE_NAME, Init)
 }
```

We can quickly see that two methods have been scoped: Add and Subtract (Subtract is defined nearly identically with Add, with only a change of operator). Within the Add method, we see an Arguments object (reminiscent of Javascript's arguments object) that is checked for length (we expect two arguments) and argument type (we want numbers: !args[0]->IsNumber() || !args[1]->IsNumber()). Take a good look at how this method closes out:

```
   Local<Number> num = Number::New(args[0]->NumberValue() +
   args[1]->NumberValue());
    return scope.Close(num);
```

While there seems to be a lot going on, it is really rather simple: V8 is instructed to allocate space for a Number with name num, to be assigned the value of adding our two numbers together. When this operation has been completed, we close out the execution scope and return num. We don't have to worry about memory management for this reference, as that is automatically handled by V8.

Finally, we see in the following chunk not only how this particular program defines its interface, but how, at a deep level, Node modules and the exports object are in fact associated:

```
   void Init(Handle<Object> exports) {
     exports->Set(String::NewSymbol("add"),
       FunctionTemplate::New(Add)->GetFunction());
     exports->Set(String::NewSymbol("subtract"),
       FunctionTemplate::New(Subtract)->GetFunction());
   }
```

As in our "hello" example, here we see the new symbols (these are just types of strings) `add` and `subtract`, which represent the method names for our new Node module. Their function signature is implemented using the easy-to-follow `FunctionTemplate::New(Add)->GetFunction())` blueprint.

Using our calculator from a Node program is now easy:

```
let calculator = require('./build/Release/calculator');
console.log(calculator.add(2,3));
console.log(calculator.subtract(3,2));
// 5
// 1
```

With just this simple start, we can already implement useful C++ modules. We'll go deeper now, and we'll get some help from **nan (Native Abstractions for Node)**.

Using NAN

nan (`https://github.com/nodejs/nan`) is a collection of header files providing helpers and macros aimed at simplifying the creation of add-ons. According to the documentation, nan was created primarily in order to preserve compatibility of your C++ code across different Node versions:

Thanks to the crazy changes in V8 (and some in Node core), keeping native add-ons compiling happily across versions, particularly 0.10 to 0.12 to 4.0, is a minor nightmare. The goal of this project is to store all logic necessary to develop native Node.js add-ons without having to inspect `NODE_MODULE_VERSION` and get yourself into a macro-tangle.

In the examples that follow, we will use nan to build some native add-ons. Let's rebuild our `hello world` example using nan.

Hello, nan

Create a folder for your project, and add the following package.json file:

```
// package.json
{
  "name": "hello",
  "version": "1.0.0",
  "description": "",
  "main": "index.js",
  "scripts": {
```

```
      "build": "node-gyp rebuild",
      "start": "node index.js"
    },
    "keywords": [],
    "author": "",
    "license": "ISC",
    "dependencies": {
      "nan": "^2.8.0",
      "node-gyp": "^3.6.2"
    },
    "gypfile": true
}
```

We've added a couple of new things here, such as indicating that there exists a `gypfile`. More importantly, we create some convenience scripts for compiling and running our module: `build` and `start`. Also, of course, we indicate that the module's main execution file is `index.js` (we'll create that soon). Note as well that, when you `npm install` this package, GYP will notice the `binding.gyp` file and automatically build—a `/build` folder will be created along with the install.

Now, create our GYP binding file. Note the addition of `include_dirs`. This ensures that `nan` headers are made available to the compiler:

```
// binding.gyp
{
  "targets": [{
    "include_dirs": [
      "<!(node -e \"require('nan')\")"
    ],
    "target_name": "hello",
    "sources": [
      "hello.cc"
    ]
  }]
}
```

Now, we rewrite the main C++ file to take advantage of the **nan** helpers:

```
#include <nan.h>

NAN_METHOD(sayHello) {
    auto message = Nan::New("Hello Node from NAN code!").ToLocalChecked();
    // 'info' is an implicit bridge object between JavaScript and C++
    info.GetReturnValue().Set(message);
}
```

```
NAN_MODULE_INIT(Initialize) {
    // Similar to the 'export' statement in Node -- export the sayHello
method
    NAN_EXPORT(target, sayHello);
}

// Create and Initialize function created with NAN_MODULE_INIT macro
NODE_MODULE(hello, Initialize);
```

Here, we can see that the long list of inclusions isn't necessary. The rest of the code follows the same pattern as our original example, but with the initialization and function definitions now running through NAN-prefixed shortcuts. Note that, we can directly type the sayHello method on the module object (NAN_EXPORT(target, sayHello)), rather than requiring us to specify "sayHello" on the interface that a require statement will receive.

The final step is to prove that this module can be bound to Node. Create the following index.js file:

```
const {Hello} = require('./build/Release/hello');
console.log(Hello());
```

Now, all we have to do is build:

```
$ npm run build
```

Then, we'll run it:

```
$ node index.js
// Hello Node from NAN code!
```

Asynchronous add-ons

In keeping with the typical pattern of a Node program, add-ons also implement the notion of asynchronous callbacks. As one might expect in a Node program, a C++ add-on performing an expensive and time-consuming operation should comprehend the notion of asynchronously executing functions.

Let's create a module that exposes two methods that ultimately call the same function, yet one method does it synchronously and the other asynchronously. This will allow us to demonstrate how to create native modules with callbacks.

We're going to break our module up into 4 files, separating functionality. Create a new directory and copy the `package.json` file from the previous example (changing `name` to something else), and add the following `binding.gyp` file:

```
{
  "targets": [
    {
      "target_name": "nan_addon",
      "sources": [
        "addon.cc",
        "sync.cc",
        "async.cc"
      ],
      "include_dirs": ["<!(node -e \"require('nan')\")"]
    }
  ]
}
```

When we're done, your module folder will look something like this:

We're going to create one file containing the asynchronous method (`async.cc`), one for synchronous (`sync.cc`), the common function each will call differently in `addon.h`, and the main `addon.cc` file that will "bind" everything together.

Create `addons.h` in the module folder:

```
// addons.h
using namespace Nan;

int Run (int cycles) {
    // using volatile prevents compiler from optimizing loop (slower)
    volatile int i = 0;
    for (; i < cycles; i++) {}
    return cycles;
}
```

In this file is where we will create a "mock" function, whose responsibility is simply to waste cycles (time). So, we create an inefficient function `Run`. Using the `volatile` keyword, we spook V8 into de-optimizing this function (we are warning V8 that this value will change unpredictably, scaring off the optimizer). The rest will simply run the number of requested cycles and reflect the value it was sent...slowly. This is the function that both our async and sync code will execute.

To execute `Run` synchronously, create the following **sync.cc** file:

```
// sync.cc
#include <nan.h>
int Run(int cycles);

// Simple synchronous access to the `Run()` function
NAN_METHOD(RunSync) {
  // Expect a number as first argument
  int cycles = info[0]->Uint32Value();
  int result = Run(cycles);

  info.GetReturnValue().Set(result);
}
```

As we saw earlier, `info` will contain arguments passed to this `RunSync` method. Here, we grab the number of cycles requested, pass those arguments to `Run`, and return whatever that function call produced.

Now, create the file for our asynchronous method, `async.cc`. Creating asynchronous code is slightly more complex:

```
// async.cc
#include <nan.h>

using v8::Local;
using v8::Number;
using v8::Value;
using namespace Nan;

int Run(int cycles);

class Worker : public AsyncWorker {
 public:
  Worker(Callback *callback, int cycles)
    : AsyncWorker(callback), cycles(cycles) {}
  ~Worker() {}

  // This executes in the worker thread.
```

```
// #result is being place on "this" (private.result)
void Execute () {
  result = Run(cycles);
}

// When the async work is complete execute this function in the main
event loop
// We're sending back two arguments to fulfill standard Node callback
// pattern (error, result) -> (Null(), New<Number>(result))
void HandleOKCallback () {
  HandleScope scope;
  Local<Value> argv[] = {
      Null()
    , New<Number>(result)
  };
  callback->Call(2, argv);
}

private:
  int cycles;
  int result;
};

NAN_METHOD(RunAsync) {
  int cycles = To<int>(info[0]).FromJust();
  Callback *callback = new
Callback(To<v8::Function>(info[1]).ToLocalChecked());

  AsyncQueueWorker(new Worker(callback, cycles));
}
```

Starting from the bottom, you see that we're creating a method that expects the first argument (info[0]) to be an integer, which is assigned to `cycles`. We then create a new `Callback` object as `callback`, and pass `callback` and `cycles` to the `Worker` constructor, passing the resulting instance to `AsyncQueueWorker` (setting up our asynchronous method).

Now, let's examine how to configure an asynchronous `Worker`.

Jump to the bottom of `Worker` and note the establishment of private attributes `cycles` and `result` for this class. In JavaScript, the equivalent would be to create a local variable context with `this.cycles` and `this.result` -- local variables to use in what follows.

To fulfill the worker template we need to implement two key functions: Execute and HandleOKCallback. Execute executes our Run function (from addons.h) in a worker thread (the power of C++ at work) and assigns to result the returned value. Once Run has completed we need to send this result back to the original JavaScript callback our Node module interface will have sent. HandleOKCallback prepares the argument list (argv) as expected by standard error-first Node callback pattern: we set the first error argument to Null(), and the second argument to the result. Via callback->Call(2, argv) the original callback is called with these 2 arguments, and proceeds accordingly.

The last step is to create the module export file, index.js:

```
const addon = require('./build/Release/nan_addon');
const width = 1e9;

function log(type, result, start) {
    const end = Date.now() - start;
    console.log(`${type} returned <${result}> in ${end}ms`)
}

function sync() {
    const start = Date.now();
    const result = addon.runSync(width);
    log('Sync', result, start);
}

function async() {
    const start = Date.now();
    addon.runAsync(width, (err, result) => {
        log('Async', result, start);
    });
}

console.log('1');
async();
console.log('2');
sync();
console.log('3');
```

Once you've created this file, go ahead and build your module via `npm run build.` (or `node-gyp rebuild`) and execute this file with `node index.js`. You should see something like this in your terminal:

```
1
2
Sync returned <1000000000> in 1887ms
3
Async returned <1000000000> in 1889ms
```

What's the point of that? We're proving that we can create C++ functions that run independently of the single Node process thread. If `addon.runAsync` was not running asynchronously, the output would have looked like this:

```
1
Async returned <1000000000> in 1889ms
2
Sync returned <1000000000> in 1887ms
3
```

However, we see that the runtime logged **1**, `runAsync` went off into threads land, 2 was logged, followed by the synchronous function `runSync`, blocking the event loop (which runs in the same single JavaScript thread). When finished, this sync function announces its result, and the loop continues with its next instruction to log **3**, until, finally, pending callbacks are executed, when the result of `runAsync` makes an appearance, last.

There is a lot of room here for exploration, even if you aren't a C++ programmer. From these simple building blocks, aided by `nan`, you can build add-ons with increasingly complex behavior. And, of course, the largest advantage is this ability to pass long running tasks off onto the OS, to run in a very fast, compiled language. Your Node project can now fully harness the power of C++.

Closing thoughts

Being able to easily link C++ modules with your Node program is a powerful new paradigm. It may be tempting, then, to exuberantly begin writing C++ add-ons for every identifiable segment of your programs. While this might be a productive way to learn, it is not necessarily the best idea in the long run. While it is certainly true that, in general, compiled C++ will run more quickly than JavaScript code, remember that V8 is ultimately using another type of compilation on the JavaScript code it is running. JavaScript running within V8 runs very efficiently.

As well, we don't want to lose the simplicity of organization and predictable single-threaded runtime of JavaScript when designing complex interactions within a high-concurrency environment. Remember that Node came into being partly as an attempt to save the developer from working with threads and related complexities when performing I/O. As such, try and keep some rules in mind.

Will a C++ module actually run more quickly? The answer isn't always yes. The extra step of jumping into a different execution context and then back into V8 takes time. *Felix Geisendorfer's* talk describing his work with building fast MySQL bindings provides some insight into how one should think when making these decisions, at: `http://www.youtube.com/watch?v=Kdwwvps4J9A`. In general, stick with JavaScript until you need to really do something deep and expensive where getting *closer to the metal* makes sense.

How does splitting up your code base affect maintainability? While it would be hard for any developer to suggest using less-efficient code, sometimes a negligible performance gain does not overcome an increase in complexity that can lead to harder-to-find bugs or difficulties with sharing or otherwise managing your code base (including with future team members you haven't even hired yet!).

Node has merged a beautiful JavaScript API with an enormously powerful and easily extensible application stack. Given the ability to integrate C++ into your applications, there is no reason to exclude Node from the list of technologies to consider for your next project.

Links and resources

Additional guides and resources for writing Node add-ons can be found on the web:

- The Node documentation for add-ons is excellent: `https://nodejs.org/dist/latest-v9.x/docs/api/addons.html`
- The nan repository contains many examples: `https://github.com/nodejs/nan`
- An excellent resource for those learning C++: `http://www.learncpp.com/`
- When you're feeling more confident, the source code for Node's core modules is an excellent place to both explore and learn from: `https://github.com/nodejs/node/tree/master/src`

Index

Made in the USA
Middletown, DE
16 July 2018